EMPIRICAL APPROACHES TO FISCAL POLICY MODELLING

INTERNATIONAL STUDIES IN ECONOMIC MODELLING

Series Editor
Homa Motamen-Scobie

Executive Director
European Economics and Financial Centre
London
P. O. Box 2498
London W2 4LE
Tel: (071)229-0402
Fax: (071)221-5118

Empirical Approaches to Fiscal Policy Modelling

Edited by

Alberto Heimler

Director,
Research Department,
Antitrust Authority,
Rome, Italy

and

Daniele Meulders

Professor of Economics, Free University of Brussels
Belgium

An Applied Econometrics Association Volume

CHAPMAN & HALL

London · Glasgow · New York · Tokyo · Melbourne · Madras

Published by Chapman & Hall, 2–6 Boundary Row, London SE1 8HN

Chapman & Hall, 2–6 Boundary Row, London SE1 8HN, UK

Blackie Academic & Professional, Wester Cleddens Road, Bishopbriggs, Glasgow G64 2NZ, UK

Chapman & Hall, 29 West 35th Street, New York NY10001, USA

Chapman & Hall Japan, Thomson Publishing Japan, Hirakawacho Nemoto Building, 6F, 1–7–11 Hirakawa-cho, Chiyoda-ku, Tokyo 102, Japan

Chapman & Hall Australia, Thomas Nelson Australia, 102 Dodds Street, South Melbourne, Victoria 3205, Australia

Chapman & Hall India, R. Seshadri, 32 Second Main Road, CIT East, Madras 600 035, India

First edition 1993

© 1993 Chapman & Hall

Typeset in 10/12 Times by Pure Tech Corporation, India
Printed in Great Britain by T.J. Press, Padstow, Cornwall

ISBN 0 412 44990 0

A catalogue record for this book is available from the British Library

Library of Congress Cataloging-in-Publication data available

Contents

Part Three Fiscal Reform in Four EEC Countries 183

Contributors

P. Artus
E. Bleuze
J. P. Nicolai
F. Legros
J. M. Bekkering

F. Bourguignon
P. A. Chiappori

P. Capros
G. N. Mentzas
P. Karadeloglou

A. Duncan

M. Gerard

A. Heimler

Caisse des Dépôts et Consignations Paris
195 Boulevard Saint Germain
75007 Paris
FRANCE
Wetenschappelijke Raad voor het Regeringsbeleid
Plein 1813 n°2
Postbus 20004
2500EA s Gravenhage
THE NETHERLANDS
DELTA: Département et Laboratoire d'économie
théorique et appliquée
48 Boulevard Jourdan
75014 Paris
FRANCE
National Technical University of Athens
Dep. of Electrical Engineering
42, 28th Octoviriou St.
106 82 Athens
GREECE
Institute for Fiscal Studies
7 Ridgmount St.
London WCIE 7AE
UK
Facultés Universitaires Catholiques de Mons
Chaussée de Binche 151
7000 Mons
BELGIQUE
Autorità Garante della Concorrenza
e del Mercato
Via Calabria, 48
00187 Roma
ITALY

Contributors

R. Hugounenq	WIFO
A. Jaeger	Postfach 91
	A-1103 Vienna
	AUSTRIA
D. Jorgenson	Harvard University
	Department of Economics
	Littauer Center 122
	Cambridge, Mass. 02138
	USA
C. Keuschnigg	Institute for Advanced Studies
	Stumpergasse 56
	A-1060 Vienna
	AUSTRIA
C. Milana	ISPE
	Istituto di studi per la Programmazione Economica
	Corso Vittorio Emanuele 282
	00186 Roma
	ITALIA
F. Padoa Schioppa Kostoris	Facoltà di Economia e Commercio
V. Patrizi	Università La Sapienza di Roma
	Via del Castro Laurenziano
	Roma
	ITALY
N. Rossi	University of Venice
	Ca Foscari-Dorsoduro 3246
	30123 Venice
	ITALIA
P. B. Spahn	University of Frankfurt
H. Kaiser	Merton Strasse 17 Postfach 111932
U. van Essen	Frankfurt am Main 11
	D-6000 GERMANY
K. Y. Yun	College of Business and Economics
	Yonsei University
	Seoul 120
	KOREA

Introduction to the Series

There has been a growing dependence in the past two decades on modelling as a tool for better understanding of the behaviour of economic systems, and as an aid in policy and decision making. Given the current state of the art globally, the introduction of a series such as this can be seen as a timely development. This series will provided a forum for volumes on both the theoretical and applied aspects of the subject.

International Studies in Economic Modelling is designed to present comprehensive volumes on modelling work in various areas of the economic discipline. In this respect one of the fundamental objectives is to provide a medium for ongoing review of the progression of the field.

There is no doubt that economic modelling will figure prominently in the affairs of government and in the running of the private sector, in efforts to achieve a more rational and efficient handling of economic affairs. By formally structuring an economic system, it is possible to simulate and investigate the effect of changes on the system. This in turn leads to a growing appreciation of the relevance of modelling techniques. Our aim is to provide sufficient space for authors to write authoritative handbooks, giving basic facts with an overview of the current economic models in specific areas and publish a useful series which will be consulted and used as an accessible source of reference.

The question may arise in some reader's minds as to the role of this series *vis-à-vis* other existing publications. At present, no other book series possesses the characteristics of *International Studies in Economic Modelling* and as such cannot fill the gap that will be bridged by it. Those journals which focus in this area do not present an exhaustive and comprehensive overview of a particular subject and all the developments in the field. Other journals which may contain economic modelling papers are not sufficiently broad to publish volumes on all aspects of modelling in a specific area which this series is designed to cover.

A variety of topics will be included encompassing areas of both micro and macroeconomics, as well as the methodological aspects of model construction. Naturally, we are open to suggestions from all readers of, and contributors to, the series reading its approach and content.

Finally, I would like to thank all those who have helped the launch of this series. The encouraging response received from authors who have contributed the forthcoming volumes and from the subscribers to the series has indicated the need for such a publication.

Homa Motamen-Scobie
European Economics and Financial Centre
London, 1992

Editors' Note

This book contains the revised versions of some of the most important papers presented at the 28th International Conference of the Applied Econometrics Association on Fiscal Policy Modelling, which took place at the Confederazione Generale dell'Industria Italiana (CONFINDUSTRIA) Roma on 30 November and 1 December 1989. This conference was organized by the Budgetary Policy Chapter of the Applied Econometrics Association.

The editors thank all the members of the Scientific Committee who have been extremely helpful in the preparation of this conference proceedings.

The editors also thank CONFINDUSTRIA and the Département d'Economie Appliquée de l'Université Libre de Bruxelles (DULBEA), who have been exceptionally generous in their support.

28TH INTERNATIONAL CONFERENCE OF THE APPLIED ECONOMETRICS ASSOCIATION

Confindustria, Roma, 30 November and 1 December 1989.

Scientific Committee

A. Heimler (Antitrust Authority, Roma)
P. Llau (Paris X)
D. Meulders (DULBEA, Bruxelles)
C. Milana (ISPE, Roma)
J. Owens (OECD, Paris)
A. Pedone (University of Rome)
R. Plasman (DULBEA, Bruxelles)
J. Ritzen (Erasmus, Rotterdam)
H. Serbat (AEA, Paris)
H. W. Sinn (University of Munchen)
V. Tanzi (IMF, Washington)
F. Thys-Clément (DULBEA, Bruxelles)

Introduction

Alberto Heimler and Danièle Meulders

In the last decade the modelling of the interrelationship between public finance and the rest of the economy has seen substantial advances, reflected in many of the papers delivered to the Applied Econometrics Association Conference held at Confindustria, Rome, on 30 November and 1 December 1989. In particular, the development of the literature on applied general-equilibrium modelling has found most of its applications in the field of taxation, enlarging and completing the estimation of the welfare loss due to distortionary taxes. In this context an important extension has been the introduction of overlapping-generation models. Furthermore, it has become clear that most individual decisions, especially the decision whether or not to work, are dependent upon the tax system, in the sense that the higher the marginal income tax the larger the wedge between labour cost and take-home pay, the last one being the decision variable in the demand for leisure. Finally, in the European context, the completion of the internal market has brought about the necessity to harmonize fiscal systems in the EEC member countries. A number of papers study, therefore, the effects of fiscal reform on efficiency, welfare and growth.

The first part of this book, 'Taxation, economic growth and welfare', consists of four chapters. The first two, 'The excess burden of taxation in the US' by Dale Jorgenson and Kun-Young Yun and 'An intertemporal general-equilibrium model of taxation in Italy' by Alberto Heimler and Carlo Milana, share the econometric approach to general-equilibrium modelling pioneered by Jorgenson and Yun (1986). As opposed to the so-called calibration methods, where, given a set of observations of the exogenous and the endogenous variables for a given year and some relevant known parameter, the model is solved analytically for the missing parameters, the econometric approach to general-equilibrium modelling is based on the econometric estimation of all the relevant parameters of the system, which is then solved analytically for the endogenous variables. In the calibration methods the parameters of the system are estimated with zero degrees of freedom and the observations for a given year are assumed to be consistent with a general economic equilibrium. On the other hand, in the econometric approach the parameters of the model are econometrically estimated and no assumption has to be made about the actual exact realization of a general economic equilibrium.

The central idea in the chapter by Jorgenson and Yun is the measurement of the excess burden of taxation in the US by using a hypothetical undistorting tax system as a standard. In this tax system all revenue is raised by a lump-sum levy that does not distort private decisions and involves no loss of efficiency. The most important conclusion of the chapter is that the excess burden imposed on the US economy is quite large and involves a welfare loss equivalent to 18% of the government tax revenue. Furthermore, by considering marginal effects, Jorgenson and Yun find that the cost of raising a dollar of government tax revenue at the margin is 38.3 cents, implying that the potential gains of a tax reform are quite large.

Heimler and Milana (Chapter 2) apply the methodology of Jorgenson and Yun (1986) to the study of fiscal behaviour of the Italian economy. They introduce the foreign trade sector to the Jorgenson and Yun model. This extension is crucial because it allows them to consider offsetting effects stemming from external trade, which may eliminate the domestic gains potentially arising from an isolated national fiscal reform. Furthermore, for representing the cost and expenditure functions, they use the functional forms proposed by Diewert and Wales (1987), which have the advantage of imposing concavity without losing completely their flexibility. The structure of the model is thoroughly discussed and the simulations presented evaluate the effects on the Italian economic growth and national wealth arising from the existence of a distortionary tax structure. They find that in Italy the distortionary effects of capital income taxes are approximately equal to 1% of the full wealth. On the other hand, if all taxes were substituted by a non-distortionary lump-sum levy, the welfare gain for the Italian economy would reach 3% of the full wealth.

The third chapter, 'Crowding out in a two-country overlapping-generations model' by Albert Jaeger and Christian Keuschnigg, is an extension of the Auerbach and Kotlikoff (1987) analysis of the crowding-out effects of tax cuts to a two-country model framework. Jaeger and Keuschnigg apply numerical techniques to study the effects of public debt on capital accumulation. The experiment is conducted both on the assumption of two equally sized countries as well as the case of a small open economy. The model, which is an intertemporal open-economy model of the world economy, requires a predetermination of the parameters of the system and of the exogenous variables. The main conclusion of the chapter is that the portion of public debt perceived as net wealth by the private sector is quite low and varies between zero and 0.5. Furthermore, confirming the results of Auerbach and Kotlikoff (1987), crowding-out effects of a tax cut appear to be rather small and dependent on the size of the country cutting taxes. In the extreme case, a small country does not experience any crowding-out. However, a part of the additional consumption stimulated by the tax cut is satisfied through imports. As a consequence, foreign debt accumulates. Therefore, in the new final steady state, a part of the home country capital stock is owned by the foreign country.

Finally, in the fourth chapter, 'Cost of capital, investment location and marginal effective tax rate: methodology and application', Marcel Gérard extends the methodology of King and Fullerton (1984) to a transnational context, where, assuming perfect mobility of capital, the effective tax rates on capital income depend on the fiscal systems of a number of countries. Gérard demonstrates how in such a world the effective rates of capital income taxation differ with respect to the more traditional measure proposed by King and Fullerton (1984). Furthermore, his results show that the harmonization of the corporate income tax and of interest and dividend income taxation does not exhaust the possibilities for co-ordination. Indeed, the corporate tax basis, as well as the structure of subsidies, determines very important differences in the effective corporate income tax among countries, influencing investment and locational decisions.

The second part of the book focuses on the impact of taxation on individual behaviour.

The contribution of Artus, Bleuze, Legros and Nicolai, 'Household saving, portfolio selection and taxation in France', examines French household consumption and portfolio selection decisions. Special attention is paid to the Ricardian equivalence theory, the impact of tax measures, and the perception of risk. The implications of the findings of this study for fiscal and monetary policy are discussed. It appears that the household saving rate is not largely affected by tax incentives, the growth of mutual funds, the expansion of short-term consumer credit and the inflation rate. Its main determinants are macroeconomic, such as the increase in wealth and disposable income, and the inflation rate. The asset allocation of household wealth is not influenced by incentive policy measures or taxation; it is determined by the return on each asset, the weight attributed to capital gains or losses being asset-specific.

The following three contributions of this part of the book are devoted to the impact of taxation on labour supply.

An econometric model explaining the transition probabilities between different categories of the labour force (full-time workers, disabled, unemployed) has been estimated by J.M. Bekkering for The Netherlands in Chapter 6, entitled 'Incomes and transitions within the labour force in Holland'. Emphasis is laid on the effect of financial variables on the transition probabilities. The simulation of individual reactions to changes in the system of taxes, benefits and subsidies shows a strong effect of financial incentives on the behaviour of women, but men seem to be less sensitive.

In Chapter 7, entitled 'Labour supply decisions and non-convex budget sets: the case of national insurance contributions in UK', Alan Duncan examines explicitly the decision-making process governing labour supply around points of discontinuity in the budget constraint and derives an algorithm by which non-convex budget sets can be incorporated into the estimation procedures. This is particularly interesting for the study of the impact, on labour supply, of the national insurance contributions in the United Kingdom, where single parents and married women are noted to display particular sensitivity to a national insurance regime, which renders the budget constraint discontinuous at a low income level. Taking a sample of married women from the 1984 Family Expenditure Survey, a comparison of model predictions reveals a consistent underestimation of the desired hours by continuous labour supply functions. Moreover, the omission of a mechanism to account for a national insurance regime such as the one enforced in 1984 is seen to mask a significant degree of backward-bending labour supply behaviour.

In Chapter 8, entitled 'Income taxation and the supply of labour in West Germany', P. Bernd Spahn, Ulrich van Essen and Helmut Kaiser analyse the impact of the revision of the German income tax law on labour supply decisions and evaluate the welfare gains. They combine an explicit tax simulation model representing the full scale of actual tax policy measures, validated on a microeconomic database, with a second-generation labour supply model to investigate the impact of the full reform on their welfare effect, taking behavioural reactions into account. Economic welfare is measured by the equivalent variation, and efficiency gains are insulated by comparing measures for the excess burden before and after the reforms. They conclude that the reforms have substantially reduced the excess burden for married women in all income groups.

The third part of the book is concerned with tax reforms, especially in the perspective of the fiscal harmonization necessary for the completion of the internal market.

In Chapter 9, entitled 'Tax rate progressivity and de-facto fiscal indexation in ten European countries', Fiorella Padoa Schioppa Kostoris estimates the total burden of taxation on the workers of ten European countries for the period 1960–88. In particular, in order to provide a better approximation to the tax wedge facing European workers, she estimates the marginal income tax in all countries and concludes that, with the exception of Denmark, Spain and Sweden, the degree of progressivity has strongly declined in the last decade. However, in the perspective of the fiscal harmonization of EEC member countries, direct income taxes show a much higher coefficient of variation than all other taxes (indirect and social-security contributions) which are, in fact, much more similar in the EEC. As a consequence, harmonization is a much more difficult task for direct income taxes than for all other ones. In any case, also with respect to direct income taxes, fiscal systems of EEC countries appear to be much closer now than ever before, implying that now the accomplishment of harmonization could be easier.

In Chapter 10, entitled 'Tax policy at the bifurcation between equity and efficiency: lessons from the German income tax reform', Helmut Kaiser, Ulrich van Essen and P. Bernd Spahn discuss the recent revision of income taxation in West Germany. The main feature of the reform was the reduction of marginal tax rates combined with the broadening of the tax base. These authors stress that such a reform cannot be evaluated without considering both labour supply reactions and distributional effects. They propose to utilize a microsimulation model of income taxation so that the computation of equivalent variations on an individual basis can be accomplished. The results of the simulation of the German tax reform, reported only for single families, show that the equivalent variation rises with income and is positive with all taxpayers. The welfare gain associated with the reform is quite substantial and equal to 18.8% of tax collections.

Various simulations to evaluate the equity and efficiency consequences of a reform of the French tax system that would lower VAT rates and increase the income tax, in an effort to make it closer to other EEC systems while maintaining tax-revenue neutrality, are presented by Bourguignon, Chiappori and Hugounenq in Chapter 11, entitled 'Exploring the distribution and incentive effects of tax harmonization'. This is done by the SYSIFF micro-model developed by the authors on the basis of a sample of French households which emphasizes equity considerations. The efficiency issues are also analysed through a thorough examination of the distribution of marginal tax rates.

The welfare effect on Italian consumers due to the harmonization of indirect taxes is estimated by Vincenzo Patrizi and Nicola Rossi in Chapter 12, entitled 'The European internal market and the welfare of Italian consumers'. Following the methodology pioneered by Jorgenson *et al.* (1988), they combine time-series aggregate data with cross-sectional consumer information. However, the empirical analysis, instead of being based on the translog, is based on Rossi's (1988) almost-ideal demand system. The model chosen allows them to examine equity and efficiency effects of the EEC Commission harmonization proposal. Furthermore, they extend the analysis to include the abolition of subsidies for public services, which in Italy are quite substantial, and calculate the derived welfare effects. The main result of the chapter is that the harmonization of indirect taxes would mostly have a redistributing effect, shifting the burden of indirect taxation from the poor to the rich. If subsidies to public services were eliminated as well, such a result would be strengthened, showing that the whole system of Italian indirect taxation is quite regressive.

To study the empirical effects of the tax reform within the process of the completion of the internal market, Pantelis Capros, Pavlos Karadeloglou and Gregory Mentzas, in Chapter 13, entitled 'Tax reform within the EC internal market: empirical analysis with two macroeconomic modelling approaches', introduce alternative modelling approaches. They build and estimate a neo-Keynesian and a general-equilibrium model and use them for the analysis of the impacts of some of the issues of the year 1992, especially those related to fiscal policy. Empirical analysis is carried out by comparing the behaviour of the different modelling approaches and the alternative ways of price and wage determination in the context of a general-equilibrium model. The alternative variants are an attempt to represent in a formal manner the rigidities and imperfections in the markets and evaluate their policy impacts. The impacts of tax policy modifications are evaluated with and without a public budget constraint and considering alternative ways to finance it.

Public finance and the effect it has on individuals' and firms' behaviour is very important for understanding growth possibilities. The studies in this volume represent some of the most advanced pieces of academic research on the interrelationship between taxation, welfare and economic growth. In this respect, they shed light on several issues important for fiscal policy; however, they also illustrate how substantial is the remaining research agenda and how deep the analysis still required.

REFERENCES

Auerbach, A. J. and Kotlikoff, L. J. (1987) *Dynamic Fiscal Policy*. Cambridge University Press, Cambridge.

Diewert, W. E. and Wales, T. J. (1987) Flexible Functional Forms and Global Curvature Conditions. *Econometrica*, **50**, 43–68.

Jorgenson, D. W. and Yun, K. Y. (1986) The Efficiency of Capital Allocation. *Scandinavian Journal of Economics*, **88**, 85–107.

Jorgenson, D. W., Lau, L. J. and Stocker, T. W. (1988) Welfare Comparisons and Exact Aggregation. *American Economic Review*, **70**, 268–72.

King, M. and Fullerton, D. (1984) *The Taxation of Income from Capital: A Comparative Study of the United States, the United Kingdom, Sweden and West Germany*. The University of Chicago Press, Chicago.

Rossi, N. (1988) Budget share demographic translation and the aggregrate almost ideal demand system, *European Economic Review*, **31**, 1301–18.

Part One

Taxation, Economic Growth and Welfare

1

The excess burden of taxation in the US

Dale W. Jorgenson and Kun-Young Yun

1.1 INTRODUCTION

The topic of discussion in this chapter is the measurement of the excess burden of taxation in the United States. Excess burden is one of the the central concepts in public finance. The concept is employed in optimal taxation, where the government meets given revenue requirements by choosing taxes so as to maximize social welfare. The closely related concept of the marginal cost of public funds is employed in the cost–benefit analysis of public expenditure; the benefits of a programme are balanced against the costs of raising tax revenue to finance it. In both applications it is necessary to measure the social cost of raising tax revenue.[1]

The government sector of the US economy raises revenues through taxes on income from capital and labour services. Corporate capital income is taxed at both corporate and individual levels, non-corporate capital income is taxed only at the individual level, and household capital income is not taxed at either level. In addition, the government sector imposes sales taxes on the production of consumption and investment goods and property taxes on assets held by the business and household sectors. Taxes insert wedges between demand and supply prices for investment and consumption goods and for capital and labour services. These tax wedges distort private decisions and lead to losses in efficiency.[2]

In measuring the excess burden of taxation in the US, we use a hypothetical non-distorting tax system as a standard. In this tax system all revenue is raised by means of a lump-sum levy that does not distort private decisions and involves no loss in efficiency. Our most important conclusion is that the excess burden imposed on the US economy by the current tax system is very large. The welfare loss is equivalent to 18% of the government tax revenue. Each dollar of tax revenue costs the private sector a dollar of foregone expenditure and an average

---

[1] Important progress has been made in measuring the excess burden of the US tax system, beginning with the work of Harberger (1966). Recent contributions include Shoven (1976), Ballard *et al*. (1985b, c), Ballard (1988), and Auerbach (1989a). An excellent survey is presented by Auerbach (1985).
[2] See Jorgenson and Yun (1991) for a detailed description of the US tax system.

loss in efficiency due to tax-induced distortions of 18 cents. Our estimate is based on the **average excess burden**. This is the gain in efficiency that would result from replacing the US tax system by a lump-sum levy.

The concept of efficiency loss relevant to tax reform is the **marginal excess burden**. The marginal excess burden of the US tax system is defined in terms of the efficiency loss per dollar for the last dollar of revenue raised. We find that the cost of raising a dollar of government tax revenue at the margin is 39.1 cents. In addition, there are large differences in marginal excess burdens among different types of taxes. For example, the marginal efficiency cost of raising a dollar of government revenue for taxes on capital income at the individual level is 101.7 cents for each dollar of revenue. Since marginal excess burdens must be equalized for an optimal tax system, this is an indication of important opportunities for gains in efficiency from future tax reform.[3]

In order to measure the average and marginal excess burdens of taxation, we employ a dynamic general-equilibrium model of the US economy.[4] In this highly schematic representation of the US economy, a single representative producer employs capital and labour services to produce outputs of consumption and investment goods. We have simplified the representation of technology in the model by introducing a single stock of capital at each point of time. This capital is perfectly malleable and allocated so as to equalize after-tax rates of return to equity in the corporate, non-corporate and household sectors. By modelling the substitution between consumption and investment goods, we introduce costs of adjustment in the response of investment to changes in tax policy.[5]

Our model includes a representative consumer who supplies labour services, demands consumption goods, and allocates income between consumption and saving. This model of consumer behaviour is based on an intertemporally additive utility function that depends on levels of full consumption in all time periods. Full consumption is an aggregate of consumption goods, household capital services, and leisure. To simplify the representation of preferences, we endow the representative consumer with an infinite lifetime and perfect foresight about future prices and rates of return.[6] We have fitted econometric models of producer and consumer behaviour to data for the US economy covering the period 1947–86.

In our model of the US economy, equilibrium is characterized by an intertemporal price system. This price system clears the markets for all four commodity groups included in the model – labour and capital services and consumption and investment goods. Equilibrium at each point of time links the past and the future

---

[3] See Diamond and Mirrlees (1971a, b) and Stiglitz and Dasgupta (1971). A survey of optimal tax theory is given by Auerbach (1985).

[4] See Jorgenson and Yun (1986a) for a detailed discussion of the model. The results presented by them are based on econometric models fitted to data for the period 1955–80. Alternative approaches to dynamic general-equilibrium modelling of US tax policy are presented by Auerbach and Kotlikoff (1987) and Goulder and Summers (1989).

[5] For alternative approaches to costs of adjustment, see Summers (1981) and Auerbach (1989b).

[6] Perfect foresight models of tax incidence have been presented by Hall (1971), Chamley (1981), Judd (1987), Sinn (1987), Lucas (1990) and many others.

through markets for investment goods and capital services. Assets are accumulated as a result of past investments, while the prices of assets must be equal to the present values of future capital services. The time path of full consumption must satisfy the conditions for intertemporal optimality of the household sector under perfect foresight.

In order to measure the excess burden of taxation in the US, we first consider the intertemporal equilibrium associated with a reference tax policy. In this chapter we consider the excess burden of taxation for tax policies that prevailed before and after the Tax Reform Act of 1986. We refer to the tax policy before the 1986 reform as the 1985 Tax Law, since this policy remained in force until the end of calendar year 1985.[7] Under perfect foresight, there is a unique transition path to balanced-growth equilibrium for any tax policy and any initial level of capital. The growth path of the US economy consists of a plan for consumption of goods and leisure at every point of time by the representative consumer and a plan for production of investment and consumption goods from capital and labour services at every point of time by the representative producer. These plans are brought into consistency by the intertemporal price system.

Associated with the reference tax policy and the corresponding intertemporal equilibrium is a level of welfare for the representative consumer. This can be interpreted as a measure of economic efficiency, corresponding to the potential level of welfare for society as a whole. The actual level of welfare also depends on the distribution of welfare among consuming units. To measure the excess burden of taxation, we substitute a non-distorting tax for all or part of the reference tax system. We then consider the level of welfare associated with this alternative tax system. We evaluate the excess burden of taxation in terms of the difference in wealth required to attain levels of potential welfare before and after the tax substitution.

This chapter is organized as follows. In section 1.2 we present an analytical framework for comparison of alternative tax policies. This framework is based on our model of consumer behaviour. Using the intertemporal welfare function for the representative consumer and the corresponding budget constraint, we derive an intertemporal expenditure function. This expenditure function gives the wealth required to achieve a given level of consumer welfare as a function of future prices and rates of return. We then define an intertemporal counterpart of Hicks's equivalent variation.[8] This can be interpreted as a money metric of the difference in levels of consumer welfare between the reference tax policy and the alternative tax policy.

[7] Detailed descriptions of the 1985 Tax Law and the Tax Reform Act of 1986 are given in Jorgenson and Yun (1990). In this paper we have utilized our dynamic general equilibrium model of the US economy to assess the impact on US economic growth of tax reform proposals leading to the Tax Reform Act of 1986. A detailed survey of alternative appraisals of the 1986 reform is presented by Henderson (1991). In Jorgenson and Yun (1986b) we used an earlier version of our model to analyse the tax reform of 1981.

[8] See Hicks (1942). The expenditure function has been utilized in measuring the excess burden of taxation by Diamond and McFadden (1974) and Kay (1980).

In section 1.3 we apply our analytical framework to the 1985 Tax Law and the Tax Reform Act of 1986. For this purpose we hold government expenditure, government deficit, and the net foreign investment constant. We then measure the excess burden of taxation for each of the major programmes included in the US tax system. We also consider the excess burden of the tax system as a whole. For this purpose, we simulate the growth of the US economy under each of the two reference tax policies and alternative policies incorporating a non-distorting tax. We then compare these tax policies by means of the equivalent variation in wealth.

In section 1.4 we summarize our main results. We find that the US tax system imposes a very substantial excess burden on the economy. However, the average burden was substantially reduced by the Tax Reform Act of 1986. Second, we find that marginal excess burdens differ substantially among alternative tax programmes, both before and after the 1986 tax reform. This suggests that important opportunities still remain for gains in efficiency from future tax reforms. The most important of these is to correct the excessive reliance on income taxation at both federal and state and local levels. Further gains are possible to reducing taxes on capital income at both corporate and individual levels relative to taxes on labour income.

1.2 ANALYTICAL FRAMEWORK

We represent the household sector by a representative consumer who takes prices and rates of return as given. We also assume that the representative consumer has an infinite time horizon and is endowed with perfect foresight. The assumption of an infinite time horizon can be interpreted as a way of explaining intergenerational transfers of wealth through bequests.[9] This assumption appears to be a viable alternative to the life-cycle theory in modelling consumer behaviour.[10] Finally, we assume that the services provided by the government sector enter the utility function of the consumer in an additively separable manner. This implies that the marginal utility of private consumption is independent of the level of public consumption.

To represent our model of consumer behaviour we introduce the following notation:

F_t = full consumption per capita with population measured in efficiency units,
PF_t = price of full consumption per capita,

[9] Barro (1974) has provided a rationale for the infinite-horizon representative consumer model in terms of intergenerational altruism. Intergenerational altruism has implications that are very different from those of the life-cycle theory, based on a finite lifetime for each consumer. Examples of these implications are distortions in intertemporal consumption by a social-security tax, considered by Feldstein (1974), the burden of national debt, analysed by Barro (1974), and dynamic tax reform and intergenerational distribution of the tax burden, studied by Auerbach and Kotlikoff (1987) and Auerbach (1989a).

[10] For example, Kotlikoff and Summers (1981) have suggested that life-cycle saving accounts for only a small fraction of the total saving, so that a significant fraction of saving is motivated by bequests.

n = rate of population growth,
μ = rate of Harrod-neutral productivity growth,
ρ = nominal private rate of return.

In our model of consumer behaviour the representative consumer maximizes the **intertemporal welfare function**:

$$V = \frac{1}{(1-\sigma)} \sum_{t=0}^{\infty} \left(\frac{1+n}{1+\gamma}\right)^t U_t^{1-\sigma}, \tag{1.1}$$

where σ is the inverse of the intertemporal elasticity of substitution and γ is the subjective rate of time preference. These two parameters describe the preferences of the representative consumer. The intertemporal welfare function is a discounted sum of products of total population, which grows at a constant rate, n, and per capital atemporal welfare functions, U_t ($t = 0, 1, \ldots$). These welfare functions depend on full consumption per capita, F_t, with population measured in efficiency units:

$$U_t = F_t(1+\mu)^t \quad (t = 0, 1, \ldots). \tag{1.2}$$

In this expression the term $(1+\mu)^t$, involving the rate of Harrod-neutral productivity growth μ, converts the population from efficiency units to natural units.

The representative consumer maximizes the welfare function [equation (1.1)] subject to the **intertemporal budget constraint**:

$$W = \sum_{t=0}^{\infty} \frac{PF_t F_t (1+\mu)^t (1+n)^t}{\prod_{s=0}^{t} (1+\rho_s)}, \tag{1.3}$$

where W is full wealth. Full wealth is the present value of full consumption over the whole future of the US economy. The current value of full consumption is discounted at the nominal private rate of return ρ.

The intertemporal welfare function V is additively separable into the atemporal welfare functions U_t ($t = 0, 1, \ldots$). These functions depend on the consumption of leisure, consumption goods, and capital services in each period, so that we can divide the representative consumer's optimization problem into two stages. In the first stage, the consumer allocates full wealth among consumption levels of different time periods. In the second stage, the consumer allocates full consumption among leisure, consumption goods, and household capital services in each period.

The necessary conditions for a maximum of the intertemporal utility function, subject to the constraint on full wealth, are given by the discrete-time Euler equation:

$$\frac{F_t}{F_{t-1}} = \left[\frac{PF_{t-1}}{PF_t} \cdot \frac{1+\rho_t}{(1+\gamma)(1+\mu)^\sigma}\right]^{1/\sigma}, \quad (t = 1, 2, \ldots). \tag{1.4}$$

Equation (1.4) describes the optimal time path of full consumption, given the sequence of prices of full consumption and nominal rates of return. We refer to this equation as the **transition equation** for full consumption. The growth rate of full consumption is uniquely determined by the transition equation, so that we need to determine only the level of full consumption in any one period in order to find the whole optimal time path.

In a steady state with no inflation, the level of full consumption per capita with population measured in efficiency units is constant. Therefore, the only private nominal rate of return consistent with the steady state, say $\tilde{\rho}$, is

$$\tilde{\rho} = (1 + \gamma)(1 + \mu)^{\sigma} - 1. \tag{1.5}$$

This rate of return depends on the rate of Harrod-neutral productivity growth and the parameters of the intertemporal welfare function, but is independent of tax policy.

We denote the rate of inflation in the price of full consumption by π_t, where:

$$\pi_t = \frac{PF_t}{PF_{t-1}} - 1 \quad (t = 1, 2, \ldots).$$

In a steady state with a constant rate of inflation, say $\tilde{\pi}$, the nominal private rate of return is

$$\tilde{\rho} = (1 + \gamma)(1 + \mu)^{\sigma}(1 + \tilde{\pi}) - 1. \tag{1.6}$$

If we denote the real private rate of return by r_t, where

$$r_t = \frac{PF_{t-1}}{PF_t}(1 + \rho_t) - 1 \quad (t = 1, 2, \ldots),$$

the steady-state real private rate of return, say $\tilde{r}$, is

$$\tilde{r} = (1 + \gamma)(1 + \mu)^{\sigma} - 1 \tag{1.7}$$

This rate of return is independent of tax policy and the rate of inflation.

The transition equation for full consumption implies that if the real private rate of return exceeds the steady-state rate of return, full consumption rises; conversely, if the rate of return is below its steady-state value, full consumption falls. To show this, we take the logarithm of both sides of the transition equation, obtaining

$$\ln \frac{F_t}{F_{t-1}} = \frac{1}{\sigma}[\ln(1 + r) - \ln(1 + \tilde{r})]. \tag{1.8}$$

To a first-order approximation, the growth rate of full consumption is proportional to the difference between the real private rate of return and its steady-state value.[11] The constant of proportionality is the intertemporal elasticity of substitution, $1/\sigma$. The greater this elasticity, the more rapidly full consumption approaches its steady-state level.

---

[11] Chamley (1981) derives this formula in a continuous-time framework with a single good and fixed labour supply.

In order to evaluate alternative tax policies, we compare the levels of social welfare associated with these policies. We can translate welfare comparisons into monetary terms by introducing the intertemporal counterpart of Hicks's equivalent variation. For this purpose, we express the full wealth required to achieve a given level of intertemporal welfare in terms of the time path of future prices of full consumption and rates of return. Since full wealth is the present value of full consumption over the whole future of the US economy, we refer to this expression as the **intertemporal expenditure function**. Using this expenditure function, we can express differences in welfare in terms of differences in wealth.

To derive the intertemporal expenditure function, we first express the time path of full consumption in terms of the initial level and future real private rates of return:

$$\frac{F_t}{F_0} = \prod_{s=0}^{t}\left[\frac{1+r_s}{(1+\gamma)(1+\mu)^\sigma}\right]^{1/\sigma}, \quad (t=1,2,\dots).$$ (1.9)

Using this expression, we can write the intertemporal welfare function as

$$V = \frac{F_0^{1-\sigma}}{1-\sigma}D,$$ (1.10)

where

$$D \equiv \sum_{t=0}^{\infty}\left[\frac{1+n}{(1+\gamma)^{1/\sigma}}\right]^t \prod_{s=0}^{t}(1+r_s)^{(1-\sigma)/\sigma}.$$

The function D summarizes the effect of all future prices and rates of return on the initial level of full consumption F_0 associated with a given level of welfare V.

Since the optimal time path for full consumption must satisfy the intertemporal budget constraint, we can express the initial level of full consumption in terms of full wealth and all future real private rates of return:

$$F_0 = \frac{W}{PF_0}\frac{1}{D}.$$

Combining this expression with the intertemporal welfare function [equation (1.10)] and solving for full wealth, we obtain the intertemporal expenditure function, say $W(PF, D, V)$, where

$$W(PF,D,V) = PF_0\left[\frac{(1-\sigma)V}{D^\sigma}\right]^{1/(1-\sigma)},$$ (1.11)

We employ the intertemporal expenditure function to provide a money metric of differences in levels of welfare associated with alternative tax policies. For this purpose we first calculate the solution to our dynamic general-equilibrium model of the US economy for the reference tax policy. We denote the resulting prices and discount rates by PF_0 and D_0 and the corresponding level of welfare by V_0. We then solve the model for an alternative tax policy and denote the resulting level of welfare by V_1. Finally, we calculate the **equivalent variation in full wealth**, say ΔW, where

$$\Delta W = W(PF_0, D_0, V_1) - W(PF_0, D_0, V_0) \tag{1.12}$$

$$= W(PF_0, D_0, V_1) - W_0.$$

The equivalent variation in full wealth, described by equation (1.12), is the wealth required to attain the welfare associated with the alternative tax policy at prices of the reference policy, $W(PF_0, D_0, V_1)$, less the wealth for the reference policy W_0. In calculating the excess burden associated with the US tax system, we consider two reference policies – the 1985 Tax Law and the Tax Reform Act of 1986. The alternative policies involve replacing distorting taxes by non-distorting taxes. If the equivalent variation is positive, a change in policy produces a gain in welfare; otherwise, the policy change results in a welfare loss. The equivalent variations in full wealth enable us to rank the reference policy and any number of alternative policies in terms of a money metric of the corresponding welfare levels.

In order to measure the efficiency cost associated with tax-induced distortions in private decisions, we replace distorting taxes by a lump-sum levy. We express the gain in welfare in terms of the equivalent variation in wealth [equation (1.12)]. We find it useful to compare this excess burden with the present value of the tax revenue generated from the lump-sum tax. For this purpose we add the time path of the lump-sum levy to the time path of full consumption under the reference tax policy. We then evaluate the level of welfare associated with the composite time path consisting of the lump-sum tax and full consumption. We obtain a monetary equivalent of this level of welfare by evaluating the intertemporal expenditure function at prices and rates of return of the reference tax policy. The difference between this level of wealth and the wealth of the reference policy, W_0, is the present value of the lump-sum tax in terms of full consumption.

More formally, we can express the difference in levels of intertemporal welfare between a reference tax policy and an alternative policy with a lump-sum tax in terms of the equivalent variation [equation (1.12)]. Similarly, we can express the present value of the time path of the lump-sum tax as the equivalent variation

$$T = W(PF_0, D_0, V_2) - W_0 \tag{1.13}$$

where V_2 is the welfare corresponding to the composite time path of the lump-sum tax and full consumption under the reference tax policy.

Finally, we define the **average efficiency cost**, say AEC, imposed on the US economy by the taxes we have replaced by a lump-sum levy, as follows:

$$AEC = \frac{\Delta W}{T}, \tag{1.14}$$

where ΔW and T are defined by equations (1.12) and (1.13), respectively. This is the ratio of the gain in welfare achieved by replacing distorting taxes by a non-distorting tax to the corresponding tax revenue. Both the welfare gain and the tax revenue are expressed in terms of the prices and rates of return of the reference tax policy. Similarly, we can define the **marginal efficiency cost**, say *MEC*, as follows:

$$MEC = \frac{\Delta(\Delta W)}{\Delta T}. \tag{1.15}$$

This is the ratio of the incremental gain in welfare achieved by replacing distorting taxes by a non-distorting tax to the incremental tax revenue.

Obviously, there are many different ways of expressing the average and marginal excess burdens of the US tax system. An alternative approach has been proposed by Ballard *et al.* (1985a, Chapter 7). This approach is based on the difference between present values of time paths of full consumption associated with alternative tax policies. Although there are important similarities between comparisons of present values of full consumption and comparisons of full wealth by means of the intertemporal expenditure function, these two approaches do not coincide. Only comparisons based on the expenditure function provide a money metric of differences in intertemporal welfare.

The first proposal of Ballard *et al.* (1985a) is to calculate the present value of differences in full consumption at prices of the reference tax policy. This amounts to replacing the present value of the full consumption, $W(PF_0, D_0, V_1)$, required for the level of welfare under the alternative tax policy [equation (1.12)] with the present value of the time path of full consumption associated with that policy. Since the representative consumer minimizes the present value of the full consumption required to attain any level of welfare, this overstates welfare gains and understates welfare losses. The second proposal of Ballard *et al.* is to calculate the present value of differences in full consumption at prices of the alternative tax policy. This measure understates welfare gains and overstates welfare losses and has the added disadvantage of producing welfare comparisons among alternative tax policies that are intransitive.

1.3 EFFICIENCY COSTS OF TAXATION

The welfare level of the US economy depends on both private and public consumption. Since we have assumed that the intertemporal welfare function is additively separable in these two components of consumption, we did not include public consumption in the welfare function [equation (1.1)] for private consumption. When we compare the performance of the US economy under alternative tax policies, it is essential to fix the size and composition of government spending, so that welfare derived from public consumption is held constant. For this purpose, we introduce a welfare function for public consumption.

We assume that the allocation of total government expenditures in any time period, net of interest payments on government debt, is based on a linear logarithmic welfare function. This implies that shares of consumption goods, investment goods, labour services, transfer payments to US citizens, and transfer payments to foreigners are unaffected by changes in the corresponding prices. Under the reference policy, we set the steady-state level of government spending at a fixed fraction of private national income. Along the transition path, the level of government spending is determined by the sum of tax revenue and the government deficit. When we solve the model under alternative tax policies, we set the level of public consumption in each period at the same value as under the reference policy.

On the revenue side of the government budget, there are two alternative sources of income – tax revenues and borrowing from the public. The government budget constraint requires that the present value of government spending must be equal to the present value of government receipts plus the net worth of the government sector. In our model, tax and debt financing are not equivalent. Barro's (1974) Ricardian equivalence theorem fails to hold, since taxes distort private decisions. To take account of this aspect of the revenue side of the government budget, we hold the time path of the government deficit for the reference tax policy constant for all alternative tax policies.

Our model of the US economy achieves a steady state within about 35 years after a change in tax policy. We assume that the level of government debt reaches its steady-state value in 35 years after introduction of a new policy. We close the gap between the initial and the steady-state levels of government debt by reducing the gap at an annual rate equal to 1/35 of the gap at the beginning of the transition path. Since the time paths of government spending and the government budget deficit are fixed at the levels of the reference tax policy, tax revenue must be adjusted to meet the government budget constraint under the alternative policies.

Trade with the rest of the world sector need not be balanced in our model of the US economy. From the viewpoint of an individual, it does not matter whether a given amount of saving is invested domestically or abroad. However, for the economy as a whole it does make a difference for at least two reasons. First, capital employed abroad does not generate corporate tax revenue. Second, this capital does not affect domestic output. Therefore, we control the time path of claims on the rest of the world in the same way as the time path of government debt. To keep the trade deficit on a time path implied by claims on the rest of the world for the reference tax policy, we adjust the net exports of consumption and investment goods and labour services for the alternative policies.

It is worth noting that there is no reason to believe that the actual levels of the government budget deficit and net foreign investment will follow the paths we have employed in simulating the reference tax policies. The purpose of controlling government budget deficit and the deficit of the rest of the world sector is to eliminate the effects of changes in government budget policy or trade policy on consumer welfare, so that we can concentrate on the effects of tax policy changes. The accuracy of our projections of the future time paths of the two deficits is a secondary consideration.

In this section, we estimate the efficiency costs for various parts of the US tax system under the 1985 Tax Law and the Tax Reform Act of 1986. For this purpose, we carry out alternative simulations of the US economy under reductions of tax rates for the following nine components of the US tax system: (1) the corporate income tax; (2) capital income taxes at the individual level, including taxes levied on non-corporate capital income and taxes on individual capital income originating in the corporate sector; (3) property taxes on corporate, non-corporate, and household assets; (4) capital income taxes at both corporate and individual levels; (5) labour income taxes; (6) capital and labour income taxes; (7) the individual income tax; (8) sales taxes on consumption and investment goods; and (9) all taxes.

In each simulation we reduce the tax rates and evaluate the average efficiency cost (*AEC*) and marginal efficiency cost (*MEC*) generated by tax distortions. When the corporate income tax is reduced, we also reduce the tax credits on corporate investment in the same proportion. Similarly, when the capital income tax at the individual level is reduced, we reduce the tax credits on non-corporate investment. We consider 11 points between the reference tax policy and the alternative tax policy in which the relevant tax rates are reduced to zero. The excess burdens are evaluated with tax rates reduced by 5%, 10%, 20% . . ., 90% and 100%. Except for the first two points, which are only five percentage points apart, the points for measuring the excess burdens are ten percentage points apart. The first two intervals are shorter, so that we can measure the efficiency cost of each tax program more precisely at rates prevailing under the reference tax policy.

In the first set of simulations, we evaluate the efficiency cost of all nine components of the US tax system under the 1985 Tax Law. Each of the alternative tax policies for evaluation of the excess burdens is obtained by lowering the average and marginal rates of the relevant taxes and replacing the lost revenue by a lump-sum levy. For each alternative policy, the average efficiency cost is defined relative to the tax revenue replaced by the lump-sum tax. We consider the growth of the US economy with the 1985 Tax Law as the reference tax policy. The present value T of the lump-sum tax is evaluated along the corresponding time path of full consumption, as indicated in equation (1.13).

Table 1.1 presents the average and marginal efficiency costs of the various components of the US tax system under the 1985 Tax Law. We begin by considering the marginal and average efficiency costs at the tax rates prevailing under the 1985 Tax Law. The first column of Table 1.1 shows that the marginal efficiency cost for all taxes is 0.472 when these taxes are increased from 95% to 100% of their 1985 levels. If the government increases all taxes in the same proportion, the burden imposed on the US economy in excess of the tax revenue raised is 47.2 cents per dollar of revenue. Since this efficiency cost is measured relative to the 1985 Tax Law as the reference tax policy, the estimated marginal and average efficiency costs are the same.

Table 1.1   Efficiency cost of the US tax revenues: 1985 Tax Law

Tax Bases		*Reduction in Tax Rates (%)*										
		5	*10*	*20*	*30*	*40*	*50*	*60*	*70*	*80*	*90*	*100*
1. Corporate	MEC	0.842	0.786	0.719	0.647	0.594	0.551	0.516	0.492	0.467	0.451	0.440
income	AEC	0.842	0.815	0.770	0.734	0.706	0.683	0.665	0.650	0.637	0.627	0.619
2. Ind. Cap.	MEC	1.128	1.103	1.061	1.016	0.969	0.926	0.885	0.845	0.810	0.774	0.740
income	AEC	1.128	1.116	1.089	1.065	1.042	1.020	0.999	0.979	0.960	0.941	0.923
3. Property	MEC	0.186	0.183	0.181	0.176	0.173	0.169	0.166	0.161	0.157	0.154	0.149
value	AEC	0.186	0.185	0.183	0.181	0.179	0.177	0.175	0.173	0.171	0.169	0.167
4. All Cap.	MEC	0.975	0.913	0.848	0.773	0.714	0.669	0.631	0.601	0.574	0.554	0.537
income	AEC	0.975	0.945	0.898	0.860	0.828	0.802	0.779	0.760	0.744	0.729	0.717
5. Labour	MEC	0.488	0.457	0.414	0.365	0.322	0.285	0.259	0.230	0.209	0.194	0.184
income	AEC	0.488	0.473	0.444	0.418	0.394	0.373	0.355	0.338	0.323	0.310	0.299
6. 1 + 2 + 5	MEC	0.651	0.593	0.519	0.434	0.361	0.299	0.246	0.200	0.161	0.128	0.102
= 4 + 5	AEC	0.651	0.622	0.572	0.528	0.489	0.455	0.424	0.397	0.372	0.350	0.331
7. Ind. income	MEC	0.616	0.573	0.515	0.445	0.383	0.327	0.278	0.235	0.196	0.163	0.135
	AEC	0.616	0.595	0.555	0.519	0.486	0.456	0.428	0.402	0.379	0.358	0.339
8. Sales value	MEC	0.260	0.256	0.252	0.245	0.239	0.232	0.227	0.220	0.215	0.209	0.203
	AEC	0.260	0.258	0.255	0.251	0.248	0.245	0.242	0.239	0.236	0.233	0.230
9. All Tax	MEC	0.472	0.424	0.361	0.286	0.223	0.169	0.125	0.090	0.069	0.055	0.045
Bases	AEC	0.472	0.449	0.405	0.367	0.333	0.304	0.277	0.255	0.237	0.224	0.214

Next, we consider the results presented in the last column of Table 1.1. This column gives the efficiency loss when tax revenue is raised by increasing all taxes in the same proportion from zero to 10% of the 1985 levels. For all taxes that make up the US tax system the marginal efficiency cost drops to 0.045, which implies that the efficiency cost is only 4.5 cents per dollar of tax revenue. However, the average efficiency cost is 0.214, so that the loss in efficiency from all distorting taxes is 21.4 cents per dollar of tax revenue. This is the difference in wealth corresponding to differences in welfare between the growth of the US economy under the 1985 Tax Law and economic growth with all tax revenue obtained from a non-distorting lump-sum levy.

For all the taxes we consider in Table 1.1, the marginal efficiency cost declines with the size of the tax revenue replaced by a lump-sum levy. This cost is lower than the average efficiency cost, except for the first tax reduction in each set of simulations. The average efficiency cost drops much less precipitously than the marginal efficiency cost. This corresponds to the standard result of partial equilibrium analysis of tax policy that total welfare cost increases more than in proportion to the increase in the tax rate. We conclude that the efficiency cost of the US tax system is rising at a rapidly increasing rate as we approach tax rates like those actually prevailing in the 1985 Tax Law. From this finding we would anticipate considerable gains in efficiency from the reductions in marginal tax rates embodied in the Tax Reform Act of 1986.

From the marginal efficiency costs presented in the first column of Table 1.1 we can see that the 1985 Tax Law placed excessive reliance on income taxes. Marginal and average efficiency costs for all income taxes on capital and labour income at both corporate and individual levels are given in the sixth panel of Table 1.1. The marginal efficiency cost of these taxes at rates prevailing in the 1985 Tax Law is 0.651, so that a proportional change in these taxes from 95% to 100% of the 1985 levels costs 65.1 cents for each dollar of tax revenue raised. By contrast, marginal efficiency costs of property taxes, in the third panel and sales taxes in the eighth panel, under the 1985 Tax Law were only 18.6 cents per dollar of property tax revenue and 26 cents per dollar of sales tax revenue. A shift from income taxes towards sales and property taxes would have reduced the overall excess burden of the US tax system considerably.

A third conclusion from the results given in Table 1.1 is that the allocation of income taxes under the 1985 Tax Law between capital and labour income and between corporate and individual income led to further losses in efficiency. Capital income taxes in the fourth panel of Table 1.1 had a marginal efficiency cost of 0.975 so that the efficiency loss for each dollar of revenue raised by taxing capital income was 97.5 cents. By contrast, the marginal efficiency cost of labour income taxes was only 0.488 leading to a loss in efficiency of 48.8 cents for each dollar of labour income tax revenue. Gains in efficiency could have been achieved by substituting taxes on labour income for taxes on capital income. At the other extreme, the marginal efficiency cost of all income taxes at 10% of the rates under the 1985 Tax Law was only 0.102 or 10.2 cents per dollar of tax revenue, while the costs of capital and labour income taxes were, respectively, 0.537 and 0.184 or 53.7 cents and 18.4 cents per dollar of tax revenue. These results illustrate the fact that the marginal efficiency costs of mutually exclusive sets of taxes are not additive, so that combining the results of partial equilibrium measures of tax distortions can be grossly misleading.

The results given in Table 1.1 show that the allocation of taxes on capital income between corporate and income levels was far from optimal. The marginal efficiency cost of taxes on capital income at the individual level was 1.128, so that the efficiency losses for each dollar of revenue raised actually exceeded a dollar. At this margin, the cost of each dollar of tax revenue was one dollar removed from the private sector plus one dollar and 13 cents of loss in efficiency due to tax distortions. For the corporate income tax the marginal efficiency cost was 0.842, so that the excess burden of taxation for each additional dollar of corporate tax revenue was 84.2 cents. There would have been a gain in efficiency from transferring a part of the burden of taxation on capital income from the individual to the corporate level.

We have carried out a parallel set of simulations to estimate the average and marginal efficiency costs of the various components of the US tax system under the Tax Reform Act of 1986. The results are summarized in Table 1.2. Overall, we find that this tax reform significantly reduced the average and marginal efficiency costs of taxation. An important exception is sales taxes, where the estimated efficiency costs are slightly higher. Beginning with the average and marginal efficiency costs of the whole US tax system in the ninth panel of Table 1.2, we find that the marginal efficiency cost at rates prevailing under the

1986 tax act was 0.391, so that the loss in efficiency for each dollar of tax revenue raised was 39.1 cents. This is a considerable reduction from the loss in efficiency under the 1985 Tax Law and reflects the drastic decline in marginal tax rates under the 1986 tax reform. The average efficiency cost for the whole tax system fell to 0.180, so that replacing all taxes by a lump sum levy would have increased consumer welfare by an average of 18 cents per dollar of tax revenue.

Table 1.2. Efficiency cost of the US Tax Revenues: Tax Reform Act of 1986

Tax Bases		*Reduction in Tax Rates (%)*										
		5	*10*	*20*	*30*	*40*	*50*	*60*	*70*	*80*	*90*	*100*
1. Corporate	MEC	0.448	0.435	0.418	0.397	0.379	0.363	0.348	0.334	0.322	0.310	0.301
income	AEC	0.448	0.442	0.431	0.421	0.412	0.404	0.397	0.391	0.384	0.379	0.374
2. Ind. Cap.	MEC	1.017	0.989	0.951	0.904	0.853	0.812	0.767	0.727	0.688	0.650	0.613
income	AEC	1.017	1.003	0.977	0.953	0.928	0.906	0.884	0.863	0.842	0.822	0.803
3. Property	MEC	0.176	0.174	0.171	0.168	0.164	0.160	0.157	0.153	0.149	0.145	0.142
value	AEC	0.176	0.175	0.173	0.171	0.169	0.168	0.166	0.164	0.162	0.160	0.158
4. All Cap.	MEC	0.675	0.650	0.616	0.573	0.533	0.498	0.466	0.435	0.407	0.382	0.359
income	AEC	0.675	0.663	0.640	0.619	0.600	0.582	0.566	0.551	0.537	0.524	0.512
5. Labour	MEC	0.376	0.358	0.333	0.303	0.276	0.253	0.237	0.216	0.201	0.190	0.183
income	AEC	0.376	0.367	0.350	0.334	0.320	0.307	0.296	0.285	0.275	0.266	0.259
6. 1 + 2 + 5	MEC	0.497	0.462	0.414	0.355	0.301	0.254	0.212	0.175	0.142	0.114	0.091
= 4 + 5	AEC	0.497	0.480	0.448	0.418	0.391	0.366	0.343	0.323	0.304	0.287	0.271
7. Ind. income	MEC	0.520	0.490	0.449	0.396	0.349	0.305	0.265	0.229	0.196	0.167	0.140
	AEC	0.520	0.505	0.477	0.451	0.426	0.403	0.381	0.361	0.342	0.325	0.308
8. Sales value	MEC	0.262	0.259	0.254	0.249	0.242	0.236	0.230	0.224	0.218	0.211	0.205
	AEC	0.262	0.261	0.257	0.254	0.251	0.248	0.245	0.242	0.239	0.236	0.232
9. All Tax	MEC	0.391	0.356	0.308	0.249	0.197	0.151	0.113	0.082	0.063	0.048	0.040
Bases	AEC	0.391	0.374	0.342	0.312	0.285	0.260	0.238	0.220	0.204	0.190	0.180

The Tax Reform Act of 1986 did not successfully address the issue of excessive reliance of the US tax system on income taxes. The marginal efficiency cost of sales taxes given in the eighth panel of Table 1.2 was 0.262 after the reform, while the cost of property taxes given in the third panel was 0.176. By contrast, the marginal efficiency cost of all income taxes given in the sixth panel of Table 1.2 was 0.497. The efficiency losses were 49.7 cents per dollar of income tax revenue, only 17.6 cents per dollar of property tax revenue, and only 26.2 cents per dollar of sales tax revenue. A substantial increase in efficiency could have been realized by reducing income tax rates and increasing the rates of sales and property taxes. Similarly, the structure of the income tax itself remained out of balance with marginal efficiency costs of labour income taxes at 0.376, individual capital income taxes at 1.017, and corporate income taxes at 0.448. Gains in efficiency could have been realized by further reductions in marginal tax rates on individual and corporate taxes on capital income and increases in marginal tax rates on labour income.

1.4 CONCLUSION

Our overall conclusion is that the Tax Reform Act of 1986 led to improvements in efficiency, mainly through reductions in marginal income tax rates. However, the basic structural defects in the US tax system were unaffected by the tax reform. The US tax system relies much too heavily on income taxes, relative to sales and property taxes. Since income taxes are used almost exclusively at the federal level, while sales and property taxes are employed at the state and local level, one way to achieve better balance among these tax programmes would be to shift the tax burden from the federal to the state and local level. Within the income tax at both federal and state and local levels there is excessive reliance on taxes on capital income at the individual level. Taxes on capital income at both corporate and individual levels are too burdensome, relative to taxes on labour income.

ACKNOWLEDGEMENTS

Financial support from the Program on Technology and Economic Policy of Harvard University is gratefully acknowledged.

REFERENCES

Auerbach, A. J. (1985) The Theory of Excess Burden and Optimal Taxation, in *Handbook of Public Economics*, (eds. A. J. Auerbach and M. S. Feldstein), Vol. 1, North-Holland, Amsterdam, pp. 61–127.

Auerbach, A. J. (1989a) The Deadweight Loss from 'Non-Neutral' Taxation. *Journal of Public Economics*, **40**, 1–36.

Auerbach, A. J. (1989b) Tax Reform and Adjustment Costs: The Impact on Investment and Market Value. *International Economic Review*, **30**, 939–63.

Auerbach, A. J., and Kotlikoff, L. J. (1987), *Dynamic Fiscal Policy*. Cambridge University Press, Cambridge.

Ballard, C. L. (1988) The Marginal Efficiency Cost of Redistribution. *American Economic Review*, **78**, 1019–33.

Ballard, C. L., Fullerton, D., Shoven, J. B. and Whalley, J. (1985a) *A General Equilibrium Model For Tax Policy Evaluation*, University of Chicago Press, Chicago.

Ballard, C. L., Shoven, J. B. and Whalley, J. (1985b) General Equilibrium Computations of the Marginal Welfare Costs of Taxes in the United States. *American Economic Review*, **75**, 128–38.

Ballard, C. L., Shoven, J. B., and Whalley, J. (1985c) The Total Welfare Cost of the United States Tax System: A General Equilibrium Approach. *National Tax Journal*, **38**, 125–40.

Barro, R. (1974) Are Government Bonds Net Wealth? *Journal of Political Economy*, **82**, 1095–118.

Chamley, C. (1981) The Welfare Cost of Capital Income Taxation in a Growing Economy, *Journal of Political Economy*, **89**, 468–96.

Diamond, P. A. and McFadden, D. L. (1974) Some Uses of the Expenditure Function in Public Finance. *Journal of Public Economics*, **3**, 3–21.

Diamond, P. A. and Mirrlees, J. A. (1971a) Optimal Taxation and Public Production I: Production Efficiency. *American Economic Review*, **61**, 8–27.

Diamond, P. A. and Mirrlees, J. A. (1971b) Optimal Taxation and Public Production II: Tax Rules. *American Economic Review*, **61**, 261–78.

Feldstein, M. S. (1974) Social Security, Induced Retirement, and Aggregate Capital Accumulation. *Journal of Political Economy*, **82**, 905–26.

Goulder, L. H. and Summers, L. H. (1989) Tax Policy, Asset Prices, and Growth: A General Equilibrium Analysis. *Journal of Public Economics*, **38**, 265–96.

Hall, R. E. (1971) The Dynamic Effects of Fiscal Policy in an Economy with Perfect Foresight, *Review of Economic Studies*, **38**, 229–44.

Harberger, A. C. (1966) Efficiency Effects of Taxes on Income from Capital, in *Effects of Corporation Income Tax*, (ed. M. Krzyzaniak), Wayne State University Press, Detroit.

Henderson, Y. K. (1991) Applications of General Equilibrium Models to the 1986 Tax Reform Act in the United States. *de Economist*, **139**, 147–68.

Hicks, J. R. (1942) Consumers' Surplus and Index-Numbers. *Review of Economic Studies*, **9**, 126–37.

Jorgenson, D. W. and Yun, K.-Y. (1986a) The Efficiency of Capital Allocation *Scandinavian Journal of Economics*, **88**, 85–107.

Jorgenson, D. W. and Yun, K.-Y. (1986b) Tax Policy and Capital Allocation. *Scandinavian Journal of Economics*, 355–77.

Jorgenson, D. W. and Yun, K.-Y. (1990) Tax Reform and U.S. Economic Growth. *Journal of Political Economy*, **98**, S151–93.

Jorgenson, D. W. and Yun, K.-Y. (1991) *Tax Reform and the Cost of Capital*. Oxford University Press, Oxford.

Judd, K. L. (1987) The Welfare Cost of Factor Taxation in a Perfect Foresight Model. *Journal of Political Economy*, **95**, 675–709.

Kay, J. A. (1980) The Deadweight Loss from a Tax System. *Journal of Public Economics*, **13**, 111–19.

Kotlikoff, L. J. and Summers, L. H. (1981) The Role of Intergenerational Transfers in Capital Accumulation. *Journal of Political Economy*, **89**, 706–32.

Lucas, R. E. (1990) Supply-Side Economics: An Analytical Review. *Oxford Economic Papers*, **42**, 293–316.

Shoven, J. B. (1976) The Incidence and Efficiency Effects of Taxes on Income from Capital. *Journal of Political Economy*, **84**, 1261–84.

Sinn, H. W. (1987) *Capital Income Taxation and Resource Allocation*, North-Holland, Amsterdam.

Stiglitz, J. E. and Dasgupta, P. S. (1971) Differential Taxation, Public Goods and Economic Efficiency. *Review of Economic Studies*, **38**, 151–74.

Summers, L. H. (1981) Capital Taxation and Accumulation in a Life-Cycle Growth Model. *American Economic Review*, **71**, 533–44.

2

An intertemporal general-equilibrium model of taxation in Italy

Alberto Heimler and Carlo Milana

2.1 INTRODUCTION

In this chapter we present an intertemporal general-equilibrium model of the Italian economy, with a special emphasis on taxation. The purpose of this model is to evaluate the effects, on national wealth and welfare, arising from the existence of a distortionary tax structure.

The size of waste induced by an inefficient system of taxation is controversial and its estimates vary widely among the empirical investigations, reflecting not only institutional differences in the national systems of taxation but also differences in methods of evaluation, data, disaggregation between sectors, industries and factors of production. Fullerton and Henderson (1989) review some of these studies, most of which use static general-equilibrium models based on the so-called calibration approach and find that the effects of tax distortions are much smaller than previously thought. Distortions among assets seem to be the most important, but the total of all these welfare costs would remain below 1% of income. One exception is the study by Jorgenson and Yun (1986b, 1989), where an intertemporal general-equilibrium model based on the econometric approach is used for the US economy. This study finds that the elimination of effective taxation on capital income (offset by other distorting taxes) produces a substantial gain in potential welfare. This result is confirmed (deductively) by Diewert (1988), who also suggests that the efficiency gains obtained from the reduction of capital income taxes are likely to be large rather than small.

The difference in the results obtained in the empirical literature in this field is due to the fact that the evaluation of the effects of a tax on national wealth is extraordinarily difficult, not only for the complexity of the taxation system but also for the problem of determining the contribution of the tax system on investments demand and on the future growth of income. This is, in fact, the major issue that should be addressed when welfare impacts of changes in taxation are to be evaluated. The interactions through time between saving, rate of return, capital accumulation, resource allocation and time path of income can be taken into account within intertemporal models. In particular, in this type of models investments do not passively adjust to saving, but are determined by production decisions as well. Moreover, the evolution of the economy depends upon capital formation, which in turn is related to saving behaviour. The issue of capital taxation can, therefore, be correctly addressed by models which incorporate a dynamic structure of the accumulation process and at the same time describe the allocation of resources in the different sectors of the economy.[1]

We take advantage of the better descriptive power of intertemporal models and follow, in particular, the Jorgenson and Yun (1986a, b, 1989) methodology.[2] However, with respect to the Jorgenson and Yun model, we take into account the foreign trade sector, thus introducing an additional constraint to the balanced-growth equilibrium. This extension is rather crucial because it allows us to consider offsetting effects stemming from external trade which may dwarf the domestic gains potentially arising from an isolated national fiscal reform. In this respect, our results may be significantly different from those measured with a model of a closed economy. Furthermore, we use functional forms for repres-enting the cost and expenditure functions which belong to the same class as that of Jorgenson and Yun, but have the advantage of imposing concavity without losing completely their flexibility.

The main features of our approach are the following:

1. The parameters of producer and consumer behaviour are econometrically estimated and, thus, our model differs from the most common computable general-equilibrium (GE) models which are based on the so-called calibration method, where some of the parameters are deterministically estimated.
2. The functional forms of behavioural equations are sufficiently general as they include a wide range of classes of technological relations and preferences.
3. Investment decisions are forward-looking and a solution method for rational expectation models is used to find the optimal initial value of decision variables.

To our knowledge, no other GE model based on the econometric approach has ever been constructed for the Italian economy. Furthermore, in Italy the debate about tax reforms has been mainly concentrated on equity issues and very few analyses have attempted to estimate efficiency gains from non-distortionary taxes. Recently, some general studies on institutional aspects of capital taxation have appeared. Examples are given by Alworth and Castellucci (1987) and Gian-nini (1989), who followed the King and Fullerton (1984) methodology in order to examine the tax treatment of savings and investment in Italy since 1960, and

---

[1] See Sinn (1987) for a theoretical analysis of the influence of taxation on the allocation of the factor capital, and Pereira and Shoven (1988) for a survey of dynamic general-equilibrium models used for tax policy evaluation.
[2] For another interesting intertemporal general-equilibrium model, see Goulder and Summers (1989).

to provide various estimates of effective tax rates and of the cost of capital. The aim of our analysis is much broader, since we attempt to evaluate the impact of the existence of positive effective rates of taxation on economic growth and social welfare.

2.2 THE INTERTEMPORAL GENERAL-EQUILIBRIUM MODEL

The model has the fundamental structure of general-equilibrium models, which are based on four essential elements:

1. resource endowments of the economy;
2. producer behaviour;
3. consumer behaviour;
4. market equilibrium.

The numéraire used to express prices in the economy is a fifth less important element.

The model is intertemporal, where the resource endowments are not exogenous, but change through time via an accumulation process. Two kinds of resources are considered: the first is time endowment, which grows at the rate of population growth, and the second is capital stock, which grows through investments. Time endowment is given by

$$T_t = (1 + n)T_{t-1} \tag{2.1}$$

where

T = time endowment,
n = rate of population growth.

Supply of labour is given as the difference between time endowment and leisure time:[3]

$$L_S = T - L_T \tag{2.2}$$

where

L_S = labour supplied by consumers,
L_T = leisure time.

Fixed capital of the economy is determined by an identity between capital stock at the end of each period and the sum of beginning of period capital stock and investment net of replacement:

$$K_t = I + (1 - \delta)K_{t-1} \tag{2.3}$$

---

[3] Subscript *t*, which denotes time periods, will be dropped hereafter in all variables whenever possible.

where

K = total asset of fixed capital,
I = investment,
δ = replacement rate.

The total available amount of capital services which are supplied to the economy is, therefore,

$$K_{St} = A_K K_{t-1} \tag{2.4}$$

where

A_K = coefficient that converts capital stock at the beginning of the period (K_{t-1}) into a flow of capital services (K_{St}).

Producer behaviour is specified by taking into account the production technology and deriving the long-run output-supply and factor-demand equations. Let us assume that technology is characterized by the **production possibility set** $\Phi_t \equiv \{(X_S, M, K_{DP}, L_D, t)\}$, where $X_S \equiv [X_{SC}, X_{SI}, X_{SE}]^T$ (with X_{SC} as the quantity of supplied non-durable consumer goods, X_{SI} the supplied investment goods, and X_{SE} the supplied exported goods), M is the demanded imported inputs, L_D is the demanded quantity of labour services, K_{DP} is a J-dimensional vector of demanded quantities of capital services, t denotes technical progress. Assuming Harrod-neutral technical progress, the production possibility set can be written as $\Phi \equiv \{(X_S, M, K_{DP}, \bar{L}_D)\}$, where

$$\bar{L}_D \equiv a(t) L_{Dt} \tag{2.5}$$

where

$\bar{L}_D$ = labour input measured in efficiency units,
$a(t)$ = labour-augmenting technical progress.

We also define the price of labour input measured in efficiency units as

$$\bar{w}_L \equiv w_L \frac{1}{a(t)} \tag{2.6}$$

Assuming that input-demand and output-supply decisions are made by profit-maximizing producers under perfect competition in all commodity and factor markets, we can define the country's wage function as

$$w_L = \bar{\omega}(c, p_M, w_{KP}) \tag{2.7}$$

where

p_M = market price of aggregated imported inputs,
$c \equiv [c_C, c_I, c_E]^T$ = vector of output producer prices (with c_C as an N-dimensional vector of producer prices of non-durable consumer goods, c_I the producer price of investment goods, c_E the producer price of aggregated exported goods)

Applying the modified Hotelling's lemma to equation (2.7), the economy's observed net output-supply functions and the Hicksian compensated input-demand functions per unit of employed labour in efficiency units are derived:

$$x_{SC} = \partial_{c_C}\bar{\omega}(c_C, c_I, c_E, p_M, w_{KP}) \tag{2.8a}$$

$$x_{SI} = \partial_{c_I}\bar{\omega}(c_C, c_I, c_E, p_M, w_{KP}) \tag{2.8b}$$

$$x_{SE} = \partial_{c_E}\bar{\omega}(c_C, c_I, c_E, p_M, w_{KP}) \tag{2.8c}$$

$$m_{DM} = -\partial_{p_M}\bar{\omega}(c_C, c_I, c_E, p_M, w_{KP}) \tag{2.8d}$$

$$k_{DP} = -\nabla_{w_K}\bar{\omega}(c_C, c_I, c_E, p_M, w_{KP}) \tag{2.8e}$$

where

$w_{KP} = J$-dimensional vector of price indexes of capital services demanded by producers,

$X_S \equiv X_S \bar{L}_D^{-1} \equiv [x_{SC}, x_{SI}, x_{SE}]^T =$ vector of supplied, quantities of outputs per unit of employed labour in efficiency units, where $x_{SC} \equiv X_{SC}/\bar{L}_D$, $x_{SI} \equiv X_{SI}/\bar{L}_D$ and $x_{SE} \equiv X_{SE}/\bar{L}_D$,

$m \equiv M/\bar{L}_D =$ imported inputs per unit of employed labour in efficiency units,

$k_{DP} \equiv K_{DP}\bar{L}_D^{-1} = J$-dimensional vector of quantities of capital services demanded by producers per unit of employed labour in efficiency units.

Since $\bar{\omega}(c, p_M, w_K)$ is linearly homogeneous in c, P_M and w_K, the optimal ratios x_S, m and k_{DP} given by equations (2.8a–e) are homogeneous of degree zero in c, p_M and w_{KP} and, therefore, are determined only by relative prices. By Euler's theorem, the price of labour in efficiency units can also be obtained as

$$\bar{w}_L = c^T x_S - p_M m - w_{KP}^T k_{DP} \tag{2.9}$$

Consumer behaviour can be described by dividing the allocation process between intertemporal and atemporal stages. At an intertemporal stage, we assume the existence of an additive utility function as discussed by Arrow and Kurz (1970) and recently used by Jorgenson and Yun (1986a). With this assumption, full wealth is allocated among time periods according to the following linear logarithmic intertemporal utility function:

$$U = \sum_{t=0}^{\infty} \left(\frac{1+n}{1+\alpha}\right)^t \ln \frac{\bar{F}_t}{P_t} \tag{2.10}$$

where

$\bar{F} =$ full consumption in real terms defined as the sum of consumption of goods and capital services plus leisure,

$P =$ population,

$\alpha =$ rate of time preference.

Full wealth is given by

$$W = \sum_{t=0}^{\infty} \frac{P_{Ft} \bar{F}_t}{\prod_{s=0}^{t} (1 + \rho_s)} \tag{2.11}$$

where

P_F = price index of full consumption,
ρ_s = nominal private rate of return.

Maximization of equation (2.10) subject to equation (2.11) leads to the following path of full consumption expressed at current prices:

$$F_t = \frac{(1 + \rho_t)(1 + n)}{(1 + \alpha)} F_{t-1} \tag{2.12}$$

where

$F \equiv P_F \bar{F}$ = full consumption at current prices.

In the atemporal stage, consumer preferences are defined over a set of non-negative quantities $X_D \equiv [X_{DC}, K_{DC}^T, L_T]^T \geq 0_{H+2}$, where X_{DC} is the quantity of non-durable consumer goods, and K_{DC} is an H-dimensional vector of consumer capital services. Let us define a vector of strictly positive consumer prices $p \geq 0_{H+2}$, where $p \equiv [p_C, w_{PC}^T, \bar{w}_T]^T$, p_C being the market price index of consumer goods and w_{KC} the H-dimensional vector of price indexes of capital services demanded by consumers. Moreover, let us define the $(H+2)$-dimensional vector of normalized commodity prices as

$$v \equiv \hat{p} f^{-1} \tag{2.13}$$

where

$$f \equiv F/\bar{L}_D \tag{2.14}$$

with f as full consumption per unit of employed labour in efficiency units.
We can define the **reciprocal indirect utility function** as

$$h(v) \equiv 1/g(v) \tag{2.15}$$

where $g(v)$ is the **direct utility function**, which is continuous, positive, non-decreasing and quasi-concave (Diewert, 1974, pp. 125–26). It is assumed that $h(v)$ is differentiable and that $\nabla h(v) \equiv [\partial h(v)/\partial v_1, \ldots, \partial h(v)/\partial v_{H+2}]^T \neq 0_{H+2}$. In the case of homothetic preferences it can be easily demonstrated that $g(v) = F/h(p)$. Applying the Modified Roy's Identity (see Diewert, 1974, p. 126), the system of Marshallian uncompensated consumer demand functions can be obtained as follows:

$$x_D = \nabla h(v)/v^T \nabla h(v) \tag{2.16}$$

where

$$x_D \equiv [x_{DC}, k_{DC}, l_T] \equiv X_D \bar{L}_D$$

which in the homothetic case becomes

$$x_{DC} = \frac{\partial p_C h(p_C, w_{KC}, \bar{w}_T)f}{h(p_C, w_{KC}, \bar{w}_T)} \tag{2.17a}$$

$$k_{DC} = \frac{\nabla w_{KC} h(p_C, w_{KC}, \bar{w}_T)f}{h(p_C, w_{KC}, \bar{w}_T)} \tag{2.17b}$$

$$l_T = \frac{\partial \bar{w}_T h(p_C, w_{KC}, \bar{w}_T)f}{h(p_C, w_{KC}, \bar{w}_T)} \tag{2.17c}$$

where

$x_{DC} \equiv X_{DC}/\bar{L}_D$ = demanded quantity of non-durable goods per unit of employed labour in efficiency units,

$k_{DC} \equiv K_{DC}/\bar{L}_D$ = H-dimensional vector of demanded quantities of capital services per unit of employed labour in efficiency units,

$l_T \equiv L_T/\bar{L}_D$ = demand of leisure time per unit of employed labour in efficiency units,

$\bar{w}_T$ = price of leisure defined in terms of labour measured in efficiency units.

Since $h(v)$ is linearly homogeneous in v, consumer demand functions given by equations (2.17a)–(2.17c) are homogeneous of degree zero in f, p_C, w_{KC} and w_T and, therefore, are determined only by relative prices. Moreover, by Euler's theorem, $p \nabla h(p) = h(p)$ and this leads to $f = p_C x_{DC} + w_{KC}^T k_{DC} + \bar{w}_T l_T$.

The **conditions of equilibrium** are specified by distinguishing market equilibrium in the atemporal stage from the intertemporal equilibrium. In the **atemporal stage**, both commodity and factor service markets clear. In particular, supply and demand for consumption goods are equal, so that

$$x_{SC} = x_{DC} + g_C \tag{2.18}$$

where

$$g_C = (\gamma_C g)p_C \tag{2.19}$$

with

γ_C = share of consumption goods in g,

g = government expenditure per unit of employed labour in efficiency units.

Similarly, supply and demand for exported goods are equal, so that

$$x_{SE} = e \tag{2.20}$$

and demand and supply for imported goods are also equal:

$$m_{DM} = m \qquad (2.21)$$

where

m = supply of imported goods per unit of employed labour in efficiency units.

Combining equations (2.20) and (2.21), nothing guarantees that the value of imports will be equal to the value of exports. An additional equation has to be added in order to take into account the balance of trade. We distinguish two different exchange rate regimes for maintaining the equilibrium in the balance of trade:

1. The flexible-exchange-rate regime, where the price of imports (p_M) is given in foreign currency (small-country assumption) and the exchange rate changes so as to guarantee the equilibrium in the balance of trade:

$$\frac{p_E e - \bar{b}}{\bar{p}_M m} = r_M \qquad (2.22)$$

where

$\bar{b}$ = (exogenous) level of the balance of trade (assumed equal to zero),
$\bar{p}_M$ = exogenous border price of imported goods in foreign currency,
r_M = exchange rate.

2. The fixed-exchange-rate regime, where, for a fixed level of $r_M(\bar{r}_M)$ we have

$$\frac{p_E e - \bar{b}}{\bar{r}_M m} = p_M \qquad (2.22a)$$

and p_M (the price of imports expressed in foreign currency) is endogenous, implying that the home and foreign countries keep relative prices fixed (international co-ordination of fiscal policies).

The supply of capital services is equal to the sum of capital services demanded by consumers and producers:

$$k_S = \iota_J^T k_{DP} + \iota_H^T k_{DC} \qquad (2.23)$$

where

$$k_S \equiv K_S / \bar{L}_D \qquad (2.24)$$

with

k_S = total capital services supplied by consumers per unit of employed labour in efficiency units,
$\iota_H \equiv H$-dimensional unit vector,
$\iota_J \equiv J$-dimensional unit vector.

By Hicks aggregation theorem, equation (2.23) implies that the prices of the different capital services are proportional to each other.

Supply and demand for investment goods are equal, so that

$$x_{SI} = i + g_1 \tag{2.25}$$

where

$$i \equiv I/\bar{L}_D \tag{2.26}$$

$$g_1 \equiv (\gamma_1 g)/p_1 \tag{2.27}$$

with

p_1 = market price of investment goods,
γ_1 = share of investment demand in government expenditure.

Private demand for investment goods at current prices is equal to saving minus the balance of payments, i.e.

$$p_1 i = s - b \tag{2.28}$$

Government expenditure is related to total tax revenue, i.e.

$$g = r_\tau \eta \tag{2.29}$$

where

r_τ = total tax revenue,
η = proportion parameter (which could be different from one),

so that, when $\eta > 1$, the budget deficit is given by

$$d \equiv g - r_\tau = r_\tau(\eta - 1) \tag{2.30}$$

Labour supply is equal to the sum of total labour demand plus a given proportional unemployment:

$$l_S = (1 + l_G)(1 + l_U) \tag{2.31}$$

where l_G, the government labour demand per unit of employed labour in efficiency units, is given by

$$l_G = \gamma_l g / \bar{w}_L \tag{2.32}$$

with

γ_l = share of cost of labour in total government expenditure,
$l_S \equiv L_S/\bar{L}_D$ = labour supplied per unit of employed labour in efficiency units,
$l_U \equiv$ ratio of unemployment with respect to total employed labour.

Taking account of equation (2.2), time endowment is equal to the sum of labour supply and demand for leisure; thus,

$$T = l_S + l_T \tag{2.33}$$

where $T \equiv T/\bar{L}_D$ = time endowment per unit of employed labour in efficiency units. This can be rewritten as

$$\bar{L}_D \equiv T/T \tag{2.34}$$

with T as time endowment per unit of employed labour in efficiency units.

The above equations hold with market prices equal to producer prices plus indirect taxes:

$$p_C = [I + {}_C\hat{t}_{IND}]c_C \tag{2.35a}$$

$$p_I = [I + {}_I\tau_{IND}]c_I \tag{2.35b}$$

$$p_E = [I + {}_E\tau_{IND}]c_E \tag{2.35c}$$

$$p_M = [I + {}_M\tau_{IND}]\bar{p}_M \tag{2.35d}$$

where ${}_r\tau_{IND}$ (for $r = C, I, E, M$) = vector of effective indirect tax rates. The revenue form indirect taxes are given by

$$r_{IND} = {}_C\tau_{IND}c_Cx_{SC} + {}_I\tau_{IND}c_Ix_{SI} + {}_E\tau_{IND}c_Ex_{SE} + {}_M\tau_{IND}p_Mm \tag{2.36}$$

The price of capital services is equal to the *ex ante* user cost of capital, i.e.

$$w_{KP} = [I + \hat{\epsilon}_{KP}]\hat{p}_I[\rho\iota_J - \Pi\iota_J + \delta_{KP}] \tag{2.37a}$$

$$w_{KC} = [I + \hat{\epsilon}_{KC}]\hat{p}_I[\rho\iota_H - \Pi\iota_H + \delta_{KC}] \tag{2.37b}$$

where Π is the exogenous rate of inflation and ϵ_{KP} and ϵ_{KC} are vectors of tax-induced distortions of prices of capital services, determined by the following functions:[4]

$$\epsilon_{KP} = (\rho - \Pi)[\rho I_J - \Pi I_J + \hat{\delta}_{KP}]^{-1}\tau_{KP} \tag{2.38a}$$

$$\epsilon_{KC} = (\rho - \Pi)[\rho I_H - \Pi I_H + \hat{\delta}_{KD}]^{-1}\tau_{KC} \tag{2.38b}$$

where

τ_{KP}, τ_{KC} = vectors of effective rates of taxation of income from capital assets,
δ_{KP}, δ_{KC} = vectors of economic rates of depreciation,
I_J, I_H = unit matrices of order J and H, respectively.

In our model we consider four types of producer capital assets – corporate long- and short-lived and non-corporate long- and short-lived assets – and two types of consumer capital assets: consumer long- and short-lived assets. Effective rates of taxation differ widely between these different categories of assets.[5]

Tax revenue from interests on loaned capital is given by

---

[4] Equations (2.38a) and (2.38b) are, respectively, derived from $w_{KP} = \hat{p}_I[(\iota_J + \tau_{KP})(\rho - \Pi) + \delta_{KP}]$ and $w_{KC} = \hat{p}_I[(\iota_H + \tau_{KC})(\rho - \Pi) + \delta_{KC}]$, where τ_{KP} and τ_{KC}, the effective rates of taxation, are related to ϵ_{KP} and ϵ_{KC} as shown in equations (2.37a) and (2.37b):
[5] The definition of the effective tax rates for the Italian case is available from the authors in an extended version of this chapter.

$$r_{SOST} = \tau_{SOST}(p_1 k \rho \beta_K) \tag{2.39}$$

where

τ_{SOST} = rate of taxation of interest income,
β_K = share of debt on total value of capital.

Thus, tax revenue from capital income (r_K) is given by

$$r_K = \hat{\varepsilon}_{KP}^T[I + \hat{\varepsilon}_{KP}]^{-1} w_{KP} + \hat{\varepsilon}_{KC}^T[I + \hat{\varepsilon}_{KC}]^{-1} w_{KC} + r_{SOST} \tag{2.40}$$

Marginal and average tax rates on labour income are determined, following Jorgenson and Yun (1986a), through the following system of equations:

$$\bar{\tau}_{IRPEF}^{(L)} = \lambda_0 + \lambda_1(1 + \tau_{SOCSEC})^{-1}\bar{w}_L(1 + l_G) \tag{2.41a}$$

$$\tau_{IRPEF}^{(L)} = \lambda_0 + 1/2\,\lambda_1(1 + \tau_{SOCSEC})^{-1}\bar{w}_L(1 + l_G) \tag{2.41b}$$

where

$\bar{\tau}_{IRPEF}^{(L)}$ = marginal effective tax rate on labour income,
$\tau_{IRPEF}^{(L)}$ = average effective tax rate on labour income,
τ_{SOCSEC} = exogenous effective rate for social-security contributions.

Total tax revenue on labour income (r_L) is then defined as

$$r_L = (\tau_{IRPEF}^{(L)} + \tau_{SOCSEC})(1 + \tau_{SOCSEC})^{-1}\bar{w}_L(1 + l_G) \tag{2.42}$$

The price of labour input is equal to the price of time endowment plus total marginal taxes on labour income and social-security contributions, so that, in terms of employed labour in efficiency units, we have

$$\bar{w}_T = (1 + \varepsilon_T)^{-1}\bar{w}_L \tag{2.43}$$

where

$$\varepsilon_T \equiv \frac{(1 + \tau_{SOCSEC})}{(1 - \hat{\tau}_{IRPEF}^{(L)})} - 1 \tag{2.44}$$

Total tax revenue per unit of employed labour in efficiency units is given by the sum of the revenue from indirect taxes, the tax revenue from labour income and the tax revenue from capital income:

$$r_\tau = r_{IND} + r_L + r_K \tag{2.45}$$

Total disposable income is given by the sum of values of services obtained from the supplied resources net of direct taxes:

$$y = \bar{w}_T l_T + w_L(1 + l_G) + w_{KP}^T k_{DP} + w_{KC}^T k_{DC} - (r_\tau - g_{TR} - r_{IND}) - d \tag{2.46}$$

where

y = total disposable income per unit of employed labour in efficiency units,

g_{TR} = government expenditure on transfer payments to consumers per unit of employed labour in efficiency units.

Government expenditure on transfer payments to consumers is related to total government expenditure as follows:

$$g_{TR} = \gamma_{TR} g \tag{2.47}$$

where

γ_{TR} = share of transfers in government expenditure.

Total private disposable income is allocated to private full-consumption expenditure, and saving, i.e.

$$y = f + s \tag{2.48}$$

All quantities are determined by relative prices, while all financial variables (such as income, full consumption, tax bases and others) are homogeneous of degree one in prices. Therefore, we can express all prices in terms of a numéraire commodity. We take the price of labour in efficiency units as the numéraire, so that

$$\bar{w}_{Lt} = 1 \tag{2.49}$$

thus obtaining all prices and financial magnitude relative to this price.

The **intertemporal equilibrium** is consistent with the one-period market-clearing conditions under the perfect-foresight assumption, which also guarantees that the time path of full-consumption expenditure is consistent with the condition (2.13) for intertemporal optimality. In this context, the time path of the capital stock is described by equation (2.3), which relates changes in capital stock to investment net of replacement.

For a given stationary policy there exists a **unique balanced-growth equilibrium** under the assumptions of constant returns to scale, Harrod-neutral technical change, and homothetic consumer preferences. In this equilibrium the absolute levels of all quantities grow at the same rate, equal to $[a(t)(1 + n) - 1]$, all relative prices remain constant, while absolute prices grow at an exogenous inflation rate and the nominal private rate of return depends only on the rate of technical change, the rate of time preference and the rate of inflation, so that

$$(1 + \rho) = a(t)(1 + \alpha)(1 + \Pi) \tag{2.50}$$

In this balanced-growth equilibrium we have $f_t = f_{t-1}$, as we can easily see by taking into account equations (2.12), (2.14) and (2.50). Furthermore, in this equilibrium investment net of replacement permits total supply of capital services to grow at the same rate as employed labour in efficiency units, so that

$$k = \frac{1}{\delta + n} i \tag{2.51}$$

where $k \equiv K/\bar{L}_D$, while we can rewrite equation (2.4) as follows:

$$k_S \equiv A_K k \tag{2.52}$$

The balanced-growth equilibrium of the economy can be found, for a given stationary policy and assuming a flexible exchange rate regime, with a model made of equations (2.8a)–(2.8e), (2.9), (2.17)–(2.23), (2.25), (2.27)–(2.33), (2.35)–(2.49), (2.51) and (2.52). On the other hand, when the exchange rate is assumed to be fixed, p_M becomes endogenous and equation (2.22) is substituted by equation (2.22a). We note that this model has the nature of a static general-equilibrium model. We note also that we have $4J + 4H + 32$ equations and $4J + 4H + 31$ unknowns, so that we have one more equation than we have unknowns. However, by Walras law the number of the independent equations is equal to the number of the unknowns.[6] Therefore, one equation of the model, chosen arbitrarily, can be eliminated from the rest of the system.

Time endowment is the only resource variable which grows at an exogenously given rate of growth. Under the assumptions of constant returns to scale in production, Harrod-neutral technical change and homothetic preferences, the quantities of consumption and investment goods and of capital and labour services in the balanced-growth equilibrium are homogeneous of degree one in the time endowment. Thus, we scale all these quantities relative to time endowment by dividing all the quantity equations by time endowment per unit of employed labour in efficiency units given by equation (2.34).

A policy change is evaluated by computing two balanced-growth equilibria associated, respectively, with the old and new policies. Given the change in the balanced-growth equilibrium, there is a unique **transition path** to the new equilibrium under the above-mentioned assumptions. The new balanced-growth equilibrium is associated with a different level of capital intensity. Under perfect foresight, at the initial time period full-consumption expenditure is adjusted to such a level that the economy can follow that unique transition path. The change in full consumption brings about a change in the rate of return and this results in a movement of the supply of capital stock towards its new optimal level. As the economy approximates the new equilibrium, the nominal rate of return tends to the level given by equation (2.50), which is determined only by the rate of inflation, technical change and the rate of time preference.

The intertemporal model describing the transition path can be obtained from the balanced-growth model by adding equations (2.1), (2.13), (2.26) and (2.35) and substituting the steady-state equation (2.51) with the dynamic equation (2.3), equation (2.52) with equations (2.4) and (2.24), and equation (2.48) with equation (2.12). For given balanced-growth values of the endogenous variables the initial level of full-consumption expenditure must be found. The problem of solving our

---

[6] The dependency of the complete system of the model equations can be proved by showing that in equilibrium the value of full-consumption expenditure determined through the income equation can also be obtained by the sum of the value of consumer demanded goods and services.

intertemporal model is, therefore, similar to the two-point boundary value problems, where initial conditions are provided for some variables while terminal conditions are provided for others.

The main difficulty arises from the fact that our model is a saddle-point system so that the transition path is unstable. It is, in fact, a typical dynamic rational-expectations model which is usually more difficult to solve than a standard dynamic system of equations. Small deviations of initial guesses from the unknown unique level of the so-called jumping variable (in our case, the full-consumption expenditure) lead to huge errors which accumulate through time. As a result, the traditional solution methods cannot be used since these become so ill-conditioned as to cause the approximating computation to move in the wrong direction or to show overflow problems. Various alternative methods are available for solving this type of model.[7] Among these, the 'multiple shooting' technique proposed by Lipton *et al.* (1982) is particularly useful.[8]

Specifically, the technique developed by Lipton *et al.* (1982) has been applied by dividing the transition time interval into short subintervals. An iterative computation procedure was used to find capital stock and full consumption at the terminal and initial periods of each subinterval, respectively. Full wealth was computed as the present value of all future full-consumption flows, which were discounted at the endogenous private rates of return of each subinterval.

2.3 SPECIFICATION AND ECONOMETRIC ESTIMATION OF PRODUCER AND CONSUMER EQUATIONS

The model specification is completed by choosing the functional forms of the producer and consumer behaviour equations. This can be done by specifying the wage function [equation (2.8)] and the reciprocal indirect utility function [equation (2.16)] in explicit form. A convenient functional form is the **normalized quadratic semi-flexible** form proposed by Diewert and Wales (1988a), who advocated its use for the econometric estimation of general-equilibrium models. This functional form is flexible enough to be able to represent a wide range of technologies and to include complementarity phenomena and variability of demand and supply elasticities. It also permits us to impose global curvature conditions derived from the theory of producer and consumer behaviour without losing flexibility completely (as, for example, in the translog and other flexible functions). Moreover, it requires fewer free parameters than other flexible forms, thus allowing empirical applications of larger systems of equations.

The normalized quadratic semi-flexible wage function is an adaptation of a special case of the normalized quadratic profit function proposed by Diewert and Wales (1987) and is formulated as follows:

---

[7] See, for example, Keller (1976) and Blanchard (1985) for a survey on this subject.
[8] Another convenient method is based on the Fair and Taylor (1983) algorithm.

$$\bar{\omega}(q) \equiv \omega(q, t)\frac{1}{a(t)} \tag{2.53}$$

where

$$\omega(q, t) = e^{\alpha_T t}[q^T a^{(p)} + (1/2)(q^T \alpha^{(p)})^{-1} q^T B^{(p)} q] \tag{2.54}$$

with

$q \equiv [c_C, c_I, c_E, p_M, w_{KP}^T]^T$,
$a(t) = e^{\alpha_T t}$,
$\alpha^{(p)} \equiv [\alpha_1^{(p)}, \ldots, \alpha_{J+4}^{(p)}]^T$ = predetermined parameter vector,
$a^{(p)} \equiv [a_1^{(p)}, \ldots, a_{J+4}^{(p)}]^T$ = unknown parameter vector,
$B^{(p)} \equiv (J+4) \times (J+4)$ symmetric positive semi-definite matrix of unknown parameters,
$\alpha_T \equiv \ln(1 + \alpha_H$, with α_H = rate of Harrod-neutral technical change.

The parameters in equation (2.54) satisfy the following restrictions:

$$q*^T \alpha^{(p)} = 1 \tag{2.55}$$

where $q*$ is the vector of reference prices,

$$B^{(p)} q* = 0_{J+4} \tag{2.56}$$

$$B^{(p)} = B^{(p)T} \tag{2.57}$$

and, in order to impose concavity conditions,

$$\tilde{B}^{(p)} = CC^T \tag{2.58}$$

where

C = lower triangular matrix of order $[(J+4) - 1]$,
$\tilde{B}^{(p)}$ = matrix of order $[(J+4) - 1]$ obtained from $B^{(p)}$ by eliminating the last row
  and the last column from this matrix.

In particular, as discussed by Diewert and Wales (1987), condition (2.58) imposes concavity on the estimated cost function when the coefficients of matrix C are directly estimated. Symmetric price elasticities are imposed with condition (2.65) and the price normalization is made with respect to a reference price vector.

We recall that the wage function defined by equations (2.54)–(2.58) exists only if producer competitive equilibrium is achieved and extra profits are zero. Equation (2.54) gives the effective price of labour input, while equation (2.53) is expressed in a form that is invariant with respect to time as it refers to the price of labour input measured in efficiency units. To assure the existence of a balanced-growth equilibrium in our intertemporal general-equilibrium model, we have imposed the condition that technical change must be Harrod-neutral.

Differentiating $\omega(q)$ with respect to the prices q yields the functions of output-supply and input-demand per unit of employed labour, that is: (i) the domestic supply function for non-durable consumer goods; (ii) the supply function for investment goods; (iii) the supply function for exported goods; (iv) (minus) the producer demand function for imported inputs; and (v) (minus) the producer demand function for capital services. These functions are given by

$$z = e^{\alpha_T t}[a^{(p)} + (q^T \alpha^{(p)})^{-1} B^{(p)} q^T - (1/2) q^T B^{(p)} q \alpha^{(p)}] \tag{2.59}$$

Appending a stochastic error to each of the above functions, we get the system of producer output-supply and input-demand equations to be econometrically estimated. Taking into account the Harrod-neutral technical change, we can express the above quantities in terms of employed labour in efficiency units by means of the following transformation:

$$[x_D, x_E, x_I, -m, -k_{KP}^T]^T = e^{-\alpha_T t} z \tag{2.60}$$

On the consumers side we assume that preferences are represented by the homothetic normalized quadratic semi-flexible reciprocal indirect utility function, which is a special case of the homothetic normalized quadratic reciprocal indirect utility function proposed by Diewert and Wales (1988b):

$$u = g(v) \equiv v^T a^{(c)} + (1/2)(v^T \alpha^{(c)})^{-1} v^T B^{(c)} v \tag{2.61}$$

where

$\alpha^{(c)} \equiv [\alpha_1^{(c)}, \dots, \alpha^{(c)}]^T$ = predetermined parameter vector,
$a^{(c)} \equiv [a_1^{(c)}, \dots, a_{H+2}^{(c)}]^T$ = unknown parameter vector,
$B^{(c)} \equiv (H+2) \times (H+2)$ symmetric negative semi-definite matrix of unknown parameters.

The parameters of equation (2.61) satisfy the following restrictions:

$$v*^T \alpha^{(c)} = 1 \tag{2.62}$$

$$v*^T a^{(c)} = 1 \tag{2.63}$$

where $v*$ is the vector of reference normalized prices, and

$$B^{(c)} v* = 0_{J+4} \tag{2.64}$$

$$B^{(c)} = B^{(c)T} \tag{2.65}$$

and, in order to impose concavity on the expenditure function,

$$\tilde{B}^{(c)} = -SS^T \tag{2.66}$$

where

S = lower triangular matrix of order $[(H+2)-1]$,
$\tilde{B}^{(c)}$ = matrix of order $[(H+2)-1]$ obtained from $B^{(c)}$ by eliminating the last row and the last column from this matrix.

We note, in particular, that, as discussed by Diewert and Wales (1988b), condition (2.66) imposes the concavity conditions on the expenditure function. Symmetric price elasticities are imposed with equation (2.66) and the price normalization is made with a weighted average index of normalized prices, which is equal to 1 with a reference normalized price vector as in equation (2.62).

Applying the Modified Roy's Identity to equation (2.61) we obtain the consumer demand per unit of employed labour in efficiency units. Taking account of equation (2.14), where the normalized prices v are defined, we have

$$x_D = f[a^{(c)} = (p^T\alpha^{(c)})^{-1}B^{(c)}p - (1/2)(p^T\alpha^{(c)})^{-1}p^TB^{(c)}p\alpha^{(c)}]$$
$$\times [p^Ta^{(c)} + (1/2)(p^T\alpha^{(c)})^{-1}p^TB^{(c)}p]^{-1} \tag{2.67}$$

which is our explicit form of equations (2.18a)–(2.18c). Multiplying both sides of equation (2.67) by $(\hat{p}f^{-1})$, we get functions giving the shares of consumer demands in the value of full consumption. Appending a stochastic error to each of these functions, we obtain the system of consumer budget-constraint demand equations to be econometrically estimated. We also impose the condition that the sum of the stochastic errors of the value share equations of consumer demands sum to zero.

Table 2.1 Econometric model of producer behaviour

Parameter	Estimate	Standard error
α_T	0.0244740	0.0010627
$a_{CS}^{(P)}$	-0.2564700	0.0149910
$a_{NL}^{(P)}$	-0.0959790	0.0080020
$a_{CL}^{(P)}$	-0.0388510	0.0024485
$a_{E}^{(P)}$	-0.0502870	0.0046203
$a_{NS}^{(P)}$	0.1322100	0.0237560
$a_{I}^{(P)}$	-0.0242500	0.0061515
$a_{C}^{(P)}$	0.4515200	0.0125580
$a_{M}^{(P)}$	0.7092600	0.0200200
$b_{CS,CS}^{(P)}$	0.0824160	0.0037068
$b_{CS,NL}^{(P)}$	0.0143990	0.0007559
$b_{CS,CL}^{(P)}$	0.0318770	0.0016924
$b_{CS,E}^{(P)}$	-0.1438200	0.0106100
$b_{CS,NS}^{(P)}$	0.0532410	0.0030684
$b_{CS,I}^{(P)}$	-0.0331380	0.0050162
$b_{CS,C}^{(P)}$	-0.1407000	0.0065366
$b_{CS,M}^{(P)}$	0.1357200	0.0073380
$b_{NL,NL}^{(P)}$	0.0037045	0.0003886
$b_{NL,CL}^{(P)}$	0.0072895	0.0006770
$b_{NL,E}^{(P)}$	-0.0287600	0.0035892
$b_{NL,NS}^{(P)}$	0.0068489	0.0005231
$b_{NL,I}^{(P)}$	-0.0057089	0.0019989
$b_{NL,C}^{(P)}$	-0.0194250	0.0020159
$b_{NL,M}^{(P)}$	-0.0463640	0.0034244
$b_{CL,CL}^{(P)}$	0.0148190	0.0013108
$b_{CL,E}^{(P)}$	-0.0608830	0.0070821

$b_{CL,NS}^{(P)}$	0.0170430	0.0011980
$b_{CL,I}^{(P)}$	-0.0127000	0.0034117
$b_{CL,C}^{(P)}$	-0.0469580	0.0038167
$b_{CL,M}^{(P)}$	0.0495140	0.0044036
$b_{E,E}^{(P)}$	0.2620700	0.0378560
$b_{E,NS}^{(P)}$	-0.0854090	0.0069613

Table 2.1—*contd.*

Parameter	Estimate	Standard error
$b_{E,I}^{(P)}$	0.0575800	0.0109340
$b_{E,C}^{(P)}$	0.2297600	0.0174550
$b_{E,M}^{(P)}$	-0.2305400	0.0230320
$b_{NS,NS}^{(P)}$	0.0394550	0.0025375
$b_{NS,I}^{(P)}$	-0.0215740	0.0033706
$b_{NS,C}^{(P)}$	-0.1015300	0.0049146
$b_{NS,M}^{(P)}$	0.0919270	0.0055171
$b_{I,I}^{(P)}$	0.0133300	0.0039353
$b_{I,C}^{(P)}$	0.0569230	0.0080120
$b_{I,M}^{(P)}$	-0.0547120	0.0083067
$b_{C,C}^{(P)}$	0.2625600	0.0126690
$b_{C,M}^{(P)}$	-0.2406400	0.0132810
$b_{M,M}^{(P)}$	0.2950900	0.0197420

Notation
C = non-durable consumer goods
I = investment goods
E = exported goods
M = imported inputs
CS = corporate short-lived capital goods services
CL = corporate long-lived capital goods services
NS = non-corporate short-lived capital goods services
NL = non-corporate long-lived capital goods services

Table 2.2   Econometric model of consumer behaviour

Parameter	Estimate	Standard error
$a_C^{(C)}$	0.2659300	0.0054951
$a_T^{(C)}$	0.6696800	0.0112970
$a_S^{(C)}$	0.0241510	0.0031983
$a_L^{(C)}$	0.0402320	0.0051643
$b_{C,C}^{(C)}$	-0.0147380	0.0042235
$b_{C,T}^{(C)}$	0.0462490	0.0095375
$b_{C,S}^{(C)}$	-0.0047392	0.0013924
$b_{C,L}^{(C)}$	-0.0267720	0.0058684
$b_{T,T}^{(C)}$	-0.1461100	0.0267360
$b_{T,S}^{(C)}$	0.0139770	0.0050364
$b_{T,L}^{(C)}$	0.0858800	0.0167100
$b_{S,S}^{(C)}$	-0.0023508	0.0012038
$b_{S,L}^{(C)}$	-0.0068868	0.0032921
$b_{L,L}^{(C)}$	0.0522210	0.0104220

Notation
C = non-durable consumer goods
S = consumer short-lived capital goods services
L = consumer long-lived capital goods services
T = leisure

The econometric estimation of the systems of producer output-supply and input-demand functions [equation (2.59)] and of consumer demand share functions derived from equation (2.67) was performed by applying the method of full-information maximum likelihood on a time-series of statistical observations for the period 1959–88. The predetermined parameters $\alpha^{(p)}$ and $\alpha^{(c)}$ were set equal to $[0 \ 0 \ \dots \ 1 \ 0]^T$, so that $q^T \alpha^{(p)} = p_M$, which is the price of imported inputs, and $[0 \ 1 \ 0 \ 0]^T$, so that $p^T \alpha^{(c)} = w_{KD(1)}$, which is the rental price of the consumer long-lived assets. The reference price vectors in the equations (2.63)–(2.64) were set respectively equal to $q_{1988}(= [1 \ 1 \ \dots \ 1]^T)$ and to $p_{1988}(= [1 \ 1 \ 1 \ 1]^T)$. During estimation the likelihood function was maximized with respect to the elements of C and S. Furthermore, we imposed each of the last $[(J + 4) - 3]$ columns of C to be equal to 0_{J-1} and the last $[(H + 2) - 3]$ columns of S to be equal to 0_{H+1}, thus obtaining an underlying *2-column Normalized Quadratic Flexible wage function* and an underlying *2-column Homothetic Normalized Quadratic Flexible reciprocal indirect utility function*. In this way we overcome the difficulties due to the lack of degrees of freedom usually encountered with the traditional flexible functional forms. With $J = 4$, we have in fact a system of 8 producer supply-demand equations, and with H = 2 we have 4 consumer demand (share) equations. In each of the producer and consumer sub-systems we were able to estimate the unknown parameters without the necessity of assuming two-stage allocation processes with nested functions, which are often used to solve the problem arising from the lack of degrees of freedom.

The estimates of the parameters of the producer and the consumer behavioural equations are given in Tables 2.1 and 2.2. These estimates satisfy the restrictions of homogeneity of degree zero and concavity in prices of the supply and demand functions, symmetry of the matrices $B^{(p)}$ and $B^{(c)}$, and summability of the value shares of consumer demands.

2.4 EFFECTIVE TAX RATES AND SIMULATION PARAMETERS

Our intertemporal general equilibrium model can be implemented by using the econometrically estimated parameters of producer and consumer submodels as well as other parameters which describe (see Table 2.3):

the composition of government expenditures;
the supply of labour (unemployment rate, rate of population growth);
the rates of economic depreciation for the six classes of assets;

the current tax policy;
relative prices of assets and other constants.

The rate of time preference α, representing intertemporal preferences in the household sector, is set equal to such a level that the rate of return is consistent with the capital stock available in 1988 at a 5% inflation rate. This means that the 1988 capital stock is in balanced growth. At this equilibrium the rate of return, corrected for inflation, is equal to 4.3%.

Table 2.3   Simulation parameters

Government expenditures
$\gamma_C = 0.1187$ share of consumption goods
$\gamma_I = 0.0837$ share of investment goods
$\gamma_l = 0.2966$ share of labour services
$\gamma_{TR} = 0.501$ share of transfer services

Labour services
$l_U = 0.1368$ unemployment rate
$n = 0.005$ rate of population growth

Economic depreciation rates
$\delta_{KP}(1) = 0.0914$ short-live corporate assets
$\delta_{KP}(2) = 0.1044$ short-live non-corporate assets
$\delta_{KP}(3) = 0.0249$ long-live corporate assets
$\delta_{KP}(4) = 0.0234$ long-live non-corporate assets
$\delta_{KD}(1) = 0.1366$ short-live consumer assets
$\delta_{KD}(2) = 0.0227$ long-live consumer assets

Tax parameters
$_C\tau_{IND} = 0.0933$ indirect tax on consumption goods
$_I\tau_{IND} = 0.0464$ indirect tax on investment goods
$_E\tau_{IND} = 0.0179$ indirect tax on exports
$_M\tau_{IND} = 0.0181$ indirect tax on imports
$\tau_{SOST} = 0.3$ tax rate on interest income

Relative price of assets and other constants
$\chi_P^{(1)} = 0.9$ price of short-live assets/price of investment goods
$\chi_P^{(2)} = 1.03$ price of long-live assets/price of investment goods
$\chi_C^{(1)} = 0.89$ price of consumer short-live assets/price of investment goods
$\chi_C^{(2)} = 1.04$ price of consumer long-live assets/price of investment goods
$\alpha = 0.0176$ rate of time preference

We also calculate the capital consumption allowances and the effective tax rates, which are used to measure tax-induced distortions of prices of capital services as shown by equations (2.38a)–(2.38b). At different inflation rates we obtain different levels of these two variables. Differences can also be observed between assets and sectors. Short-live assets present a very favourable treatment of capital consumption allowances. At rates of inflation close to zero the present value of capital consumption allowances is close to one, approximating a situation of immediate expensing (Table 2.4). As a consequence, their effective tax rate at all rates of inflation is almost four times lower than that of long-live assets.

The Italian capital income tax system is also characterized by a very favourable tax treatment of unincorporated business. At all rates of inflation unincorporated business presents an effective tax rate which is less than half that of the corporate sector. Furthermore, consumer long-live assets are taxed at rates which approximate zero at high inflation rate, the reason being that the imputation of income to owners that occupy their own house is fixed in nominal terms and, also initially, at levels which are below the market returns.

Table 2.4 Tax parameters

	Capital consumption allowances					
	Corporate		*Non-corporate*		*Consumer*	
Rate of inflation	*Short*	*Long*	*Short*	*Long*	*Short*	*Long*
0	0.93290	0.63028	0.93026	0.63028	0.0	0.0
5	0.85860	0.41367	0.85331	0.41367	0.0	0.0
10	0.79153	0.30435	0.78412	0.30435	0.0	0.0
	Effective tax rate					
	Corporate		*Non-corporate*		*Consumer*	
Rate of inflation	*Short*	*Long*	*Short*	*Long*	*Short*	*Long*
0	0.06131	0.32782	0.03198	0.17404	0.0	0.21240
5	0.12989	0.52695	0.06701	0.27292	0.0	0.17361
10	0.19250	0.63341	0.09824	0.32018	0.0	0.13719

2.5 WELFARE EFFECTS OF A TAX POLICY CHANGE

In order to assess the welfare effects of a tax policy change we have to adopt some kind of money metric representation of utility levels. Following Jorgenson and Yun (1986a, b, 1989), we express the effects on social welfare in terms of changes in full wealth defined by equation (2.11) and evaluated at the consumer prices before the policy change. This is an extension of the well-known procedure in welfare economics based on the *money metric indirect utility function* and leading to the Hicksian *equivalent variation* of utility level. We first evaluate the time path of the consumer prices associated with the current policy. Secondly, we determine the *money metric social welfare* associated with the tax policy change by measuring the difference between full wealth after the policy change and the wealth obtained before the change, both evaluated at pre-change prices. A positive value of this difference means that the change in policy brings about an increase in social welfare due to an efficiency gain. Since we do not disaggregate the consumer sector we cannot evaluate the equity effect on welfare due to distributive effects. The total impact to social welfare, which is given by the sum of efficiency and equity gains, can be evaluated only by considering different groups of consumers.

In our model, by eliminating the tax induced distortions, we find a new balanced growth equilibrium with higher full consumption and capital stock per unit of time endowment. In order to reach that new equilibrium, disposable income at the beginning of the transition path must be allocated in such a way that full consumption falls to a level, which is lower than the previous one. The rate of return rises initially with a higher demand for investments. The drop in full consumption and the rise in the rate of return is therefore associated with an increase in the rate of growth of capital stock. As full consumption begins to rise again during the transition path the rate of return falls while the rate of growth of capital stock approximates the new balanced equilibrium level.

Our estimate was done by evaluating all future consumption flows at the 1988 prices and by discounting these values with the simulated rates of return in each future period. The combined simulated values of consumption flows and rates of return gave us our estimate of full wealth at constant prices. The simulations show that the potential welfare change due to efficiency effects obtained by eliminating distortions in the prices of different types of capital services is not independent from the assumptions made about the determination of the exchange rate. In particular, when exchange rates are assumed to be fixed, with the effective rates of taxation on capital income equal to zero and replacing them with a lump sum tax we get an equivalent variation which increases with the rate of inflation. At 0% inflation the elimination of the non-neutrality of the capital income tax leads to a welfare gain of approximately 32,000 billions of lire at 1988 prices. This gain becomes 67,000 billions of lire with 5% inflation and 105,000 billions of lire with the 10% inflation. These magnitudes account respectively to 0.2, 0.5 and 0.9% of full private economic wealth (Table 2.5).

Moreover, in order to provide a point of reference to these figures, we have calculated the welfare gains obtained by replacing all the existing taxes with a lump sum tax. The obtained levels of the equivalent variation is extremely high and for all inflation rates greater than 350,000 billions of lire. In relative terms the results of the simulations lead to a welfare gain of 2.9% with 0% inflation, 3.1% with 5% inflation and 3.4% with 10% inflation with respect to full private economic wealth (Table 2.5).

Table 2.5 Potential economic welfare gains (billions of lire in 1988 prices and, in parenthesis, % of full wealth)

| | With inflation rate: | | |
	0%	5%	10%
With substitution of capital income tax with a lump-sum tax	32,543 (0.3%)	67,203 (0.5%)	105,964 (0,9%)
With substitution of all taxes with a lump-sum tax	355,962 (2.9%)	375,965 (3.1%)	424,125 (3.4%)

On the other hand, when we assume a flexible exchange rate, the removal of distortionary taxes does not provide any efficiency gain for the Italian economy, since the domestic currency revalues. This result represents an indirect indication of the importance of country coordination in fiscal reform. In an open economy, like that of Italy, autonomous changes of fiscal policy would produce no significant welfare gains, while if the policy changes are coordinated with the trading partners, thus permitting the exchange rate to remain fixed, the welfare gains would be substantial.

2.6 CONCLUSION

In this chapter we have measured the distortionary effects on full wealth in Italy of existing tax laws. The model which we used is an an extension of the Jorgenson and Yun (1986a) intertemporal general equilibrium model of the US economy. The results we have obtained are in line with those of most studies in this field, which, however, use the calibration method applied to static evaluation models. Our welfare gains, measured from an intertemporal model constructed with the econometric approach, are significantly lower than those obtained, for the US economy, by Jorgenson and Yun (1986b, 1989). We believe that a different specification of our cost and expenditure functions and the assumption of an economy open to external trade represent the major reasons for the emergence of these differences.

However, our results are still preliminary, since some strong assumptions in the model should be relaxed in order to consider more complex aspects of the Italian economic system that were not taken into account. In particular, we did not consider equity effects and, as a consequence, the policy change is not examined from the point of view of redistributive effects on economic welfare.

REFERENCES

Alworth, J. S. and Castellucci, L. (1987) The Taxation of Income from Capital in Italy, 1960–86. Paper prepared for the International Conference on the Cost of Capital, Kennedy School of Government, Harvard University, Cambridge, MA.

Arrow, K. J. and Kurz, M. (1970) *Public Investment, the Rate of Return, and Optimal Fiscal Policy*. Johns Hopkins University Press, Baltimore.

Blanchard, O. J. (1985) Methods of Solution for Dynamic Rational Expectations Models: A Survey, in *Economic Equilibrium Model Formulation and Solution* (ed. A. S. Manne), North-Holland, Amsterdam, pp. 210–25.

Diewert, W. E. (1974) Applications of Duality Theory in *Frontiers of Quantitative Economics* Vol. II, (eds. M. D. Intriligator and D. A. Kendrick), Amsterdam, North-Holland, pp. 106–99.

Diewert, W. E. (1988) On Tax Reform. *Canadian Journal of Economics*, 21, 1–40.

Diewert, W. E. and Wales, T. J. (1987) Flexible Functional Forms and Global Curvature Conditions. *Econometrica*, 50, 43–68.

Diewert, W. E. and Wales, T. J. (1988a) A Normalized Quadratic Semi-Flexible Functional Form. *Journal of Econometrics*, 37, 327–42.

Diewert, W. E. and Wales, T. J. (1988b) Normalized Quadratic Systems of Consumer Demand Functions. *Journal of Business and Economic Statistics.*

Diewert, W. E. and Woodland, A. D. (1977) Frank Knight's Theorem in Linear Programming Revisited. *Econometrica,* **45,** 375–98.

Fair, R. C. and Taylor, J. B. (1983) Solution and Maximum Likelihood Estimation of Dynamic Non-linear National Expectations Models. *Econometrica,* **51,** 1169–85.

Fullerton, D. and Kondrzycki Henderson, Y. (1989) A Disaggregate Equilibrium Model of the Tax Distortions Among Assets, Sectors, and Industries. *International Economic Review,* **30,** 391–413.

Giannini, S. (1989) *Imposte e finanziamento delle imprese.* Il Mulino, Bologna.

Goulder, L. H. and Summers, L. H. (1989) Tax Policy, Asset Prices, and Growth: A General Equilibrium Analysis. *Journal of Public Economics,* **38,** 265–96.

Jorgenson, D. W. and Yun, K.-Y. (1986a) The Efficiency of Capital Allocation. *Scandinavian Journal of Economics,* **88,** 85–107.

Jorgenson, D. W. and Yun, K. Y. (1986b) Tax Policy and Capital Allocation, *Scandinavian Journal of Economics,* **88,** 355–77.

Jorgenson, D. W. and Yun, K. Y. (1989) Tax Reform and U. S. Economic Growth. *Discussion Paper No. 1459,* Harvard University, Harvard Institute of Economic Research, Cambridge, MA.

Keller, H. B. (1976) *Numerical Solution of Two-Point Boundary Value Problems.* Society for Industrial and Applied Mathematics, Philadelphia, PA.

King, M. A. and Fullerton, D. (1984) *The Taxation of Income from Capital.* University of Chicago Press, Chicago.

Lipton, D., Poterba, J., Sachs, J. and Summers, L. (1982) Multiple Shooting in Rational Expectations Models. *Econometrica,* **50,** 1329–33.

Pereira, A. M. and Shoven, J. B. (1988) Survey of Dynamic Computational General Equilibrium Models for Tax Policy Evaluation. *Journal of Policy Modeling,* **10,** 401–36.

Sinn, H.-W. (1987) *Capital Income Taxation and Resource Allocation.* North-Holland, Amsterdam.

3

Crowding out in a two-country overlapping-generations model

Albert Jaeger and Christian Keuschnigg

3.1 INTRODUCTION

Overlapping-generations (OLG) models have recently emerged as the unifying framework for studying a wide range of fiscal policy issues including the crowding out effects of budget deficits (e.g. Auerbach and Kotlikoff, 1987; Frenkel and Razin, 1987). As their most attractive features, OLG models stress the intertemporal effects of fiscal policy changes and allow theoretical analyses to be based on solid microfoundations. In this chapter, we study the effects of public debt on capital accumulation in a numerical two-country OLG model. The fiscal policy experiment considered is a lump-sum tax cut over a specified number of periods in one of the two countries. We consider the case of two equally sized countries as well as the case of a small open economy. The model assumes that both countries produce the same good and that capital is perfectly mobile between the two countries. Crowding out of real capital is exclusively related to finite horizons of private households because we do not allow for Barro-type intergenerational transfers (Barro, 1974).

We view this chapter as an extension of the work by Auerbach and Kotlikoff (1987). They analyse the crowding-out effects of tax cuts in a closed-economy framework. Related work using analytical models is presented by Giovannini (1988) and Obstfeld (1989). The use of numerical techniques allows one to evaluate crowding-out effects quantitatively. To shed light on the extent of public debt neutrality in multiperiod OLG models, we calculate the portion of public debt perceived as net wealth by private households. This exercise may be of some interest because several authors, including Poterba and Summers (1987), have argued that finite horizons may not be an appropriate device to model substantial deviations from debt neutrality.

The main results reported here can be summarized as follows: The portion of public debt perceived as net wealth by private households is small indeed for realistic parameterizations of the model. Crowding out of real capital is stretched over many time periods in open OLG economies. The extent of real capital crowding out depends critically on the size of the country cutting the taxes. In the extreme case of the small open economy, however, ownership crowding out substitutes for real capital crowding out and tax cuts may require a substantial long-run trade surplus to service the accumulated foreign debt.

The rest of the chapter is organized as follows. Section 3.2 outlines the model. In section 3.3 we report the simulation results. Section 3.4 concludes the results.

3.2 THE MODEL

The world economy considered comprises a home country and a foreign country, both producing the same good. Each country is made up of three sectors: private household sector, a production sector and a government sector. We start by describing the behaviour of the private household sector in the home country.

3.2.1 Private household behaviour

The private household sector is populated by 55 generations. Generations are indexed by $i = 0, \ldots, 54$, where i denotes the planning horizon over the rest of their life. Each new generation has a certain lifetime of 55 years. In the first 45 years of their lifespan, a member of the youngest generation supplies one unit of labour inelastically. The remaining ten years of life are spent in retirement. Labour supply of a representative member of generation i at date t is, therefore,

$$L_{i,t} = \begin{cases} 0 & \text{if } 0 \leqslant i < 10 \\ 1 & \text{if } 10 \leqslant i \leqslant 54 \end{cases} \tag{3.1}$$

If we assume that each generation comprises one member, aggregate labour supply at time t is

$$L_t^s = \sum_{i=0}^{54} L_{i,t} = 45 \tag{3.2}$$

Savings decisions of private households are determined by the life-cycle motive. Generation i maximizes the utility index

$$U_i[C_{i,t}, \ldots, C_{i,t+i}] = \sum_{s=t}^{t+i} \frac{C_{i,s}^{1-1/\beta}}{1 - 1/\beta} \frac{1}{(1+\delta)^{s-t}} \tag{3.3}$$

$C_{i,t}$ is the consumption of generation i in time period t, β is the intertemporal elasticity of substitution, and δ denotes the time preference rate. The utility index given by equation (3.3) is maximized subject to the intertemporal wealth constraint of generation i:

$$W_{i,t} = (1 + r_t) A_{i,t} + \sum_{s=t}^{t+i} \frac{w_s L_{i,s}}{d_{t+1,s}} - \sum_{s=t}^{t+i} \frac{T_{i,s}}{d_{t+1,s}} = \sum_{s=t}^{t+i} \frac{C_{i,s}}{d_{t+1,s}} \tag{3.4}$$

Here $W_{i,t}$ denotes the total wealth as perceived by generation i, r_t is the one-period interest rate, $A_{i,t}$ are the accumulated financial assets of generation i, w_t is the real wage, $L_{i,t}$ is labour supply, and $T_{i,t}$ is the amount of lump-sum taxes paid by generation i. The discount factor is defined as

$$d_{t,s} = \prod_{u=t}^{s} 1 + r_u \quad \text{and} \quad d_{t+1,t} = 1 \tag{3.5}$$

Setting up a Lagrange function to maximize equation (3.3) subject to the constraint given by equation (3.4) results in the consumption decision rule

$$C_{i,t} = \Gamma_{i,t} W_{i,t} \tag{3.6}$$

The marginal propensity to consume out of total wealth, denoted by $\Gamma_{i,t}$, depends non-linearly on current and future interest rates and the time preference rate and declines with age.

The next step is to aggregate the wealth constraints in equation (3.4) over all generations:

$$W_t = (1+r_t) \sum_{i=0}^{54} A_{i,t} + \sum_{i=0}^{54} \sum_{s=t}^{t+i} \frac{w_s L_{i,s}}{d_{t+1,s}} - \sum_{i=0}^{54} \sum_{s=t}^{t+i} \frac{T_{i,s}}{d_{t+1,s}} \tag{3.7}$$

Finally, aggregating financial assets and consumption over generations, we have

$$A_t = \sum_{i=0}^{54} A_{i,t} \quad \text{and} \quad C_t = \sum_{i=0}^{54} C_{i,t} \tag{3.8}$$

The household sector of the foreign country is set up symmetrically. Preference parameters, wage rates, lump-sum tax rates, and the number of members per generation may take different values in the home and foreign country. Arbitrage behaviour, however, equates home and foreign interest rates.

3.2.2 Production sector behaviour

The single good in the world economy is produced in the home and foreign country by a Cobb–Douglas technology. In the home country, the output, or more precisely, the domestic product is determined by

$$Y_t = K_t^\alpha [L_t(1+g)^t]^{1-\alpha} \tag{3.9}$$

where Y_t is the output, K_t the capital stock and g the exogenously given rate of Harrod-neutral technological progress. Profit maximization implies that factors are paid their marginal products

$$w_t = (1-\alpha)K_t^\alpha [L_t(1+g)^t]^{-\alpha}(1+g)^t \tag{3.10}$$

$$r_t = \alpha K_t^{\alpha-1}[L_t(1+g)^t]^{1-\alpha} \tag{3.11}$$

Investment in new capital is denoted by I_t, and the capital stock develops according to

$$K_{t+1} = I_t + K_t \tag{3.12}$$

The production sector in the foreign country is specified analogously.

3.2.3 Government behaviour

The government may raise lump-sum taxes or make lump-sum transfers, spend on government consumption, and issue public debt. Given our intention to analyse the crowding-out effects of lump-sum tax cuts, we find it convenient to set government consumption equal to zero. The period-to-period government budget constraint under this assumption is

$$B_{t+1} = (1 + r_t)B_t - \sum_{i=0}^{54} T_{i,t} \tag{3.13}$$

where B_t denotes the public debt. The government plans over an infinite horizon. If the real interest rate exceeds the exogenous growth rate, a case always appearing in our simulations, we have to rule out explosive public debt paths. Assuming that debt does not increase asymptotically at a rate faster than the interest rate gives the intertemporal government budget constraint

$$B_t = \sum_{s=t}^{\infty} \frac{T_s}{d_{t,s}} \tag{3.14}$$

where T_s denotes lump-sum taxes aggregated across generations at time s.

To define a measure of the amount of public debt perceived as net wealth in this economy, consider equations (3.7) and (3.14). The proportion of public debt perceived as net wealth by the private sector is given by

$$k_t = \left[(1 + r_t)B_t - \sum_{i=0}^{54} \sum_{s=t}^{t+i} \frac{T_{i,s}}{d_{t+1,s}} \right] \Big/ \left[(1 + r_t)B_t \right] \tag{3.15}$$

Under Ricardian equivalence, k_t would be zero because households would expect to pay exactly the present value of taxes given in equation (3.14). Patinkin (1965) suggested k as a measure of the net-wealth proportion of the public debt. For this reason we will refer to k in the following as Patinkin's k.

3.2.4 Balance-of-payments determination

The balance-of-trade surplus TB_t is the excess of domestic product Y_t over domestic absorption $C_t + I_t$. In a one-good world, we have

$$TB_t = Y_t - C_t - I_t \tag{3.16}$$

By definition, the trade surplus of the foreign country must be the negative of the home country's surplus, $TB_t^* = TB_t$. In what follows, the starred variables denote variables of the foreign country. The current account surplus, CA_t, is the excess of national product, which is the sum of domestic product and income from foreign assets, over domestic absorption:

$$CA_t = Y_t + r_t Z_t - C_t - I_t \qquad (3.17)$$

Z_t denotes the home country's ownership of real assets of the foreign country; by symmetry, $Z_t^* = -Z_t$ and $CA_t^* = -CA_t$. Because of perfect capital mobility, arbitrage dictates that real interest rates are equal in both countries. The current account determines the accumulation of net foreign assets

$$Z_{t+1} = (1 + r_t) Z_t + TB_t \qquad (3.18)$$

Solving equation (3.18) and assuming that the foreign asset position of the home economy cannot grow asymptotically at a rate faster than the interest rate, the intertemporal constraint on the accumulation of net foreign wealth is

$$Z_t = \sum_{s=t}^{\infty} \frac{-TB_s}{d_{t,s}} \qquad (3.19)$$

This intertemporal constraint means that a country with positive foreign assets Z_t runs future trade deficits with a present value equal to the value of current assets.

3.2.5 Market-clearing conditions and equilibrium

Market clearing requires that the following equations hold for each date t:
Labour markets in home and foreign country

$$L_t^s = L_t \quad \text{and} \quad L_t^{s*} = L_t^* \qquad (3.20)$$

World capital market

$$A_{t+1} + A_{t+1}^* = K_{t+1} + K_{t+1}^* + B_{t+1} + B_{t+1}^* \qquad (3.21)$$

World goods market

$$TB_t + TB_t^* = 0 \qquad (3.22)$$

The world capital market-clearing equation (3.21) is obtained by summing home and foreign asset holdings $A_{t+1} = K_{t+1} + B_{t+1} + Z_{t+1}$ and $A_{t+1}^* = K_{t+1}^* + B_{t+1}^* - Z_{t+1}$. All assets are perfect substitutes.

An intertemporal equilibrium for the world economy consists of infinite sequences for all variables in the model fulfilling the following conditions:

1. For correctly anticipated paths of prices and tax rates, the consumption and asset paths for all generations as well as the investment and labour demand paths for all firms must solve the relevant optimization problems.

2. Market-clearing conditions [equations (3.20)–(3.22)] must hold at each date.
3. The transversality conditions for the intertemporal constraints [equations (3.14) and (3.19)] must hold for $t \to \infty$.

In summary, we use the concept of a perfect-foresight general equilibrium for solving the model. In the long-run or steady-state equilibrium the world economy will exhibit balanced growth at the rate g. We use the iterative techniques discussed by Auerbach and Kotlikoff (1987) to solve the model for its steady state as well as for transition paths between steady states.[1] Conceivably, our comparative dynamic analyses could suffer from indeterminacy of equilibrium. Laitner (1984), however, computed a linearized version of a closed-economy OLG model almost identical to ours, and found stable and determinate eigenvalue configurations for the linearized system. Testing for local stability and uniqueness of equilibrium over a wide range of parameter constellations, he could not find any case of indeterminacy.

3.3 SIMULATION RESULTS

3.3.1 Parameterization of the model

To solve the model numerically, values for the parameters and exogenous variables must first be assigned. The parameterization is symmetrical for both countries except when we consider the case of the small open economy. To model the small open-economy case, the population of the foreign country is assumed to be 50 times larger than the population of the home country.

Empirical estimates have reached no firm conclusion concerning the size of the intertemporal elasticity of substitution (β). But most studies, including Hall (1988) and Campbell and Mankiw (1989), interpret the time-series evidence on interest rates and consumption to suggest that this parameter is likely to be small. We fix the value of β at 0.40.[2] The rate of time preference is assigned a value of 0.02. The production elasticity of capital (α) in the Cobb–Douglas production function is probably not as controversial and is fixed at 0.30. The rate of technological progress is set to 0.02. Finally, we have chosen the size of the public debt in the initial steady state to give a debt–income ratio of 0.20.

3.3.2 The initial steady state

Table 3.1 presents the initial steady-state solution of the model for the home economy. Because the parameterization is symmetrical, the same solution is

---

[1] The model is programmed in GAUSS 2.0.
[2] Jaeger and Keuschnigg (1988) show that the extent of crowding out in a closed OLG economy may depend critically on this parameter. Lower values of β imply *ceteris paribus* larger crowding-out effects. Auerbach and Kotlikoff (1987) fix β at 0.25 and report substantial long-run crowding out. Some work on numerical overlapping-generations models uses logarithmic utility functions, thereby fixing β at 1.0 (e.g. Van De Klundert and Van De Ploeg, 1989).

obtained for the foreign country. The symmetrical parameterization also implies that there is no incentive for trade in goods or assets between the home and the foreign country. The net foreign asset position, the current account, and the trade balance are all zero.

Table 3.1 Initial steady state of home country

Capital stock	231.76	Private savings[a]	6.70
Labour supply	45.00	Budget surplus[a]	−0.40
Domestic product	73.58	Current account[a]	0.00
Public debt	14.72	Trade balance[a]	0.00
Net foreign assets	0.00	Investment[a]	6.30
Interest rate	9.53	Lump-sum taxes	1.11
Wage	1.15	Patinkin's k	0.17

[a] In percentages of domestic product.

The portion of public debt perceived as net wealth in the initial steady state is 0.17. We have investigated the sensitivity of Patinkin's k to different values of the preference and the technological parameters. The results are presented in Table 3.2. The first row of the table gives the parameter values chosen for the initial steady state and the values of Patinkin's k and the interest rate from Table 3.1. The other rows of Table 3.2 contain alternative configurations of parameters as well as the resulting values of k and the interest rate.

Table 3.2 Sensitivity analysis for Patinkin's k

	Parameters[a]				Patinkin's k	Interest rate
	β	δ	α	g		
Base case	0.40	0.02	0.30	0.02	0.17	9.53
Low β	**0.20**	0.02	0.30	0.02	0.03	16.92
High β	**1.50**	0.02	0.30	0.02	0.50	4.69
Low δ	0.40	**0.00**	0.30	0.02	0.25	7.79
High δ	0.40	**0.05**	0.30	0.02	0.07	12.47
Low α	0.40	0.02	**0.10**	0.02	0.41	5.55
High α	0.40	0.02	**0.40**	0.02	0.10	11.43
Low g	0.40	0.02	0.30	**0.00**	0.25	6.01
High g	0.40	0.02	0.30	**0.05**	0.02	16.72

[a] Parameters: β = intertemporal elasticity of substitution; δ = time preference rate; α = capital income share; g = rate of technological progress.

Two main results emerge from the sensitivity analysis. First, the portion of public debt perceived as net wealth by the private sector can vary from low values close to zero to values up to 0.50 for the parameter configurations considered in Table 3.2. It appears to be difficult to find reasonable parameter configurations where more than 50% of the public debt is perceived as net wealth.[3] Second, the

[3] Jaeger (1991) reports approximate estimates of k using time-series data for the United Kingdom and USA running from 1900 to 1987. If war years are excluded from the sample, estimates of k for both countries are close to 0.80. Standard errors of the estimates are, however, large.

size of Patinkin's k is inversely related to the interest rate. The higher the interest rate, the more heavily households discount future tax liabilities. With high interest rates, a finite-horizon household may face approximately the same tax liability as an infinite-horizon household. A numerical example illustrates this point. An infinite-horizon household facing an interest rate of 15% and a tax liability of 1 dollar per period has a discounted tax liability of 7.67 dollars. A finite-horizon household with 30 years left to live faces a discounted tax liability of 7.55 dollars under the same circumstances. If the interest rate is 5%, however, discounted tax liabilities are 21.00 dollars for the infinite-horizon household and only 16.14 dollars for the finite-horizon household.

3.3.3 The tax cut experiments

We consider the following fiscal policy experiment: The world economy is in an initial steady-state equilibrium, and lump-sum taxes in both countries are determined by the requirement of a constant long-run debt–income ratio of 0.20. In any period, per capita tax liabilities are the same for all age cohorts. The government of the home country announces a new fiscal policy regime. Lump-sum taxes are set for a specified number of years such that the budget surplus is − 5.0% of domestic output. Given our specification of the model with zero government expenditures, the tax cut is a lump-sum transfer over the horizon of the tax cut. We consider a 'short-run' tax cut over five years and a 'long-run' tax cut in effect for 20 years. At the end of the tax cut horizon, taxes are set to fix the debt–income ratio at the newly reached level. Fiscal policy in the foreign country is assumed not to react to the new fiscal policy regime announced in the home country.

Table 3.3 Transition path of home country for five-year tax cut[a]

Period	Debt output ratio	Budget surplus	Saving rate	Invest. rate	Current account	Trade balance	Capital labour ratio	Patinkin's k
	(1)	(2)	(3)	(4)	(5)	(6)	(7)	(8)
ISS[b]	0.20	− 0.4	6.7	6.3	0.0	0.0	5.15	0.17
1	0.20	− 5.0	10.5	6.0	− 0.4	− 0.4	5.15	0.42
2	0.25	− 5.0	10.6	6.0	− 0.4	− 0.4	5.14	0.33
3	0.29	− 5.0	10.6	6.0	− 0.4	− 0.3	5.14	0.28
4	0.33	− 5.0	10.6	6.0	− 0.4	− 0.3	5.13	0.23
5	0.38	− 5.0	10.6	6.0	− 0.3	− 0.2	5.13	0.17
6	0.42	− 0.8	6.5	6.0	− 0.3	− 0.2	5.13	0.17
10	0.42	− 0.8	6.6	6.1	− 0.3	− 0.1	5.11	0.16
30	0.42	− 0.8	6.6	6.1	− 0.3	0.4	5.07	0.16
60	0.42	− 0.8	6.8	6.2	− 0.2	1.0	5.03	0.16
90	0.42	− 0.8	6.8	6.2	− 0.2	1.0	5.03	0.16
FSS[b]	0.42	− 0.8	6.8	6.2	− 0.2	1.0	5.03	0.16

[a] Home and foreign country are equally sized. Budget surplus, saving rate, investment rate, current account, and trade balance are in percentages of domestic output.
[b] ISS: initial steady state; FSS: final steady state.

3.3.4 Transition paths for the tax cut experiments

We start by reporting the results for the case where home and foreign country are equally sized. Table 3.3 traces the evolution of the home country for the five-year tax cut from the initial steady state to the final steady state. The transition paths for the public debt ratio and the budget surplus in percentages of domestic product are given in columns 1 and 2. The debt–income ratio increases to 0.42 in period 6 and is fixed at this new level.

The crowding-out effects of the fiscal policy experiments are compactly described by the path of the capital–labour ratio in column 7. The change in the world interest rate is inversely related to the change in the capital–labour ratio via the marginal productivity condition. There are two main results. First, crowding out is a slow process. Second, the crowding-out effect of the tax cut appears to be rather small even in the final steady state. The first result is also stressed by Auerbach and Kotlikoff (1987) in a closed-economy framework. The logic of life-cycle consumption behaviour explains the slow crowding-out process. The tax cut is perceived as transitory by households, and the additional consumption possibilities are spread out over the remaining life cycle by the existing generations. This effect is clearly captured by the path of the private savings rate in column 3. The small long-run crowding-out effect is explained by the workings of two factors. While the portion of public debt perceived as net wealth in column 8 increases transitorily, only a small part of the additional public debt is taken to represent net wealth by households after the tax cut is phased out. Further, part of the additional consumption triggered by the tax cut is satisfied by importing goods (column 6). The accumulated foreign debt has, however, to be serviced, and the trade deficits at the beginning of the transition path have eventually to give way to trade surpluses in later periods. This open-economy effect also reduces crowding out of the capital stock. But because of foreign debt accumulation, part of the home country capital stock in the new final steady state will effectively be owned by the foreign country.

In Table 3.4, we report qualitatively similar results for the 20-year tax cut. The debt–income ratio increases to almost 1.0. The portion of public debt perceived as net wealth increases substantially at the beginning of the transition path because many generations expect to pay no taxes or at least face a reduced discounted tax liability. Crowding-out effects are more pronounced than for the five-year tax cut. The home country has to run a substantial trade surplus in the final steady state to service the accumulated foreign debt.

Table 3.5 reports the results for a 20-year tax cut for the case when the home country is a small open economy and the foreign country represents the world economy with a population 50 times larger than in the home country. As the world interest rate is now approximately exogenous from the viewpoint of the small open economy, crowding out of real capital is approximately zero. The increase in consumption in the initial years is financed by accumulating foreign debt,

Table 3.4   Transition path of home country for 20-year tax cut[a]

Period	Debt output ratio	Budget surplus	Saving rate	Invest. rate	Current account	Trade balance	Capital labour ratio	Patinkin's k
	(1)	(2)	(3)	(4)	(5)	(6)	(7)	(8)
ISS[b]	0.20	−0.4	6.7	6.3	0.0	0.0	5.15	0.17
1	0.20	−5.0	10.1	5.8	−0.7	−0.7	5.15	0.72
2	0.25	−5.0	10.0	5.8	−0.7	−0.7	5.14	0.60
3	0.29	−5.0	10.0	5.8	−0.7	−0.6	5.13	0.52
19	0.89	−5.0	9.6	5.7	−1.1	0.2	5.00	0.18
20	0.93	−5.0	9.6	5.7	−1.1	0.3	4.99	0.17
21	0.96	−1.9	6.5	5.7	−1.1	0.4	4.99	0.16
30	0.96	−1.9	6.3	5.7	−1.3	1.0	4.93	0.15
60	0.96	−1.9	6.6	5.8	−1.2	3.1	4.76	0.15
90	0.96	−1.9	7.0	5.9	−0.9	3.6	4.75	0.15
FSS[b]	0.96	−1.9	7.0	6.0	−0.9	3.6	4.75	0.15

[a] Home and foreign country are equally sized. Budget surplus, saving rate, investment rate, current account, and trade balance are in percentages of domestic output.
[b] ISS: initial steady state; FSS: final steady state.

Table 3.5   Transition path of small open economy for 20-year tax cut[a]

Period	Debt output ratio	Budget surplus	Saving rate	Invest. rate	Current account	Trade balance	Capital labour ratio	Patinkin's k
	(1)	(2)	(3)	(4)	(5)	(6)	(7)	(8)
ISS[b]	0.20	−0.4	6.7	6.3	0.0	0.0	5.15	0.17
1	0.20	−5.0	9.9	6.3	−1.4	−1.4	5.15	0.74
2	0.25	−5.0	9.9	6.3	−1.4	−1.3	5.15	0.61
3	0.29	−5.0	9.8	6.3	−1.5	−1.2	5.15	0.53
19	0.89	−5.0	9.1	6.3	−2.2	0.4	5.14	0.19
20	0.92	−5.0	9.1	6.3	−2.2	0.5	5.14	0.18
21	0.95	−1.9	6.0	6.3	−2.2	0.7	5.14	0.17
30	0.95	−1.9	5.7	6.3	−2.4	1.8	5.14	0.17
60	0.95	−1.9	6.0	6.3	−2.2	5.6	5.13	0.17
90	0.95	−1.9	6.5	6.3	−1.7	6.4	5.13	0.17
FSS[b]	0.95	−1.9	6.5	6.3	−1.7	6.4	5.13	0.17

[a] Budget surplus, saving rate, investment rate, current account, and trade balance are in percentages of domestic output.
[b] ISS: initial steady state; FSS: final steady state.

which has eventually to be serviced by running a large trade balance surplus. Since the demand for real capital is fixed by the world interest rate and labour is inelastically supplied, output and investment remain unchanged in the small open economy. From the commodity market condition, we, therefore, see that the change in aggregate consumption must be inversely related to the trade balance position.

3.4 CONCLUSIONS

In this chapter we studied the crowding-out effects of a transitory cut in lump-sum taxes in an intertemporal open-economy model. Numerical simulation techniques were used to solve the model. We found that only a small portion of the public debt is perceived as net wealth by the private sector for realistic values of preference and technology parameters. Crowding out of real capital may be a slow process stretched over many time periods in open overlapping-generations economies. The extent of real capital crowding out depends critically on the size of the country cutting the taxes. A small open economy experiences no capital crowding out at all. But tax cuts will lead to foreign debt accumulation that may require substantial steady-state trade surpluses to service the foreign debt.

ACKNOWLEDGEMENTS

We are grateful to Wolfgang Peters for helpful comments. The usual disclaimer applies. The first author thanks the Erwin Schroedinger Foundation for granting a fellowship at Princeton University, and the second author thanks the Alexander von Humboldt Foundation for granting a research fellowship at the University of Bonn.

REFERENCES

Auerbach, A. J. and Kotlikoff, L. J. (1987) *Dynamic Fiscal Policy*. Cambridge University Press, Cambridge.

Barro, R. J. (1974) Are Government Bonds Net Wealth? *Journal of Political Economy*, **82**, 1095–117.

Campbell, J. Y. and Mankiw, N. G. (1989) Consumption, Income, and Interest Rates: Reinterpreting the Time Series Evidence, in *Macroeconomics Annual* (eds. O. J. Blanchard and S. Fischer), MIT Press, Cambridge, MA, pp. 185–216.

Frenkel, J. A. and Razin, A. (1987) *Fiscal Policies and the World Economy*. MIT Press, Cambridge, MA.

Giovannini, A. (1988) The Real Exchange Rate, the Capital Stock, and Fiscal Policy. *European Economic Review*, **32**, 1747–67.

Hall, R. E. (1988) Intertemporal Substitution in Consumption. *Journal of Political Economy*, **96**, 339–57.

Jaeger, A. (1991) Debt Neutrality, Finite Horizons, and Private Savings Behaviour, in *The Political Economy of Public Debt* (eds. H. Verbon and F. van Winden), North Holland, Amsterdam (forthcoming).

Jaeger, A. and Keuschnigg, C. (1988) Adjusting Unsustainable Budget Deficits and Crowding-Out. *Jahrbücher für Nationalökonomie und Statistik*, **205**, 492–505.

Laitner, J. (1984) Transition Time Paths for Overlapping-Generations Models. *Journal of Economic Dynamics and Control*, **7**, 111–29.

Obstfeld, M. (1989) Fiscal Deficits and Relative Prices in a Growing World Economy. *Journal of Monetary Economics*, **23**, 461–84.

Patinkin, D. (1965) *Money, Interest and Prices*, 2nd edn. Harper & Row, New York.
Poterba, J. and Summers, L. H. (1987) Finite Lifetimes and the Effects of Budget Deficits on National Savings. *Journal of Monetary Economics*, **20**, 369–91.
Van de Klundert, T. and Van de Ploeg, F. (1989) Finite Lives in Interdependent Economies with Real and Nominal Wage Rigidity. *Oxford Economic Papers*, **41**, 459–89.

4

Cost of capital, investment location and marginal effective tax rate: methodology and application
Marcel Gérard

4.1 INTRODUCTION

The cost of capital is deemed to be a key variable in the choice of the location of an investment, as well as of its financing, especially in an area where both labour and capital are easily mobile. Since taxation plays a central role among the determinants of that cost, measuring the **effective tax rate on investment income** and, in particular, its marginal value, the **marginal effective tax rate** (hereafter METR), is an important issue. The problem of an efficient allocation of resources in an open area is intrinsically related to this issue, making it quite critical in the prospect of the building of a large and open transnational market as it is the case in Western Europe now.

Effective tax rate on capital income has been defined by Feldstein and Summers (1979) and Feldstein *et al.* (1983) as depending on the direct taxes paid by the corporation itself as well as by its shareholders and creditors. We adopt this definition here. In their seminal book, King and Fullerton (1984) suggested a methodology for computing marginal effective tax rate on investment income and proposed figures for Germany, Sweden, United Kingdom and the United States. More recently, attempts have been made to extend this exercise to transnational investment.

Despite its merit in terms of inner consistency, the King–Fullerton METR is not just a description of how tax systems operate. Rather, it vehicles an assumption, common in neoclassical microeconomics, including Jorgenson's (1963) definition of the cost of capital that the marginal unit of investment is the one for which return equals cost. Such a definition of marginality ignores the possible non-price rationing phenomena. In view of what happens in most economies where different forms of rationing exist, or coexist, the King–Fullerton METR might lead to an underestimation of the true METR. This chapter tries to clarify this point by presenting a new and more general derivation of METR which incorporates rationing phenomena and produces the King–Fullerton METR as a particular case. Section 4.2 deals with this methodological issue.

On the other hand, attempts made to extend this methodology to transnational capital income, e.g. Alworth (1988) and Devereux and Keen (1989), usually consist in formalizing tax treaties provisions. Such an approach to transnational investment income taxation might be a bit unrealistic when suppliers of invest-ment funds are private people as well as too restrictive since it is limited to bilateral flows. This chapter suggests an alternative view based on the long-held Belgian tradition of perfect capital mobility, i.e. that tax treaties matter only for institutions and big capitalists (we also use the term 'dominant shareholder') while most individual savers pay only the withholding tax, if any, retained when and where interest or dividend is paid. Combined with a 'superarbitrage' mech-anism, which implies the endogenization of domestic interest rate, this view has the two following properties. First, it allows us to investigate such situations as an investment decided by a resident of country *a*, located in country *b* and financed by funds supplied by savers from various countries; therefore, we move from bilateral flows of funds to multilateral flows. Second, the model built up on that assumption seems to be well-suited to study harmonization proposals like the one recently issued by EEC Commissioner, Mrs Scrivener, regarding a uniform and flat withholding tax on capital income amongst the EEC members or the Giovannini and Hines (1990) clearing system. Section 4.3 proposes a (possibly Belgian-biased) model of transnational investment income taxation consistent with that view.

Section 4.4 completes the chapter with an application to two transnational triangles where factors are especially mobile: the Aken(D) – Liège(B) – Maas-tricht(Nl) Euregio on the one hand and the Arlon(B) – Longwy(F) – Luxem-burg(L) or Rodange(L) triangle on the other. The latter triangle is already organized as *Pôle Européen de Développement*.[1]

4.2 AN ALTERNATIVE DERIVATION OF MARGINAL EFFECTIVE TAX RATE (METR)

The alternative derivation of the marginal effective tax rate proposed in this section incorporates the rationing phenomena as well as produces the King–Fullerton METR as a particular case. It is shown that under some conditions the King–Fullerton METR might be an underestimation of the true METR. The derivation is conducted under the following assumptions, which help focusing on the effects of tax parameters:

[1] Policy instruments especially designed for the Euregio or the *Pôle Européen de Développement* are not considered in the study. Therefore, the places mentioned are just representative locations in their respective countries.

— H1: infinite horizon;
— H2: one factor of production – capital goods;
— H3: shareholders are households with tax residence in the country where the firm is currently operating (this assumption will be relaxed in section 4.3);
— H4: firm is initially unlevered;
— H5: marginal rate of return on investment is decreasing; and
— H6: there is no uncertainty.

4.2.1 Definition and arbitrage

Let p be the pre-tax rate of return on a marginal project of investment, net of deterioration but before financial liabilities: interest payment, dividend and opportunity cost of self-financing. Let s' be the post-tax real rate of return to the decider of the project, i.e. the so-called dominant shareholder. Let s'' be the post-tax real rate of return to the supplier of the funds, possibly the same agent as the decider. Then the marginal effective tax rate is defined as

$$t = \frac{p - s' - s''}{p} \tag{4.1}$$

the numerator being the tax wedge, also denoted as w.

Now it seems natural to require that

$$s' \geq 0 \tag{4.2}$$

as the dominant shareholder will not decide on an investment involving losses. In a price-regulated economy, s' is known to be zero, involving further the definition of a marginal project as a project such that return (the so-called marginal productivity in value in a competitive economy or in income if some degree of monopolization is at work) equals cost (the so-called marginal cost). Unlike that, in the case of non-price rationing such as quantity rationing, e.g. when some upper limit to sales is expected for the future, one easily imagines that the decider of an investment will be more pessimistic and stops earlier on his marginal return curve, deemed to be decreasing, thus deciding of a marginal project such that s' might be positive. Similarly, one assumes that

$$s'' \geq (1 - m^i)(r + \pi) - \pi \tag{4.3}$$

so that the real after-tax return for the supplier of the funds is not smaller than the return on alternative forms of saving. If there is no disequilibrium on the stock market, equation (4.3) holds as a strict equality, which means that the return on any asset has to be identical irrespective of the form of saving. Actually, in the rest of the chapter we postulate such an equilibrium, thus assuming $s'' = (1 - m^i)(r + \pi) - \pi$.

In equation (4.3), m^i stands for the marginal personal income tax rate on interest for a representative saver i (e.g. in Belgium m^i is a flat rate of 0.10 for virtually all taxpayers). Moreover, r is the real rate of interest and π is the rate of inflation.

Let us now turn to p and explore the relation between p, s' and s''.

4.2.2 Value of a marginal project

The value of a marginal project for the private sector is the difference between the discounted flow of benefits that the project generates for both the owner of the firm and the supplier of the funds on the one hand, and the sacrifice made by the supplier of the funds on the other. Assuming the invested marginal amount equal to unity, this value, which we know equals zero in a competitive world, is MV such that

$$MV = (1 - m_1)\left[\int_0^\infty (1 - \tau)(p + \delta)e^{-(\rho + \delta - \pi)u}\, du + A - C \right] + R - 1 \qquad (4.4)$$

or

$$MV = (1 - m_1)\left[\frac{(1 - \tau)(p + \delta)}{\rho + \delta - \pi} + A - C \right] + R - 1 \qquad (4.5)$$

where the term between brackets is the value of the marginal project for the decider, a value deemed to be zero in standard price-regulated microeconomics but permitted to be positive when non-price rationing like quantity rationing is at work. It turns out that in standard microeconomics one has an additional equation which makes p a function of the cost of capital C; this additional equation plays a key role in the King–Fullerton way to derive METR. Otherwise, $R - 1$ is the value of the marginal saving for the supplier of the funds; again, in standard microeconomics R equals 1 so that at equilibrium: (i) equation (4.3) is a strict equality, and (ii) MV is definetly zero. As stated before, we will regard equation (4.3) as a strict equality in the rest of the chapter.

Symbols in equations (4.4) and (4.5) are:

p = marginal productivity in value (viz. in income) in the first period of operation, net of deterioration,
δ = rate of deterioration of the capital good,
ρ = discounting rate,
u = time index,
A = present value of tax shields,
C = present value of the corporate financial liabilities,
R = present value of net income for the supplier of the funds,
τ = corporate tax rate,
m_1 = personal tax rate on corporate profits defined by

$$1 - m_1 = (1 - m^i) \frac{1 - \tau + x\tau}{1 - \tau} d + (1 - z)(1 - d) \tag{4.6}$$

with

m^i = marginal personal income tax rate on interest,
x = imputation rate, $0 \leqslant x \leqslant 1$,
d = pay-out ratio,
z = tax rate on (accrued) capital gains.

It is to be observed that equation (4.6) authorizes different dividend policies ranking from full distribution ($d = 1$) to full accumulation ($d = 0$).

Due to our definition of the value of a project, equation (4.5) might be rewritten as

$$V = \frac{s' + s'' + \pi}{\rho} - 1 \tag{4.7}$$

so that

$$s' = (1 - m_1) \left[\frac{(1 - \tau)(p + \delta)}{\rho + \delta - \pi} \rho + \rho A - \rho C \right] \tag{4.8}$$

and

$$s'' = \rho R - \pi \tag{4.9}$$

Obviously, there is a link between C and R, which in turn depends on the way the project has been financed and on the arbitrage equation (4.3).

In the rest of the chapter we consider three financing policies, i.e. issuing new shares, a policy referred to by $f = 1$, issuing bonds (actually perpetuities), a policy denoted by $f = 2$, and using the available current profits or self-financing ($f = 3$).

New shares issue

In case of new shares issue, the return for the saver will, in general, be characterized by

$$\rho R = (1 - m_1)\rho C \tag{4.10}$$

so that, by the arbitrage equation (4.3) taken as a strict equality and using equation (4.9) which links s'' to R,

$$\rho C = \frac{1 - m^i}{1 - m_1}(r + \pi) \equiv i/\vartheta \tag{4.11}$$

where, on the right-hand side of $\equiv$,

$$i = r + \pi \tag{4.12}$$

so that i is the nominal rate of interest, and ϑ is such that

$$\vartheta = \frac{1-\tau+x\tau}{1-\tau} d + \frac{1-z}{1-m^i}(1-d) \qquad (4.13)$$

Note that particular values of ϑ deserve special interest. These are:

— classical tax system with capital gains taxed like other capital income: $x=0$, $z=m^i$; then $\vartheta=1$ and $\rho C = i$;
— same but no tax on capital gain (Belgium after 1983); then $\vartheta=d + (1-d)/(1-m^i)$ and cost of finance ρC goes up when the pay-out ratio increases and *vice versa*;
— $x=0.5$ and $z=0$ (Belgium before 1983); then ρC goes up when pay-out ratio increases if $m^i > 0.5\tau/(1-0.5\tau)$;
— full imputation (e.g. Germany after 1977) and $z=0$; then the above result occurs if $m^i > \tau$;
— same but $z=m^i$; then the above result never occurs, the converse is true.

It turns out that one way to render C independent of d is to set $x=0$ and $m^i = z$, although there are still other ways of realizing the irrelevance of dividend policy set forth by Modigliani and Miller (1958).

Otherwise, some incentives to equity finance recently taken, among others, in Belgium and France require a revision of equations (4.10)–(4.13). They are characterized by the following three elements to be considered separately or to be combined:

— non-taxation at corporate level of dividends paid to newly issued shares, at least during a given number of years,
— non-taxation at recipient level of dividends paid to newly issued shares;
— tax credit at personal level proportional to the amount devoted to purchasing shares.

They provide tax systems which are neutral with respect to equity and debt finance, under the assumption of full distribution.

New debt (perpetuities) issue

As interest liabilities are usually deductible against the corporate tax base, we have here that

$$\rho R = \frac{1-m^i}{1-\tau}\rho C \qquad (4.14)$$

and, by equations (4.3) and (4.9) again,

$$\rho C = i(1-\tau) \qquad (4.15)$$

However, it is well-known that under a cash flow tax system, equation (4.15) becomes $\rho C = i$ as interest is no longer deductible against corporate tax base. Then a classical tax system provides neutrality with respect to equity and debt finance under full distribution.

Using retained earnings

This financing policy enables the supplier of funds, now the owner of the corporation, to avoid taxation on distributed profits or/and capital gains at personal level. Then

$$\rho R = (1 - m_1)\rho C \qquad (4.16)$$

but as the sacrifice is $1 - m_1$ instead of 1, the arbitrage condition now implies

$$\rho R = (1 - m^i)(1 - m_1)i \qquad (4.17)$$

and

$$\rho C = (1 - m^i)i \qquad (4.18)$$

Again, $m^i = \tau$ might be a condition of tax neutrality with respect to corporate financing policies.

4.2.3 Return on a project and METR

As a consequence of equations (4.11), (4.15) and (4.18), the return on a project for the owner of the company depends on the financing policy chosen and might be written as

$$s'_f = (1 - m_1)\left[\frac{(1 - \tau)(p + \delta)}{\rho + \delta - \pi} \rho + \rho A - \gamma_f i \right] \qquad (4.19)$$

with γ_f depending on the financing policy of the company, i.e.

$$\gamma_f = \begin{cases} 1/\vartheta, & f = 1, \text{ new shares} \\ 1 - \tau, & f = 2, \text{ new debt} \\ 1 - m^i, & f = 3, \text{ retained earnings} \end{cases} \qquad \begin{matrix} (4.20) \\ (4.21) \\ (4.22) \end{matrix}$$

while the return of the same project for the supplier of the funds is

$$s'' = (1 - m^i)i - \pi \qquad (4.23)$$

irrespective of financing policy f.

In addition, by equation (4.2), i.e. $s' \geqslant 0$, we have

$$p \geqslant \left[\frac{\gamma_f i}{\rho} - A \right] \frac{\rho + \delta - \pi}{1 - \tau} - \delta \qquad (4.24)$$

Equations (4.19), (4.23) and (4.24) are central for the rest of the chapter.

In view of equation (4.1), marginal efective tax rate also depends on the financing policy and becomes

$$t = 1 - \frac{(1 - m_1)\left[\dfrac{(1 - \tau)(p + \delta)}{\rho + \delta - \pi} \rho + \rho A - \gamma_f i \right]}{p} - \frac{(1 - m^i)i - \pi}{p} \qquad (4.25)$$

We can now show that the King–Fullerton marginal effective tax rate, hereafter KF-METR, is a particular case of equation (4.25) and even a minimal case.

4.2.4 King–Fullerton METR as a particular (neoclassical) METR

As stated above, the King–Fullerton METR vehicles the assumption common in neoclassical microeconomics that the marginal unit of investment is the one for which return equals cost. Such a definition implies that the owner of the company does not draw any profit for himself from the marginal unit of investment. Then KF-METR might be generated from equation (4.25) by just substituting

$$s'_f = 0 \qquad (4.26)$$

for equation (4.2), i.e. for $s'_f \geqslant 0$. Clearly, this corresponds to an economy, sometimes called notional or Walrasian, in which the behaviour is totally and exclusively ruled by costs and prices, no form of non-price rationing being permitted.

A consequence of the substitution of equation (4.26) for equation (4.2) is that equation (4.24) is now the strict equality

$$p = \left[\frac{\gamma_f i}{\rho} - A \right] \frac{\rho + \delta - \pi}{1 - \tau} - \delta \qquad (4.27)$$

and as i, the nominal rate of interest, is the sum of the real rate of interest r and the rate of inflation π, equation (4.27) implies a fixed link between r and p, permitting the so-called King–Fullerton (KF) **fixed-p** case and **fixed-r** case.

In the rest of the chapter we will denote by p_f^* the value of p defined by equation (4.27).

Another, important, consequence of equation (4.26) and, thus, equation (4.27) is that METR defined by equation (4.25) now reduces to

$$t_f^{\mathrm{KF}} = 1 - \frac{(1 - m^i)i - \pi}{p_f^*} \qquad (4.28)$$

At this stage the relevance of the King–Fullerton assumption that $s'_f = 0$ might be questioned at least from two points of view: because it is required for **every finance policy** on the one hand and because it ignores **rationing phenomena** e.g. in terms of funds availability or in terms of expected upper limit to sales opportunities on the other. Moreover, one can show that under some actual tax designs the King–Fullerton METR underestimates the true METR.

To illustrate this point, consider the following numerical example inspired from actual Belgian tax figures, i.e. $\tau = 0.39$, $m^i = 0.10 \ \forall_i$ (a flat withholding and final tax on interest income), $m_1 = 0.25$ and $z = 0$. Note that if full distribution, $d = 1$, is assumed as is the case in this example, $m_1 = 0.25$ not because any imputation system is at work but simply because since the spring of 1990, the withholding final tax rate has been reduced from 0.25 to 0.10 for interest but has remained unchanged at 0.25 for dividend income. Moreover, assume $p = 0.20$, $\rho = 0.06$ and $r = 0.0667 \, [\rho/(1 - m^i)]$ and suppose $\pi = \delta = A = 0$. Then we observe the KF-METR values shown in Table 4.1. that the reader might compare with similar figures computed in Gérard (1989) for a period where $m^i = m_1$.

Table 4.1 King–Fullerton METR values for the case $\tau = 0.39$, $m^i = 0.10$ and $\pi = \delta = A = 0$

	General case p and r exo	KF fixed-r case $p* = \gamma r/(1 - \tau)$, r exo	KF fixed-p case $r* = (1 - \tau)p/\gamma$, p exo
$f = 1$	0.4925	0.4510	0.4510
$f = 2$	0.3950	0.1000	0.1000
$f = 3$	0.4675	0.3900	0.3900

4.3 EXTENSION TO TRANSNATIONAL CAPITAL INCOME

Based on the Belgian long experience of capital mobility, one can issue an apparently radical assumption, i.e. that tax treaties provisions matter only for institutional agent and big capitalist, another name for the so-called dominant shareholder. Unlike these agents, most savers only pay withholding tax – if any – when and where interest or dividend is paid.

Extension to transnational investment income first needs to introduce an additional arbitrage condition adapted to a setting where capital is transnationally mobile and second to formalize repatriation tax mechanism, including relevant sections of tax treaties.

Otherwise, in order to help concentrating on taxation, the following two additional assumptions are introduced:
— H7: exchange rates are fixed;
— H8: inflation is identical across countries.

4.3.1 A transnational arbitrage condition

The following transnational arbitrage condition or **superarbitrage** condition is introduced which implies an endogenization of the domestic interest rate.

Assume that i_w^i is the highest net of tax nominal rate of interest a saver i can obtain in a transnational area. Then a condition for that economic agent to be indifferent between saving domestically and abroad is that the nominal net domestic rate of interest i_d is such that

$$(1 - m^i)i_d = i_w^i \qquad (4.29)$$

If i_w^i is obtained from saving in a country w where the gross nominal rate is i_w,

$$i_w^i = (1 - m_{dw}^i)i_w \qquad (4.30)$$

where m_{dw}^i is the income tax rate paid on interest received in country w by a resident i of country d. In view of what has been experienced by Belgian savers, it is realistic to assume that, at least for non-dominant shareholders, $m_{dw}^i = m^w$, where m^w is the rate of the withholding tax on interest income paid to non-residents in country w irrespective of tax treaties provisions. Then $(1 - m^w)i_w$ might be regarded as a benchmark rate of interest. As m^i in Belgium is equal to a flat rate for virtually all taxpayers – alternatively m^i might be viewed as an average marginal rate or the marginal rate for the most representative agent – it turns out from equations (4.29) and (4.30) that

$$i_d = i_w(1 - m^w)/(1 - m^i) \tag{4.31}$$

and **domestic interest rate has become an endogenous variable**.

Accordingly, equation (4.3) is now

$$s'' = i_w(1 - m^w) - \pi \tag{4.32}$$

4.3.2 Cost of transnational investment

Consider a prospective dominant shareholder who is a resident of country d. He considers investing in country g, where he owns a resident company, the money collected on the international market and, thus, subject to the superarbitrage condition. Note that unlike other studies – e.g. Devereux and Keen (1989) – funds are not assumed to be supplied either by residents of country d or by residents of country g. Therefore, the model developed in this section is actually a model of **multilateral** investment. The investor has to provide the suppliers of the funds with a return equal to $(1 - m^w)i_w$. Now if he decides to finance his project using new shares, new debt or retained earnings, the cost of the source of finance will be, subject to the qualifications issued in section 4.2:

New shares

$$\rho C = i_w/\vartheta^g \tag{4.33}$$

with

$$\vartheta^g = \frac{1 - m_d^g}{1 - m^w} d + \frac{1 - z}{1 - m^w}(1 - d) \tag{4.34}$$

m_d^g being the withholding tax rate on dividend in country g and z^g being the possible withholding rate on capital gains (measured on accrued gains).

New debt

$$\rho C = (1 - \tau^g)\frac{1 - m^w}{1 - m^g}i_w \tag{4.35}$$

where τ^g and m^g stand, respectively, for the corporate tax rate and the withholding tax rate on interest income in country g.

Retained earnings

In the case of retained earnings, our investor will take into account his own net sacrifice in terms of unpaid dividend or immediate capital gain. However, unlike the saver, he cannot avoid personal income tax in either his country of business or his country of residence. Therefore, his net sacrifice is

$$1 - m_1^{dg} \tag{4.36a}$$

where m_1^{dg} is the repatriation tax rate on dividend and capital gain paid in country g and taxed in possibly both the country of origin g and the country of residence of the shareholder, d. This rate is a statistic encompassing relevant provisions of the tax treaty between country g and country d (see, among others, Alworth, (1988), for more details). To alleviate the notation, we have omitted the superscript i suggesting that such a repatriation tax rate might vary from one investor to another. Similarly, m_1^{dg} is also the tax the investor will have to pay on his return on equity. Then we have

$$\rho C = (1 - m^w) i_w \tag{4.36b}$$

4.3.3 METR on transnational investment income

As a consequence of equations (4.33)–(4.36a), the return on a project located in country g, for its decider deemed to be a resident of country d, might now be rewritten as

$$s_f' = (1 - m_1^{dg}) \left[\frac{(1 - \tau^g)(p + \delta)}{\rho + \delta - \pi} \rho + \rho A^g - \gamma_f^g i_w \right] \tag{4.37}$$

with

$$\gamma_f^g = \begin{cases} 1/\vartheta^g, & f = 1, \text{ new shares} & (4.38) \\ (1 - \tau^g)(1 - m^w)/(1 - m^g), & f = 2, \text{ new debt} & (4.39) \\ 1 - m^w, & f = 3, \text{ retained earnings} & (4.40) \end{cases}$$

and, thus, by equation (4.2), i.e. $s' \geq 0$,

$$p \geq \left[\gamma_f^g i_w / \rho - A^g \right] \frac{\rho + \delta - \pi}{1 - \tau^g} - \delta \tag{4.41}$$

so that METR on transnational investment income becomes

$$t = 1 - \frac{(1 - m_1^{dg}) \left[\dfrac{(1 - \tau^g)(p + \delta)}{\rho + \delta - \pi} \rho + \rho A^g - \gamma_f^g i_w \right]}{p} - \frac{i(1 - m^w) - \pi}{p} \tag{4.42}$$

to be compared with equation (4.25) of section 4.2.

Now if we further adopt the King–Fullerton classical view that $s' = 0$, equation (4.42) reduces to formula (4.43), defining what we name **classical METR on transnational investment income**, a concept which combines the superarbitrage mechanism and the King–Fullerton classical view,

$$t_f^* = 1 - \frac{i_w(1 - m^w) - \pi}{p_f^*} \qquad (4.43)$$

with

$$p_f^* = \left[\gamma_f^g i_w / \rho - A^g \right] \frac{\rho + \delta - \pi}{1 - \tau^g} - \delta \qquad (4.44)$$

which again creates a clear link between p_f^* and i_w. Equation (4.43) exhibits the important property for the ease of computation, that **combining the superarbitrage mechanism and the classical view produces a classical METR which is independent of tax treaties**. Indeed, parameter m_1^{dg} no longer appears in equation (4.43).

4.4 APPLICATION TO TWO AREAS WITH HIGH TRANSNATIONAL MOBILITY

This application consists in computing METR figures for two transnational triangles where factors are highly mobile: the Aken(D)–Liège(B)–Maastricht(Nl) Euregio on the one hand and the Arlon(B)–Longwy(F)–Luxemburg(L) or Rodange(L) *Pôle Européen de Développement*, on the other. However, policy instruments especially designed for the Euregio or the *Pôle Européen de Développement* are not considered in the study. Therefore, the places mentioned above are just representative locations in their respective countries.

The application is organized in four steps[2] illustrated in Tables 4.2–4.5.

In the **first step**, countries are deemed to be closed economies where taxpayers are individuals who strictly obey the domestic tax law. Residents of the various countries, however, share in common discount future costs and earnings at an identical net rate of interest fixed at 8%.

Frontiers open when **second step** begins. Then we enter a multilateral setting in the sense that debt issued by any company in any country might be purchased by any resident of any country. In line with our apparently radical assumption that tax treaties provisions matter only for institutional agent and dominant shareholder, only withholding tax, if any, is paid by savers on interest income, irrespective of the legal status of this tax – a legal final tax or just a prepayment – and of the residence of the saver, whether or not it is the country where the issuing company is located. However, shareholders are still supposed to have the same residence as the company and, thus, obey domestic tax law as to their dividend income.

[2] This application differs from the one we originally produced in Gérard (1989) and is adapted – actually translated – from Gérard and Valenduc (1990).

Table 4.2 Closed economies: taxpayers obey domestic tax law

Country	p_1	p_2	p_3	t_1	t_2	t_3	t_{weight}
Inflation: 0%. No special incentive							
BEL	0.1382	0.0463	0.0930	0.4211	− 0.7280	0.1398	0.0066
FRA	0.1434	0.0690	0.0880	0.4422	− 0.1595	0.0912	0.0581
LUX	0.1838	0.1009	0.1036	0.5647	0.2075	0.2279	0.2314
FRG	0.1165	0.1050	0.1851	0.3131	0.2382	0.5679	0.5101
NL	0.1778	0.1039	0.0936	0.5500	0.2300	0.1457	0.1673
AVG	0.1519	0.0850	0.1127	0.4582	− 0.0424	0.2345	0.1947
DIS	0.1665	0.2766	0.3246	0.2011	8.8280	0.7351	0.9062
Inflation: 0%. Special incentives introduced							
BEL	0.1300	0.0392	0.0848	0.3847	− 1.0392	0.0568	− 0.1120
FRA	0.1434	0.0690	0.0880	0.4422	− 0.1595	0.0912	0.0581
LUX	0.1819	0.0990	0.1017	0.5601	0.1921	0.2132	0.2168
FRG	0.1165	0.1050	0.1851	0.3131	0.2382	0.5679	0.5101
NL	0.1571	0.0833	0.0730	0.4908	0.0391	− 0.0959	− 0.0626
AVG	0.1458	0.0791	0.1065	0.4382	− 0.1459	0.1666	0.1221
DIS	0.1547	0.2979	0.3788	0.1941	3.2067	1.3415	1.8408
Inflation: 3%. Special incentives introduced							
BEL	0.0813	0.0245	0.0530	0.3847	− 1.0392	0.0568	− 0.1120
FRA	0.0896	0.0431	0.0550	0.4422	− 0.1595	0.0912	0.0581
LUX	0.1137	0.0619	0.0636	0.5601	0.1921	0.2132	0.2168
FRG	0.0728	0.0656	0.1157	0.3131	0.2382	0.5679	0.5101
NL	0.0982	0.0520	0.0456	0.4908	0.0391	− 0.0959	− 0.0626
AVG	0.0911	0.0494	0.0666	0.4382	− 0.1459	0.1666	0.1221
DIS	0.1547	0.2979	0.3788	0.1941	3.2067	1.3415	1.8408

AVG = average value; $DIS = [\Sigma(XXX - AVG)^2]^{1/2}/AVG$.

p = minimal return required to avoid marginal corporate loss.

t = marginal effective tax rate, financed by a new share issue (t_1), financed by long-term corporate debt (t_2), and financed by retaining current profits (t_3).

At **step three**, the multilateral setting is extended to share and only withholding tax is paid on dividend income too. The exercise is then fully consistent with the apparently radical view of tax treaties mentioned above.

Step four investigates the case of a uniform and final withholding tax fixed to 15%, both on interest income and on dividend income. This allows us to evaluate the contribution of this measure of tax harmonization to the convergence of effective tax rates, as well as its limits.

Data used in this empirical investigation refer to tax year 1991 or, if information is not available for that year, to the most recent year for which data are available.

Each table consists of three parts and each part has eight columns. The top part provides computations made neglecting tax and industrial policy incentives which are not of automatic and general application, like regional or sectoral incentives, and assuming zero inflation ($\pi = 0$) as well as a zero rate for δ.[3]

---

[3] As we assume δ to be zero, the value of the rate of inflation does not influence the value of the effective tax rate, and this is one of the reasons why we decided to set δ equal to zero in this study.

Industrial policy incentives are introduced in the central part of the table; however, as such the matter is institutionally much complicated, misunderstanding or misvaluing of some incentives might not be excluded. In the bottom part, the rate of inflation is changed from zero to three points. In each part, columns p_1–p_3 provide figures for the corresponding statistics p_f, i.e. the minimum pre-tax real return required for the company to avoid losses on the marginal investment, defined by equation (4.44) – recall that subscripts 1, 2 and 3 refer to equity financing, debt financing and self-financing, respectively. The next three columns provide numerical figures for the corresponding marginal effective tax rates (METR), t_f; they are based on equation (4.43). Finally, the last column suggests values for a summarizing statistics, i.e. the weighted average over t_f. The weights used to produce this statistics are those used by de Callataÿ and Gérard (1990) for Belgium, i.e. 0.02 for equity finance, 0.16 for debt finance and 0.82 for self-financing.

Table 4.3 Open economies: withholding tax is final for interests

Country	p_1	p_2	p_3	t_1	t_2	t_3	t_{weight}
Inflation: 0%. No special incentive							
BEL	0.1382	0.0463	0.0930	0.4211	− 0.7280	0.1398	0.0066
FRA	0.1434	0.0690	0.0880	0.4422	− 0.1595	0.0912	0.0581
LUX	0.1838	0.0505	0.1036	0.5647	− 0.5851	0.2279	0.1046
FRG	0.1165	0.0483	0.1851	0.3131	− 0.6578	0.5679	0.3667
NL	0.1778	0.0506	0.0936	0.5500	− 0.5820	0.1457	0.0374
AVG	0.1519	0.0529	0.1127	0.4582	− 0.5425	0.2345	0.1147
DIS	0.1665	0.1548	0.3246	0.2011	0.3666	0.7351	1.1337
Inflation: 0%. Special incentives introduced							
BEL	0.1300	0.0392	0.0848	0.3847	− 1.0392	0.0568	− 0.1120
FRA	0.1434	0.0690	0.0880	0.4422	− 0.1595	0.0912	0.0581
LUX	0.1819	0.0485	0.1017	0.5601	− 0.6482	0.2132	0.0823
FRG	0.1165	0.0483	0.1851	0.3131	− 0.6578	0.5679	0.3667
NL	0.1571	0.0299	0.0730	0.4908	− 1.6738	− 0.0959	− 0.3367
AVG	0.1458	0.0470	0.1065	0.4382	− 0.8357	0.1666	0.0117
DIS	0.1547	0.2758	0.3788	0.1941	0.6026	1.3415	19.849
Inflation: 3%. Special incentives introduced							
BEL	0.0813	0.0245	0.0530	0.3847	− 1.0392	0.0568	− 0.1120
FRA	0.0896	0.0431	0.0550	0.4422	− 0.1595	0.0912	0.0581
LUX	0.1137	0.0303	0.0636	0.5601	− 0.6482	0.2132	0.0823
FRG	0.0728	0.0302	0.1157	0.3131	− 0.6578	0.5679	0.3667
NL	0.0982	0.0187	0.0456	0.4908	− 1.6738	− 0.0959	− 0.3367
AVG	0.0911	0.0294	0.0666	0.4382	− 0.8357	0.1666	0.0117
DIS	0.1547	0.2758	0.3788	0.1941	0.6026	1.3415	19.849

The tables also give the average values across countries as well as the relative standard deviation around the mean, denoted as *DIS* (the standard deviation divided by the mean). A decrease in the latter statistics illustrates that minimal requirements on p (viz. effective rates t) are closer to each other, thus revealing a more harmonized transnational tax system or less tax discrimination.

Table 4.4 Open economies: withholding tax is final for interests and dividends, or the application of the source principle

Country	p_1	p_2	p_3	t_1	t_2	t_3	t_{weight}
Inflation: 0%. No special incentive							
BEL	0.1382	0.0463	0.0930	0.4211	− 0.7280	0.1398	0.0066
FRA	0.1433	0.0690	0.0880	0.4418	− 0.1595	0.0912	0.0581
LUX	0.1274	0.0505	0.1036	0.3719	− 0.5851	0.2279	0.1007
FRG	0.1552	0.0483	0.1851	0.4845	− 0.6578	0.5679	0.3701
NL	0.1363	0.0506	0.0936	0.4132	− 0.5820	0.1457	0.0346
AVG	0.1401	0.0529	0.1127	0.4265	− 0.5425	0.2345	0.1140
DIS	0.0652	0.1548	0.3246	0.0863	0.3666	0.7351	1.1552
Inflation: 0%. Special incentives introduced							
BEL	0.1300	0.0392	0.0848	0.3847	− 1.0392	0.0568	− 0.1120
FRA	0.1433	0.0690	0.0880	0.4418	− 0.1595	0.0912	0.0581
LUX	0.1254	0.0485	0.1017	0.3622	− 0.6482	0.2132	0.0784
FRG	0.1552	0.0483	0.1851	0.4845	− 0.6578	0.5679	0.3701
NL	0.1157	0.0299	0.0730	0.3084	− 1.6738	− 0.0959	− 0.3403
AVG	0.1339	0.0470	0.1065	0.3963	− 0.8357	0.1666	0.0109
DIS	0.1035	0.2758	0.3788	0.1549	0.6026	1.3415	21.554
Inflation: 3%. Special incentives introduced							
BEL	0.0813	0.0245	0.0530	0.3847	− 1.0392	0.0568	− 0.1120
FRA	0.0896	0.0431	0.0550	0.4418	− 0.1595	0.0912	0.0581
LUX	0.0784	0.0303	0.0636	0.3622	− 0.6482	0.2132	0.0784
FRG	0.0970	0.0302	0.1157	0.4845	− 0.6578	0.5679	0.3701
NL	0.0723	0.0187	0.0456	0.3084	− 1.6738	− 0.0959	− 0.3403
AVG	0.0837	0.0294	0.0666	0.3963	− 0.8357	0.1666	0.0109
DIS	0.1035	0.2758	0.3788	0.1549	0.6026	1.3415	21.554

Note that we do not have to be aware of a negative value for the marginal effective tax rates; such a value simply means that the marginal investment is subsidized. And this does not rule out that the average effective tax rate might be non-negative.

4.4.1 Closed economies

As mentioned above, in this first step countries are deemed to be closed economies where taxpayers are individuals who strictly obey the domestic tax law. This implies that both interest and dividend income are to be entered in one's tax return wherever it is required to do so, i.e. in all investigated countries but Belgium and, in part, France. In Belgium, the withholding tax levied at a 25% rate on dividend income and a 10% rate on interest is legally final. In France, a global system applies to dividend income while both that system and a final withholding tax are permitted for interest income; the rate of the latter tax is 27%. We use this rate value in this exercise.

Let us now examine the key figures in the top part of Table 4.2.

The difference in the ways interest income is taxed in Belgium and France on the one hand, and in the other counties on the other, explains why p_2 and t_2 are smaller in the first two countries. Otherwise, p_2 and t_2 are usually smaller than other p_f and t_f due to the allowed deductibility of interest against the corporate income tax. Values of p_1 and t_1 are the highest in The Netherlands and Luxemburg as these two countries experiment economic double taxation of dividend income. This double taxation is mitigated in France by the *avoir fiscal* mechanism – a system equivalent to a 69% imputation in terms of the paid-out dividend – and is completely cancelled out in Germany by the application of the full-imputation system. In Belgium, double taxation actually applies but the personal tax is relatively low as it is limited to the 25% rate withholding tax on dividend income. Finally, p_3 and t_3 are smaller than p_1 and t_1 in all but one countries due to the avoidance of personal taxation when profit is kept in the company in order to provide internal financing of an investment rather than distributed to shareholders. The exception of Germany is due to a higher corporate tax rate on retained profit than on distributed earnings.

Table 4.5 Harmonized economies: a uniform 15% withholding tax assumed to be final, or the harmonized application of the source principle

Country	p_1	p_2	p_3	t_1	t_2	t_3	t_{weight}
Inflation: 0%. No special incentive							
BEL	0.1169	0.0515	0.0930	0.3158	− 0.5527	0.1398	0.0325
FRA	0.1217	0.0535	0.0880	0.3425	− 0.4947	0.0912	0.0025
LUX	0.1274	0.0654	0.1036	0.3719	− 0.2228	0.2279	0.1587
FRG	0.1327	0.0634	0.1851	0.3971	− 0.2617	0.5679	0.4318
NL	0.1168	0.0647	0.0936	0.3152	− 0.2368	0.1457	0.0879
AVG	0.1231	0.0597	0.1127	0.3485	− 0.3537	0.2345	0.1427
DIS	0.0501	0.0995	0.3246	0.0919	0.3973	0.7351	1.0976
Inflation: 0%. Special incentives introduced							
BEL	0.1087	0.0445	0.0848	0.2644	− 0.7993	0.0568	− 0.0760
FRA	0.1217	0.0535	0.0880	0.3425	− 0.4947	0.0912	0.0025
LUX	0.1254	0.0635	0.1017	0.3622	− 0.2600	0.2132	0.1405
FRG	0.1327	0.0634	0.1851	0.3971	− 0.2617	0.5679	0.4318
NL	0.0962	0.0440	0.0730	0.1682	− 0.8166	− 0.0959	− 0.2060
AVG	0.1169	0.0538	0.1065	0.3069	− 0.5265	0.1666	0.0586
DIS	0.1109	0.1597	0.3788	0.2668	0.4659	1.3415	3.7200
Inflation: 3%. Special incentives introduced							
BEL	0.0680	0.0278	0.0530	0.2644	− 0.7993	0.0568	− 0.0760
FRA	0.0760	0.0335	0.0550	0.3425	− 0.4947	0.0912	0.0025
LUX	0.0784	0.0397	0.0636	0.3622	− 0.2600	0.2132	0.1405
FRG	0.0829	0.0396	0.1157	0.3971	− 0.2617	0.5679	0.4318
NL	0.0601	0.0275	0.0456	0.1682	− 0.8166	− 0.0959	− 0.2060
AVG	0.0731	0.0336	0.0666	0.3069	− 0.5265	0.1666	0.0586
DIS	0.1109	0.1597	0.3788	0.2668	0.4659	1.3415	3.7200

In terms of the weighted average statistics, Belgium exhibits the smallest marginal effective tax rate, mainly because the personal tax rate is limited to a flat and rather moderate withholding tax. Conversely, Germany shows the largest value; this is due to the combined effect of a higher corporate tax rate on undistributed profit and of the largest influence of this source of funds on the average METR on the one hand, and of the German business tax on the other. The latter tax exists in Germany and Luxemburg; its base is the corporate tax base plus half the interest paid on the long-run corporate debt and its revenue is for local authorities who decide its rate. The average rate of this tax in Germany is 15%. Subsequent parts of the table reveal that when industrial policy incentives are introduced, The Netherlands defeat Belgium in the least-tax race. However, as stressed above, these incentives are very complicated and, thus, subject to possible misunderstanding or misvaluing. Therefore, the central and the bottom parts of the table are to be considered with care, *cum grano salis*.

4.4.2 Multilateral debt finance and domestic equity

With the second step we enter a multilateral setting where corporate debt issued by any company in any country might be purchased by any resident of any country. Then, in line with the assumption that tax treaties provisions matter only for institutional agent and dominant shareholder, only withholding tax, if any, is paid by savers on interest income, irrespective of the legal status of that tax and of the residence of the saver. However, shareholders are yet supposed to have the same residence as the company and, thus, to obey domestic tax law as to their dividend income.

Therefore, the figures in Table 4.3 are similar to those of Table 4.2 for equity financing and self-financing. Values of p_2 and t_2 are reduced in those countries where interest income was supposed to be included in individual tax return, i.e Luxemburg, Germany and The Netherlands. The average values over countries and over sources of funds are modified accordingly and the deviation around the mean, *DIS*, sharply decreases for p_2 and t_2.

4.4.3 Open economies: perfectly mobile saving and the source principle

The extension of the multilateral setting to equity finance characterizes the third step. Now, only withholding tax, if any, is paid by individual saver on both his dividend and interest income. The exercise is then fully consistent with the view of tax treaties developed earlier in this chapter.

A comparison of the upper parts of Tables 4.3 and 4.4 shows little change in figures, the only clear result being the decrease in the deviation around the mean, *DIS*, in case of equity finance.

Actually, changes appear only for p_1 and t_1, except in Belgium, since withholding tax on dividend was already a final tax in that country, and they are balanced. These statistics go down significantly in Luxemburg and The Netherlands, where double taxation of dividends is at work, so that the institutional change investigated here really means the substitution of a 15% or 25% flat rate for the marginal personal income tax rate. In France, the substitution of a 25% flat rate – actually the standard rate for non-resident individuals – for the combination of the marginal individual income tax rate and the *avoir fiscal* produces quasi-unchanged figures. Maybe surprising is the German case, where the statistics go up: German shareholder has no interest to give up the full imputation of the corporate tax on his individual tax liabilities.

4.4.4 Harmonized economies: a uniform withholding tax

In the fourth step the case of a uniform and final 15% withholding tax on both interest and dividend income is investigated. This step enables one to evaluate the contribution of a measure of tax harmonization in line with the one issued recently by EEC Commissioner, Mrs Scrivener, to the convergence of marginal effective tax rates, as well as its limits. For this reason, it deserves special attention: it permits one to draw an important **lesson for tax harmonization**.

If we confine the comparison to the upper parts of Tables 4.4 and 4.5, we observe, as a consequence of the measure, a general downward movement in p_1 and t_1 with the sole exception of Luxemburg, where the withholding tax rate on dividend income was already 15% (compared to 25% in other countries) and a general upward movement in p_2 and t_2, with the exception of France, where the converse movement is observed. This is due to the fact that the actual withholding tax rate on interest income in France is above 15%, unlike other countries, where it is below this value, being either 10% in Belgium or 0% in Luxemburg, Germany and The Netherlands. Thus, a merit of the proposal might be to make the tax system more neutral, or less non-neutral or discriminating, between equity and debt finance.

A global comparison of Tables 4.2–4.5 shows that the relative deviations have decreased significantly for equity and debt finance from Table 4.2 to Table 4.5. However, we are, obviously, still left with non-zero relative deviations. These residual deviations set forth the limits of such a measure of portfolio income tax harmonization if not performed in the framework of a global harmonization of METRs.

The latter observation is largely due to the great heterogeneity among tax systems which prevails in the investigated areas, especially because regional and sectoral incentives currently at work vary much across countries.

4.5 CONCLUSION

Based on the last observation of section 4.4, it turns out that **harmonization of the system of interest and dividend income taxation does not exhaust harmonization of capital income taxation**. Indeed, corporate tax bases as well as depreciation allowance mechanisms and other tax and non-tax industrial policy incentives remain very different, and there is a need for co-ordination in this matter, too, if one aims at designing a tax system as neutral as possible with respect to corporate finance and location decision.

However, harmonization of METRs is attainable also by just determining common desirable values for marginal effective tax rates and then allowing each country to design freely its own capital income tax system under the restriction on the values of METRs.

Two important limits of the approach, which open avenues for further research, are now to be stressed.

First, some countries like France have substituted incentives to create new firms with incentives to invest, so that two cases should be distinguished depending upon whether investment is made in an existing company or in a newly created one.

Second, some countries have substituted incentives to create jobs with incentives to invest. A second factor should then be introduced in the production process, i.e. labour.

In the same context, it is to be noted that the actual ranking of locations depends also on the cost of labour and, consequently, on the level of social-security and other employers' and employees' contributions, where presumably a large heterogeneity appears also across countries.

Therefore, an extension of the METR methodology should be a relevant research agenda, especially to draw particularly meaningful figures for the designers and deciders of harmonization policies in the European Community.

From a methodological point of view, the notion of marginal effective tax rate should be extended and redefined as **the difference between the social return of a unit-valued marginal investment** – measured by its return before payments to the suppliers of the funds, to the suppliers of the labour and to the tax and social-security administrations – **and its net real return to the suppliers of factors divided by the social return**.

Finally, the research reported in this chapter focused on domestic and transnational saving by individuals. It is only one aspect of the problem of transnational saving and investment. Thus, another natural extension of the present research, and a relevant research agenda as well, should be based on the assumption **that not only are individuals permitted to save either domestically or abroad, but also that companies might invest the collected funds either domestically or abroad**.

ACKNOWLEDGEMENTS

This chapter elaborates on a conversation with Mervyn King on the occasion of a conference held at Harvard's JFK School in November 1987. I have benefited from the stimulating discussions held during the presentation of the successive versions of this paper and from the comments by colleagues at ZIF, University of Bielefeld, Erasmus University, CORE, AFFI meeting at Paris-Dauphine and ESEM89 in Munich, among others, by Charles Stuart, Myron Scholes, Hans-Werner Sinn and Käre Hagen. I am also much indebted to my associates in this line of research, Etienne de Callataÿ, Isabelle Pireau and Christian Valenduc. However, and obviously, errors remain mine.

REFERENCES

Alworth, J. (1988) *The Finance Investment and Taxation Decision of Multinationals*. Basil Blackwell, Oxford.

de Callataÿ, E. and Gérard, M. (1990) La Taxation Effective des Revenus de l'Investissement en Belgique. *Bulletin de Documentation du Ministère des Finances*, **3**, 170–93.

Devereux, M. and Keen, M. (1989) Corporate Tax, Transnational Investment and Welfare (mimeo).

Feldstein, M., Dicks-Mireaux, L. and Poterba, J. (1983) The Effective Tax Rate and the Pretax Rate of Return. *Journal of Public Economics*, **21**, 129–58.

Feldstein, M. and Summers, L. (1979) Inflation and the Taxation of Capital Income in the Corporate Sector, *National Tax Journal*, **32**, 445–70.

Gérard, M. (1989) Cost of Capital, Investment Location and the Marginal Effective Tax Rate: Methodology and Two Applications. A Paper presented at the XXVIIIth AEA Conference on Fiscal Policy Modelling, Confindustria, Rome, Nov. 30–Dec. 1.

Gérard, M. and Valenduc, C. (1990) La Taxation Marginale Effective des Revenus de l'Investissement Transfrontalier, in *Rapport de la Commission 1 Préparatoire au 9ème Congrès des Economistes Belges de Langue Française* (ed. F. Thys-Clément), CIFOP, Charleroi.

Giovannini, A. and Hines, J. (1990) Capital Flight and Tax Competition: Are There Viable Solutions to Both Problems? *NBER Working Paper, No. 3333*, National Bureau of Economic Research, Cambridge, MA.

Jorgenson, D. W. (1963) Capital Theory and Investment Behavior. *American Economic Review*, **53**, 247–67.

King, M. and Fullerton, D. (1984) *The Taxation of Income from Capital: a Comparative Study of United States, the United Kingdom, Sweden and West Germany*. The University of Chicago Press, Chicago.

Modigliani, F. and Miller, M. (1958) The Cost of Capital, Corporation Finance and the Theory of Investment. *American Economic Review*, **48**, 261–97.

Part Two

Taxation and Individual Behaviour

5

Household saving, portfolio selection and taxation in France

P. Artus, E. Bleuze, F. Legros and J.-P. Nicolaï

5.1 INTRODUCTION

Two major types of explanation have been put forward to explain the fall in the French saving rate: (a) the decline in real income, combined with the determination to maintain a constant consumption level; and (b) the structural changes in the financial markets, notably the increase in risk. Our study seeks to compare the explanatory power of these two phenomena.

Household behaviour is generally represented as a two-stage process consisting of the consumption/saving allocation decision, followed by the allocation of saving among available assets. We adopt this model, demonstrating its suitability to France. Our analysis, therefore, begins with the determination of the saving rate, followed by the selection of financial assets – namely, liquid instruments, bonds, equities and life insurance policies[1] – for inclusion in the portfolio.

The conventional life-cycle models are based on household-consumption specifications that incorporate both asset–stock variables and current-income variables. This requires an exact definition of what agents regard as their 'wealth' and what they regard strictly as income flows. This distinction is important to avoid double-counting the impact of the ownership of a real or financial asset on consumption – since, if the markets are efficient, an asset's value reflects the future income it will procure to its holder. In the first stage, therefore, we begin by classifying the components of wealth – housing, equities, bonds, money and credit and life insurance – into two groups: the components that have a wealth effect, and those that influence consumption solely through the income flow they generate. If the two-stage decision-making model is valid, the wealth structure has no influence on consumption. Initially, therefore, we test for the presence of income structure or wealth structure effects. The form finally adopted will allow us, in the second stage, to examine various hypotheses concerning household

[1] Life insurance is defined here in a broad sense, including instruments such as with-profits policies, annuities, or individual retirement accounts, as they are variously referred to in the US and Britain.

expectation formation. We focus on the Barro (1974; 1981) equivalence hypothesis, and investigate the extent to which households take into account the information available on changes in the main taxation variables. Finally, we analyse the impact of specific economic-policy measures relevant to saving allocation.

In section 5.3, we study allocation decisions concerning four financial assets: liquid instruments, bonds, equities and life insurance. We take as our reference the standard portfolio management model based on comparative net returns and behavioural inertia. As with consumption, we examine the impact of saving-specific tax policy command variables on the wealth structure.

5.2 THE CONSUMPTION/SAVING ALLOCATION DECISION

5.2.1 Broad trends

As Table 5.1 shows, the household saving rate has steadily declined over the period studied, with a particularly sharp downturn from 1983 onwards: by year-end 1988, it stood at more than six points below its 1970 level. In this section we try to assess the impact of income variables and wealth variables – which are in turn largely influenced by the corresponding taxation – on the French house-hold saving rate. It is clear from our analysis that the growth rates of both sets of variables do not suffice to explain the observed discontinuities.

Table 5.1   Saving, income and wealth (% average rates)

	70–78	79–83	84–88	86	87	88
Saving rate	19.3	17.5	13.1	13.2	11.5	12.4
Real wealth growth	5.6	3.1	4.4	6.5	4.4	4.0
Real earned-income growth[a]	4.1	0.5	1.1	2.6	−0.6	3.1

[a] Disposable income in the national accounts, minus property income and rent (actual and imputed, representing income from all forms of housing ownership). For an explanation, see section 5.2.3.

5.2.2 A simple life-cycle model

Our starting point is the standard life-cycle model, which has given rise to recent developments in the consumer theory (Hall, 1978). Let C_t denote the consumption in t. The instantaneous utility function of households is

$$U(C_t) = \frac{1}{\gamma} C_t^{\gamma}$$

and we assume the time separability of the utility function. The consumer's program is, thus:

$$\text{Max } U = \sum_{i=0}^{\infty} \frac{1}{(1+\rho)^i} \frac{1}{\gamma} C_{t+i}^{\gamma} \tag{5.1}$$

under the constraints

$$C_{t+i} + S_{t+i} = R_{t+i} + S_{t+i-1}(1 + r_{t+i}) \tag{5.2}$$

S_t is real 'saving,' which is positive or, in the case of debt, negative. R_t is the real income in t, unrelated to financial assets. r_t is the real interest rate in t. ρ is the discount rate.

We assume perfect expectations of future incomes and rates, and perfect financial markets. The i budget constraints can, therefore, be written as a single intertemporal constraint:

$$\sum_{i=0}^{\infty} \frac{C_{t+i}}{\prod_{j=0}^{i}(1 + r_{t+j})} = S_{t-1} + \sum_{i=0}^{\infty} \frac{R_{t+i}}{\prod_{j=0}^{i}(1 + r_{t+j})} = W \tag{5.3}$$

W comprises the initial real wealth and the discounted future real income. Maximizing equation (5.1) under the constraint given by equation (5.3), we obtain

$$C_{t+i} = \frac{W}{\sum_{i=0}^{\infty}(1+\rho)^{-i/(1-\gamma)}\left[\prod_{j=0}^{i}(1+\hat{r}_{t+j})\right]^{\gamma/(1-\gamma)}} \frac{(1+\rho)^{-i/(1-\gamma)}}{\left[\prod_{j=0}^{i}(1+r_{t+j})\right]^{\gamma/(1-\gamma)}} \tag{5.4}$$

Assuming a constant expected real rate $\hat{r}_{t+j} = \hat{r}_t$ and linearizing around $\hat{r} = \rho$ and $R = \bar{R}$, we obtain

$$C_t = \frac{\rho}{1+\rho}\bar{W} - \theta(\hat{r}_t - \rho), \quad \text{where } \theta = \frac{\bar{W}}{(1+\rho)^2}\frac{\gamma}{(1-\gamma)} \tag{5.5}$$

$\bar{W}$ is the discounted income plus the initial wealth calculated at the point $(\rho, \bar{R})$.

5.2.3 Income/wealth allocation: the basic model

Before analysing the impact of taxation, we would like to construct a properly tested basic model for consumption. What is the ideal content of the initial real wealth variable S_{t-1}? The most comprehensive definition includes the following positive elements: corporate securities (equities and bonds), housing, currency, government securities and life insurance assets (actuarial reserves).

Minczeles and Sicsic (1988), examining whether capital gains should be included in disposable income, have shown the absence of a capital gains effect. However, we are not satisfied with the income specifications in book terms or 'economic' terms – the latter comprising not only actual flows but also capital gains and losses on stocks of goods, financial assets and debt (Sterdyniak, 1986). We would argue that if stocks of assets held by households may legitimately be included in wealth, one should then subtract the corresponding income from the total-income variable used. For example, if equities are included in household wealth, equity dividends must not be included in household income.

We, therefore, test a 'basic' specification of income/wealth in which 'wealth' comprises all household assets – equities, bonds, transactions money and investment money, housing and life insurance – minus short-and long-term loans. The corresponding 'basic income' specification thus includes disposable income minus property income and rent. We then subtract asset stocks (or add debt stocks) to wealth and add the corresponding income flows (or subtract the corresponding interest flows on debt) to income.

To perform the econometric test, we start with the linearized form [equation (5.5)]. Let R^H be the 'basic income', W^a the corresponding wealth, specified above, $R^H x$ the earned income plus the current income x linked to the holding of a specific asset, WX^a the wealth excluding the asset considered (held in the amount of X). We obtain $R^H x = R^H + x$ and $WX^a = W^a - X$ Hence, $\log R^H x \approx \log R^H x + x/R^H$ and $\log WX^a \approx \log W^a - X/W^a$.

The principle adopted is, therefore, to test the hypothesis of joint nullity of the x/R^H and X/W^a coefficients in the estimate of equation (5.5). If the hypothesis is accepted, we reject the notion that the asset studied is not regarded as a wealth component. If the hypothesis is rejected, the asset's significance lies in its income and not – or at least not entirely – in its market value.[2,3]

The estimates were performed on quarterly data covering 1970:I–1989:I. The main statistical sources are the quarterly national accounts compiled by the French Statistics Institute (Insee), the Bank of France Financial Transactions Tables (Tableaux d'Equilibre des Relations Financières: hereafter TERFs), insurance company accounts, and the reports of the French National Accounting Board.

Income/wealth allocation

The basic specification defines earned income as disposable income minus the net property income, net interest and the 'actual' rent booked in the national accounts.

---

[2] Strictly speaking, we should use perfect expectations of future income to estimate equation (5.5). However, we decided to reject the perfect-expectations hypothesis. To begin with equation (5.5) implies that:

$$C_t = (1 + \rho)C_{t-1} = -\rho RC_{t-1} - \theta[r_t - r_{t-1}(1 + \rho)] + \text{constant}$$

$$+ \frac{\rho}{1+\rho}\left[\sum_{i=0}^{\infty} \frac{R_{t\,t+1}}{(1+\rho)^i} - \sum_{i=0}^{\infty} \frac{R_{t-1\,t+1-1}}{(1+\rho)^i}\right] \tag{5.6}$$

where $R_{t\,t+1}$ is the expectation formed in t of real income in $t + i$. If expectations are rational, the last term – i.e. the revision of future-income expectations between $t-1$ and $t-2$ is independent of the information available in $t-1$, $t-2$ and so on. In our findings, however, that assumption is clearly rejected. We conducted standard rationality tests, which consist in estimating equation (5.6) with the inclusion of variables known in $t-1$. If expectations are rational, the variables should not be significant, since they do not influence the expectations revision. But, in practice, the significance of these variables as a group shows that households do not seem to form rational income expectations. We, therefore, adopted an autoregressive specification to model expectation formation.

[3] The market value of an asset is equal to the discounted total future it provides, which can obviously differ from its discounted current income. However, if we assume naive expectations, we can compare the current financial income and the market value of the corresponding asset.

The corresponding definition of wealth, therefore, includes the value of the housing stock[4] plus the value of stocks of equities, bonds, transactions money and life insurance actuarial reserves, minus loans outstanding.

Table 5.2

Income	Wealth	Fisher	Conclusion
+ Actual rent	– Housing stock	0.42	H_0 not rejected
– Interest paid	+ Credit	1.42	H_0 not rejected
+ Dividends	– Equities	1.28	H_0 not rejected
+ Interest received	– Bonds	1.56	H_0 not rejected
	– Transactions money	0.81	H_0 not rejected
+ Interest on	– Life insurance	1.92	H_0 not rejected
life insurance	actuarial reserves		

The five tests may, therefore, be tabulated as shown in Table 5.2. Each line describes an alternative income/wealth allocation to the H_0 **reference**, in which **wealth includes all components** and income does not include asset-linked transfers. The third column lists the value of the Fisher statistic linked to the nullity of the x/R^H and X/W^a coefficients (see above). If the nullity is accepted, the H_0 hypothesis is accepted as well.

We are, therefore, led to accept a definition of wealth that includes all the components. Correspondingly, income includes only 'earned' components, leaving out resources linked to asset holding. We, therefore, adopt the most conventional life-cycle model. This also means that we can keep the two-stage household behaviour model, since the wealth structure has no effect on the saving rate.

The saving rate and asset stocks are, therefore, independent. This is because we assume that, according to the standard portfolio selection model, the savings allocation decision bears on financial-asset holdings, not on flows.

Basic equation adopted

We find no effect of short- or long-term interest rates, real or nominal. In contrast, we obtain a robust negative effect for the previous year's inflation rate. Price increases, therefore, brake consumption more than the loss of purchasing power of liquid assets or earned income. We can also demonstrate that the propensity to consume transfer income (social benefits) is slightly greater than for average income.

As shown earlier, credit effectively has the expected negative effect on household income. If households are subjected to a liquidity constraint that does not jeopardize the wealth effect, credit has a different impact on consumption: the credit variation obtained during a given period allows higher consumption, since

---

[4] We derived the housing stock value from the balance sheets as a simple total of residential gross fixed-capital formation flows, without a scrapping hypothesis. The valuation uses the residential gross fixed-capital formation deflator.

the liquidity constraint – or the constraint of maximum obtainable indebtedness – is loosened (Hayashi, 1985). We test this hypothesis by adding the following variable to the basic equation: $\Delta\,credit_t/$(nominal) $consumption_{t-1}$, where 'credit' is either short-term loans or long-term loans (mortgages) to households, or both. These variables never appeared to be significant. While we find that **transitory income affects consumption** (as suggested earlier), we believe that this is not due to a credit shortage, but more likely to households' relative lack of foresight in forming income expectations.

Our final basic equations work out as follows:

$$\log C = 0.75 + 0.67 \log C_{-1} + 0.20 \log R - 0.15 \log R_{-1} + 0.19 \log S \quad (5.7)$$
$$ (4.2) \quad (9.4) \quad\quad (2.7) \quad\quad\quad (2.1) \quad\quad\quad (4.6)$$

$R^2 = 0.99$ DW $= 2.23$ Durbin $h = 1.21$ SEE $= 0.0061$

$$\log C = 0.57 + 0.68 \log C_{-1} + 0.19 \log R - 0.10 \log R_{-1} + 0.16 \log S + 0.0007\dot{p}$$
$$ (0.42) \quad (9.4) \quad\quad (2.7) \quad\quad\quad (2.1) \quad\quad\quad (4.6) \quad\quad\quad (5.8)$$

$R^2 = 0.98$ DW $= 2.31$ Durbin $h = 1.65$ SEE $= 0.0059$

$$\log C = 1.11 + 0.64 \log C_{-1} + 0.21 \log R - 0.09 \log R_{-1}$$
$$ (3.2) \quad (9.0) \quad\quad (3.0) \quad\quad\quad (1.2)$$
$$ + 0.12 \log S - 0.006\dot{p} + 0.19RT \quad\quad\quad\quad (5.9)$$
$$ (2.7) \quad\quad (1.8) \quad\quad (2.0)$$

$R^2 = 0.998$ DW $= 2.31$ Durbin $h = 1.68$ SEE $= 0.0058$

where

$\log C =$ consumption logarithm,
$\dot{p} =$ occurred inflation rate,
$\log R =$ earned-income logarithm,
$\log S =$ logarithm of total wealth (defined above),
$RT =$ share of transfer income in earned income.

For equation (5.9), effects on consumption (%); obtained from the simulations, are shown in Table 5.3.

Table 5.3

	Short-term	Long-term
+ 1% earned income	0.21	0.33
+ 1% wealth	0.12	0.33
+ 1-point inflation (annual rate)	− 0.06	− 0.17
+ 1-point transfer income/earned income	0.19	0.53

The sum of the long-term elasticities of consumption to income and wealth is less than unity. This result is not compatible with balanced growth, but is due to the fact that wealth grew faster than income in the period studied. From 1970 to 1988, the wealth/earned income ratio rose from 3 to 4.5. According to our estimates, this generated 12% more consumption than if wealth and income had grown at the same pace. Having determined these basic equations, we can now use them to study the impact of taxation and various economic-policy measures concerning saving.

5.2.4 Consumption and equivalence

We begin by examining the impact of public deficits on consumption. If the private sector has rational expectations, and if the government faces a solvency constraint, government securities are not perceived as net wealth since the interest and principal will need to be financed by future taxes. This argument has been widely challenged. Among the most recent studies, that of Nicoletti (1988) on the OECD countries concludes that 'for most countries, as well as for all the countries as a group, the Barro model is clearly rejected'. Evans (1988), however, does not discard the Ricardian equivalence hypothesis. Theoretically, it has been shown that whenever households apply a different discount rate from the government's, there is no equivalence (for example, the 'finite lives' approach of Blanchard (1985) and the 'distortion taxation' approach of Judd (1987)). Barro's equivalence theorem assumes that

$$\forall t, \quad B_t = \sum_{i=0}^{\infty} (T_{t+1}^{H} + T_{t+i}^{E} - D_{t+i}) p_{t+i} / (1+r)^i$$

T^{H} represents the net transfers (in real terms) from households to government, T^{E} the transfers from firms to government, D the real government expenditures, B the nominal government debt, and p the price level.

We deliberately omit social security fund deficits on the assumption that they are covered on an *ad hoc* basis by an increase in social-security contributions. The recent pattern in France does not invalidate this hypothesis.

Conventional theoretical models neglect the distribution of taxes between firms and households, and the breakdown of GDP into wages and cash flow. We get

$$C_t = c \left(\sum_{i=0}^{\infty} \frac{P_{t+i}\bar{Y}_{t+i} - p_{t+i}\bar{T}_{t+i}}{P_t(1+\rho)^i} \right)$$

where Y and T are real GDP and real taxes, W is the wealth other than government securities, and ρ the nominal discount rate. The solvency constraint is

$$B_t = \sum_{i=0}^{\infty} \frac{P_{t+i}(\bar{T}_{t+i} - D_{t+i})}{(1+\rho)^i}$$

To study household behaviour, we incorporate VAT on goods at the rate τ. $T_t^{H} = \mu T_t$ are the taxes paid by households, B_t^{H} their government securities holdings and P_t the price level net of VAT at date t. We have the following solvency constraint in real terms:

$$\frac{B_t}{P_t(1+\tau_t)} = \sum_{i=0}^{\infty} \frac{\left[\dfrac{\tau_{t+i}}{(1+\tau_{t+i})}\bar{Y}_{t+i}+\bar{T}_{t+i}-D_{t+i}\right]}{(1+\rho)^i}$$

where ρ is the real discount rate. This gives us

$$C_t = c\left[\sum_{i=0}^{\infty}\bar{R}^H_{t+i}+\frac{\mu\bar{T}_{t+i}}{(1+\rho)^i}+\frac{W_t}{P_t(1+\tau_t)}+\sum_{i=0}^{\infty}\frac{[\tau_{t+i}/(1+\tau_{t+i})]\bar{Y}_{t+i}+\bar{T}_{t+i}-D_{t+i}}{(1+\rho)^i}\right.$$
$$\left.+\frac{B^H_t-B_t}{P_t(1+\tau_t)}\right]$$

Households pay $T^H = \mu T$ taxes (in real terms) and hold $B^H = B + (B^H - B)$ government securities. Hence,

$$C_t = c\left[\sum_{i=0}^{\infty}\frac{\bar{R}^H_{t+i}+\dfrac{\tau_{t+i}}{(1+\tau_{t+i})}\bar{Y}_{t+i}+\bar{T}_{t+i}(1-\mu)-D_{t+i}}{(1+\rho)^i}+\frac{W_t+B^H_t-B_t}{P_t}\right] \quad (5.10)$$

The income variable is, therefore, the earned income of the previous estimates $(R^H - T^H)$ plus the wealth variable, total wealth $(W + B^H)$ minus total public debt B and the budget surplus:

$$[\tau/(1+\tau)]\bar{Y}+\bar{T}-D.$$

We, therefore, test the equivalence hypothesis by adding the following ratios to the basic equation: (i) the ratio of general government net lending to earned income, and (ii) the ratio of public debt (with or without Treasury bonds issued) to total household wealth.

If there is equivalence, the first variable must have the same coefficient as the earned-income logarithm, while the second variable must have the opposite sign of the wealth logarithm. In fact, we accept the hypothesis of joint nullity of the two coefficients. For example, we obtain

$$\log C = 0.97 + 0.05 \log C_{-1} + 0.19 \log R - 0.07 \log R_{-1} + 0.12 \log S$$
$$(2.6) \quad (7.9) \qquad\quad (2.6) \qquad\quad (0.9) \qquad\quad (2.5)$$
$$+ 0.20\, CAPU/R - 0.01\, B/S - 0.08p + 0.17RT \qquad\qquad (5.11)$$
$$(1.4) \qquad\qquad (0.1) \qquad\quad (1.4) \quad (1.5)$$
$$R^2 = 0.998 \quad DW = 2.34 \quad Durbin\, h = 2.31 \quad SEE = 0.0058$$

$$\log C = 0.74 + 0.68 \log C_{-1} + 0.19 \log R - 0.15 \log R_{-1} + 0.19 \log S$$
$$(4.0) \quad (9.4) \qquad\quad (2.6) \qquad\quad (2.0) \qquad\quad (4.7)$$
$$+ 0.09\, CAPU/R + 0.04(CAPU/R)_{-1} \qquad\qquad (5.12)$$
$$(0.5) \qquad\qquad (0.2)$$
$$R^2 = 0.928 \quad DW = 2.26 \quad Durbin\, h = 1.43 \quad SEE = 0.0062$$

where *CAPU* is the general government net lending and *B* the total government debt outstanding.

We do find a very slight positive effect of *CAPU* but it is neither significant nor robust; the government debt has no effect. This leads us to reject the overall equivalence hypothesis – a fairly logical conclusion since we previously rejected the assumption of rational income expectations.

5.2.5 Expectations about taxation and transfer income

It might be argued that households have advance notice (for example, from parliamentary budget debates) of the tax changes that will affect them. This implies that future changes in taxes or transfer income influence current consumption, while present changes do not affect it (Wilcox, 1989). Because future changes are very hard to measure accurately, we used a statistical method to determine how they fit in with the total information available to households.

Our series of tests seeks to examine consumption behaviour in terms of expectations about direct-tax pressure, transfer income and social-security contributions. First, we regress the variables for compulsory levy rates and transfer rates (as a ratio of income) on their lagged values. We then calculate the differences between the variable and its expected value forecast over three quarters, and substitute the results into the regression. The differences, expressed as a ratio of income, are supposed to represent future tax measures affecting households. If the expectations of future tax measures are perfect, they must influence current consumption.

We also represented new tax measures simply as the future variation in the rates of tax pressure or transfers. We obtained no result for transfers (social benefits) or social-security contributions. For indirect taxes, on the other hand, we found interesting results such as

$$\log C = 0.53 + 0.68 \log C_{-1} + 0.23 \log R - 0.13 \log R_{-1} + 0.16 \log S$$
$$ (2.3) \quad (9.6) \qquad (3.0) \qquad (0.17) \qquad (3.6)$$
$$ - 0.0006p - 0.14\Delta(DT/R)_{+1} - 0.23\Delta(DT/R)_{+2} \qquad (5.13)$$
$$ (1.7) \qquad (1.2) \qquad \qquad (2.0)$$

$R^2 = 0.998$ DW = 2.20   Durbin $h = 1.10$ SEE = 0.0059

where *DT* represents direct taxes, *R* the earned income, and $\Delta(DT/R)_{+i}$ the change in the *DT/R* ratio in $t + i$.

We performed the same tests for current – rather than future – tax measures. If the expectations of the measures are perfect, the measures should not modify consumption, since they are already known and incorporated into the expected level. Here again, transfer income and social-security contributions do not seem to be expected, since a reduction in their rates causes consumption to vary. That is not the case with direct taxes: we can also assume rational expectations about taxation limited to the expectation of direct taxes (income taxes).

5.2.6 Economic policy measures affecting savings

Returning to our basic specification, we test the incidence of three government policy command variables: the real cap on the tax-exempt 'Livret A' savings account, the minimum required balance on time deposits to qualify for unregulated interest, and the rate of the tax relief (income tax deduction) granted to life insurance policy holders. Later, we shall analyse the effects of these variables on household investment.

We also examined the improvement provided by the addition of a dummy variable to proxy the 1978 introduction of the 'Monory Law' and the subsequent creation of an equity-invested savings account (Compte d'Epargne en Actions or CEA).[5]

There is no noticeable effect of the dummy variable, the Livret A cap or the tax relief on life insurance premiums. The time deposit floor variable, expressed in real terms, gives better results, with a positive sign as expected: this means that a raising of the minimum required balance on unregulated-interest-bearing accounts may be perceived as an apparent fall in the mean return on time deposits, and thus as an incentive to save less. The variable's weight, however, is weak, as shown by the Student's t-value: the household saving rate displays very weak sensitivity to institutional measures to promote saving. Lastly, we found no significant impact on the saving rate of the proportion of equities held by households in mutual-fund form.

5.2.7 Conclusions regarding consumption

1. Consumers are not very rational. They form naive expectations about income, and do not perceive that public deficits and public debt will generate future taxes. The sole variables for which their expectations are correct – indeed, only partly so – are the changes in the direct taxation burden in the near future (one or two quarters). Since no active liquidity constraints seem to be at work, the apparent non-equivalence seems to result more from irrationality than from these constraints.
2. The net wealth structure has no effect on consumption, which depends solely on total assets – cash, equities, bonds, housing and life insurance, minus loans – and earned income. We find a small income structure effect for social benefits. We can also detect a moderate specific inflation effect in addition to the real balance effect. The real interest rate appears to have no effect on the saving rate.

These findings would imply that the influence of monetary policy on household behaviour is relatively indirect. Monetary authorities have long argued that monetary asset holdings are a greater incentive to consume than ownership of long-term securities and assets. This claim is not supported by our estimates.

---

[5] The Monory law grants tax deductions to share purchasers provided the shares are held for a minimum prescribed time.

Moreover, the absence of wealth structure and interest rate effects seems to indicate that neither an open-market policy (substituting securities for cash) nor direct rate control are effective in modifying the saving rate. One should not conclude, however, that monetary policy has no incidence on the saving rate. To begin with, a rise in interest rates causes stock market wealth to fall and, therefore, depresses consumption, since we have found a strong wealth effect on consumption. Also, inflation seems to have a significant effect on saving, both directly and via real wealth. This represents a second mechanism for transmitting monetary movements.

3. From a technical standpoint, the lack of effect of wealth structure or liquidity constraints (new loans do not influence consumption) justifies the two-stage model of saving rate choice followed by portfolio selection.
4. Structural measures designed to modify the saving rate – such as tax exemptions and relief, changes in deposit caps, or regulatory changes – have no detectable effect either. The saving rate is determined by macroeconomic factors such as the rise in real wages, inflation, and capital gains or losses on assets. It is difficult to control through specific economic-policy measures. These can influence only the portfolio structure, as we shall see in section 5.3.

5.3 HOUSEHOLD PORTFOLIO SELECTION

In section 5.2, we showed the validity of the consumption–decision separability assumption, and the lack of influence of financial tax provisions on household saving volume. We must now examine the effects of taxation on the structure of household financial assets. For this purpose, we adopt a model based on the portfolio selection model for financial agents, which has been frequently described in the literature (for its application to France, see Artus and Bleuze, 1989). This is a pure demand model that seeks to explain the share of each financial asset in total wealth by expected returns, adjustment costs, and 'regulatory' variables – in other words, variables reflecting official regulatory measures. Taxation, therefore, exerts a twofold effect: (a) the weight of taxation on the income generated by different financial assets; and (b) the influence of the regulatory measures described in section 5.2, such as the cap on tax-sheltered passbook accounts, and the minimum balance required on unregulated-interest-bearing time deposits.

5.3.1 Financial asset structure and returns

Household financial assets

The series for household financial asset holdings are derived from the Bank of France Quarterly Tables of Financial Transactions (TERF), available from 1970 to

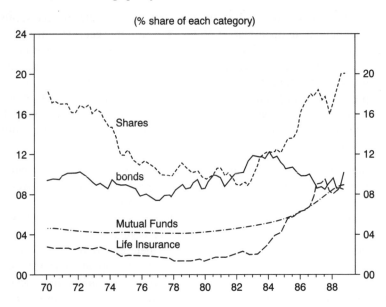

Fig. 5.1 Household wealth structure, treating mutual funds as separate assets.
[Source: TERF (Bank of France).]

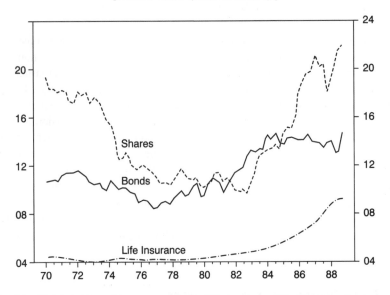

Fig. 5.2 Household wealth structure, consolidating mutual funds with others assets.
[Source: TERF (Bank of France).]

1988. Apart from unlisted securities, the equities and bonds held by individuals are
marked to market. The first problem encountered relates to the treatment of mutual

Table 5.4 Household financial wealth at year-end 1988 (FF billion)[a]

	Households including mutual funds	Mutual funds	Households and mutual funds
Liquidity of:			
Coins and paper currency in circulation	232.8	—	232.8
Demand deposits	704.2	22.8	714.2
Tax-sheltered passbook accounts	1066.6	—	1066.6
Ordinary passbook accounts	223.7	—	223.7
Foreign-currency liquidity	1.5	1.4	2.1
Non-negotiable investments	447.1	111.7	496.1
Savings plans	408.7	—	408.7
Total	3048.7	135.9	3144.3
Money-market securities of:			
Certificates of deposit and related instruments	—	142.3	62.4
Treasury bills	—	85.0	37.3
Commercial paper	—	30.2	13.3
Total	—	257.6	113.0
Long-term securities of:			
French bonds	539.4	564.5	787.1
French shares of:	1746.8	186.6	1304.7
Mutual funds	524.0	—	—
Other equities	1.0	1.0	1.4
Foreign bonds	90.6	15.0	97.2
Foreign shares and other equities	0.4	34.3	15.1
Total	2377.2	801.4	2204.6
Actuarial reserves	554.5	—	554.5
Total holdings	11967.2	1194.1	6016.4

[a] The first and second columns show household and mutual-fund financial assets as estimated by the Bank of France TERF tables. The third column is calculated by subtracting mutual-fund shares from French shares held by households, and adding these mutual-fund shares to each financial instrument category in proportion to that instrument's share of mutual-fund assets.

funds owned by households.[6] Should mutual-fund shares be regarded as financial assets with clearly distinctive return and risk characteristics, or, on the contrary, should they be made 'transparent' in the calculation of household financial assets?

In the second method, households are regarded as purchasing mutual-fund shares – hitherto transparent from a tax standpoint – for the deliberate purpose of holding a portion of fund assets invested in money market securities, bonds and/or equities. This choice is of some importance for the rest of our study, as Figures 5.1 and 5.2 show. The change in the percentage of equities and bonds in household financial assets differs according to whether mutual-fund shares are treated as a separate asset (Figure 5.1) or whether the financial assets of mutual funds and households are 'consolidated' (Figure 5.2 and Table 5.4). The consoli-

[6] The TERFs do not distinguish mutual-fund shares from non-mutual-fund shares and other equities. We have calculated them from the annual reports of the Conseil National du Crédit (CNC).

dation method notably eliminates the rather steep fall in bonds as a proportion of total wealth when mutual funds are counted as a separate asset – from 12% in 1983 to 8.9% in early 1987. Earlier studies (Artus and Bleuze, 1989) have shown the great difficulty, from an econometric standpoint, of isolating mutual funds as a distinct asset. The reason is that the rate-of-return series for mutual-fund assets actually consist of linear combinations of returns on liquidity, equities, bonds and other assets. As a result, the return on mutual-fund assets cannot be clearly identified. We have, therefore, chosen a model in which mutual-fund shares held by households are consolidated. The financial wealth thus measured is aggregated into four asset categories: liquidity, equities, bonds and life insurance policies. The proportion of mutual funds in household wealth is, however, regarded as a supplementary explanatory variable for the breakdown into these four categories.

Lastly, we calculate the value of life insurance policies held by households. Our sources are the French national accounts and the annual accounts of life insurance companies provided by the Finance Ministry's insurance industry bureau. We constructed an actuarial-reserves series for life insurance policies alone. The actuarial reserves outstanding at the end of the period studied come to approximately FF550 billion or 9% of household financial assets.

Returns

To obtain returns net of tax, we calculate the weighted nominal returns for each category of assets except for life insurance actuarial reserves. The weightings are based on the detailed splitting of the TERF data into 13 assets (Figure 5.3).

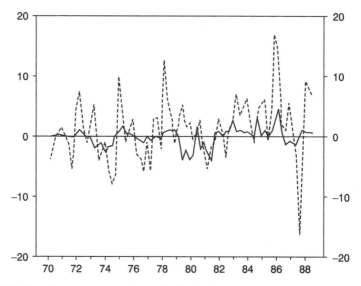

Fig. 5.3 Gross/net return spreads: capital gains/losses on equities (– – – –); capital gains/losses on bonds (———). [Source: TERF (Bank of France) and CDC computations.]

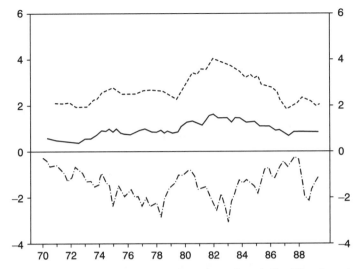

Fig. 5.4 Gross/net return spreads: bonds coupons (−−−); liquidity (——); share dividends (−·−·−). [Source: TERF (Bank of France) and CDC computations.]

Appendix B shows the year-end 1988 breakdown of household assets and the corresponding gross and net returns, after isolating the consolidation effect.

For liquidity, our computations are fairly straightforward. We have assumed that time deposits are unregulated and yield the three month interbank prime rate. For all liquid assets, the gross/net return spread is small, owing to the large proportion of assets carrying zero or tax-free yields (Figure 5.4). Risky securities are harder to assess. We decided to separate the yield portion from the potential capital gain/loss portion, and then to make an econometric estimate of the weight assigned by households to the potential capital gain/loss portion, which is obviously more volatile. If this estimated weight reaches unity, our method is equivalent to assuming perfect return expectations. If it is significantly lower than unity, several assumptions are possible. Either the capital gains/losses expectations are incomplete, or they are correctly forecast, but households smooth them, for example if households' investment horizons exceed one quarter.

For bonds, we have distinguished between fixed-rate issues, floating-rate issues indexed on long-term rates, and floating-rate issues indexed on short-term rates. We have assumed that coupons are subjected to a withholding tax that exempts from further taxation. This choice is based on tax statistics, in particular the estimated amounts of withholding taxes levied.

Potential capital gains/losses on bonds are calculated for fixed-rate issues on the basis of yield variations, assuming a mean maturity of five years.[7] In France, sales of securities are exempt from capital gains tax provided the total value of redemptions within the calendar year does not exceed an annually adjusted

---

[7] This is the mean maturity of fixed-rate bonds over the period studied.

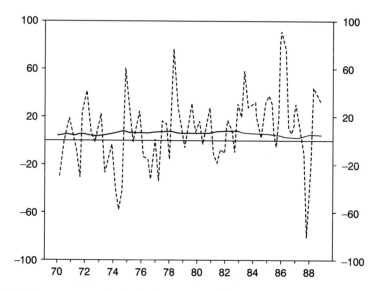

Fig. 5.5 Net returns: capital gains/losses on equities (– – –); share dividends (———).
[Source: TERF (Bank of France) and CDC computations.]

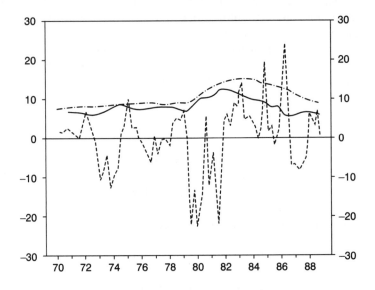

Fig. 5.6 Net returns: bond coupons (———); life insurance (—·—·); capital
gains/losses on bonds (– – –). [Source: TERF (Bank of France) and CDC computations.]

ceiling. We apply a tax rate of 16% to the capital gains on bonds, thereby
assuming that the redemptions exceed the annual limit. Capital losses are sub-

tracted from capital gains. Figure 5.5 shows that in a capital loss period such as 1979 or 1987, the tax rules reduce the losses since they ease the tax burden on later capital gains.

For equities, we use the Bank of France figure for the average rate of return including the dividend tax credit. The gross return is recalculated from the dividends received by households as measured in the national accounts. Capital gains or losses on French stocks are proxied by the change in the CAC Paris Bourse index, and the corresponding tax regime is identical to that of capital gains/losses on bonds.

For life insurance actuarial reserves, the gross rate of return is calculated from the interest paid out by insurance companies. The corresponding tax relief is estimated from government budget documents itemizing tax deductions for premiums on life insurance policies, annuities and disablement insurance savings plans.

Figures 5.5 and 5.6 show the net return series for the four assets studied. After hitting an 8% peak in 1981–82, the net return on liquid assets has moved down to a level close to that of the early 1970s. For equities and bonds, we observe the high volatility of potential capital gains/losses, which, in the case of equities, can reach $\pm 60\%$. Compared to these potential gains/losses, yields seem to be a much more important factor for bonds than for shares.

The return on life insurance increased sharply in the early 1980s, stimulated by rising bond yields and the introduction of tax relief. Over the entire period, the life insurance return stayed below the level observed for the coupon portion of bond returns.

'Regulatory' variables

The government command variables used here are the same as those mentioned in section 5.2.5. The changes in time-deposit regulations are erratic. These regulatory modifications, in particular those of 1981, help to explain the growth in short-term (money market) mutual funds.

5.3.2 Econometric results

Description of the model

We have tested a model comprising three asset categories: bonds (po), equities (pa) and life insurance (pv). A well-known feature of the portfolio selection model is that the additivity constraint is met even when the same explanatory variables are present in all asset shares. We can, therefore, deduce the liquidity share from the three other shares. The equations used are:

$$po = \sum_{i=1}^{4} a_i rd_i + a_5 po_{-1} + a_6 pa_{-1} + a_7 pv_{-1} + cst$$

$$pa = \sum_{i=1}^{4} b_i rd_i + b_5 pa_{-1} + b_6 po_{-1} + b_7 pv_{-1} + cst$$

$$pv = \sum_{i=1}^{4} C_i rd_i + C_5 pv_{-1} + C_6 po_{-1} + C_7 pa_{-1} + cst$$

with

rd_i = net return on asset i (1 = liquidity; 2 = bonds; 3 = equities; 4 = life insurance)
rd_2 = return on bonds = $rd_{21} + L_1 rd_{22}$,
rd_{21} = coupon portion of return on bonds,
rd_{22} = potential capital gains/losses on bonds,
L_1 = weighting of capital gains on bonds,
rd_3 = return on equities = $rd_{31} + L_2 rd_{32}$,
rd_{31} = dividend portion of return on equities,
rd_{32} = potential capital gains/losses on equities,
L_2 = weighting of capital gains on equities,
cst = constant.

The introduction of lagged shares is explained by the fact that the model allows for adjustment costs (Artus and Bleuze, 1989).

In the standard theoretical model (Friedman and Roley, 1985; Roley, 1981; Courakis, 1988), the returns vector is multiplied by the inverse of the conditional variance–covariance matrix of the returns. Naturally, it would be desirable to compare these coefficients with the observed second-order moments as in Frankel (1985). Unfortunately, the French experience (Lantieri and Riviere, 1989) shows that it is impossible to achieve consistency between the returns effects and the moments. In particular, the observed relative risk of equities and fixed-rate bonds compared with other investments is far too great. The implicit variance–covariances used seem very different from the empirical ones, or from those obtained with the estimate. Any comparison, therefore, is likely to be unsuccessful.

We estimate the model using the seeming unrelated regressions (SURE) method. To maximize the model's likelihood, we estimate the L_i parameters using an iterative procèdure: the parameters represent the weight of potential capital gains/losses in total expected returns on bonds and equities.

Estimate of the basic model

We begin by testing the most general form of the model (Table 5.5). The results obtained are disappointing. While the return on each asset does have the expected positive effect on the corresponding asset share, these effects are econometrically of little significance (bonds) or largely offset in the short run by the inertia of each share (life insurance).

The simplest portfolio selection model would, therefore, appear to be of limited efficiency except, perhaps, for equities. It seems to give an inadequate explanation of the sharp growth in life insurance as a share of household financial assets. It would also tend to show that the portfolio selection inertia is high, as indicated by the lagged-share coefficients.

We try to introduce as an exogenous variable the share of mutual funds in household wealth. To avoid collinearity problems, we estimate this share separately. The effect on the equity and bond percentage shares does carry the expected negative sign but is of little significance.

Table 5.5 Estimate of the basic model (period: 1971:I–1988:IV, quarterly data)

	cste	rd_1	rd_2	rd_3	rd_4^a	po_{-1}	pa_{-1}	pv_{-1}	R^2	*SEE*	*DW*
po	−0.013	2.5×10^{-3}	6.2×10^{-4}	2.2×10^{-5}	1.0×10^{-3}	0.81	0.04	0.06	0.95	0.005	1.9
	(1.5)	(1.2)	(0.8)	(0.9)	(1.3)	(9.7)	(0.7)	(0.5)			
pa	0.003	6.3×10^{-4}	-1.7×10^{-3}	1.5×10^{-4}	-1.2×10^{-4}	0.15	0.76	0.5	0.98	0.006	2.5
	(0.3)	(0.3)	(2.1)	(5.7)	(0.1)	(1.6)	(12.0)	(3.3)			
pv	−0.004	3.9×10^{-5}	1.4×10^{-5}	-1.2×10^{-5}	3.1×10^{-4}	0.01	0.01	0.98	0.99	0.0006	1.9
	(3.3)	(0.1)	(0.2)	(4.2)	(3.5)	(0.7)	(1.1)	(59.4)			

[a] Return smoothed over 2 years.
Notes: rd_1 = return on liquidity; rd_2 = return on bonds; rd_3 = return on equities; rd_4 = return on life insurance; *po* = share of bonds; *pa* = share of equities; *pv* = share of life insurance.

Estimation of a model without life insurance return

The life insurance return is approximately a linear combination of the other returns, calculated from the asset structure of life insurance companies. We, therefore, assumed the econometric difficulties could be partly eased by removing the life insurance return from our estimates – a procedure allowed by the theoretical model. The results are indeed much more satisfactory (Table 5.6).

Returns on risky assets (equities and bonds) have a positive effect on the respective shares of these assets, and a negative effect on the life insurance share. A change in the liquidity return, therefore, tends to separate bonds and life insurance (positive sign) from equities (negative sign). That is not surprising, given the comparative risks of the three assets.

We observe a strong inertia of portfolio selection in the short run, and a general substitution between liquidity and other assets, since the cross-effects of other asset shares (bonds, equities, life insurance) on each other are generally positive. The saving rate has a negative influence on the three estimated shares and hence, a sharply positive effect on the liquidity share. This may represent the 'buffer' effect of liquidity as a store for supplementary saving – a surplus that household may regard as temporary. The share of mutual funds in household financial assets exerts a negative effect on risky securities – despite the consolidation of the balance sheets – and a positive effect on life insurance and liquidity, possibly because of the surge in money market funds. The introduction of the money

Table 5.6 Estimate of a model without life insurance return (Period: 1971:I–1988:IV, quarterly data)

		cste	rd_1	rd_2	rd_3	po_{-1}	pa_{-1}	pv_{-1}	txp	ps	R^2	SEE	h
(1)	po	0.3	4.1×10^{-4}	1.1×10^{-3}	2.3×10^{-5}	0.78	0.06	−0.05	−0.12		0.95	0.0047	0.1
		(1.5)	(0.3)	(2.0)	(1.1)	(11.4)	(1.6)	(0.5)	(2.1)				
	pa	0.016	−0.003	-4.2×10^{-4}	1.4×10^{-4}	0.10	0.85	0.20	−0.02		0.98	0.0057	−0.3
		(0.7)	(1.6)	(0.6)	(5.3)	(1.2)	(17.2)	(1.7)	(0.3)				
	pv	0.002	2.6×10^{-4}	-1.6×10^{-4}	-1.0×10^{-5}	0.02	−0.01	1.02	−0.02		0.99	6.3×10^{-3}	0.2
		(3.3)	(1.3)	(2.1)	(3.5)	(2.0)	(1.1)	(80.1)	(2.8)				
(2)	po	0.3	4.5×10^{-4}	9.9×10^{-4}	2.3×10^{-5}	0.80	0.07	0.05	−0.13	−0.09	0.95	0.0047	0.1
		(1.5)	(0.3)	(1.6)	(1.0)	(11.2)	(1.7)	(0.3)	(2.3)	(0.8)			
	pa	0.01	-3.0×10^{-3}	-8.8×10^{-4}	1.4×10^{-4}	0.16	0.88	0.50	−0.073	−0.26	0.98	0.0056	−0.4
		(0.6)	(1.6)	(1.2)	(5.4)	(1.9)	(17.6)	(2.8)	(1.0)	(2.1)			
	pv	0.003	2.2×10^{-4}	-4.3×10^{-4}	-1.0×10^{-5}	0.005	−0.013	0.95	−0.007	0.073	0.99	0.0005	0.3
		(1.5)	(1.4)	(0.6)	(4.1)	(0.6)	(2.8)	(55.2)	(1.0)	(5.6)			

market mutual-fund growth variable is necessary, in particular because it stabilizes the life insurance share equation, which would otherwise display a lagged-variable coefficient greater than unity. It is clear that, in so doing, we regard the mutual-fund growth as exogenous. We have been unable to obtain a satisfactory equation for the mutual-fund share; we, therefore, conclude that the level of mutual-fund holdings is perhaps determined more by supply than by demand.

Using this model, we have tried to define the optimal weight of potential capital gains or losses. The best result obtained gives a very small weighting for bonds (0.1) and a very large one for equities (0.9). Households would, therefore, seem to take into account virtually all potential capital gains/losses in their perception of return on equities. A 10-point rise in the total return on equities would generate 0.15-point growth in the proportion of equities in the very short run (one quarter), or approximately FF8 billion at year-end 1988. Bond holding, by contrast, seems motivated by a search for steady income, since capital gains/losses play a minimal role. For equities, the difference between dividends and potential capital gains/losses means that a change in the weight assigned to the latter – in other words, the risk perception – leads to a symmetrical adjustment of the estimated coefficient. Thus, for an 0.9 weighting, the estimated coefficient for the stock yield is 1.4×10^{-4}, whereas for a weighting of, for example, 0.3, the estimated coefficient rises to 4.2×10^{-4}.

Homogeneity constraint

Before performing specific tests on the tax variables, we incorporated the homogeneity constraint into the portfolio model. The constraint requires that the sum of the coefficients estimated for the various returns affecting one asset-category share should equal zero; in other words,

$$\left[\sum_{i=1}^{4} a_i = \sum_{i=1}^{4} b_i = \sum_{i=1}^{4} c_i = 0 \right]$$

The model can accordingly be rewritten in terms of the spreads between non-liquid asset returns and the liquidity return $(rd_i - rd_1)$. If the constraint is respected, a uniform rise of all returns will not distort the portfolio structure. We subjected the model to a likelihood ratio test that enabled us not to reject the homogeneity constraint (Table 5.7). The result is satisfactory with respect to the theoretical model, for the rejection of the homogeneity assumption would have cast doubt on the model specification.

Some versions of the theoretical model specify identical adjustment costs for new saving and the existing saving. These versions involve a symmetry constraint—namely, the effect of asset i's return on the share of asset j must be identical to the effect of asset j's return on the share of asset i (Courakis, 1988). With our specification, the symmetry constraint is systematically rejected, no doubt because of the heavier inertia on existing saving. We, therefore, decided not to introduce it here.

Table 5.7 Estimate of a model with homogeneity constraint (period: 1971:I–1988:IV, quarterly data)

	cste	$(rd_2 - rd_1)$	$(rd_3 - rd_1)$	po_{-1}	pa_{-1}	pv_{-1}	txp	ps	R^2	SEE	DW
(1) po	-0.035	1.3×10^{-5}	1.4×10^{-5}	0.80	0.03	-0.02	-0.12		0.95	0.0047	0.95
	(2.1)	(2.3)	(0.6)	(11.7)	(0.9)	(0.2)	(2.1)				
pa	-0.9×10^{-4}	-7.5×10^{-4}	1.6×10^{-4}	0.08	0.93	0.16	-0.02		0.98	0.0058	2.63
	(0.0)	(1.1)	(6.2)	(0.9)	(26.7)	(1.3)	(0.3)				
pv	0.003	-1.5×10^{-4}	-1.1×10^{-5}	0.02	-0.01	1.02	-0.02		0.99	0.0006	1.98
	(1.2)	(2.0)	(3.9)	(2.1)	(2.1)	(81.4)	(2.7)				
(2) po	0.033	1.1×10^{-3}	1.4×10^{-5}	0.81	0.04	0.09	-0.14	-0.11	0.95	0.0047	2.0
	(2.0)	(1.9)	(0.7)	(11.5)	(1.2)	(0.6)	(2.3)	(0.9)			
pa	-0.4×10^{-2}	-1.2×10^{-3}	1.6×10^{-4}	0.12	0.96	0.41	-0.07	-0.25	0.98	0.0058	2.6
	(0.2)	(1.6)	(6.3)	(1.4)	(24.8)	(2.2)	(0.9)	(1.8)			
pv	0.004	-2.7×10^{-5}	-1.1×10^{-5}	0.01	-0.02	0.95	-0.007	0.07	0.99	0.0005	2.2
	(2.1)	(0.4)	(4.7)	(0.8)	(4.8)	(55.9)	(1.0)	(5.5)			

Note: $(rd_4 - rd_1)$ disappears from the estimate owing to the additivity constraint that identifies the $(rd_4 - rd_1)$ coefficient. (1), (2): See Table 5.6.

Table 5.8 Introduction of gross return (Period: 1971:I–1988:IV, quarterly data)

	$cste$	erb_2	erb_3	ecf_2	ecf_3	po_2	pa_2	pv_2	txp	ps	R^2	SEE	DW
po	-0.03	-6.2×10^{-3}	-2.4×10^{-4}	9.3×10^{-3}	2.8×10^{-4}	0.81	0.04	0.15	-0.15	-0.12	0.95	0.0047	2.0
	(1.4)	(0.4)	(0.2)	(1.3)	(0.4)	(11.3)	(1.3)	(1.0)	(2.5)	(1.1)			
pa	0.005	-1.5×10^{-3}	1.3×10^{-4}	3.5×10^{-3}	2.9×10^{-5}	0.11	0.96	0.43	-0.07	-0.25	0.98	0.006	2.6
	(0.2)	(0.9)	(1.0)	(0.4)	(0.0)	(1.3)	(23.4)	(2.2)	(1.0)	(1.8)			
pv	-0.005	2.5×10^{-4}	9.2×10^{-6}	-1.9×10^{-3}	-1.3×10^{-4}	0.01	-0.02	0.94	-0.003	0.07	0.99	0.0005	2.3
	(2.4)	(1.7)	(0.8)	(2.5)	(1.7)	(1.2)	(4.7)	(56.4)	(0.5)	(6.0)			

$erb_i = rdb_i - rdb_1 =$ (gross return on i - gross return on liquidity) spread.
$ecf_i = cf_i - cf_1 =$ (tax component of i - tax component of liquidity) spread.
$cf_i = rdb_i - rdn_i =$ tax component of asset i return.

Introduction of gross returns

We split the net returns into gross returns and tax components, which, as we saw earlier, can be positive or negative. A negative tax component corresponds to a tax benefit, as in the case of capital losses. Using the homogeneous model, we estimated the spreads between risky-asset returns and the riskless-asset returns, but the test was unsuccessful (Table 5.8). We also conducted a direct test of the influence of the tax relief on life insurance policies. This seems to contradict the assumption that agents distinguish between gross returns and the tax component. The changes in tax legislation, however, were relatively few in number over the period. The flat withholding tax on deposits moved from 25% to 33% in early 1975, from 33% to 40% in 1978, from 40% down to 38% in 1980, and from 38% up to 45% in 1983. All levies were raised by one point in 1984 and again by one point in 1987. The absence of major or frequent tax reforms means that it may be hard to spot the taxation effects in a time series, even if the change in asset mix entails a change in the average taxation rate.

Introduction of regulatory variables

The introduction of 'regulatory' variables does not improve the model's results – either because the variables themselves display the opposite of the expected sign, or because the estimated coefficients exhibit little significance. These findings differ significantly from those of our earlier studies (Artus and Bleuze, 1989), where the real cap on tax-sheltered passbook accounts had a demonstrably negative effect on risky-asset shares, and where the minimum-balance requirement on unregulated time deposits had the opposite effect.

The disappearance of these effects is undoubtedly due to the inclusion of life insurance, an asset whose expansion is poorly explained by the model and probably disturbs the movements of other assets. We also failed to obtain significant results with the dummy variable proxying the Monory plan (section 5.2.6).

5.3.3 Conclusion concerning portfolio selection

One of the commonest goals of economic policy is to promote household saving by directing it towards long-term investments and thereby increasing its stability. Our findings in section 5.2 suggest that the saving volume is relatively unaffected by tax incentives. In section 5.3, however, we show that rates of return have a measurable influence on the asset mix, albeit with a lagged response time, at least in certain estimates such as the homogeneous model.

A permanent one-point rise in the net bond return will thus cause a 0.1-point increase in the share of bonds in household financial assets in the very short run (1 point = 1%). The long-term effect (16 quarters) may be estimated at 0.5 points. With financial wealth totaling FF6 trillion at year-end 1988, the impact of the measure can, therefore, be evaluated at about FF7 billion in the short run and FF30 billion in the long run.

The recent evolution of French financial markets has been characterized by profound changes on the supply side, including foreign-exchange deregulation, the reform of mutual funds to allow a capitalized (dividend reinvestment) structure, the creation of new products such as the tax-sheltered individual retirement plan (Plan d'Epargne Populaire or PEP), the abandonment of other products such as the PEP's precursor, the Plan d'Epargne Retraite, lower taxes on life insurance policies, and a European-oriented opening of capital markets.

To help us understand how French households have responded to these changes, portfolio models such as the one described above notably demonstrate (1) the influence of net returns, (2) the weak impact of taxation and regulatory variables when one takes into account the entire spectrum of household portfolio assets including life insurance and, (3) the strong inertia of portfolio selection in the short run, reflecting the presence of adjustment costs.

Households, therefore, appear to confuse gross returns and net returns. This finding, however, must be treated with prudence, because, as we saw earlier, the taxation effects may be poorly measured in the estimates based on time series. If it is robust, however, the finding implies that the asset mix effectively depends on interest rate and stock market price levels and movements, but not on tax incentives. Consequently, we cannot exclude the possibility that – after what may prove to be a long adjustment phase – portfolio structures could be deeply altered in response to changes in rates of return brought about by monetary-policy choices or by market developments. On the other hand, it would be very difficult to brake or stimulate such movements by specific savings-oriented measures. Indeed, it is obvious that gross-return movements are on a far higher order of magnitude than taxation rates.

This conclusion – which, we must repeat, should be interpreted with caution – also implies that monetary authorities must not neglect the financial effects of the measures that they might be led to take in pursuit of broader objectives such as exchange rate stabilization or inflation control.

The finding concerning inertia is important when assessing the risk of saving outflows abroad, or of the shift from low-yield assets such as passbook accounts into other liquid assets offering much higher yields, such as capitalized money market funds. It must be emphasized, however, that the degree of the inertia is estimated over a fairly long period and that it hides changes in household behaviour. Surveys by the CREP and Insee show, for example, that the typical Livret A holder is an elderly person residing outside the Paris area. The gradual population trends will certainly lower the overall inertia of financial behaviour.

The main advantage of portfolio selection models is to offer a comprehensive, coherent understanding of the changes in agents' financial wealth. But to use the models efficiently, one must restrict the number of assets included, and their explanatory power is reduced for the assets that expand sharply at the end of the observation period, as is the case with life insurance in France.

Breakdown of household financial wealth and returns net of tax, fourth quarter 1988

	Households including mutual funds			Mutual funds			Households and mutual funds		
	Percentage of total wealth	Return		Percentage of total wealth	Return		Percentage of total wealth	Return	
		Coupon or dividend	Capital gain/loss		Coupon or dividend	Capital gain/loss		Coupon or dividend	Capital gain/loss
Liquidity, including money market securities	51.3	3.2	—	33.0	4.1	—	54.1	3.2	—
Equities of mutual funds	29.0	3.1	31.9	18.6	3.2	26.2	21.9	3.2	31.6
	8.7	5.0	5.9	nd	5.0	5.9	—	—	—
Bonds	10.5	6.6	0.3	48.5	6.3	2.1	14.7	6.6	0.8
Life insurance	9.2	9.8	—	—	—	—	9.2	9.8	—
Total	100.0			100.0			100.0		

Source: Bank of France TERF tables and Caisse des Dépôts computations.

APPENDIX B

Detailed breakdown of gross and net returns, year-end 1988

	Asset share of total wealth	Gross return	Net return
Coins and paper currency			
Households (TERF tables)	3.9%	0	0
Consolidated mutual-fund shares	—	—	—
Demand deposits			
Households (TERF tables)	11.7%	0	0
Consolidated mutual-fund shares	0.2%	0	0
Tax-sheltered passbook accounts			
Households (TERF tables)	17.7%	4.5	4.5
Consolidated mutual-fund shares	—	—	—
Ordinary passbook accounts			
Households (TERF tables)	3.7%	4.5	2.4
Consolidated mutual-fund shares	—	—	—
Non-negotiable investments			
Households (TERF tables)	7.4%	8.2	4.3
Consolidated mutual-fund shares	0.8%	8.2	4.3
Households (TERF tables)	6.8%	6.0%	6.0
Consolidated mutual-fund shares	—	—	—
Money market securities			
Households (TERF tables)	—	—	—
Consolidated mutual-fund shares	1.9%	8.2	4.3
Total liquidity			
Households (TERF tables)	51.3%	3.9	3.2
Consolidated mutual-fund shares	2.9%	7.7	4.1

APPENDIX C

	Asset share of total wealth	Gross return		Net return	
		Coupon or dividend	Capital gain/loss	Coupon or dividend	Capital gain/loss
French bonds					
Households (TERF tables)	9.0%	8.6	3.1	6.2	2.5
Consolidated mutual-fund shares	4.1%	8.6	3.1	6.2	2.5
Foreign bonds					
Households (TERF tables)	1.5%	9.0	−13.3	9.0	−13.3
Consolidated mutual-fund shares	0.1%	9.0	−13.3	9.0	−13.3
Total bonds					
Households (TERF tables)	10.5%	8.6	0.7	6.6	0.3
Consolidated mutual-fund shares	4.2%	8.6	2.6	6.3	2.1
French shares and other equities (excluding mutual funds)					
Households (TERF tables)	20.3%	2.0	38.4	3.1	31.9
Consolidated mutual-fund shares	1.4%	2.0	38.4	3.1	31.9
Foreign shares[a]					
Households (TERF tables)	0.0%	3.7	−4.6	3.7	−4.6
Consolidated mutual-fund shares	0.2%	3.7	−4.6	3.7	−4.6
Total equities[b]					
Households (TERF tables)	20.3%	2.0	38.4	3.1	31.9
Consolidated mutual-fund shares	1.6%	3.2	31.8	3.2	26.2
Life insurance					
Households (TERF tables)	9.2%	9.1	—	9.8	—
Consolidated mutual-fund shares	0.0%	—	—	—	—
Mutual funds					
Households (TERF tables)	8.7%	7.3	7.2	5.0	5.9
Consolidated mutual-fund shares	—	—	—	—	—
Total					
Households (TERF tables)	100.0%				
Consolidated mutual-fund shares	8.7%				

[a] 'and other equities'
[b] Total shares and other equities

REFERENCES

Artus, P., Bleuze, E. (1989) Les Choix de Portefeuille des Ménages en France. *Recherches Economiques de Louvain*, **55** (2), 129–54.

Barro, R. (1974) Are Government Bonds Net Wealth? *Journal of Political Economy*, **82**, 1095–117.

Barro, R. (1981) Output Effects of Government Purchases. *Journal of Political Economy*, **89**, 1086–121.

Blanchard, O. (1985) Consumer Behaviour: Theory and Empirical Evidence, A Survey. *The Economic Journal*, XX.

Courakis, A. (1988) Modelling Portfolio Selection. *The Economic Journal*, **98**, 619–42.

Evans, P. (1988) Are Consumers Ricardian? Evidence for the United States. *Journal of Political Economy*, **96**, 983–1004.

Frankel, J. (1985) Portfolio Crowding-Out Empirically Estimated. *Quarterly Journal of Economics*, Supplement, 1041–66.

Frankel, J. and Engel, C. (1984) Do Asset Demand Functions optimize over the Mean and Variance of Real Returns? A Six-Currency Test. *Journal of International Economics*, **17**, 309–24.

Friedman, B. and Roley, V. (1985) Aspects of Investor Behavior under Risk, NBER Working Paper No. 1611, April.

Hall, R. (1978) Stochastic Implications of the Life-Cycle, permanent Income Hypothesis: Theory and Evidence, *Journal of Political Economy*, **86**, 971–87.

Hayashi, F. (1985) Tests of Liquidity Constraints: A Critical Survey, NBER Working Paper, No. 1720.

Judd, K. (1987) Debt and distortion taxation in a simple perfect foresight model. *Journal of Monetary Economics*, 51–72.

Lantieri, C. and Riviere, P. (1989) Peut-on estimer la demande d'actifs à partir d'un modèle de portefeuille? *Revue Economique*, **40**, (1), 55–79.

Minczeles, A. and Sicsic, P. (1988) Incidence de la désinflation et des plus-values sur les variables de richesse et la consommation des ménages. *Cahiers Economiques et Monétaires*, no. 29, 5–32.

Nicoletti, G. (1988) Une analyse internationale de la consommation privée, de l'inflation et de l'hypothèse de la Neutralité de la dette. *Revue économique de l'OCDE*, no. 11, 49–98.

Palm, F.C. and Winder, C. (1986) *The Stochastic Life Cycle Consumption Model: Theoretical* results and Empirical Evidence, International Conference on Modelling Dynamic Systems, Paris 1986.

Pecha, J. and Sicsic, P. (1988) Développement du crédit à la consommation et économie réelle. *Revue d'Economie Financière*, no. 5/6.

Roley, V. (1981) The Determinants of the Treasury Security Yield Curve. *Journal of Finance*, 1103–26.

Sterdyniak, H. (1986) Des conséquences patrimoniales de la désinflation. *Observations et Diagnostics Economiques*, no. 17, October.

Wilcox, D. (1989) Social Security Benefits, Consumption Expenditure and the Life Cycle Hypothesis. *Journal of Political Economy*, **97**, 288–304.

6

Incomes and transitions within the labour force in Holland

Joke M. Bekkering

6.1 INTRODUCTION

Although the Dutch economy has experienced a boom in the last half of the 1980s, there still are severe labour market problems. On the one hand, there is high unemployment among lower educated groups and ethnic minorities, and, on the other hand, the market for professional workers is tight. Unemployment is decreasing slowly, but the percentage of long-term unemployed has been fairly stable in the last few years.

In labour market policy, attention has shifted from macroeconomic to microeconomic measures, which take into account the individual circumstances of unemployed persons and their potential employers. For instance, the government supports schooling projects in computer science and in administrative professions. These projects are directed exclusively towards the long-term unemployed, and a considerable percentage of the participants succeeds in finding a job after finishing the course. Another important instrument to influence supply and demand of labour is incomes policy.

On the demand side of the labour market, incomes policy means a reduction of social-insurance premiums for employers. This leads to lower labour costs. In general, the measures are aimed especially at reducing labour costs at the minimum wage level, without any consequences for the net income the employee receives. Several studies suggest that this can boost demand for precisely those kinds of labour where excess supply is largest (e.g. van Schaaijk and Waaijers, 1989; van Soest, 1989; CPB, 1988). During recession periods, this effect seems to be stronger than during an economic boom.

On the supply side of the labour market, incomes policy is aimed at increasing the financial incentives for unemployed persons to accept a job. It is believed that the present tax and benefit system encourages inflexibility in the labour supply. Unemployment benefits are fairly high in The Netherlands, compared to those in other European countries (Department of Social Affairs, 1989b). Moreover, there exists an extensive system of income-dependent subsidies or income-dependent prices for such goods as housing and child care. A household that receives an unemployment benefit plus one or more income-dependent subsidies is confronted with an effective marginal tax rate of almost 100%. Since individual situations can differ widely, individual reactions to a change in the tax/benefit/subsidy system will probably vary too. It is almost impossible to predict behavioural reactions if one has access to only aggregate data. That is why a microsimulation model is necessary to analyse the effects of incomes policy.

The model developed in this chapter describes the transition probabilities between various categories of the labour force, such as 'working full-time', 'working part-time' or 'disabled'. These probabilities are affected by the potential income the person can receive in the different categories: if a transition is financially profitable, the transition probability will be relatively large, *ceteris paribus*.

Here we estimate an econometric model that explains the transition probabilities within the labour force. The emphasis is laid on the effect of financial variables on the transition probabilities. This chapter contains the estimation results. Although the model can – and will – be improved further, the results seem plausible and meaningful.

At the moment, we can simulate individual reactions to changes in the system of taxes/benefits/subsidies. Such simulations are useful in themselves for policy makers, and they can serve as a check on plausibility. But to be able to draw conclusions about the sum of individual reactions we have to carry out a microsimulation on a representative sample of the population.

6.2 THE DUTCH TAX AND BENEFIT SYSTEM

The income tax system in The Netherlands is progressive. Very low incomes are not taxed. If gross income exceeds a certain threshold, a marginal rate is paid which increases from 16% to 72% in the sample period. The highest rate is paid for incomes above F250 000[1] per year. The threshold above which tax is due we call the zero-bracket amount (ZBA).

In principle, the individual is the tax unit, and not the household. Nevertheless, the taxpayer's family situation does play a role in determining the amount of taxes one has to pay, because the ZBA varies with the family situation. Every Dutch citizen is entitled to a ZBA of about F7500. If the earned income of one spouse does not exceed the ZBA, the unused part may be transferred to the other spouse. Furthermore, some special groups, like single parents, have a higher ZBA. The possibility to transfer part of the ZBA means that couples have a ZBA of about F15 000. But a small income of one partner is taxed rather heavily: until his/her income has reached the ZBA, the other partner's marginal rate applies. The effective marginal rate drops to 16% when the ZBA is reached.

[1] About $112 000.

The progressivity of the tax system is counteracted by the degressive premium system for social security. Since most benefits are bound to a maximum, there is also a limit on the premium one has to pay. Employees pay about 13% of their gross income for the compulsory old-age insurance (*AOW/AWW*), about 5% for the compulsory health insurance (*ZFW*), 16% for the disability insurance (*WAO*) and about 3% for the unemployment insurance (*WW*). Until income has reached the respective thresholds, the total social-security premium percentage paid by employees can amount to 30–40%. The 'wedge' between gross labour cost and net income is larger, though, because employers pay social security taxes as well. Since these affect only labour demand, we ignore them in this study.

Taken together, income taxes and social-security premiums result in an almost constant combined marginal rate, at least in the income brackets that contain the majority of the population. In 1990, the tax and premium system has been drastically simplified. Income taxes and several social-insurance premiums are now combined into one tax. There are only three tax brackets, ranging from about 35% to about 60%. The majority of the population is in the 35% bracket. Because the reform has been combined with a reduction of total income taxes, for the majority of the population it caused an increase in net income of about 3%.

Welfare benefits are relatively high in The Netherlands. In 1987, a married couple was entitled to a net yearly benefit of 17 619 guilders (about $8000). This amount is called the 'social minimum'. Single adults receive 70% of the social minimum, and single parents 90%. Those under 23% have a lower social minimum. Unemployment and disability benefits are related to the wage the person received when employed. The social minimum defines a lower bound: if the unemployment or disability benefit is lower than the minimum, the person will receive a supplementary benefit to make up for the difference.

The net minimum wage is equal to the social minimum for a married couple. Because of the costs connected with work (like travel expenses), in some cases it is possible that the transition to work is financially disadvantageous (Department of Social Affairs, 1990). There is a law which states that the yearly increase of the social minimum should equal the rise in consumer prices; so the purchasing power of welfare recipients cannot decrease. But, for the past few years, this law was overruled and purchasing power of the real minimum wage decreased by 8.5% between 1981 and 1987.

There is an extensive system of means-tested subsidies in The Netherlands. The most important ones are rent subsidies and student grants, the latter depending on parents' income. Such subsidies are generally given to households and not to individuals. As a result, the marginal tax rate may be very high. de Kam and van Herwaarden (1988) show that rent subsidy can increase the marginal rate substantially. For the average welfare recipient the total marginal rate of taxes and premiums is 32%. Rent subsidy adds about 20–25 percentage points to this rate.

It is generally believed that the high effective marginal rates at the minimum level cause rigidities in labour supply. Since individual effective rates vary strongly, their effects must be investigated with microeconometric methods.

6.3 DATA AND MODEL

To estimate the transition probabilities within the labour force, we need a panel data set. That is, we should have observations of a fixed set of persons at more than one moment in time. Such data have become available only recently in The Netherlands. We use three waves of the Social Economic Panel (SEP) which are produced by the Dutch Central Bureau of Statistics, namely, the October 1985, 1986 and 1987 ones. After matching the cross-sections, we have data about transitions within the labour force in two one-year periods.

6.3.1 Labour force categories

To describe the transitions we should define the precise labour force categories we are interested in. Since our interest lies with individual supply choices, we define the categories in terms of supply versus non-supply. This means that a very important transition, namely the one between the categories 'unemployed' and 'employed', falls outside the scope of the model. The reason is that the decision to participate in labour supply lies with the individual itself. It can be explained by the characteristics of the individual only. But in the transition from 'unemployed' to 'employed' many other factors play an important role, e.g. the total demand for labour, expectations of potential employers, etc. That is why transitions between 'unemployed' and 'employed' are ignored in this supply model.

Note that in the foregoing discussion we make a distinction only between 'searching' and 'not searching'. In reality, unemployed persons receive a sequence of job offers and they follow a strategy to decide whether to accept an offer or not. Search intensity will depend on the supplier's perception of his own wage potential. In this chapter we ignore the search intensity of labour suppliers and investigate the effect of financial incentives on the flow between 'searching' and 'not searching'. Although the data do contain information about search intensity, in the framework of this study we choose not to pursue this subject any further.

We choose the boundaries between the labour force categories in such a way that the crossing of a boundary is caused by the specific circumstances of the individual (plus a random term). The transition from 'employed' into 'disabled' is affected mainly by characteristics of the individual itself, like age and health.[2] On the other hand, the decision whether to dismiss workers and, if so, how many, is affected mainly by factors outside the individuals. Since our model explains transitions from individual characteristics, we include only the first kind of transitions and not the second.

---

[2] In the Dutch system this assumption is disputable in a sense. Until recently applications for a disability pension were granted more easily if the applicant had a weak labour market position. For this reason it is believed that disability statistics contain a large hidden employment component. See e.g. Wong (1986)

There is, however, one strong argument to distinguish between the categories 'employed' and 'unemployed'. The effect of financial incentives will differ between them. Unemployed persons must find a job before they can collect the income that belongs to the state 'supply of labour', whereas workers have more security about the income they receive in that state. Therefore, unemployed persons will react less strongly to incentives than workers. For this reason we distinguish between 'employed' and 'unemployed' as states of origin, but combine them into 'labour supply' if we speak about states of destination.

Table 6.1 Definition of labour force categories

State of origin	State of destination
Full-time work Looking for full-time work	Full-time labour supply
Part-time work Looking for part-time work	Part-time labour supply
Disabled/retired	Disabled/retired
Household	Household
Out of labour force	Out of labour force

The definition of labour force categories we use is given in Table 6.1. 'Labour supply' is split into 'full-time' and 'part-time'. The latter state contains all jobs where the number of working hours per week is less than 30. Persons belong to the state 'unemployed' if they have no job and claim that they are actively looking for one. The question if one receives an unemployment benefit is not relevant. For a discussion about the definition of 'unemployed' in terms of Dutch labour market statistics, we refer to the Central Economic Plan (1989).

In practice, we had to combine or delete some flows between the states. 'Disabled/retired' turns out to be an absorbing state, i.e. we observe no flow out of it. For men we have not enough observations of part-time workers and of household workers, so these categories have been deleted. For the same reason the states 'out of the labour force' and 'working in household' have been combined for women, just like 'looking for full-time work' and 'looking for part-time work'. Tables 6.2 and 6.3 show the total number of transitions we are left with. It is clear that in a one-year period most people will stay in the state they were in already. Although we have a reasonable number of observations, some cells are so poorly filled that estimation results should be interpreted with more than the usual caution.

Table 6.2 Observed number of transitions, men

$t-1$	t Full-time labour supply	Out of the labour force	Disabled/retired	Total
Working full-time	3895		76	3971
Unemployed	139	23	9	171
Out of the labour force	24	53	14	91

Table 6.3   Observed number of transitions, women

$t-1$	*t* *Full-time labour supply*	*Part-time labour supply*	*Household/out of the labour force*	*Total*
Working full-time	984	46	70	1100
Working part-time	59	756	51	866
Unemployed	42	49	54	145
Out of the labour force	33	95	2209	2337

6.3.2 Income variables

The aim of our model is to find out how the numbers of transitions in Tables 6.2 and 6.3 is affected by the increase in income the persons can receive by switching from one state to another. This is the most important explanatory variable in the model. Transitions are affected not only by the potential income in the state of origin and the state of destination, but also by the potential incomes in other states. Therefore, we must calculate for every observed person what 'profit' he or she can earn by changing labour market status. Since for either sex we distinguish three states of destination, we must calculate three potential incomes for each observation.

Of course, we should reckon with net incomes and take into account the peculiarities of the tax and benefit system as described in section 6.2. For instance, the spouse of an employee with a high salary will have a lower net income in the state 'labour supply' than the spouse of a low-paid employee. We expect that the first will have a lower probability to supply labour.

Incomes in the various states are calculated in two stages. First we calculate each person's 'pure' gross income in every state. Since we do not know the wages of the persons who do not work (and there are also missing observations among the workers), we have estimated a regression equation in the gross hourly wage. Each person's gross hourly wage is calculated with the estimated regression coefficients. Gross and net incomes in other states are determined according to the rules of the tax and social-security system.[3]

In the second stage we include the family situation in the calculation. For each possible labour market state we calculate the total gross family income, taking the partner's income and labour market status as given. Welfare benefits are corrected for the size of partner's income and the appropriate tax bracket is used. From total gross income we calculate net family income in each possible labour market state. Subtracting partner's net income yields the net income that the individual itself can gain in each labour market state. Unfortunately, it has not been possible to incorporate the system of individual subsidies in the calculation. Therefore, in our data set marginal rates are underestimated.

In Table 6.4 we show how the family situation affects the potential income in each possible state. A woman with certain characteristics (35 years old, high

---

[3] See Appendix A.

Table 6.4 Potential net income in three states in various family situations

$t-1$	t Full-time labour supply (38.6 h/week)	Part-time labour supply (15.6 h/week)	Household/out of the labour force
Single woman	F31.318	F15.685	F12.333
Partner with F 17 619 net labour income	F29.833	F15.444	F0.000
Partner with F17 619 net welfare income	F12.214	F3.090	F0.000

Amounts are based on the 1987 tax and benefit system. Incomes have been calculated for a woman with the following characteristics: age: 35 years; education: academic; working in private sector; had a job last year; gross hourly wage: F26.95.

education) will earn a gross hourly wage of about 26.95 guilders[4] according to the results given in Appendix A. The first row in Table 6.4 gives the net income she will receive in the three labour market states, 'full-time', 'part-time' and 'household', if she lives alone. In the last state she will receive the welfare benefit for singles, which was about F12 333 guilders per year in 1987. If she moves from 'household' to 'part-time work', she is awarded with a F3352 profit. Moving to 'full-time work' is more advantageous: the net income is F18 985 higher than in the state 'household'.

The second and third rows show how her income would change if she lived with a partner, who has either a labour income or a welfare benefit at the minimum level. It is clear that for the welfare recipient's partner it is not very profitable to supply labour. If she works part-time, a substantial part of her own labour income is subtracted from partner's benefit. The total family income is not much lower if she does not work.

It is reasonable to expect that the woman in the last row has a smaller probability to participate in the labour force than the other two. Before we can say how large this effect is, we have to formulate and estimate an econometric model.

6.3.3 Mathematical formulation

Since we are interested in yearly transition probabilities, we choose these quantities as dependent variables in the model. The independent variables can be classified into two categories:

— Variables depending on the individual only, such as age, family situation, etc. Such variables are indicated by the symbol x.
— Variables that vary with the state the individual is in. We include only one variable of this kind, namely, the net income the person receives. This is indicated by the symbol w_j, j being the number of the labour force state.

[4] One guilder is approximately equal to $0.45.

If one is concerned with transitions between discrete states, it is natural to resort to the literature about duration models and Markov chains (Ridder, 1987). In these models the crucial variable is the transition intensity or hazard rate, generally indicated by the symbol λ_{ij}, where i and j stand for the state of origin and destination, respectively. The hazard rate is related to the transition probabilities in the following way:

$$\lambda_{ij} = \lim_{\Delta t \downarrow 0} \frac{P\{m_{t+\Delta t} = j \mid m_t = i\}}{\Delta t} \tag{6.1}$$

where m_t is the number of the state the individual is in at time t.

For the model to be well-behaved, the hazard rate should be positive and finite. We formulate the following expression for the hazard rate:

$$\lambda_{ij} = \exp(\alpha_j w_j - \alpha_i w_i + \beta_j x + \varepsilon_t) \tag{6.2}$$

where the α and β denote the parameters to be estimated and ε_t is a stochastic disturbance term with an extreme-value type I distribution. We expect the α's, the income parameters, to be positive. Thus, the hazard rate will be high if the destination state is connected with a high income, and low if the income in the state of origin is high. Under certain not unrealistic assumptions, the probability that the individual does not leave state i in a one-year period is equal to

$$P_{ii} = \exp\left\{ -\sum_{\substack{j=1 \\ j \neq i}}^{M} \lambda_{ij} \right\} \tag{6.3}$$

The probability to stay in state i is low when the λ_{ij} are high. The one-year probability to flow from state i to j (with j not equal to i) is equal to

$$P_{ij} = (1 - P_{ii}) \cdot \frac{\lambda_{ij}}{\sum_{\substack{k=1 \\ k \neq i}}^{M} \lambda_{ik}} \tag{6.4}$$

The transition probability consists of two parts: (i) the probability to leave state i and (ii) the conditional probability to flow into state j given that the individual leaves state i. The latter probability is of the well-known logit form.

It will be clear from equations (6.3) and (6.4) that the relation between the parameters α and β and the transition probabilities is a very complex one. The parameters are very difficult to interpret. That is why, in the next section, we do not present the parameter estimates themselves, but a more meaningful quantity, namely the **partial derivative** of the probabilities with respect to the independent variables:

$$\frac{\partial P_{ii}}{\partial x}, \quad \frac{\partial P_{ij}}{\partial w_j}, \quad \ldots \tag{6.5}$$

The partial derivatives tell us how the probabilities change if x or w increase by one unit. Their advantage is that they are readily understandable, but they vary with x and w. Unless stated otherwise, we always present the derivatives for the sample averages of the x and w variables.

6.4 RESULTS OF ESTIMATION

The model has been estimated on seven disjoint data sets, consisting of persons of the same sex and the same labour force state of origin. We use three waves of the Dutch Social Economic Panel (namely, the October 1985, 1986 and 1987 ones), which leaves us with observations of transitions in two years. The coefficients and other statistics are presented in Appendix B. We tried out several specifications of the explanatory variables and the coefficients were stable, although in the three smaller data sets (unemployed men, unemployed women and men out of the labour force) the results are less satisfactory than in the large data sets.

Here in this chapter we can describe only the effects on the level of individuals. Since these effects seem to vary strongly with the individual's socio-economic status and income, we cannot yet draw conclusions about aggregate behaviour. To do this, we must incorporate information or make assumptions about the distribution of incomes and benefits over households.

6.4.1 Effects of control variables

We have included the following variables in the model:

CON = constant term,
DED = dummy for 'education at middle or high level',
MAR = dummy for 'lives with partner',
CHL = dummy for 'mother of child under 12',
AGE = person's age,
$AGE2$ = square of AGE,
$INCPRT$ = partner's net income,
$INCOWN$ = own income; varies over labour market states.

In this paragraph we describe the effects of the variables $DED, \ldots, AGE2$. The income variables are described in the next section. Unfortunately, due to the distribution of the variables in the data set it was not possible to estimate all effects. For instance, since almost every woman in the state 'household' is married, it is impossible to distinguish the MAR dummy from the constant term in the data set for 'women, state of origin = household'.

The partial derivatives of the probabilities with respect to the education dummies are presented in Tables 6.5 and 6.6. Note that the derivatives sum to zero over rows; this is necessary because a rise in the transition probability into one state must be compensated by a decrease at one of the other states. The absolute value of the derivatives is not very important, because it depends on the values of the explanatory variables. But the sign and the relative size within rows tell us something about the effects of the variables.

The first row of Table 6.5 tells us that the average working man has a 98.09% probability to stay in the same state, and a 1.91% chance to become disabled. Working men with high education have an approximately 0.15% lower probability to flow into the state 'disabled' than have low educated men. This effect is small relative to the inflow in 'supply', but not relative to the inflow in 'disabled'. The most plausible explanation is that highly educated men less often have unhealthy or dangerous jobs.

Table 6.5   Effect of high education on transition probabilities, men

$t-1$	t	*Full-time labour supply*	*Out of the labour force*	*Disabled/ retired*
Working full-time		P = 98.09% (+0.15)		P = 1.91% (−0.15)
Unemployed		P = 81.29% (+6.78)	P = 13.45% (−7.64)	P = 5.26% (+0.88)
Out of the labour force		P = 26.37% (−18.64)	P = 58.24% (+6.35)	P = 15.38% (+12.29)

Table 6.6   Effect of high education on transition probabilities, women

$t-1$	t	*Full-time labour supply*	*Part-time labour supply*	*Household/out of the labour force*
Working full-time		P = 89.46% (−1.13)	P = 4.18% (+0.70)	P = 6.36% (+0.43)
Working part-time		P = 6.81% (+0.41)	P = 87.30% (+2.34)	P = 5.89 (−2.74)
Unemployed		P = 28.97% (+3.93)	P = 33.79% (+12.72)	P = 37.24% (−16.65)
Out of the labour force		P = 1.41% (−0.68)	P = 4.07 (+1.10)	P = 94.52% (−0.42)

As indicated above, the estimates for unemployed men and men out of the labour force are less reliable. The estimated education effects for these groups are inconsistent: unemployed men with low education seem to become discouraged more often (their chance to flow into 'out of the labour force' is 7.64% higher) but once they are out of the labour force, they seem to have a higher probability to return to the state 'labour supply'. This inconsistency is probably due to the lack of data in these two sets; the education coefficients do not differ significantly from zero.

This fact illustrates why the partial derivatives by themselves do not give enough information about the effect of a variable on the long-term or static behaviour: a higher chance to flow into a certain state can be compensated by higher outflow probabilities. If all derivatives in a column have a positive sign, we can conclude that this labour market state is attractive. For instance, Table

6.6 shows that 'part-time work' is more attractive to women with high education than to low-educated women. If the signs of the derivatives differ within a column, we call them 'inconsistent' because we cannot be sure about the long-term effect. We let this matter rest while we are looking at the control variables and come back on it when we proceed with the income effects.

Table 6.6 shows the estimated education effects on the transitions of women. Women with high education seem to prefer part-time over full-time jobs, and they flow less often into 'household' than low-educated women. But the effects on flows into 'full-time labour supply' are not consistent.

High education affects labour market behaviour in two distinct ways. First, there is a cultural effect: norms and preferences of highly educated and low-educated people differ. Second, there is an indirect income effect: high education means a higher wage, which will stimulate labour supply. Because education and income are correlated, we must interpret their effects with some caution.

Table 6.7 Effect of civil status on transition probabilities, men

$t-1$	t	Full-time labour supply	Out of the labour force	Disabled/ retired
Working full-time		$P = 98.09\%$		$P = 1.91\%$
		$(+0.22)$		(-0.22)
Unemployed		$P = 81.29\%$	$P = 13.45\%$	$P = 5.26\%$
		$(+3.22)$	$(+1.02)$	(-4.25)
Out of the labour force		$P = 26.37\%$	$P = 58.24\%$	$P = 15.38\%$
		$(+0.30)$	$(+23.52)$	(-23.82)

Table 6.8 Effect of civil status on transition probabilities, women

$t-1$	t	Full-time labour supply	Part-time labour supply	Household/out of the labour force
Working full-time		$P = 89.46\%$	$P = 4.18\%$	$P = 6.36\%$
		(-8.77)	$(+6.97)$	$(+1.80)$
Working part-time		$P = 6.81\%$	$P = 87.30\%$	$P = 5.89$
		$(+4.13)$	(-3.08)	(-1.05)
Unemployed		$P = 28.97\%$	$P = 33.79\%$	$P = 37.24\%$
		(-39.32)	$(+30.19)$	(-9.13)

In Tables 6.7 and 6.8 we show the estimated effects of the *MAR* dummy on the transition probabilities. Dutch labour supply studies often show that married men supply more labour than singles. The effects in Table 6.7 confirm this expectation. Single men become disabled more often than married men.

It is not immediately clear how we expect the behaviour of married women to differ from that of single women. Of course, married women participate less, but this can be due to the presence of young children or to the partner's income. The effects given in Table 6.8 do not indicate that married women prefer one specific labour market state (we were not able to estimate the effects on the subset of women in 'household'). The only conclusion we can draw is that married women

Table 6.9 Effect of young children on transition probabilities, women

$t-1$	t Full-time labour supply	Part-time labour supply	Household/out of the labour force
Working full-time	$P = 89.46\%$ (-8.28)	$P = 4.18\%$ $(+2.98)$	$P = 6.36\%$ $(+5.30)$
Working part-time	$P = 6.81\%$ (-2.86)	$P = 87.30\%$ $(+1.23)$	$P = 5.89$ $(+1.64)$
Unemployed	$P = 28.97\%$ (-20.15)	$P = 33.79\%$ $(+17.14)$	$P = 37.24\%$ $(+3.01)$
Out of the labour force	$P = 1.41\%$ (-0.80)	$P = 4.07\%$ $(+0.13)$	$P = 94.52\%$ $(+0.67)$

change labour market status more often: both in the 'full-time' and in the 'part-time' subset married women have higher probability to leave the state they are in. The implication is that married women have less strong attachment to their jobs than single women.

Table 6.9 gives the effect of the presence of children younger than 12 years on the labour market behaviour of women. As is to be expected, mothers flow less often into 'full-time supply'. Instead of this state, most mothers flow into 'household'. Only unemployed mothers, who had decided to participate already, prefer 'part-time supply'.

The last control variable we included is the age of the respondent. We have assumed that the age effect is not linear but quadratic. Tables 6.10 and 6.11 show what kind of parabola expresses the relation between age and transitions. We give the location of the minimum or maximum, if existent, on the age interval from 20 to 64 years.

Table 6.10 Effect of age on transition probablities, men

$t-1$	t Full-time labour supply	Out of the labour force	Disabled/retired
Working full-time	20 ⌒↘ 64		20 ___ 64
Unemployed	20 ___ 33 ___ 64	20 ___ 64	20 ___ 64
Out of the labour force	20 ⌒ 64	20 ⌣ 33 64	20 ___ 64

Table 6.11 Effect of age on transition probabilities, women

$t-1$	t Full-time labour supply	Part-time labour supply	Household/out of the labour force
Working full-time	20 ___ 20 64	20 ⌒ 50 64	20 ___ 64
Working part-time	20 ___ 64	20 ⌒ 48 64	20 ___ 44 64
Unemployed	20 ___ 20 64	20 ⌒ 39 64	20 ___ 44 64
Out of the labour force	20 ___ 64	20 ⌒ 64	20 ⌣

It is not surprising that the chance to become disabled increases with age. In all three data sets of men, this probability is very low for young men, and increases rapidly for the age groups above 45 years. For men above 60, the state 'disabled' is the same as 'retired'; in The Netherlands many older workers have access to generous flexible pension schemes.

Male participation seems to be highest around the age of 30. Younger men, if they are working or unemployed, prefer to keep supplying labour. But if they are 'out of the labour force' they will probably stay in that state until they are about 30. Older men often stay 'out of the labour force' once they are out.

For women the transitions vary even more strongly with age than for men. Without doubt, this is largely a cohort effect: female participation, which is traditionally low in The Netherlands, has been rising rapidly in the past. Unfortunately, because our data describe a very short period, we are not able to distinguish between a time trend and a 'real' age effect. Strictly speaking, we should control for the cohort effect when using our estimated probabilities for prediction. If we do not, predicted participation will be too low.

Table 6.11 shows that younger women of around 20 years prefer to work full-time. Part-time work is the most attractive state for women between 30 and 50, whereas older women prefer to be housewives. We can only speculate about the question if this is an age or a trend effect. Intuitively, if the life-cycle effect is the most important, we expect this to show up in the flows from 'full-time' to 'part-time' and from 'part-time' to 'household': the age effects should be very prominent in these flows if the life-cycle effect is dominant. But this is not the case. The flows from 'unemployed' and from 'household' indicate that women between 20 and 30 enter the labour market as full-timers, and between 30 and 50 as part-timers. Therefore, we can tentatively conclude that age effects reflect an overall trend of increasing female participation. But we need data over a longer period to be sure of this.

The effects of the control variables given above are plausible. But interpretation is hindered because we observe only the effect on the yearly transition probabilities. Naturally, these effects depend on the original situation. Nevertheless, we can conclude that the average, approximated effects generally have the expected sign.

6.4.2 Effect of partner's income

Tables 6.12 and 6.13 show the effects of F1000 rise in partner's net income. Our expectation, that this reduces labour supply, is not confirmed for men. For working men, partner's income has no effect. For unemployed men and men out of the labour force, the effects have the wrong sign and they are very small. This confirms the findings of other authors, that male participation does not depend on their spouse's income (e.g. Kapteyn *et al.*, 1989; Theeuwes, 1988; Renaud and Siegers, 1984). Female participation decreases (the flow into 'household' rises) when partner's income increases. This effect seems concentrated in the

Table 6.12 Effect of partner's income on transition probabilities, men (effects of an F1000 increase)

$t-1$	t	Full-time labour supply	Out of the labour force	Disabled/ retired
Working full-time		$P = 98.09\%$		$P = 1.91\%$
		. *(0.00)*		*(0.00)*
Unemployed		$P = 81.29\%$	$P = 13.45\%$	$P = 5.26\%$
		(+0.40)	*(−0.50)*	*(+0.10)*
Out of the labour force		$P = 26.37\%$	$P = 58.24\%$	$P = 15.38\%$
		(+1.57)	*(−0.92)*	*(−0.64)*

Table 6.13 Effect of partner's income on transition probabilities, women (effect of an F1000 increase)

$t-1$	t	Full-time labour supply	Part-time labour supply	Household/out of the labour force
Working full-time		$P = 89.46\%$	$P = 4.18\%$	$P = 6.36\%$
		(+0.10)	*(−0.13)*	*(+0.03)*
Working part-time		$P = 6.81\%$	$P = 87.30\%$	$P = 5.89$
		(−0.20)	*(+0.02)*	*(+0.18)*
Unemployed		$P = 28.97\%$	$P = 33.79\%$	$P = 37.24\%$
		(+1.20)	*(−1.21)*	*(+0.01)*
Out of the labour force		$P = 1.41\%$	$P = 4.07\%$	$P = 94.52\%$
		(+0.01)	*(−0.17)*	*(+0.16)*

subset of part-time workers; on the basis of Table 6.13, we can draw no conclusion about the effect of partner's income on full-time participation.

We can, however, investigate what would happen if a person is subjected to the same matrix of transition probabilities for an infinitely long time. Although this never happens in reality, it supplies information about the **direction** in which the system is going. We carried out such a simulation for women with certain characteristics (30 years old, married, with child under 12, high education). The outcome of this exercise is a **stationary state**: the long-term distribution over the states if the transition probabilities do not change. Naturally, these stationary states cannot be used for prediction, since every individual's transition probabilities change continually over time. Moreover, the characteristics vary simultaneously. But as a first approximation the stationary states can be useful, and their advantage is that they are independent of the starting position of the individual.

Figure 6.1 shows how the partner's income affects the stationary state for the woman with characteristics given above. Note that the probabilities cannot be interpreted as 'aggregate' participation rates: they are conditional on the particular characteristics we use in the simulation.

If partner's income is low, the woman will choose between all three states. Most probably, she will work part-time. Part-time participation decreases to zero when partner's income rises. Wives of very rich men seem to make more radical choices: if they supply labour, it is full-time. The full-time participation rate does

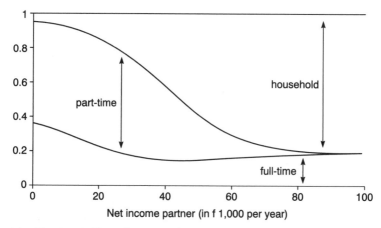

Fig. 6.1 Simulated effect of partner's income on stationary labour force states for a woman with the following characteristics – age: 30 years; marital status: married; income in 'full-time' region: F23 200; income in 'part-time' region: F10 390; children: one child under 12; education: middle or high.

Table 6.14 Effect of own income on transition probablities, men (effect of an F1000 increase)

$t-1$	t Full-time labour supply	Out of the labour force	Disabled/ retired
Working full-time	P = 98.09% (+ 0.04)		P = 1.91% (+ 0.02)
Unemployed	P = 81.29% (+ 0.79)		P = 5.26% (+ 0.99)
Out of the labour force	P = 26.37% (+ 0.43)		P = 15.38% (+ 4.32)

Table 6.15 Effect of own income on transition probablities, women (effect of an F1000 increase)

$t-1$	t Full-time labour supply	Part-time labour supply	Household/out of the labour force
Working full-time	P = 89.46% (+ 1.12)	P = 4.18% (+ 1.07)	
Working part-time	P = 6.81% (+ 0.69)	P = 87.30% (+ 0.64)	
Unemployed	P = 28.97% (+ 1.66)	P = 33.79% (+ 0.46)	
Out of the labour force	P = 1.41% (+ 0.39)	P = 4.07% (+ 0.69)	

not vary strongly with partner's income; it is almost constant for net incomes above F20 000. This indicates that the decision to supply part-time labour is affected by financial incentives whereas full-time working women have other reasons for their choice, like the expected job satisfaction, the status connected to a job or the social contacts.

Apparently, there is a group of women who will always supply labour, for other than financial reasons. This confirms the results of Siegers and his co-authors who, in a number of related studies, conclude that the so-called 'discouraged-worker effect' disappears when unemployment is very high. A certain group of women seems to be insensitive to this effect.

6.4.3 Effect of own income

The effects of the person's own income confirm our expectation as shown in Tables 6.14 and 6.15. Note that the derivatives do not sum to zero over rows, because in every column of this table a different income is used. Thus, a F1000 rise in net labour income leads to a 0.04% higher probability for working men to stay in that state, whereas the same absolute increase of disability pensions increases the flow into that state by 0.02%. Unfortunately, it was impossible to estimate the income effect in the state 'out of the labour force'. There was not enough variation in the size of the benefits within the data set.

Table 6.15 indicates that working women react more strongly to financial incentives than men. If income in a certain state increases, the inflow into that state increases too.

6.4.4 Some preliminary simulations

To translate the effects on the one-year transitions into something like 'long-term elasticities', we calculated the stationary states for women with various characteristics, and the effect of a 1% increase in net hourly wage. Thus, both full-time and part-time income rise by 1%. The effects on female participation vary strongly with the women's characteristics, as shown in Table 6.16.

Some of our earlier findings are confirmed by the effects in Table 6.16: participation decreases with age, mothers participate less, and the effect of marital status on participation is ambiguous. It is not easy to check the plausibility of the stationary states, because they vary so strongly with partner's income (Figure 6.1). To compare the figures in Table 6.16 with aggregate participation data, we must include information about the income variables in each age group. Probably, we have overestimated incomes for the younger age groups, and underestimated them for the older women. But the aim of Table 6.16 is to identify the differences in income effects for women with different characteristics, not to predict their true reaction.

Nevertheless, we can be fairly sure that the long-term stationary states in Table 6.16 are substantially higher than the observed participation rates for comparable groups. This is not a shortcoming of the model; it reflects the rising trend in female participation in The Netherlands. Since especially part-time labour supply

Table 6.16 Effect of 1% wage rise on stationary states for women with different characteristics

t – 1	t	Full-time labour supply	Part-time labour supply	Household/out of the labour force
Age: 20				
Single		$P = 98.2\%$	$P = 1.3\%$	$P = 0.5\%$
		$(+0.1)$	(-0.1)	(-0.1)
Married no child		$P = 95.3\%$	$P = 3.6\%$	$P = 1.1\%$
		$(+0.3)$	(-0.1)	(-0.1)
Married with child		$P = 50.7\%$	$P = 16.5\%$	$P = 32.7\%$
		$(+2.6)$	(-0.6)	(-1.9)
Age: 30				
Single		$P = 90.1\%$	$P = 9.5\%$	$P = 0.4\%$
		$(+0.10)$	(-0.5)	(0.0)
Married no child		$P = 71.6\%$	$P = 25.7\%$	$P = 2.6\%$
		$(+1.1)$	(-0.9)	(-0.2)
Married with child		$P = 20.0\%$	$P = 60.7\%$	$P = 19.3\%$
		$(+1.1)$	(-0.6)	(-0.4)
Age: 40				
Single		$P = 63.5\%$	$P = 35.7\%$	$P = 0.9\%$
		$(+1.4)$	(-1.3)	(-0.1)
Married no child		$P = 33.0\%$	$P = 61.2\%$	$P = 5.8\%$
		$(+1.2)$	(-1.0)	(-0.2)
Married with child		$P = 5.1\%$	$P = 79.2\%$	$P = 15.7\%$
		$(+0.3)$	(-0.01)	(-0.3)

Assumptions about other characteristics:

Education: high.
Partner's net income: F 23 200 per year
Own net fulltime income: F 22 200 per year
Own net parttime income: F 10 390 per year

is much higher in Table 6.16 than in reality, this rising trend must be concentrated in part-time jobs. This is confirmed by the findings of van Soest *et al.* (1989). The number of part-time jobs has been rising rapidly in the past years: the ratio of persons to labour years increased from 1.24 in 1988 to 1.27 in 1991 (Central Planning Bureau, 1992).

The conclusion from Table 6.16 is that, if all net incomes rise by 1% (e.g. because of a tax reform), female participation will shift from part-time to full-time. On the basis of this table we cannot make statements about the effect on the composition of labour supply; for that we must carry out a microsimulation on a data set that is representative for the Dutch population. Only then can we be sure that the distribution of income variables, which is likely to have a strong effect, is not misrepresented.

To illustrate this, Table 6.17 gives the stationary state for the three women of Table 6.4, who differ only in the socio-economic status of their husband. This affects not only their non-labour income, but also their own income in the various states, as shown in Table 6.4.

Table 6.17   Stationary states of the three women from Table 6.4

$t-1$	t Full-time labour supply (38.6 h/week)	Part-time labour supply (15.6 h/week)	Household/out of the labour force
Single woman	0.949	0.050	0.001
Partner with F17 619 net labour income	0.755	0.242	0.003
Partner with F17 619 net welfare income	0.106	0.425	0.47

Table 16.17 presents the stationary probabilities that the woman is in a certain state. Of course, the probabilities sum to one over rows. We have assumed that the women have no children, and their other characteristics are as given in Table 6.4. The single woman has the highest participation probability. The welfare recipient's wife, who has a very high marginal rate due to her partner's benefit, has almost a 50% probability to be out of the labour force. Working full-time is not an attractive state for her. But if her partner finds a job at the minimum wage, her labour supply will change drastically. Almost surely she will start looking for a job, and chances are three in four that she will want to work full-time.

6.5 CONCLUSION

In this chapter we presented the results of estimation of a model describing transitions between various states of the labour market.

The stationary states we present may not be interpreted as a prediction of labour market behaviour in the future. They function as a kind of compass: an indication in which direction a person with certain characteristics is heading. We find rather strong effects of financial incentives on labour market behaviour of women, but men are less susceptible to incomes policy. Of course, we should bear in mind that our income effects can be biased, e.g. because of the correlation between income and education or because of omitted variables. Regarding the first problem, we cannot say in which direction the bias would be, because it is possible that incomes 'take over' the education effects, but the opposite can apply too. Omitted variables will probably result in overestimation of income effects.

Nevertheless, in our data set there is a substantial variation in incomes, due to the tax and social-security system. People with otherwise equal characteristics face different choices because their potential income in each labour market state differs. Apparently, in our data set there is a tendency to flow into the labour market state where income is highest.

Female labour supply in The Netherlands is increasing autonomously at the moment; it is not clear what contribution incomes policy could have. The increase in labour supply seems especially strong in the part-time segment of the labour market.

So far, we have only been able to present conclusions on the level of individuals. All statements are conditional on the assumptions we have made about the individual characteristics. Nevertheless, we can conclude that the results seem plausible and are in accordance with the findings of other authors. To be able to make statements about aggregate behaviour, we must make assumptions about the income distribution or carry out a microsimulation.

APPENDIX A: CONSTRUCTION INCOME VARIABLES

For every person in the data set we must calculate the potential income in each possible labour market state. In this appendix we explain how the various potential incomes have been calculated.

Participation (full-time/part-time)

Respondents were asked what their net wage was and how many hours they worked. We used the yearly net wage to estimate gross wage. Then we estimated a regression on the logarithm of gross hourly wage, for the subset of working respondents. The regression results are presented in Table 6A.1. The regression coefficients are plausible and significant; the wage increases with age and education level. For women the coefficient of 'public sector worker' was very small and not significantly different from zero; therefore, we omitted this variable. Starters on the labour market receive significantly lower wages than more experienced workers. We did not include a correction for sample selection bias because in an earlier exercise this had almost no effect.

With the regression coefficients in Table 6A.1 we can calculate each respondent's potential gross hourly wage. Next we make the assumption that the labour

Table 6A.1 Regression equation in gross hourly wages (logarithmic)

Variable	Men		Women	
Constant	3.09	(103.4)	2.78	(86.4)
$1/(AGE-12)$	-6.46	(16.0)	-3.08	(9.3)
Education				
Level 2	0.11	(3.8)	0.09	(2.8)
Level 3	0.24	(9.5)	0.16	(5.2)
Level 4	0.59	(18.6)	0.41	(11.4)
Level 5	0.85	(20.6)	0.60	(9.2)
Self-employed	0.41	(10.2)	0.38	(4.2)
Public sector	-0.09	(4.8)		
Non-participant in year $t-1$	-0.13	(2.5)	-0.14	(4.3)
R^2		0.39		0.28
N		2078		1018
σ^2		0.37		0.29

t-values in brackets.

market states 'full-time' and 'part-time' are connected with a fixed number of working hours per week. This number is based on the observed average working time for men and women:

— men, full-time: 40.4 hours/week,
— women, full-time: 38.9 hours/week,
— women, part-time: 15.6 hours/week.

Multiplication of working hours and gross wage yields the potential gross yearly wage in each state. From this variable, we deduce the net yearly wage in each state. This estimated wage is used in estimating the transition probabilities.

Disabled

Persons entering this state from 'participation' receive a benefit which is related to the labour income they earned. In most cases the gross benefit is about 75% of their wage. The maximum net benefit is around F38 000 per year.

For older workers there exist very attractive pension schemes. We assume that for the age groups older than 60 years, the pensions are a substitute for a disability benefit. For these workers the income in the state 'disabled' is equal to their labour income.

For persons entering this state from 'out of the labour force' the disability pension is equal to the welfare benefit.

Household/out of labour force

This category contains housewives, but also a number of unemployed respondents who are not actively looking for work. Some respondents in this state receive a welfare or unemployment benefit. Most housewives are not entitled to welfare; their income in this state is zero.

The welfare benefit is easy to calculate, but the unemployment benefit is not. It depends on a number of unknown criteria, such as the income received when working, the labour market history and the duration of unemployment. For reasons of consistency, we should probably have estimated the unemployment benefits, but because of this practical difficulty we used the respondent's own benefit, if known.

APPENDIX B: COEFFICIENT ESTIMATES

In this appendix we give the estimates of the coefficients of formula (6.2) for each of the seven data sets we used in estimation. In most data sets there are three possible labour market states. As in normal logit models, we can estimate the coefficients for only two states. Therefore, most tables contain two columns, describing the two states of destination that are not equal to the state of origin for that particular data set.

The coefficients in this appendix have been used to calculate the derivatives and the stationary states given in section 6.4. We have experimented with various specifications of the model and the coefficients show a stable pattern. The variable definition is as follows:

CON = constant term,
DED = dummy for 'education at middle or high level',
MAR = dummy for 'lives with partner',
CHL = dummy for 'mother of child under 12',
AGE = person's age,

Table 6B.1 Estimation results for data set women, working full-time

| Variable | State of destination | | | |
	Work part-time		Household	
CON	− 6.47	(3.01)	2.86	(1.73)
DED	0.23	(0.70)	0.31	(1.08)
MAR	2.28	(3.63)	1.69	(2.51)
CHL	1.00	(2.78)	3.69	(9.53)
AGE	0.21	(1.65)	− 0.30	(2.87)
$AGE2$	− 0.22	(1.33)	0.51	(3.85)
$INCPRT$	− 0.04	(2.77)	0.01	(2.18)
$INCOWN$-full-time	− 0.25	(5.73)	− 0.25	(5.73)
$INCOWN$-part-time	0.34	(3.50)		
− Log likelihood		314.49		
N		1100		

t-values between brackets.

Table 6B.2 Estimation results for data set women, working part-time

| Variable | State of destination | | | |
	Work full-time		Household	
CON	2.42	(1.37)	0.21	(0.11)
DED	0.09	(0.16)	− 0.58	(0.87)
MAR	1.02	(1.65)	− 0.19	(0.25)
CHL	− 0.71	(1.95)	0.33	(0.96)
AGE	− 0.32	(2.31)	− 0.16	(1.21)
$AGE2$	0.28	(1.65)	0.18	(1.09)
$INCPRT$	− 0.05	(2.59)	0.04	(3.34)
$INCOWN$-full-time	0.17	(0.56)		
$INCOWN$-part-time	− 0.07	(2.03)	− 0.07	(2.03)
− Log likelihood		360.30		
N		866		

t-values between brackets.

Table 6B.3   Estimation results for data set women, unemployed

Variable	State of destination			
	Work part-time		*Household*	
CON	− 3.93	(1.52)	− 2.32	(1.13)
DED	0.34	(0.79)	− 0.48	(1.22)
MAR	1.49	(1.76)	0.79	(1.09)
CHL	0.81	(2.02)	0.36	(0.98)
AGE	0.14	(0.83)	0.10	(0.66)
AGE2	− 0.15	(0.66)	− 0.88	(0.46)
DPT	1.25	(2.93)	0.77	(2.05)
INCPRT	− 0.05	(2.01)	− 0.02	(0.77)
INCOWN-full-time	− 0.05	(0.65)	− 0.05	(0.65)
INCOWN-part-time	0.02	(0.10)		
− Log likelihood		133.15		
N		145		

t-values between brackets.

Table 6B.4   Estimation results for data set women, household

Variable	State of destination			
	Work full-time		*Work part-time*	
CON	− 5.61	(1.92)	− 6.27	(3.03)
DED	− 0.86	(1.97)	0.50	(2.03)
CHL	− 1.02	(1.88)	0.06	(0.16)
AGE	0.30	(2.04)	0.20	(1.79)
AGE2	0.22	(1.27)	− 0.32	(2.26)
INCPRT	0.01	(1.32)	− 0.08	(7.10)
INCOWN-full-time	0.50	(7.37)		
INCOWN-part-time			0.31	(3.23)
− Log likelihood		489.80		
N		2337		

t-values between brackets.

$AGE2$ = square of AGE,
DPT = (for unemployed women only) dummy for 'looking for part-time work',
$INCPRT$ = partner's net income,
$INCOWN$ = own income; varies over labour market states.

Table 6B.5 Estimation results for data set men, working full-time

Variable	State of destination Disabled	
	Disabled	
CON	− 0.60	(0.30)
DED	− 0.26	(0.91)
MAR	− 0.40	(1.15)
AGE	− 0.25	(2.63)
AGE2	0.44	(4.26)
INCPRT	− 0.00	(0.00)
INCOWN-full-time	− 0.07	(2.97)
INCOWN-disabled	0.04	(1.15)
− Log likelihood	266.70	
N	3971	

t-values between brackets.

Table 6B.6 Estimation results for data set men, unemployed

Variable	Out of labour force		Disabled	
CON	− 3.49	(1.52)	− 12.15	(1.72)
DED	− 0.87	(1.32)	0.27	(0.33)
MAR	0.10	(0.18)	− 1.49	(0.62)
AGE	0.10	(0.79)	0.28	(1.07)
AGE2	− 0.01	(0.10)	− 0.25	(0.82)
INCPRT	− 0.06	(0.97)	0.03	(0.64)
INCOWN-full-time	− 0.07	(1.65)	− 0.07	(1.65)
INCOWN-disabled			0.35	(0.81)
− Log likelihood	84.91			
N	171			

t-values between brackets.

Table 6B.7 Estimation results for data set men, out of labour force

Variable	Work full-time		Disabled	
CON	− 4.39	(1.35)	− 14.54	(0.48)
DED	− 1.55	(2.10)	2.09	(3.45)
MAR	− 0.11	(0.23)	− 4.26	(0.35)
AGE	0.23	(1.38)	0.01	(0.04)
AGE2	− 0.39	(1.88)	0.07	(0.24)
INCPRT	0.13	(1.72)	− 0.11	(0.62)
INCOWN-full-time	0.04	(0.93)		
INCOWN-disabled			0.77	(0.34)
− Log likelihood	58.01			
N	91			

t-values between brackets.

ACKNOWLEDGEMENTS

At the time of writing the chapter the author worked for The Netherlands Central Planning Bureau in The Hague. I acknowledge the help I received from H. Don, F. Huizinga and J. Kok.

REFERENCES

Central Planning Bureau (1988) *Gevolgen Verlaging Minimum-loonkosten (Effects of lower minimum wages)*, Working Document No. 25, The Hague (in Dutch).

Central Planning Bureau (1989) *Central Economic Plan 1989 and Economic Prospects 1990*. The Hague (in Dutch).

Central Planning Bureau (1992) *Central Economic Plan 1992*, The Hague (in Dutch).

Department of Social Affairs (1989a) *Rapportage Arbeidsmarkt 1989 (Report on the Labour Market 1989)*, The Hague (in Dutch).

Department of Social Affairs (1989b) *Nota Inkomensbeleid 1990 (Incomes Policy in 1990)*, The Hague (in Dutch).

Department of Social Affairs (1990) *Nota Inkomensbeleid 1991 (Incomes Policy in 1991)*, The Hague (in Dutch).

Kam, C. A. de and van Herwaarden, F. G. (1988) Belastingherziening in Nederland: Problemen en Perspectieven (Tax reform in The Netherlands, Problems and Perspectives), in *Yearbook of the Royal Society for Economics*, Leiden (in Dutch).

Kapteyn, A., Keuzenkamp, H. and van der Ploeg, F. (1989) De Hardnekkige Werkloosheid in Nederland (Persistent Unemployment in The Netherlands). *Economisch Statistische Berichten*, 794–9 (in Dutch).

Ours, J. C. van (1989), Duration of Dutch Job Vacancies. *De Economist*, **137**, 309–27.

Renaud, P. S. A. and Siegers, J. J. (1984) Income and Substitution Effects in Family Labour Supply. *De Economist*, **132**, 350–66.

Ridder, G. (1987) *Life Cycle Patterns in Labor Market Experience*. University of Amsterdam, Amsterdam.

Schaaijk, M. L. J. H. A. van and Waaijers, R. (1989) Loonkosten-differentiatie (Wage Cost Differentiation). *Economisch Statistische Berichten*, 996–1000 (in Dutch).

Soest, A. van (1989) Minimum Wage Rates and Unemployment in The Netherlands, *De Economist*, **137**, 279–308.

Soest, A. van, Woittiez, I. and Kapteyn, A. (1989) *Household Labor Supply in The Netherlands in the Eighties and Nineties*, OSA-document No. W61, The Hague.

Theeuwes, J. J. (1988) Arbeid en Belastingen (Labour and Taxes), in *Yearbook of the Royal Society for Economics*. Leiden (in Dutch).

Wong Meeuw Hing, L. (1986) *Het Discouraged Workers' en Additional Workers' Effect in de in- en Uitschrijvingen van Werklozen en Werkzoekenden bij Gewestelijke Arbeidsburaus*. Central Planning Bureau, Research Memorandum 9, The Hague (in Dutch).

7

Labour supply decisions and non-convex budget sets: the case of national insurance contributions in UK

Alan Duncan

7.1 INTRODUCTION

Recent work on the labour supply of economic agents highlights the inability of a simple Tobit specification to account for the variety of reasons for an individual being out of work. Such a model characterizes all those individuals who report zero hours of work as not wanting to work. This chapter follows the work of Blundell *et al.* (1988) in extending a labour supply model to incorporate those agents who have either been discouraged from working due to fixed and search costs, or who actively seek work but remain unemployed. Data from the UK Family Expenditure Survey (FES) includes sample separation information on those non-working individuals who are seeking work.

It has become increasingly apparent that the kinks and discontinuities inherent in the UK tax–benefit system produce groupings in the earnings distribution. Marginal wage rates fall substantially as workers cross points of discontinuity in their budget sets, and it is important to examine the effects of such non-convexities on work incentives. In this work, the decision-making process governing labour supply around points of discontinuity in the budget constraint is examined explicitly using the methodology developed by Hausman (1980, 1985).[1] By doing so, we may examine a possible bias in the estimates of continuous labour supply equations based on data that displays significant bunching at margins. Examination of the work hours distribution of married male workers in the FES indicate that they choose not to, or are not at liberty to, vary their hours of work significantly. As Figure 7.1 shows, however, the hours distribution of married women shows a much greater variation.

[1] Blundell *et al.* (1991) adopt a different approach which involves selecting those individuals above the point of discontinuity for estimation. A comparison with full-sample estimates serves to reveal the extent of bias.

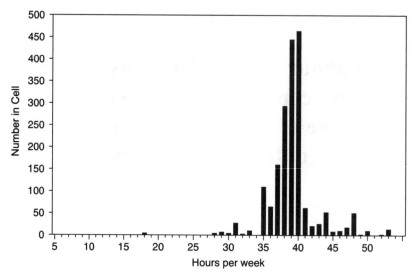

Fig. 7.1(a) Hours distribution (1984 FES): married men.

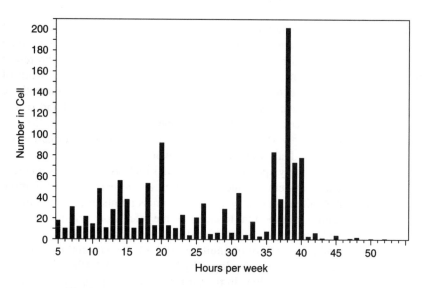

Fig. 7.1(b) Hours distribution (1984 FES): married women.

This tends to suggest that there exists a greater sensitivity of the labour supply decisions of married women to after-tax wages, other income and demographic characteristics. Furthermore, because such groups are more sensitive to their marginal wage when determining their labour supply, it is also the case that any disincentive effect associated with a tax – benefit regime will have a greater impact on work incentives for these groups than for others.

The National Insurance (NI) regime in 1984 was such that both employers and employees faced NI liabilities of 9% of gross earned income above a lower earnings limit (LEL) of £34. Below the LEL, no National Insurance contributions (NICs) were required. However, once weekly earning reached £34, NI was levied on the whole income and not just on that amount of earned income in excess of the LEL. As Dilnot and Webb (1988) point out, such an NI regime has serious implications for labour demand and supply. From the point of view of the employee, some wage/hours combinations become decidedly unattractive. As an example, a woman working 16 hours per week at an hourly rate of £2.00 would not (or, at least, ought not to) accept an extra hour of work. From a position of earning £32 per week, she would then move into the NI system, becoming liable to pay £3.06 in contributions. So, taking on an extra hour of work would, in this instance, have reduced take-home pay from £32 to £30.94. In all likelihood, however, the additional labour would not have been offered. On top of the extra £2.00 per week to pay in wages, the employer is also liable to the same NICs of £3.06. The total cost to the employer of an additional hour of labour, then, is £5.06 per week. Only if the value of the extra hour of work exceeds this figure would that labour have been offered to the employee.

Dilnot and Webb go on to provide evidence that such a distortion has a serious impact on the labour market, by highlighting the bunching of workers just below the NI LEL. Figure 7.2 supports this view, and also indicates that the distortion has more serious implications for the labour supply choices of married women than of their partners.

The UK tax system in 1984 includes a range of kinks and discontinuities, particularly at the lower end of the earnings distribution. Social-security benefits

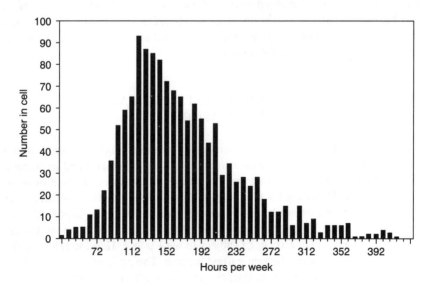

Fig. 7.2(a) Earnings distribution (1984 FES): (a) male.

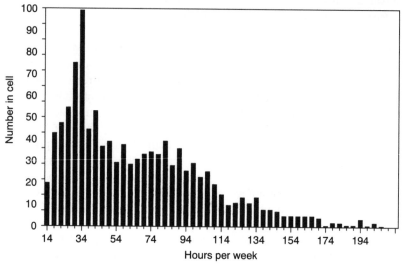

Fig. 7.2(b) Earnings distribution (1984 FES): (b) married women.

and indirect taxation combine to produce a somewhat complicated budget constraint at low income levels. Among these complications, however, the NI regime features as a distinctive, clearly understood distortion. Consideration of the impact on labour supply decisions of the NI system alone can, therefore, offer valuable insight into the behaviour of individuals facing discontinuous budget sets. Although this chapter concentrates on the distortionary impact of NI system on the hours of work of married women from a supply-side viewpoint only, it should be noted that the inclusion of demand-side features into the analysis, perhaps within the context of an applied general-equilibrium model, would provide an attractive area for future research.

7.2 DISCONTINUOUS BUDGET SETS AND LABOUR SUPPLY ESTIMATION

The modelling of the labour supply decisions of economic agents is set within a utility-maximizing framework, where the individual is characterized as using a preference function to establish an optimal supply of labour in the face of some budget constraint. Denoting by $U(c, h; \xi)$ the preference function, defined over consumption, c, hours of work, h, and subject to a set of demographic characteristics, ξ, the optimization problem facing the agent, given a linear budget constraint, is to maximize $U(c, h; \xi)$ subject to $wh + \mu \geqslant c$. Here, w refers to the market wage and μ denotes the non-earned income. The price of c is set at unity. Assumptions of budget constraint linearity and strict quasi-concavity of U combine to generate a unique tangency of the indifference curve, with the budget constraint at every wage, such that the derived labour supply function $h(w, \mu, \xi)$ is everywhere continuous. Admitting a NI system into the analysis, however, renders the budget set discontinuous.

As Figure 7.3 shows, the tangency of the indifference curve and the budget set under these circumstances is not always unique, and the derived labour supply function becomes discontinuous at the points of discontinuity of the budget set. To see this, consider the range of possible tangencies of some preference function with budget constraints at different wage rates, as described in Figure 7.4. For lower wage levels, the most likely point of tangency occurs on the first segment of the budget constraint, below the LEL of the NI regime (Figure 7.4a). As wage rates rise, the tangency (and, consequently, the desired supply of hours) moves smoothly to the point of discontinuity. Further wage rises, however, do not result in a smooth transition of earned income past the LEL. The utility enjoyed at the

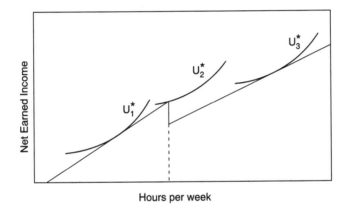

Fig. 7.3

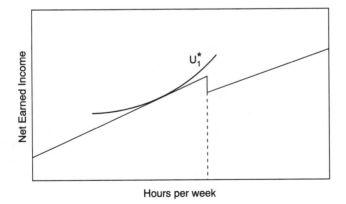

Fig. 7.4(a)

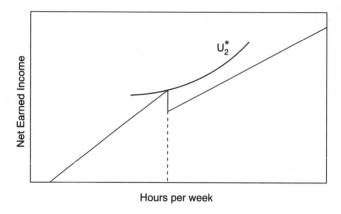

Fig. 7.4(b)

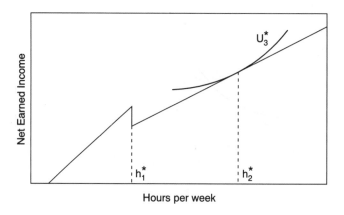

Fig. 7.4(c)

kink point of the budget set is such that, initially at least, the worker prefers to reduce her hours of work in order to remain on the LEL rather than work past it and suffer a discrete drop in net earned income (Figure 7.4b). This behaviour continues up to some critical wage level, at which point the maximum utility on the second segment of the budget constraint exceeds the utility at the LEL. The associated jump in desired hours (from h_1^* to h_2^* in Figure 7.4c) manifests itself as a point of discontinuity in the labour supply curve. The solution to the utility maximization problem, given a discontinuous budget constraint, requires a comparison of the maximum utility on each linear segment of the constraint (U_1^* and U_3^* in Figure 7.3) with the utility enjoyed at the point of discontinuity (U_2^*). The labour supply associated with the **maximum maximorum** of utilities is then taken to be the most preferred supply of hours.

An empirical application of the solution method just discussed requires a specification of the functional form for preferences. This specification need not be explicitly in the form of an indirect utility function. Given a labour supply specification, and provided that it satisfies the conditions for integrability, the indirect utility function can be derived.[2] Evidence suggests that, among different demographic groups, married women exhibit a greater tendency to reduce their hours of work as wage rates rise, so the choice of labour supply function should be sufficiently flexible so as not to preclude non-monotonicity in wages.[3] The intention of this chapter is to derive a modification of the likelihood specification for a series of labour supply models, so as to incorporate the behaviour of individuals around discontinuities in their budget sets.

7.3 LIKELIHOOD SPECIFICATIONS INCORPORATING UNEMPLOYED AND DISCOURAGED WORKERS

The labour supply equation to be used in this study takes the form introduced in Duncan (1990), such that

$$h_i^* = h(w_i, \mu_i, \xi_i; \beta) + u_i \tag{7.1}$$

where w_i represents the marginal wage, μ_i denotes the unearned income and ξ_i represents a vector of demographic characteristics. The disturbance term u_i is assumed normal, such that $u_i \sim N(0, \sigma_u^2)$, although specific tests for the normality of this and other disturbances will be provided. The density and distribution functions of u_i may then be denoted by $f(u_i) = \sigma_u^{-1} \varphi(u_i/\sigma_u)$ and $F(h_i^*) = \Phi(h_i^*)$ respectively.[4]

The simplest model to be estimated is the familiar Tobit specification. If h_i denotes the observed hours of work, this model may be defined as follows:

(L1)
$$h_i = \begin{cases} h_i^* & \text{for } h_i^* > 0 \\ 0 & \text{otherwise} \end{cases} \tag{7.2}$$

where the latent dependent variable h_i^* is described by equation (7.1). The probability of observing zero hours of work is

$$\Pr[h_i = 0] = \Pr[u_i \leqslant -h(w_i, \mu_i, \xi_i)]$$

$$= F[-h(w_i, \mu_i, \xi_i)] = 1 - F_i \tag{7.3}$$

where F_i represents the distribution function of h_i^* evaluated at $h(w_i, \mu_i, \xi_i)$. The log of the likelihood for model (L1) may then be written as

[2] The integrability conditions essentially require that the Slutsky matrix is symmetric and negative semi-definite. See, for example, Deaton and Muellbauer (1980).

[3] See Stern (1986) for an appraisal of a number of frequently used labour supply specifications.

[4] $\varphi(.)$ and $\Phi(.)$ represent the density and cumulative distribution functions of the standard normal distribution.

$$\ln(L_1) = \sum_0 \ln[\Pr(h_i^* \leq 0)] + \sum_+ \ln[\Pr(h_i^* > 0)f(h_i^* \mid h_i^* > 0)]$$

$$= \sum_0 \ln(1 - F_i) + \sum_+ \ln f(h_i^*) \tag{7.4}$$

The first term in (7.4) constitutes a summation over all those individuals who report zero hours of work, while the second term sums all those workers with positive work hours. The evaluation of (7.4) requires wage rates for all observations in the sample. Since those individuals who report zero hours of work generally do not report their market wage, a wage equation is required in order to predict wages for non-workers. A log-linear wage specification adopted is of the form

$$\ln(w_i) = z_i \cdot \alpha + v_i \tag{7.5}$$

where z_i represents a vector of individual characteristics and demand-side variables, α denotes the unknown parameter vector, and v_i represents the disturbance term, assumed normal such that $v_i \sim N(0, \sigma_v^2)^i$ and independent of u_i.

A major drawback with the Tobit model is that all those who report zero hours are considered not to want to work (desired hours $h_i^* \leq 0$). Mroz (1987) find such a specification unduly restrictive. As Blundell *et al.* (1988) point out, the Tobit model does not account for those individuals who want to work but are either discouraged from doing so through the presence of search costs, or who are unable to secure employment. An alternative model to the Tobit model (L1) can extend the analysis of labour supply to incorporate these groups in the likelihood specification, taking advantage of the sample separation information included in the FES. Specifically, the FES variable A202 separates observations in the sample according to whether the individual is non-participant in the labour market, is actively seeking work, or is currently in employment. Details of this and other variables are presented in Appendix A.

In order to model discouraged workers in the sample, one can define an indicator variable D_i to represent an individual's desire to participate in the labour market, such that

$$D_i = \begin{cases} 1 & \text{if } D_i^* > 0 \\ 0 & \text{otherwise} \end{cases}$$

with

$$D_i^* = x_i \cdot \gamma + \omega_i, \quad \omega_i \sim N(0, 1) \tag{7.6}$$

where x_i represents a vector of individual and regional characteristics, as well as economic variables. The probability of participation in the labour market is equivalent to the probability that $D_i^* > 0$. So, with positive search costs, there may exist a situation where an individual wants to work ($h_i^* > 0$) but chooses not to seek employment ($D_i^* \leq 0$). The probability of observing a discouraged worker is, therefore, $\Pr[h_i^* > 0, D_i^* \leq 0]$.

A second group not catered for in the simple Tobit formulation comprises those individuals who are looking for work, but cannot find employment, given their own demographic situation and in the face of the prevailing economic conditions. To model this group, a second reduced-form index function is defined to account explicitly for those individuals who are actively seeking employment, taking advantage of the sample separation information provided by the FES. For the subset of seekers and workers in the sample, we may define an employment probability index E_i such that

$$E_i = \begin{cases} 1 & \text{if } E_i^* > 0 \\ 0 & \text{otherwise} \end{cases}$$

where

$$E_i^* = y_i \cdot \delta + \varepsilon_i, \quad \varepsilon_i \sim N(0, 1) \tag{7.7}$$

Here, y_i represents a vector of regional, demographic and economic characteristics. Those individuals recorded as non-participant by the FES generally do not record their occupation or industry, whereas seekers tend to have an occupation to offer a potential employer. A more complete description of occupational characteristics in the employment equation can, therefore, be specified then for the full-sample participation index. With zero search costs, and for the subset of seekers and workers in the sample, the probability of observing a working woman is given by $\Pr[E_i^* > 0]$. There may then be a set of individuals for whom desired hours of work are positive $(h_i^* > 0)$, who are not discouraged from working $(D_i^* > 0)$, but who have not attained employment $(E_i^* \leq 0)$. The probability of observing an unemployed seeker will, therefore, be $\Pr[h_i^* > 0, D_i^* > 0, E_i^* \leq 0]$.

Incorporating both participation and employment indices into a general labour supply specification, we can write a more general model as

(L2)
$$h_i = \begin{cases} h_i^* & \text{for } h_i^* > 0, D_i^* > 0 \text{ and } E_i^* > 0 \\ 0 & \text{otherwise} \end{cases} \tag{7.8}$$

where h_i^*, D_i^* and E_i^* are as defined in equations (7.1), (7.6) and (7.7), respectively, and where the errors in these equations are mutually independent.

Considering first those individuals in the sample who do not seek work, the probability of observing a non-participant, P_{NP}, is defined to be

$$P_{\text{NP}} = \Pr[h_i^* \leq 0] + \Pr[h_i^* > 0, D_i^* \leq 0] \tag{7.9}$$

The first term in (7.9) identifies those women who have no desire to work. The second term defines those individuals who want to work $(h_i^* > 0)$, but for whom positive search costs discourage them from seeking work. The probability of observing an unemployed seeker in the sample, P_{US}, is defined as

$$P_{\text{US}} = \Pr[h_i^* > 0, D_i^* > 0, E_i^* \leq 0] \tag{7.10}$$

That is, the individual wants to work ($h_i^* > 0$), is not dissuaded from seeking work ($D_i^* > 0$), but cannot find employment ($E_i^* \leqslant 0$). Finally, the probability of observing a worker is

$$P_{\text{W}} = \Pr[h_i^* > 0,\ D_i^* > 0,\ E_i^* > 0] \tag{7.11}$$

Given probabilities (7.9)–(7.11), the sample likelihood for model (L2) under the assumption of mutual independence of equation errors becomes

$$\ln(L_2) = \sum_{\text{NP}} \ln[\Pr(h_i^* \leqslant 0) + \Pr(h_i^* > 0,\ D_i^* \leqslant 0)]$$

$$+ \sum_{\text{US}} \ln[\Pr(h_i^* > 0,\ D_i^* > 0,\ E_i^* \leqslant 0)]$$

$$+ \sum_{\text{W}} \ln[\Pr(h_i^* > 0,\ D_i^* > 0,\ E_i^* > 0) \cdot f(h_i^* \mid h_i^* > 0,\ D_i^* > 0,\ E_i^* > 0)]$$

$$= \sum_{\text{NP}} \ln[1 - F_i \cdot \Phi_i^{\text{D}}] + \sum_{\text{US}} \ln[F_i \cdot \Phi_i^{\text{D}} \cdot (1 - \Phi_i^{\text{E}})]$$

$$+ \sum_{\text{W}} \ln[\Phi_i^{\text{D}} \cdot \Phi_i^{\text{E}} \cdot f(h_i^*)] \tag{7.12}$$

The likelihood specifications presented above ignore the presence, in 1984, of a one-tier NI regime which taxed earned income at 9% above a weekly earnings limit of £34. There exists, therefore, a potential for bias in parameter estimates as a result of such an omission. To test this hypothesis, a method is derived for incorporating the NI regime into model sample likelihoods.

Under assumptions of linearity of budget constraint and normality of errors, the densities of h_i^* included in the likelihood specifications of models (L1) and (L2), given the general functional form for h_i^* as described in (7.1), could be written as

$$f(h_i^*) = \Pr[h_i^* > 0] \cdot f(h_i^* \mid h_i^* > 0)$$

$$= \sigma_u^{-1} \cdot \Phi\{[h_i^* - h_i(w, \mu)]/\sigma_u\} \tag{7.13}$$

Under a regime of NI, however, the density for h_i^* cannot be described so simply. Because of the discontinuity in the budget constraint, whether to use the marginal wage gross or net of NI in the evaluation of (7.13) is ambiguous. The solution, as set out in section 7.2, requires an evaluation of the maximum utilities enjoyed on each linear segment of the budget set. These are then compared with the utility gained by remaining on the LEL (i.e. at the 'kink point' of the budget set), in order to identify the correct marginal wage to use in the likelihood specification. With the NI regime included, $f(h_i^*)$ may be restated as

$$f(h_i^* = \Pr[h_i^* > 0] \cdot f(h_i^* \mid h_i^* > 0)$$

$$= \Pr[\text{below kink}] \cdot f[h_i^* \mid \text{below kink}) + \Pr[\text{at kink}]$$

$$+ \Pr[\text{above kink}] \cdot f(h_i^* \mid \text{above kink}) \tag{7.14}$$

Let U_i^{LEL} denote the utility at the kink point of the budget set, and let $V_i(w)$ represent the maximum utility enjoyed at some wage level w. Furthermore, with a NI rate of t_{NI}, let the wage rate net of NI be written as $w_{NI} = w(1 - t_{NI})$. In order to remain at the kink point of the budget set (i.e. earning at the LEL, desired hours must be such that earned income is at least equal to the LEL, and, at the same time, the utility enjoyed at the kink point must exceed the maximum utility available on the second budget segment. To reside above the kink point of the budget set, the maximum utility on the second budget segment must exceed that at the LEL. The density (7.14) may, thus, be written as

$$f(h_i^*) = \Pr[wh_i^* > 0, \ wh_i^* < LEL] \cdot f_i(h_i^* \mid \text{below kink})$$

$$+ \Pr[wh_i^* \geq LEL \text{ and } U_i^{LEL} \geq V_i(w_{NI})]$$

$$+ \Pr[wh_i^* \geq LEL \text{ and } U_i^{LEL} < V_i(w_{NI})] \cdot f_i(h_i^* \mid \text{above kink}) \qquad (7.15)$$

7.4 LABOUR SUPPLY SPECIFICATION AND MODEL ESTIMATES

The labour supply equation to be used for estimation is a semi-log quadratic function of the form

$$h_i(w, \mu, \xi) = \alpha \ln w_i + \beta (\ln w_i^2) + \gamma(\mu_i/w_i) + \delta + u_i \qquad (7.16)$$

where w_i is the marginal wage and μ_i denotes the non-earned or **virtual** income, defined to be the difference between the total expenditure and earned income. Examination of the wage derivative of (7.16) reveals that the specification is non-monotonic in w, the term in $\ln w^2$ serving to give an extra degree of wage responsiveness, while the virtual income derivative is negative for $\gamma < 0$. Given this restriction and for positive μ, the labour supply function is forward-sloping for lower wages, a feature which is necessary for the model to remain theory-consistent. Indeed, the indirect utility function is explicitly available (Appendix B), a feature which is important for the application of a Hausman utility-maximizing algorithm.

Demographic variables ξ enter into the hours equation through each of the parameters α to δ, using a system of **demographic translation** as suggested in Pollak and Wales (1981). The presence and age of children in the household would seem intuitively to be a major consideration in married womens' labour supply decisions, and to reflect this the following variables are included in the demographic specification. η_1, η_2, η_3 and η_4 represent the number of children in each of the age groups 0–2, 3–4, 5–10 and 11 upwards. The total number of children in the household is represented by η. Furthermore, age dummies d_1, d_2, d_3 and d_4 identify into which age category the youngest child falls. The parameter α is specified thus:

$$\alpha(\xi) = \alpha 0 + \alpha(ED) \cdot ED_i + \alpha(ED_2) \cdot ED_i^2 + \alpha(TK)\eta_i + \alpha(Srv) \cdot Serv_i$$

$$+ \alpha(SKM) \cdot SkMan_i + \alpha(Man) \cdot Manual_i \qquad (7.17)$$

where ED_i describes the level of education. The parameter β is defined as

$$\beta(\xi) = \beta(0) + \beta(K_1)\eta_{1i} + \beta(K_2)\eta_{2i} + \beta(K_3)\eta_{3i} + \beta(TK) \cdot \eta_i$$
$$+ \beta(A)AGE_i + \beta(MH)MHrs_i \qquad (7.18)$$

where AGE_i represents (female age 35) and $MHrs_i$ records the number of hours worked by the partner.

$$\gamma(\xi) = \gamma(0) + \gamma(d_1)d_{1i} + \gamma(d_2)d_{2i} + \gamma(d_3)d_{3i} + \gamma(A)AGE_i + \gamma(A_2)AGE_i^2$$
$$+ \gamma(ED) \cdot ED_i + \gamma(MH) \cdot MHrs_i + \gamma(MMan) \cdot MMan_i \qquad (7.19)$$

Here, $MMan_i$ is an occupational dummy to identify whether the partner is engaged in manual work. Finally, δ comprises the following demographic characteristics.

$$\delta(\xi) = \delta(0) + \delta(dk_1) \cdot d_{1i}\eta_{1i} + \delta(dk_2) \cdot d_{2i}\eta_{2i} + \delta(dk_3) \cdot d_{3i}\eta_{3i}$$
$$+ \delta(SKM) \cdot SkMan_i + \delta(Man) \cdot Manual_i \qquad (7.20)$$

For estimation, a sample of married women from the 1984 FES was taken, the characteristics of which are summarized in Appendix A. Dilnot and Kell (1987) note the fact that in a household where the husband is unemployed, social-security benefits fall sharply as the wife begins to earn any income. The marginal wage facing the married women in this circumstance is subject to wide fluctua-

Table 7.1   The participation probability index

Variable	Parameter	T-statistic
Constant	3.470	3.028
AGE	−0.306	−2.229
AGE^2	0.095	1.208
Number of children	0.322	2.980
Education	0.088	0.520
Education^2	−0.011	−0.685
d_1	−1.994	−8.233
$(d_2\eta_2)^{1/2}$	−1.267	−4.302
$(d_3\eta_3)^{1/2}$	−0.517	−2.803
Male services	0.146	0.604
Male manual	−0.060	−0.358
London	−0.122	−0.359
South	−0.200	−0.637
Vacancies/region	0.003	0.203
Redundancies/region	0.006	0.390
Male unemployment/occupation	−5.378	−4.742
Male unemployment/region	−0.054	−0.957
Female unemployment/region	0.480	0.298
Female unemployment/age	−6.315	−4.554
Observations		1889
Skewness (d.f. = 1)		6.882
Kurtosis (d.f. = 1)		0.181
Normality (d.f. = 2)		7.311

tions, and so, in order to avoid complications, the sample is drawn only from those households where the husband is in employment. The participation and employment probability indices contain a selection of the demographic variables presented above, together with a series of regional and economic characteristics. Since the employment index is estimated over the subsample of unemployed seekers and workers only, and since seekers generally report their occupation or industry, a more complete occupational specification for that index than for the participation index is possible. Finally, the sample likelihood for model (L2) relies on the assumption of independence between errors in the participation index and in the desired hours equation. To assess the implications of this assumption, the model is re-estimated under dependence, asserting that the two errors u_i and ω_i possess a bivariate normal distribution.

7.4.1 Results

Estimates of the labour supply equation (7.16) corresponding to each of the likelihood specifications (L1) and (L2), under the assumption of linear budget constraints, are given in Table 7.3. Probits were run to estimate the probability of participation in the labour market and the probability of finding employment. Tables 7.1 and 7.2 report estimates for these two indices, the latter probit being

Table 7.2   The employment probability index

Variable	Parameter	T-statistic
Constant	2.227	3.048
AGE	− 0.020	− 1.559
Number of children	0.282	2.714
Education	0.040	0.833
d_1	− 1.954	− 7.912
$(d_2\eta_2)^{1/2}$	− 1.149	− 3.631
$(d_3\eta_3)^{1/2}$	− 0.581	− 2.854
Male services	0.155	0.542
Male manual	− 0.151	− 0.871
Female services	− 0.259	− 1.034
Female skilled manual	− 0.452	− 1.167
Female semi-skilled	− 0.175	− 0.726
Female non-skilled	− 0.479	− 0.868
London	0.009	0.028
South	0.116	0.320
Vacancies/region	0.004	0.350
Redundancies/region	0.006	0.530
Female unemployment/occupation	− 0.961	− 0.473
Male unemployment/occupation	3.296	1.143
Female unemployment/age	− 5.893	− 3.904
Observations		1259
Skewness (d.f. = 1)		0.014
Kurtosis (d.f. = 1)		0.084
Normality (d.f. = 2)		0.173

run over the subsample of workers and only those seeking work. All estimates were obtained via algorithms written in the GAUSS programming language (Version 1.49b).

The parameter estimates for this index seem intuitively appealing. In line with other studies (for example, Kell and Wright, 1988), the probability of labour market participation is greater for younger women with a higher level of education. As expected, the presence of young children in the household reduces the likelihood of participation. Married women are more likely, however, to enter into the labour market the greater the number of children in the household. This

Table 7.3

	MODEL L1		MODEL L2	
	Parameter	*T-statistic*	*Parameter*	*T-statistic*
$\alpha(0)$	-53.762	-9.857	2.821	0.767
$\alpha(ED)$	3.223	3.428	-0.168	-0.249
$\alpha(ED_2)$	-0.309	-3.544	-0.041	-0.668
$\alpha(TK)$	-0.494	-0.318	-4.496	-4.638
$\alpha(Srv)$	-2.217	-1.399	-0.934	-1.012
$\alpha(SKM)$	-13.163	-2.228	-8.124	-2.863
$\alpha(Man)$	13.969	-4.101	2.634	1.297
$\beta(0)$	19.968	5.920	-1.924	-0.981
$\beta(K_1)$	1.538	0.969	-1.504	-1.312
$\beta(K_2)$	-3.067	-1.482	-4.049	-2.779
$\beta(K_3)$	-0.978	-0.848	-1.334	-2.300
$\beta(TK)$	0.308	0.201	2.693	3.286
$\beta(A)$	-1.536	-2.789	-1.100	-2.803
$\beta(MH)$	2.712	0.414	5.943	1.899
$\gamma(0)$	-0.393	-3.823	-0.268	-3.462
$\gamma(d_1)$	-0.033	-0.948	-0.013	-0.346
$\gamma(d_2)$	0.011	0.171	0.014	0.339
$\gamma(d_3)$	-0.127	-4.111	-0.051	-2.615
$\gamma(A)$	0.032	2.497	-0.004	-0.447
$\gamma(A_2)$	-0.064	-6.298	-0.007	-0.933
$\gamma(ED)$	-0.001	-0.178	-7.9×10^{-5}	-0.019
$\gamma(MH)$	0.497	2.084	0.411	2.216
$\gamma(MMan)$	-0.072	-2.618	-0.025	-1.432
$\delta(0)$	52.878	18.297	32.015	19.864
$\delta(dk_1)$	-27.216	-11.520	-4.572	-2.081
$\delta(dk_2)$	-16.330	-4.996	-3.968	-1.739
$\delta(dk_3)$	-3.078	-2.434	-1.450	-1.895
$\delta(SKM)$	8.755	1.626	7.148	2.791
$\delta(Man)$	5.151	1.855	-6.128	-3.848
σ	16.132	18.914	8.828	20.481
Observations	1889		1889	
Log likelihood	-5392.582		-4595.770	
Skewness (d.f. = 1)	4.739		0.063	
Kurtosis (d.f. = 2)	23.580		4.503	
Normality (d.f. = 2)	31.479		6.598	

is partly an 'income effect', reflecting the fact that larger families require a greater income to maintain a certain living standard.

A comparison of models L1 and L2, as displayed in Table 7.3 shows that a simple Tobit specification is decisively rejected in favour of the more general model. (Although a formal comparison of the two models is impossible given the non-nested nature of their likelihoods, examination of the standard errors reveals that the parameters of the more general model are almost universally better defined.) Non-normality of errors is generally taken as an indication of model misspecification, and score tests for normality following Bera *et al.* (1984) indicate a strong preference for model L2. This supports the view that the decision to participate in the labour market should be modelled as separate from the choice of hours of work. Inclusion of a separate participation equation in (L2) serves to lessen the importance of certain parameters in the labour supply equation. The education variables, although significant in L1, become insignificantly different from zero in L2. This suggests that the importance of education in labour supply is more in the probability of participation rather than the decision of how many hours per week to work. As expected, the presence of children in the household has a strong negative effect on the number of hours worked, with younger children placing a greater demand on non-work time. Noting that the number and ages of children have a strong negative effect through the β parameters, it seems that the inclusion of the term in $\ln w^2$ serves to heighten the sensitivity of the labour supply equation to family size. From an examination of the occupational variables, skilled manual workers seem to display maximum sensitivity to marginal wages in their hours of work decisions.

Model L2 was estimated on the basis of independence between errors in the participation and desired-hours equations. To investigate whether this is a valid assumption, the model was re-estimated under dependence. The results of this re-estimation were reassuring in two respects. Firstly, the estimated correlation of 0.438 is well-defined and positive, in accord with expectations. Secondly, although the correlation is quite strong, no significant change in the signs or magnitudes of the parameter estimates were apparent. In fact, the labour supply elasticities for model L2 prove to be virtually identical with or without dependence (Table 7.4). In what follows, therefore, the independence assumption is

Table 7.4 A comparison of elasticities with and without dependence

MODEL L2	Independence	Dependence
Mean	0.200	0.192
M25	− 0.012	− 0.010
M50	0.091	0.086
M75	0.270	0.269
Std deviation	0.806	0.781
Prop(+)	0.733	0.728
Failures	0.275	0.293
Total	1173	1173

maintained in the belief that parameter estimates remain consistent. As an aid to understanding the effects of demographics on hours of work, Table 7.5 categorizes wage elasticities separated according to a series of demographic characteristics. The tables evaluate means, medians ($M50$), 25- and 75-percentile points ($M25$, $M75$), the proportion of positive elasticities (Prop +) and the proportion of concavity failures (Failures) associated with each separation.

Skilled manual workers demonstrate the greatest willingness to reduce hours of work as wages rise, only 6.1% of the subsample having positive elasticities. As expected, families with large numbers of children have elasticities which are predominantly large in magnitude and negative in sign. The mean elasticity for families without children is smaller than for larger families. The magnitudes of elasticities for the former group, however, are significantly smaller and display little variation. The implication of these findings, therefore, is that couples without children are more at liberty to take on a full working week than are larger families.[5] Surprisingly, children between the ages of two and four seem to have a greater negative effect on hours elasticities than do younger children. One possible explanation is that a very young child is most likely to persuade the parent not to work at all, rather than to reduce hours of work. (Examination of the distribution of female hours against the child age shows that 72.2% of married women with a child aged less than two years do not work.) Those married women who remain at work may have made child care arrangements in order that they may continue with their normal working week. Unfortunately, further investigation of this claim through the analysis of household expenditure on child care is made difficult through constraints on the available data.

7.5 LABOUR SUPPLY ESTIMATES TAKING ACCOUNT OF BUDGET CONSTRAINT DISCONTINUITY

To examine the possibility of bias in the parameter estimates of the models presented above, the algorithm set out in section 7.3 is applied to the re-estimation of model L2 taking account of the 1984 NI regime.[6] This system of direct taxation levied a Ni rate of 9% on all earned income above a LEL of £34.00 per week. Table 7.5 presents the results of this re-estimation, on the assumption that an individual grossing an income within a range of £4.00 around the LEL is deemed to reside at the kink point of their budget set. Using this definition, a total of 53 workers occupy the kink point of their budget constraint, representing 4.51% of the sample of workers. As Table 7.5 shows, the parameter estimates of model L2 undergo a marked change once the discontinuity of the NI regime has been accounted for, reinforcing the contention that model specifications which do not recognize bunching at discontinuities in workers' budget sets can produce

---

[5] The cross tabulation of female hours versus number of children presented in Appendix A bears out this result.
[6] A derivation of the modified sample likelihood corresponding to functional form [(equation 7.1)] is supplied in Appendix B.

significantly biased estimates. Of the demographic variables included in the desired-hours equation, those pertaining to family size seem to change most dramatically, although no explanation is offered for this result.

In order to relate these changes more directly to the modelled labour supply behaviour of all the married women in the sample, Table 7.6 compares the wage elasticities of workers implied by the two estimated equations in Table 7.5. The most important result here is the much increased proportion of negative hours elasticities generated by the labour supply model which takes account of NICs, yielding as a consequence a much smaller mean elasticity.

As an example of the striking impact of a modified estimation procedure on the labour supply behaviour of married women, consider the hours of work of a 25-year-old woman with no children. Having left school at 16, both herself and her partner are engaged in manual work. Given a continuous labour supply function, the desired-hours schedule may be generated simply by feeding these demographic characteristics into the estimated equation for different wage levels. However, in the presence of the 1984 NI regime, a more complicated derivation is required. At a given wage, if desired hours imply gross weekly earnings of

Table 7.5 Wage elasticities by children and age of youngest child

Age	<20	20–30	30–40	40–50	50+
Mean	0.235	0.205	0.203	0.224	0.145
M25	0.053	0.013	−0.025	0.016	−0.090
M50	0.116	0.084	0.101	0.119	0.047
M75	0.272	0.168	0.324	0.303	0.305
Std deviation	0.319	1.373	0.524	0.400	0.382
Prop(+)	0.875	0.775	0.724	0.778	0.596
Failures	0.250	0.206	0.251	0.354	0.365
Total	8	306	438	243	178
No. kids	*0*	*1*	*2*	*3*	*4+*
Mean	0.094	0.224	0.343	0.163	0.013
M25	−0.030	0.017	0.012	−0.019	−0.220
M50	0.063	0.116	0.181	0.111	−0.037
M75	0.143	0.301	0.427	0.312	0.228
Std deviation	0.244	0.446	1.340	0.416	0.354
Prop(+)	0.686	0.787	0.772	0.727	0.389
Failures	0.301	0.246	0.228	0.330	0.778
Total	488	211	368	88	18
Youngest	*0–2*	*2–4*	*4–11*	*11–18*	*No kids*
Mean	0.415	−0.150	0.334	0.291	0.094
M25	−0.025	−0.346	0.024	0.055	−0.030
M50	0.083	−0.169	0.182	0.164	0.063
M75	0.269	0.056	0.446	0.379	0.143
Std deviation	2.616	0.523	0.521	0.430	0.244
Prop(+)	0.735	0.266	0.799	0.897	0.686
Failures	0.301	0.456	0.207	0.252	0.301
Total	83	79	309	214	488

Table 7.6 A comparison of estimates of L2 with and without NI

	With NI discontinuity		Without NI		Percentage change
	Parameter	T-statistic	Parameter	T-statistic	
$\alpha(0)$	− 1.842	− 0.798	2.821	0.767	− 165.29
$\alpha(ED)$	0.169	0.265	− 0.168	− 0.249	− 200.66
$\alpha(ED_2)$	− 0.065	− 1.098	− 0.041	− 0.668	58.37
$\alpha(TK)$	− 3.413	− 6.301*	− 4.496	− 4.638*	− 24.09
$\alpha(Srv)$	− 1.422	− 1.483	− 0.934	− 1.012	52.16
$\alpha(SKM)$	− 10.096	− 3.771*	− 8.124	− 2.863*	24.28
$\alpha(Man)$	2.870	1.708	2.634	1.297	8.96
$\beta(0)$	− 1.225	− 0.827	− 1.924	− 0.981	− 36.34
$\beta(K_1)$	− 0.170	− 0.175	− 1.504	− 1.312	− 88.68
$\beta(K_2)$	− 2.968	− 2.093*	− 4.049	− 2.779*	− 26.71
$\beta(K_3)$	− 1.030	− 2.006*	− 1.334	− 2.300*	− 22.85
$\beta(TK)$	1.794	3.457*	2.693	3.286*	− 33.38
$\beta(A)$	− 0.956	− 2.362*	− 1.100	− 2.803*	− 13.06
$\beta(MH)$	5.839	1.677	5.943	1.899	− 1.74
$\gamma(0)$	− 0.279	− 3.899*	− 0.268	− 3.462*	4.34
$\gamma(d_1)$	0.008	0.305	− 0.013	− 0.346	− 159.62
$\gamma(d_2)$	0.061	2.021*	0.014	0.339	348.80
$\gamma(d_3)$	− 0.044	− 3.829*	− 0.051	− 2.615*	− 13.91
$\gamma(A)$	0.006	0.865	− 0.004	− 0.447	− 260.60
$\gamma(A_2)$	− 0.007	− 1.264	− 0.007	− 0.933	− 1.65
$\gamma(ED)$	0.000	0.094	-7.90×10^{-5}	− 0.019	− 419.20
$\gamma(MH)$	0.409	2.366*	0.411	2.216*	− 0.60
$\gamma(MMan)$	− 0.029	− 2.041*	− 0.025	− 1.432	15.88
$\delta(0)$	35.588	34.352*	32.015	19.864*	11.16
$\delta(dk_1)$	− 6.751	− 4.206*	− 4.572	− 2.081*	47.67
$\delta(dk_2)$	− 6.718	− 3.387*	− 3.968	− 1.739	69.30
$\delta(dk_3)$	− 1.966	− 3.526*	− 1.450	− 1.895	35.62
$\delta(SKM)$	7.735	3.436*	7.148	2.791*	8.21
$\delta(Man)$	− 6.602	− 5.976*	− 6.128	− 3.848*	7.74
σ	8.764	20.946*	8.828	20.481*	− 0.72
Observations	1889		1889		
Log likelihood	− 4552.525		− 4595.770		

* Significant at 5% level.

Table 7.7 A comparison of wage elasticities for model
L2 with and without NI

MODEL L2	With NI	Without NI
Mean	0.011	0.200
M25	− 0.134	− 0.012
M50	− 0.019	0.091
M75	0.112	0.270
Std deviation	0.732	0.806
Prop(+)	0.450	0.733
Failures	0.359	0.273
Total	1173	1173

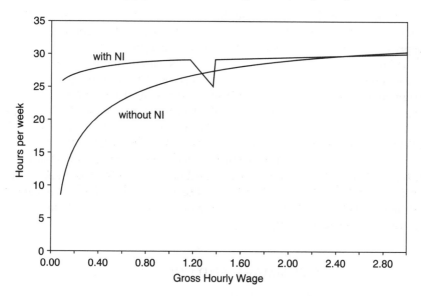

Fig. 7.5 A comparison of hours schedules.

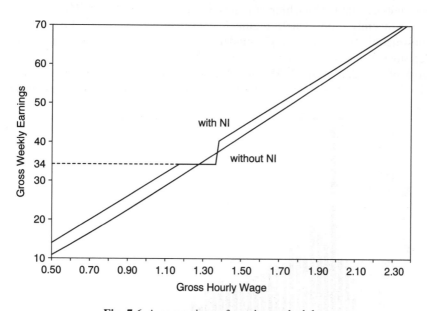

Fig. 7.6 A comparison of earnings schedules.

more than £34.00, then a comparison of the utility at £34.00 per week with the maximum utility enjoyed on the second segment of the budget constraint will reveal whether the woman works past the kink point of her budget set. Figures 7.5 and 7.6 describe the modelled hours and gross-earnings schedules of a woman with the demographic features described above, and expose a consistent under-estimation of the hours of work and gross weekly income by a continuous labour supply estimated on data which display bunching at the NI margin.

The implication of these results, at least in the case of married women, is that a continuous desired-hours function estimated on data with grouping at the NI margin masks a significant degree of backward-bending labour supply behaviour. Bearing this in mind, it is quite possible than simulations of the labour supply behaviour of married women based on continuous desired hours schedules may underestimate the efficiency loss associated with a NI regime. By predicting desired hours using the more general NI model, incorporating a comparison of maximum utilities on different linear segments of the budget constraint, a fitted earnings distribution may be generated. The success with which this earnings distribution (Figure 7.7) reproduces the features of the actual distribution (Figure 7.2) can be seen quite clearly.

7.6 SUMMARY AND CONCLUSIONS

The hypothesis on which this chapter is based is that a labour supply model which does not account for bunching at points of the budget set rendered discontinuous by the incumbent tax–benefit regime may display bias. Section 7.3 describes the construction of a labour supply model designed to describe the hours of work decisions of married women in a fairly complete fashion, leaning heavily on the work of Blundell *et al.* (1988). An algorithm is then derived to modify sample likelihoods in order to account for a one-tier NI regime. Estimates using a

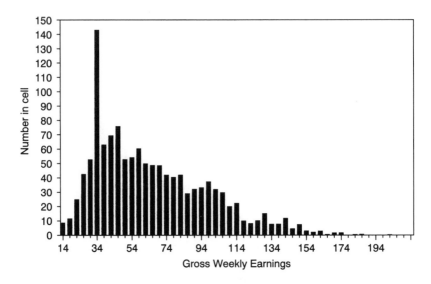

Fig. 7.7 Married women: predicted earnings distribution.

semi-log quadratic labour supply specification are presented in section 7.4, using a sample of married women from the 1984 FES. Finally, a re-estimation of the model using the modified sample likelihood is compared with previous estimates to examine the extent of possible parameter bias.

The results presented here strongly support the contention that a continuous labour supply model estimated on data grouped at the NI margin produces biased parameter estimates. A comparison of the predicted hours elasticities reveals a significantly higher degree of backward-bending labour supply behaviour when the more general NI model is used – a feature which has important implications for the assessment of efficiency losses associated with a particular tax–benefit regime. It is certainly true that the labour supply specification ignores the presence of a large number of lump-sum and means-tested social-security benefits. As has been suggested, however, the system of NI is perceived by the worker (and the employer) as an unambiguous, clearly understood distortion. Although means-tested benefits may reimburse to some extent the loss in net earned income, this additional payment will certainly not cover in full the NIC. Reference to the distribution of earnings in 1984 supports the view that the distortion is not diluted by means-tested benefits. Analyses of labour supply behaviour, and investigations into the reform of direct taxation should, therefore, recognize the sensitivity of certain demographic groups to the NI regime, and estimation procedures designed to account for bunching at NI margins should be carefully considered.

APPENDIX A

A sample of data from the 1984 FES was drawn according to the following criteria:

1. Male partner employed.
2. Retired and self-employed excluded.
3. Female hours < 60; male hours < 60
4. Female wage < £8.00 per hour; Male wage < £8.00 per hour.
5. Age at departure from full-time education > 12 and < 25

According to these selection criteria, a sample of 1889 was generated.

Cross-tabulation of female hours versus number of children

| No. kids | *Female hours* | | | | | | |
	0	*1–10*	*11–20*	*21–30*	*31–40*	*41 +*	*Total*
0	118	13	74	59	345	11	620
1	183	34	74	43	80	1	415
2	256	86	154	67	67	3	633
3	82	24	36	14	17	2	175
4 +	28	3	7	3	3	2	46
Total	667	160	345	186	512	19	1889

Cross-tabulation of female hours versus age of youngest child

	Female hours						
Youngest	*0*	*1–10*	*11–20*	*21–30*	*31–40*	*41 +*	*Total*
0–2	267	31	31	12	29	—	370
2–4	109	21	40	8	13	1	192
4–11	121	71	134	55	55	3	439
11–18	52	24	66	52	70	4	268
No Kids	118	13	74	59	345	11	620
Total	667	160	345	186	512	19	1889

Cross-tabulation of female hours versus occupation

	Female hours						
Occupation	*0*	*1–10*	*11–20*	*21–30*	*31–40*	*41 +*	*Total*
Prof/tech	5	7	33	18	67	4	134
Admin/man	2	1	1	2	43	3	52
Teachers	2	15	17	23	18	2	77
Clerical	15	25	75	50	236	3	404
Shop asst.	3	8	52	21	15	—	99
Man/skill	10	5	12	12	38	2	79
Man/semi	9	56	91	51	87	4	298
Man/non sk.	1	43	64	9	8	1	126
Unoccupied	620	—	—	—	—	—	620
Total	667	160	345	186	512	19	1889

Separating the data set into workers, unemployed seekers and non-participants, the following descriptive statistics are obtained

Working women; *observations*: 1173

Variable	*Mean*	*Standard deviation*	*Minimum*	*Maximum*
Hours	25.70	11.78	1.00	55.00
Income	70.26	48.08	0.67	283.63
Other income	97.82	51.96	20.30	496.03
Children aged 0–2	0.08	0.28	0.00	2.00
Children aged 2–4	0.09	0.29	0.00	2.00
Children aged 5–11	0.47	0.75	0.00	4.00
Children aged 11–18	0.46	0.77	0.00	4.00
Age	36.95	10.02	18.00	59.00
Age left education	16.19	1.97	13.00	24.00
Male hours	39.21	4.22	4.00	58.00
Male wage	4.09	1.34	0.40	7.96

APPENDIX B

In order to evaluate the probabilities in equation (7.15), the specific functional form and distribution for the indirect utility $V(w)$ is required. With the particular

Unemployed seeking women; observations: 86

Variable	Mean	Standard deviation	Minimum	Maximum
Other income	109.43	60.67	31.85	460.97
Children aged 0–2	0.51	0.55	0.00	2.00
Children aged 2–4	0.15	0.39	0.00	2.00
Children aged 5–11	0.34	0.66	0.00	2.00
Children aged 11–18	0.17	0.51	0.00	3.00
Age	31.59	9.44	20.00	58.00
Age left education	16.21	1.80	14.00	23.00
Male hours	39.34	3.59	27.00	52.00
Male wage	4.11	1.47	1.75	7.88

Non-participating women; observations: 630

Variable	Mean	Standard deviation	Minimum	Maximum
Other income	82.22	41.60	20.21	433.16
Children aged 0–2	0.43	0.58	0.00	2.00
Children aged 2–4	0.30	0.49	0.00	3.00
Children aged 5–11	0.58	0.77	0.00	4.00
Children aged 11–18	0.29	0.62	0.00	3.00
Age	35.23	10.27	18.00	59.00
Age left education	15.98	1.71	13.00	24.00
Male hours	39.51	4.94	2.00	58.00
Male wage	4.24	1.47	1.30	7.95

specification for $h_i^*(w, \mu)$ as given in equation (7.16), application of Roy's identity yields the indirect utility function $V_i(w)$ as

$$V_i(w) = \frac{w^{1+\gamma}}{1+\gamma} [w^{-1}\mu(1 + \gamma + \beta \ln w)^2 + B \ln w + \Gamma) \qquad (7\text{B}.1)$$

where

$$B = \alpha - 2\beta/(1 + \gamma)$$

and

$$\Gamma = \delta - \alpha/(1 + \gamma) + 2\beta/(1 + \gamma)^2$$

Given that the additive error in equation (7.16) is normal, $V_i(w)$ may be decomposed into $V_i(w) = V_i^*(w) + u_i^*$, from which the probabilities in equation (7.14) can be written as

$$\Pr[\text{below kink}] = \Pr[u_i > -h_i(w, \mu), \; u_i < (LEL/w) - h_i(w, \mu)]$$

$$= \Phi\left(\frac{LEL}{\sigma_u w_i} - \frac{h_i(w, \mu)}{\sigma_u}\right) - \Phi\left(\frac{-h_i(w, \mu)}{\sigma_u}\right) \qquad (7\text{B}.2)$$

Estimated wage equation

Variable	Estimate	Standard error	T-statistic
Constant	3.0946	0.1854	16.6872
Age	0.0059	0.0015	3.8961
Age^2	−0.0005	0.0001	−4.7249
Number of children	−0.0818	0.0144	−5.6985
Male wage	0.0117	0.0074	1.5778
Education	0.0615	0.0204	3.0075
Education^2	−0.0026	0.0020	−1.3015
d_1	0.2046	0.1643	1.2456
d_2	0.0904	0.0815	1.1094
d_3	−0.0399	0.0416	−0.9588
η_1	−0.1554	0.1467	−1.0594
η_2	−0.0919	0.0699	−1.3135
η_3	0.0167	0.0249	0.6693
Quarter 2	0.0121	0.0254	0.4748
Quarter 3	0.0234	0.0248	0.9403
Quarter 4	0.0559	0.0276	2.0215
Male service occupation	−0.0190	0.0353	−0.5388
Male manual occupation	0.0032	0.0253	0.1264
Female service occupation	−0.3218	0.0292	−11.0344
Female skilled manual	−0.3228	0.0484	−6.6745
Female manual occupation	−0.4816	0.0313	−15.3770
North	0.0239	0.0774	0.3092
Yorkshire	−0.0531	0.0429	−1.2380
London	0.2614	0.0524	4.9881
South	0.0213	0.0664	0.3208
North–West	0.0418	0.0658	0.6348
Female unemployment/region	0.0683	0.0477	1.4315
Female unemployment/age	0.0143	0.1686	0.0847
Male unemp/occupation	0.1660	0.2141	0.7753
Male unemployment/region	−0.0291	0.0214	−1.3555
Vacancies/region	0.0008	0.0032	0.2512
Redundancies/region	0.0013	0.0033	0.3880

Diagnostics

Adj. R^2: 0.401   Dep. Var. Mean: 3.176   SE of Reg'n: 0.310
SSR: 110.25   Skewness: −0.551   Kurtosis: 2.946

$$\Pr[\text{at kink}] = \Pr[u_i \geqslant (LEL/w) - h_i(w, \mu),\ u_i \leqslant U_i^{\text{LEL}} - V_i^*(w_{\text{NI}})]$$

$$= \Phi\left(\sigma_{u^*}^{-1} \cdot [U_i^{\text{LEL}} - V_i^*(w_{\text{NI}})]\right) - \Phi\left(\frac{LEL}{\sigma_u w_i} - \frac{h_i(w, \mu)}{\sigma_u}\right) \quad (7\text{B}.3)$$

$$\Pr[\text{above kink}] = \Pr[u_i \geqslant (LEL/w) - h_i(w, \mu),\ u_i^* > U_i^{\text{LEL}} - V_i^*(w_{\text{NI}})]$$

$$= \Phi\left(\sigma_{u^*}^{-1} \cdot [V_i^*(w_{\text{NI}}) - U_i^{\text{LEL}}]\right) - \Phi\left(\frac{LEL}{\sigma_u w_i} - \frac{h_i(w, \mu)}{\sigma_u}\right) \quad (7\text{B}.4)$$

The final step required in order to completely specify the modified density (7.3) is to derive the densities of h_i^* conditional on residing below or above the LEL.

$$f(h_i^* \mid h_i^* \text{ below kink}) = \sigma_u^{-1} \cdot \emptyset\left(\frac{h_i - h_i^*(w, \mu)}{\sigma_u}\right) \cdot \frac{1}{\Pr[\text{below kink}]}$$

and

$$f(h_i^* \mid h_i^* \text{ above kink}) = \sigma_u^{-1} \cdot \emptyset\left(\frac{h_i - h_i^*(w_{\text{NI}}, \mu)}{\sigma_u}\right) \cdot \frac{1}{\Pr[\text{above kink}]}$$

ACKNOWLEDGEMENTS

I thank Richard Blundell, Andrew Dilnot, John Hutton, Peter Lambert and participants at the Applied Econometrics Association Meeting, Rome, 1989, for useful comments. Financial support from the ESRC under project B00222009 at IFS is gratefully acknowledged. We are also grateful to the Department of Employment for providing the FES data used in this study. All errors and opinions are the sole responsibility of the author.

REFERENCES

Bera, A. K., Jarque, C. M. and Lee, L-F. (1984) Testing the Normality Assumption in Limited Dependent Variable Models. *International Economic Review*, **25**, 563–78.

Blundell, R. W., Ham, J. and Meghir, C. (1988) Unemployment, Discouraged Workers and Female Labour Supply, Discussion Paper No.88–19, University College, London.

Blundell, R. W., Duncan, A. S. and Meghir, C. (1991) *Endogeneity, Selectivity and Taxes in Female Labour Supply Models.* Institute for Fiscal Studies, London.

Deaton, A. and Muellbauer, J. (1980) *Economics and Consumer Behaviour.* Cambridge University Press, Cambridge.

Dilnot, A. and Kell, M. (1987) Male Unemployment and Female Labour Supply. *Fiscal Studies*, **8**, 1–17.

Dilnot, A. and Webb, S. (1988) Reforming National Insurance Contributions. *Fiscal Studies*, **9**, 1–24.

Duncan, A. S. (1990), The Dependence of Labour Supply Behaviour on Family Composition – The Case of the Single Parent, in *Dependency To Enterprise* (eds J. Hutton *et al.*), Routledge.

Hausman, J. A. (1980) The Effects of Wages, Taxes and Fixed Costs on Womens' Labour Force Participation. *Journal of Public Economics*, **14**, 161–194.

Hausman, J. A. (1985) The Econometrics of Nonlinear Budget Sets. *Econometrica*, **53**, 1255–1282.

Kell, M. and Wright, J. (1988), Benefits and the Labour Supply of Women married to Unemployed Men, IFS Working Paper No. 88/12, Institute for Fiscal Studies, London.

Mroz, T. A. (1987) The Sensitivity of an Empirical Model of Married Women's Hours of Work to Economic and Statistical Assumptions. *Econometrica*, **55**, 765–800.

Pollak, R. A. and Wales, T. J. (1981) Demographic Variables in Demand Analysis. *Econometrica*, **49**, 1533–1554.

Stern, N. H. (1986) On the Specification of Labour Supply Functions, in *Unemployment, Search and Labour Supply* (eds R. W. Blundell and I. Walker), Cambridge University Press. Cambridge.

8

Income taxation and the supply of labour in West Germany: A microeconometric analysis with special reference to the West German Income Tax Reforms 1986–1990

Helmut Kaiser, Ulrich van Essen
and P. Bernd Spahn

8.1 INTRODUCTION

Many recent attempts to reform income taxes in OECD countries have stressed the importance of allocative aspects related to the tax system. In particular, the reforms aimed at mitigating possible distortive effects on saving decisions and on labour supply. It is well-understood that income taxes drive a wedge between the prices of leisure and consumption, and that this may reduce the supply of labour whenever the substitution effect dominates the income effect. It is less well understood as to what extent such an effect is relevant for a tax system in a given historical context. Only empirical research may help to shed some light on this question.

This chapter tries to contribute to this issue in the light of the West German experience with a major revision of the tax law in recent times.[1] The analysis is based on microeconomic data for representative households that are evaluated applying the Frankfurt income tax simulation (FITS) model for the calculation of marginal tax rates. This model has been used earlier to study distributional aspects of tax reforms.[2] It incorporates the full set of rules governing the German income tax system and, by applying these rules to a representative sample of

[1] The German income tax code was revised in three major steps 1986–90.
[2] See van Essen et al. (1988, 1990a, b, 1993), Kaiser et al. (1989, 1991), Kaiser and Spahn (1991) and Spahn et al. (1990).

households, it allows one to assess, in any detail, the effect of changes of the tax code on the distribution of income. Furthermore, it is capable of monitoring certain behavioural reactions of taxpayers; hence, it allows one to trace back allocative effects of the German income tax reform.

The plan of the chapter is as follows. The first part is concerned with some methodological remarks about the analysis of tax systems and their effects on labour supply. We begin with the concept of measurement of the welfare effects of tax systems (section 8.2) and present our labour supply model, which is used to capture behavioural responses of the taxpayers (section 8.3). Moreover, we present the FITS model (section 8.4) and the data on which it is based (section 8.5). The second part of the chapter focuses on the empirical results of our study for the labour supply function (section 8.6) and for the induced welfare effects of the recent tax reforms in West Germany (section 8.7). Finally, the main findings and conclusions are summarized (section 8.8).

8.2 THE MEASUREMENT OF ECONOMIC WELFARE

Suppose that we perceive a change in prices and income due to a tax reform. In order to obtain an indicator for the economic welfare effects of the considered reform, we could ask what variation in income will generate the same improvement of well-being but on the basis of the initial set of prices?

This variation in income is defined as the equivalent variation (*EV*). *EV* is, hence, the amount of money that has to be given to (or taken away from) the taxpayer in order to leave him in his original utility position – assuming the prevalence of pre-reform prices. This compensation payment is also sometimes called the equivalent gain ($EV > 0$) or loss ($EV < 0$).[3] The whole income that a household would have to obtain in order to achieve his post-tax-reform level of utility with pre-reform prices, i.e. the initial income and the *EV*, is defined as the equivalent income (y_E).

Using an indirect utility function, $v(p, y)$, we obtain y_E and *EV* implicitly by

$$v(p_0, y_E) = v(p_0, y_0 + EV) = v(p_1, y_1) \tag{8.1}$$

where p_0 and y_0 are the vectors of prices and income, respectively, for a (pre-reform) basis period, and p_1 and y_1 are the vectors of prices and income after the considered reform. Given a vector of reference prices p_0, *EV* is fully determined by $v(p, y)$, which is essentially a monotonic transformation of the expenditure function. This is why the measure is sometimes simply called a 'money metric utility'.[4] As a monotonic transformation of the underlying utility function, *EV* can be used without restrictions in evaluating the changes in welfare induced by tax policy.

[3] *EV* and equivalent gain or loss are used synonymously in this chapter. Our definition of *EV* is akin to that of McKenzie (1983), Alheim and Rose (1984) and Ebert (1987).

[4] See Samuelson (1974)

In order to calculate *EV* from equation (8.1), the indirect utility function has to be inverted, which leads to the equivalent income function, y_E, and the expenditure function, e:

$$y_E = e(p_0, v_1) \tag{8.2}$$

Thus, *EV* is obtained by

$$EV = e(p_0, v_1) - e(p_0, v_0) = y_E - y_0 \tag{8.3}$$

After definition of the tax reform and its simulation, the equivalent gains and losses for private households can be calculated by equation (8.3). The welfare effects of the reform are then shown by the distribution of the *EV* in the sample and the efficiency gains can be insulated by measuring the excess burden of a tax measure.[5] Hereby, the excess burden represents the difference between the welfare loss which would prevail if taxes could be collected without affecting economic decisions, and the total loss of welfare associated with taxation – including the effect of negative incentives on economic decisions.

Since the excess burden is directly associated with the substitution effect of a tax change, the total change in income has to be corrected for by *EV* and, possibly – in the case of a tax change that is non-neutral in tax revenues – by the difference in tax yields.[6] The change in excess burden is given by

$$\Delta EB = \sum_h (y_1^h - y_0^h) - \sum_h EV^h - (t_1 - t_0) \tag{8.4}$$

It becomes clear that ΔEB as a measure of (welfare) gains and losses may be very different from pure cash gains and losses (*CG*). The latter are simply represented by the difference in disposable income before and after the tax reform; hence,

$$CG = \bar{y}_1 - y_0 \tag{8.5}$$

where $\bar{y}_1$ is an estimation for household income after the reform, assuming unchanged economic behaviour of the taxpayer.

The difference between cash gain and welfare gain is depicted in Figure 8.1. Before the tax reform, the individual is in its utility-maximizing equilibrium point A, where the slope of the indifference curve, u_0, is identical to the slope of the budget constraint, $y_0 m_0$, before the reform. A reduction of tax rates leads to the post-reform budget constraint, $y_1 m_1$. In the case described here, the new equilibrium point is B, where $y_1 m_1$ is tangent to u_1. The total effect, A → B, is decomposed in the substitution effect, A → C, and the income effect, C → B. For leisure being a normal good – as in our case – both effects are working in opposite directions. The total effect hinges on the strength (or dominance) of one of the effects. In our case, the substitution effect is dominating the income effect.

---

[5] See King (1983, p. 193).
[6] See King (1983, p. 192).

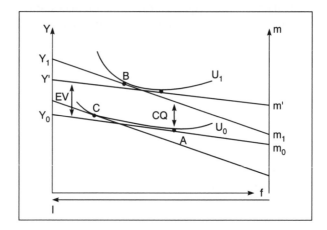

Fig. 8.1   Equivalent variation and cash gain for a change in net wages.

Cash gains disregard behavioural changes totally. In Figure 8.1 they are represented by the vertical distance between $y_0 m_0$ and $y_1 m_1$ above point A. This distance indicates the mere cash gain due to a reduction of the tax rate. On the other hand, *EV* is the income that has to be given to the individual in order to enable him to maintain its utility level after reform (u_1) under the old price regime. The compensation payment is the vertical distance between the parallel $y' m'$ and $y_0 m_0$.

As can be seen from Figure 8.1, the equivalent gain exceeds the cash gain in this case. This is not necessarily true under all circumstances. It hinges on the curvature of the indifference schedule, and on the sign and intensity of the (compound) substitution and income effects. In particular, the cash gain can exceed the welfare gain although the tax change might induce an increase in labour supply.

8.3 THE LABOUR SUPPLY MODEL: THEORY AND ESTIMATION

8.3.1 The theoretical model

It should be clear from the analysis that empirical estimates of equivalent gains and losses of a tax reform require not only a fully fledged simulation model that measures the money effects of a change in tax law, but also the estimation of labour supply behaviour in response to changes in the marginal net wage. Such estimates can be obtained using a second-generation labour supply model that is based on the utility-maximization approach under an explicit budget constraint.[7]

---

[7] The distinction between first- and second-generation models was made by Killingsworth (1983). First-generation models are based on *ad hoc* assumptions not accounting for an explicit utility-maximizing framework. In addition, they do not take into account possible sample selection biases and the tax system.

Hereby, we consider the progressivity of the West German income tax system by linearizing the budget constraint as suggested – among others – by Hall (1973) and Hausman (1981, 1983, 1985). This procedure allows a (local) linear approximation of the budget restriction using the marginal net wage

$$w = (1 - t')w_b \tag{8.6}$$

and a tax-corrected net non-labour income

$$m = m_b - (t - t'w_b l) \tag{8.7}$$

where t', w_b, m_b, t and l stand for the marginal tax rate, the gross wage rate, the gross non-labour income, the tax liability and the supply of labour, respectively.[8]

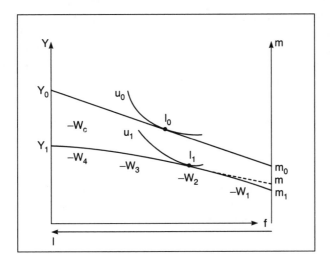

Fig. 8.2   Linearization of the budget constraint under a progressive tax schedule.

The approach is illustrated in Figure 8.2. In this figure, two indifference curves, u_0 and u_1, are plotted as well as the two budget restrictions with and without taxes. For the no-tax case, the budget constraint $y_0 m_b$ will hold. Considering a first derivative of $-w_0$ and the intercept m_b; we obtain an equilibrium point for a positive labour supply in l_0. For progressive income taxation, the constraint $y_1 m_1$ is non-linear (four segments are shown in Figure 8.2, with tangents $-w_1$, $-w_2$, $-w_3$ and $-w_4$). A tax reform that shifts the new equilibrium point for labour supply to the second segment will generate a corrected non-labour income m as a positional parameter, with the marginal wage rate $-w_2$ as a slope parameter. The reduction of the marginal wage rate resulting from a tax reform leads, in this case, to a reduction of labour supply.

[8] For details of this technique, see Killingsworth (1983, p. 331ff).

If the marginal net wage is smaller than the reservation wage, w_{ri} for the individual – which is defined as the marginal rate of substitution between leisure and consumption at which no labour is supplied – the individual does not supply labour at all at the going wage rate.

8.3.2 The econometric specification

Functional form

Our choice of the econometric specification of the labour supply function was dictated by limitations of the database,[9] and by procedural questions – like the flexibility and the manageability of the approach. It seemed appropriate to approximate the corresponding functions by a linear form, an approach that was used, for instance, by Hausman (1981, 1983, 1985). Labour hours, l, supplied are then a linear function of the marginal net wage, w, the tax-corrected non-labour income, m, socio-economic characteristics, x_j, like the number of children, age and health status, and of a disturbance term, ε_{li}:[10]

$$l_i = \alpha_0 + \alpha w_i + \beta m_i + \sum_{j=1}^{v} \delta_j x_{ji} + \varepsilon_{li}, \quad w_i > w_{ri}$$

$$l_i = 0, \qquad\qquad\qquad\qquad\qquad w_i < w_{ri} \qquad (8.8)$$

where w_{ri} is the reservation wage. The labour supply function and the corresponding utility and expenditure functions as well as the equivalent income function, EV and the relevant elasticities are depicted in Table 8.1.

Estimation procedure

The theoretical model sketched was estimated using the extended Tobit approach.[11] This procedure estimates the probability to participate in the labour force simultaneously with labour supply from the full set of data.

Since we do not know the wage rates for the non-working people, we first instrument a wage rate for this group. The imputed wage rate is estimated for the fully employed by considering possible sample selection biases. Hence, the estimated inverse of Mill's ratio, generated by the probit equation for work

---

[9] For instance, the non-availability of information on price variations within the set of cross-section data excludes all models that require the splitting up of consumer expenditures into a price and a quantity component.

[10] The latter term is supposed to be normally distributed with mean zero and a constant variance σ^2.

[11] Neither a formal analysis of the Tobit model nor the discussion of the numerical techniques related to the estimation procedure is warranted here, however. The respective discussion can be found in Maddala (1983) or Judge *et al.* (1985). The different stages of the estimation processes are sketched in Kaiser *et al.* (1989, p. 18ff.). Methodological support by J. Merz (Sonderforschungsbereich 3 der Deutschen Forschungsgemeinschaft and University of Frankfurt) is gratefully acknowledged by the authors; see also Merz (1987a, b).

Table 8.1 The linear labour supply function and the corresponding functions

---

Labour supply function

$l = \alpha w + \beta m + \delta x$

where
l = working hours
w = marginal net wage
m = corrected net non-labour income
x = socio-economic variables
α, β, δ = parameters to be estimated

Direct utility function

$$u(l, c) = \frac{1}{\beta}\left(l - \frac{\alpha}{\beta}\right)\exp\left\{\left[1 - \beta\left(c + \frac{\delta x}{\beta} - \frac{\alpha}{\beta^2}\right)\right] / \left(\frac{\alpha}{\beta} - l\right)\right\}$$

with c as the composite commodity

Indirect utility function

$$v(w, m, x) = e^{\beta w}\left(m + \frac{\alpha}{\beta} w - \frac{\alpha}{\beta^2} + \frac{\delta}{\beta} x\right)$$

Equivalent income function

$v(w_0, m_E, x) = v(w_1, m_1, x) \Rightarrow$

implies

$$e^{\beta w_0}\left(m_E + \frac{\alpha}{\beta} w_0 - \frac{\alpha}{\beta^2} + \frac{\delta}{\beta} x\right) = e^{\beta w_1}\left(m_1 + \frac{\alpha}{\beta} w_1 - \frac{\alpha}{\beta^2} + \frac{\delta}{\beta} x\right) \Rightarrow$$

which further implies that

$$m_E = e^{\beta(w_1 - w_0)}\left(m_1 + \frac{\alpha}{\beta} w_1 - \frac{\alpha}{\beta^2} + \frac{\delta}{\beta} x\right) - \left(\frac{\alpha}{\beta} w_0 - \frac{\alpha}{\beta^2} + \frac{\delta}{\beta} x\right)$$

$$= e(w_0, v_1)$$

Equivalent variation

$$EV = e^{\beta(w_1 - w_0)}\left(m_1 + \frac{\alpha}{\beta} w_1 - \frac{\alpha}{\beta^2} + \frac{\delta}{\beta} x\right) - \left(\frac{\alpha}{\beta} w_0 - \frac{\alpha}{\beta^2} + \frac{\delta}{\beta} x\right) - m_0$$

Uncompensated wage elasticity (total effect)

$$H_{l,w} = \frac{\delta l}{\delta w}\frac{w}{l} = \alpha \frac{w}{l}$$

Total income elasticity (income effect)

$$H_{l,m} = \frac{\delta l}{\delta m} w = \beta w$$

Compensated wage elasticity (substitution effect)

$$H^*_{l,w} = \frac{\delta l}{\delta w}\frac{w}{l}\bigg|_{u=u_0} = H_{l,w} - H_{l,m}$$

---

participation, enters the wage rate equation as an additional regressor. In a second step the imputed wage rates are used for the Tobit model as instruments.

Definition and measurement of the variables

An empirical study requires a thorough analysis of the database and its correspondence with conceptional elements of the theoretical model to be validated. Three main problems have to be dealt with in this context: (i) the appropriate selection of variables; (ii) the measurement unit; and (iii) possibly, problems of endogeneity.

The supply of labour is measured in hours worked per year.[12] This allows one to base the analysis on a time span that usually covers all elements of non-regular remuneration (like holiday grants or a 13th monthly income).

In order to arrive at the marginal net wage, the analysis departs from the average gross hourly wage which is obtained by dividing annual labour income by the total number of hours worked during that year. The marginal net wage w was calculated using equation (8.6). Because of the endogeneity of the wage rate as well as the fact that a wage rate could not be identified for the non-working population, we used an instrumental-variable approach,[13] according to which the marginal net wage is determined by variables as suggested by human–capital theory – work experience, age, education – and by introducing a correction for the selection bias. The 'imputed' wage thus derived is then used as a regressor in the labour supply function given in equation (8.8).

The calculation of the (linearized) net non-labour income starts with the gross non-labour income, which is the sum of income from rents and capital income plus transfer payments (related to households and individuals). In determining the (individual) labour supply it is crucial to assess the impact of total household resources on individual behaviour.[14] In particular, labour income of spouses can formally be treated like any other interest-bearing asset; this is the case for the so-called 'male-chauvinist' model (MC model) of family behaviour in which men disregard the labour income of spouses for their work decisions, whereas women add their husband's income to their own non-labour income. For the present study the MC model was chosen. The derivation of the corrected net non-labour income follows equation (8.7). The marginal tax rates are obtained from the tax assessment model.

Finally, individual utility depends on both observable socio-economic factors (like sex, age, number of children, health status), variables that are available in the microeconomic database used for this study, and on non-observable variables that are compounded in the error term ε_{li}.

---

[12] The arguments supporting this choice are convincingly put forward in Keeley (1981, p. 81ff) and Killingsworth (1983, p. 97ff).

[13] See Hall (1973), Layard *et al.* (1980), Johnson and Pencavel (1982) and Killingsworth (1983, Chapters 3 and 6).

[14] See Killingsworth (1983, p. 30ff).

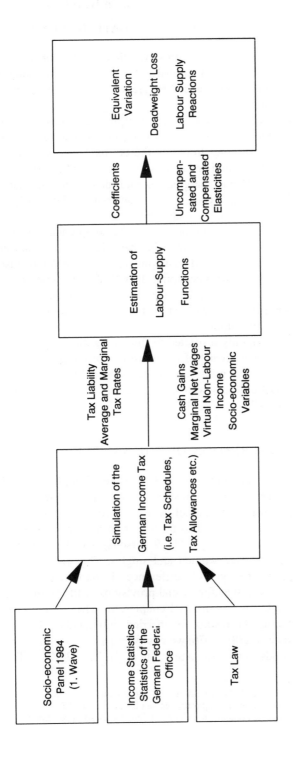

Fig. 8.3 Structure of the model.

8.4 THE FRANKFURT INCOME TAX SIMULATION (FITS) MODEL

The model discussed in the previous section shows that labour supply hinges on the tax system and, in particular, on marginal tax rates in two important ways: they determine net marginal wages and they are required in order to derive corrected non-labour income.

If taxable incomes of taxpayers were known, marginal tax rates could immediately be applied using the tax schedule. However, the income reported in the data is not taxable income; in order to obtain the tax base, one must take into account a number of allowances and deductions that are related to the socio-economic status of the taxpayer. Hence, marginal tax rates do not only depend on the level of income but also on socio-economic characteristics like family status, number of children, professional activity and age.

This calls for a fully fledged model representing the comprehensive set of tax rules governing income taxation. Such a model has been developed by the authors. The structure of the model is depicted in Figure 8.3. The model is based on the first wave of the German 'Socio-economic Panel' of 1984, comprising not only detailed information on incomes but also on socio-economic variables.[15] Furthermore, information from the income statistics was used and the tax law had to be cast into a computer algorithm.

The model is, however, not only restricted to simulating the actual tax law but also allows one to monitor the impact of tax reforms. For the present study the pre-reform tax law of 1983 was used to estimate the supply of labour and the corresponding supply elasticities as well as the welfare effects of the German Income Tax Reforms 1986–90.

8.5 DESCRIPTION OF THE SAMPLE

The database consists of a subsample of the first wave of the German 'Socio-economic Panel'.[16] Farmers, liberal professions and pensioners were excluded from the analysis since a wage rate cannot be defined for these groups. For the same reason, dependent workers who had income from independent occupation were eliminated. The remaining sample (7429 persons) was divided into three categories: married men, married women and singles. This classification was chosen in order to account for possible differences in participation rates and labour supply behaviour, as well as for special provisions of the German tax law that concedes income splitting for married couples. In what follows we shall restrict ourself to reporting the results for married individuals.[17] Of the 3321 (3360) married men (women), 2382 (1076) were fully employed over the whole year in 1983, which corresponds to a participation rate of 71.7% (32.0%).[18] Table 8.2

---

[15] See Hanefeld (1987).

[16] The complete sample comprises 5921 households and 12 246 persons.

[17] For a discussion of the results for single taxpayers, see van Essen *et al.* (1993).

[18] All persons who were unemployed one month or more are not contained in the sample.

Table 8.2 Definition and description of variables for estimating the labour supply function*

Variable	Married men	Married women
Effective number	2382	1076
	(3321)	(3360)
	Mean	Mean
Working hours	2212	1681
	(1692)	(622)
Marginal net wage in DM per hour	14.15	10.03
	(10.76)	(3.55)
Corrected non-labour income in DM	6831	38 616**
	(8832)	(37 896)
Number of children under 18 years	1.30	1.01
	(1.18)	(1.18)
Partner working (0 = No; 1 = Yes)	0.45	0.88
	(0.42)	(0.83)
Nationality (0 = foreigner; 1 = German)	0.65	0.63
	(0.68)	(0.68)
School education (1 = primary; 4 = University)	1.06	0.95
	(1.09)	(0.95)
Age in years	42.40	39.8
	(44.93)	(41.7)
Degree of physical handicap (0–100%)	2.06	1.80
	(6.57)	(3.36)

* Numbers without parantheses: fully employed persons.
   Numbers in parentheses: inclusive of non-employed persons.
** This value can be explained by the use of the male-chauvinist model.
For non-working persons the wage rate and hours worked are zero.
Source: Own calculations.

shows the mean values of the variables used in the estimations according to sex and family status. The (unweighted) data were used for estimating the microeconomic labour supply model described in section 8.3, separately for both groups.

8.6 RESULTS FOR THE LABOUR SUPPLY FUNCTION

In this section the main estimation results – using the extended Tobit approach – are compiled and briefly commented upon. Note that in all the following tables the t-values are given in parentheses, and the coefficients marked with an asterix are significant at the 99% level. The results of the maximum likelihood estimates for participation rates of male household heads and women are depicted in Table 8.3. It can be seen that all significant variables show the expected sign for both groups. With increasing number of children, the probabilty of participation in the labour market rises for married men and declines for married women, respectively. Both groups are less likely to work if they are elder and less healthy. Foreign married women tend to work more than their German counterparts. If its partner is working then it is very likely that the regarded individual is employed as well.

Table 8.3 Maximum likelihood estimation of the probit model for participation rates:

$$\Pr(I_i = 1) = \Phi\left(a_0 + \sum_{j=1}^{k} a_j z_{ji}\right), \quad i = 1, \ldots, N$$

Regressor	Married men	Married women
Intercept	1.54*	0.15
	(12.25)	(1.09)
Corrected non-labour income in DM	-0.22×10^{-4}*	0.17×10^{-5}
	(−8.18)	(1.25)
Age	−0.018*	−0.012*
	(−7.87)	(−5.26)
Nationality (0 = Foreigner; 1 = German)	0.77×10^{-2}	−0.28*
	(0.11)	(−4.14)
Number of children below 18 years	0.087*	−0.23*
	(3.61)	(−9.82)
School education (1 = Primary; 4 = University)	0.028	0.049
	(0.96)	(1.44)
Degree of handicap (0–100%)	−0.012*	−0.007*
	(−9.83)	(−3.39)
Partner working (0 = No; 1 = Yes)	0.13*	0.28*
	(2.43)	(3.82)
Number of cases	3321	3360

* Significant at 99% level.
Source: Own calculations.

Table 8.4 OLS estimation for the marginal net wage rate with correction for selection bias:

$$w_i = a_0 + \sum_{j=1}^{m} a_j x_{ji} + a_i \pi + \varepsilon_i, \quad i = 1, \ldots, n$$

Regressor	Married men	Married women
Intercept	11.46*	7.10*
	(6.16)	(2.97)
School education (1 = Primary; 4 = University)	1.89*	1.97*
	(5.36)	(5.14)
Degree of handicap (0–100%)	−0.004	−0.009
	(−0.13)	(−0.22)
Age in years	0.04	0.02
	(0.99)	(0.47)
Heckman variable for SB correction π	−1.69	0.47
	(−0.88)	(0.25)
Number of cases	2382	1076

* Significant at 99% level.
Source: Own calculations.

Non-labour income decreases the working probability for married men, while it is insignificant for married females.

From the probit model, we calculate the inverse Mill's ratio for inclusion as an additional regressor in the marginal net wage equation. The imputed marginal net wages for the fully employed men and married women are summarized in Table 8.4. According to these results the only significant variable for both groups is school education, while regressors like the degree of handicap and age turn out to have no influence on the net marginal wage rate. Note that other attempts with variables like job experience (and its square) and squared age caused multicollinearity. The inverse of Mill's ratio turns out to be insignificant in both cases.

However, these results are not very surprising. The relationship between the marginal net market wage rate and the other variables is not very strong since the effective marginal wage rate of an individual is influenced not only by personal skills and characteristics but also by institutional factors of the relevant economy, i.e. the tax and transfer system. Hence, we did not carry out the regressions for economic rather than for econometric reasons. The imputed marginal net wage rate now serves as an instrument within the estimation of the Tobit labour supply model in order to avoid endogeneity problems and in order to provide the necessary information on 'wage rate' for the non-working population. Otherwise, the Tobit model could not have been estimated anyway. The results obtained with the Tobit methodology are depicted in Table 8.5. It is noteworthy that the estimation for married men does not verify the neoclassical labour supply model. Although the coefficient for corrected non-labour income is negative and significant – revealing that leisure is a normal good – the

Table 8.5 Maximum likelihood estimation of the Tobit model for hours worked:

$$l_i = \alpha_0 + \alpha w_i + \beta m_i + \sum_{j=1}^{v} \delta_j x_{ji} + \varepsilon_{li}, \quad w_i > w_{ri}$$

$$l_i = 0, \qquad\qquad\qquad\qquad\qquad w_i \leqslant w_{ri}$$

Regressor	Married men	Married women
Intercept	1397.29*	− 439.99*
	(7.76)	(− 3.18)
IV Estimate for marginal net wage rate in DM	− 0.57	64.21*
	(− 0.04)	(4.29)
Corrected non-labour income in DM	− 0.20 × 10⁻¹*	− 0.28 × 10⁻²*
	(− 11.32)	(− 2.37)
Number of children under 18 years	223.90*	− 264.08*
	(11.31)	(− 13.61)
Partner working (0 = No; 1 = Yes)	657.33*	737.00*
	(12.80)	(12.08)
Nationality (0 = Foreigner; 1 = German)	25.06	− 626.20*
	(0.41)	(− 10.56)
Number of persons	3321	3360

Note: *t*-values in parentheses.
    * Level of significance 99%.
Source: Own calculations.

influence of marginal net wage rates cannot be ascertained: the corresponding coefficient is insignificant.

On the other hand, the estimation results are consistent and in accordance with theoretical *a priori* insights for married women. The uncompensated wage rate effect is strongly positive, and virtual non-labour income has the expected negative sign – stressing the hypothesis that leisure is a normal good for married women.

Table 8.6 shows the division of the estimated uncompensated wage rate effect into the income and substitution effects based on the sample means. Although the substitution and income elasticities exhibit the correct sign for both groups of taxpayers, it should be kept in mind that the wage elasticity for married men was statistically not significant. This is why we excluded men from the following welfare analysis.

Table 8.6   Estimated income and substitution elasticities for the linear labour supply function

	Uncompensated wage-rate elasticity	Substitution elasticity (compensated wage-rate elasticity)	Total income elasticity
Married men	– 0.004	0.28	– 0.28
Married women	1.04	1.22	– 0.18

Source: Own calculations using the arithmetic mean of hours worked and of corrected non-labour income (see Table 8.2).

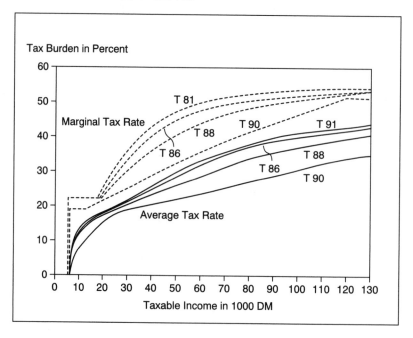

Fig. 8.4   Different income tax schedules for West Germany.

The question is: Why does the traditional labour choice model not seem to work for married men? We think that standardized work contracts as well as quantity rationing in large segments of the market imply an all-or-nothing choice for married men that largely abstracts from utility-maximizing behaviour. As long as the reservation wage is below the net market wage, the contract offered with a standardized volume of work is accepted independent of the optimizing considerations.

On the other hand, the substitution and income effects of a change in the wage rate are significant and consistent with the theory for married women. A negative total income elasticity for this group implies that leisure is a normal good for these persons in Germany. This seems to indicate that married women are less constrained by standardized work contracts, both because the husband's income, considered to be non-wage income by the spouse, renders the latter more independent from all-or-nothing considerations, which may be more typical for the 'male chauvinist' and which have to be more readily accepted in situations where basic needs have to be covered. Women, on the contrary, seem to be more sensitive to opportunity cost considerations. Married women often tend to care for the house and the children, services that are highly price-elastic. And, hence, the alternative of renting these services on the market place becomes very sensitive to changes in the tax code that may impinge heavily on the marginal net wage rate of second income earners like, often, women. This is true in particular for higher income groups where this option is more realistic, given the higher level of joint household resources.

According to the estimates, labour supply of married women is indeed reacting more strongly to changes in the wage rate than that for married men. Note that the estimated elasticities for married women come very close to those obtained by other authors, notably Franz (1981, p. 105), Franz and Kawasaki (1981, p. 141), Franz (1985), Dagsvik *et al.* (1988, p. 44), Merz (1989) and Spahn *et al.* (1990) for Germany, and Leu and Kugler (1986, p. 243) for Switzerland.[19]

8.7 THE INDUCED WELFARE EFFECTS OF THE RECENT TAX REFORMS IN WEST GERMANY

8.7.1 General remarks

The reactions of the supply of labour to changes in the marginal net wage rate are of an eminent importance for tax policy, since the income tax influences net wage rates directly for any taxpayer. Figure 8.4 shows the marginal and the average income tax schedules for West Germany before and after the Income Tax Reforms 1986–1990. This reveals that the series of recent tax reforms have

---

[19] Further comparisons relating to the results for other countries, notably the United States and United Kingdom, are beyond the scope of our study. See, however, the surveys by Pencavel (1986) and Killingsworth and Heckman (1986).

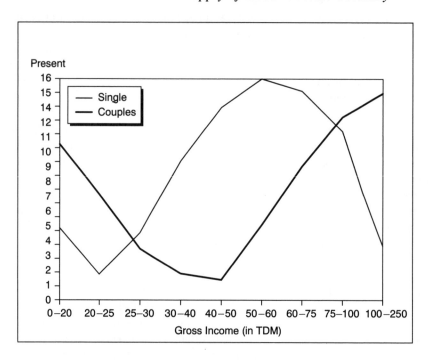

Fig. 8.5 Absolute reduction of marginal tax rates resulting from the Income Tax Reform 1986–90.

considerably reduced marginal income tax rates for middle-income brackets, less so for the top-income brackets where the reduction was only 3%. One would, therefore, expect that the reform has brought to the fore some – if not considerable – welfare gains for middle-income earners.

Studies on labour supply reactions and welfare effects have to focus on marginal tax rates in particular. The reduction of these rates after 1990 in comparison to the pre-reform tax law of 1986 is shown in Figure 8.5. It should be understood that the German tax law uses full income-splitting for married couples; hence, the marginal rates for singles (and married men under the 'male-chauvinist' model) differ from those of married women. The reduction depends very much on the level of taxable income, but it also hinges on socio-economic factors that determine the level of deductible items and, hence, the tax base effects which are crucial for the marginal rates to be applied. Contrary to most other studies, we had a comparative advantage here, since we could rely on our FITS model, where others have to use roughly approximate marginal rates.[20]

---

[20] See the studies by Franz (1981), Merz (1987a, b) and Dagsvik *et al.* (1988). To our knowledge, the only exemption – besides our own studies – is a paper by Merz (1989), who analyses the effects of the 1990 tax reform on the allocation of time spent on formal and informal activities using marginal tax rates generated by the FITS model.

8.7.2 The welfare gains for married women

Married women exhibit 'normal' and significant reactions of their labour supply and since this group of taxpayers constitutes an important segment of the labour force, it is warranted to study their welfare gains in detail. Table 8.7 indicates the change in the total number of hours supplied by married women expected as a result of the tax reform. On an average, the increase in the number of hours worked is about 98 hours per year (or 3.6%), which is in accordance with the labour supply elasticities shown in Table 8.7. The substitution effect dominates the income effect for all classes, also for the highest income group, whereas this was not true for single taxpayers, for instance.

The different income classes exhibit large variations, though. It is interesting to note that the highest class of income earners works considerably more than the average. The same is true for lower-income groups, though to a much lesser extent. This is consistent with the reduction of marginal tax rates as shown before: reactions are strongest for those income groups that benefit most from the reform.

Table 8.7 also includes information on cash gains and on *EV* for different income brackets. Both indicators rise with increasing income, yet the rise of *EV* is much steeper in relative terms. One may be tempted to compare the figures of these two colums, yet it may be difficult to convey what the difference really means. The cash gain, though economically less relevant, is a clear-cut monetary

Table 8.7 Labour supply reactions and welfare effects of the Income Tax Reforms 1986–90 for married women

Variable	*Total gross income (in DM)*							
	All house holds	*0 to 20 000*	*20 001 to 30 000*	*30 001 to 40 000*	*40 001 to 50 000*	*50 001 to 60 000*	*60 001 to 75 000*	*75 001 to 10 0000*
Absolute change of labour supply*	97.79	33.30	17.69	4.14	4.84	39.28	110.6	232.1
Relative change of labour supply**	3.6	19.5	2.7	0.1	0.9	1.6	1.3	43.7
Change of excess burden in percentage of tax yield before the reform	– 12.4	—	—	—	—	—	—	—
Yearly cash gain	2673	192	925	1466	1435	1619	2251	4306
Equivalent variation	4589	81	895	678	548	1459	4333	14398
Change of excess burden	– 1454	—	—	—	—	—	—	—

* In hours worked per year as compared to hours worked in 1983.
** In percentage of hours worked per year in 1983.
Source: Own calculations.

measure that is widely accepted by policy makers as an indicator of distributional effects. The equivalent variation, although economically much more meaningful, is more abstract for the layman, however. It is a utility measure transformed into a monetary equivalent by applying the shadow price of income which is heavily dependent on the specification of the optimization model. Furthermore, it includes the effects of behavioural reactions, and the compensation to be given to the taxpayer is again largely determined by his utility schedule before and after the reform. Such a measure may, hence, be less 'concrete' and certainly less appealing to politicians for evaluating policy results.

As far as the interpretation of these figures is concerned, a further reservation has to be made relating to the limitations of the database. Very high income earners should benefit less from the reform, since the reduction of marginal tax rates must approach the difference between the top rates before and after reform, which is rather small: 3%! Our database, however, lacks information on these high-income groups. Hence, they had to be disregarded in the analysis. As a result the value for *EV* must appear to be too high for the upper income bracket.

The reform has also reduced the excess burden for married women: On an average, the equivalent of roughly DM 1500 is obtained by the tax reform largely through mitigating distortive economic behaviour for married women. The amount is approximately 12.5% of the reductions of tax revenue acquired by this group of taxpayers, which seems to indicate remarkable additional benefits on top of the mere cash gains.

8.8 SUMMARY AND CONCLUSION

The methodology used to quantify labour supply reactions and to evaluate welfare gains of the recent German tax reforms may partly appear conventional at a first glance. Its application to the German tax reforms is innovative, though.

In contrast to the conventional labour supply studies for West Germany, we combined an explicit tax simulation model representing the full scale of actual tax policy measures (and validated on a microeconomic database) with a second-generation labour supply model to investigate the impact of the full reform (not only of changes in tax rates) on their welfare effects, taking behavioural reactions into account.

The measures derived for marginal net wage rate elasticities indicate a rather large potential for welfare gains through reforming the income tax laws in West Germany. In particular, married women benefit considerably from the tax measures and their labour supply remarkably increase. Labour supply reactions of married men do not seem to vary significantly as a function of tax rate changes.

There are visible welfare gains for married women. The tax reform is, therefore, applauded as a right move towards rendering the German labour market more efficient as well as liberalizing married women in middle-income groups from the 'family trap' in which they are locked-in by actual high marginal tax rates.

If these results are compared with those from the previous studies of the authors[21] that dealt with the distribution effects of the income tax reforms 1986–90, the classical equity efficiency trade-off becomes obvious: the welfare gains achieved have to be traded-in for a more unequal distribution of net incomes after the reform. On the other hand, greater participation of women may also be a means to achieving greater equity and social justice for society. This calls for an explicit modelling of tax reforms based on optimal-taxation rules that try to contrast the welfare gains achieved against the loss in social welfare attributable to greater inequity where it occurs. The authors have shown how this can be done in the realm of indirect taxation.[22] Similarly, the approach could be applied to more radical changes in the tax system such as a shift from direct to indirect taxation. The simulation of allocative and distributive effects of such major changes in the tax code was, however, not the subject of the present study.

REFERENCES

Alheim, M. and Rose, M. (1984) Alte und neue Maße Individueller Steuerlasten. *Finanzarchiv*, **42**, 274–349.

Dagsvik, J. K., Holst, K. Strøm, S., Wagenhals, G. and Østervald, J. (1988) Female labor supply in West Germany 1984, Discussion Paper No. 122, University of Heidelberg, Heidelberg.

Ebert, U. (1987) *Beiträge zur Wohlfahrtsökonomie*. Springer, Berlin.

van Essen, U., Kaiser, H. and Spahn, P. B. (1988) Verteilungswirkungen der Einkommensteuerreformen 1986–1990. *Finanzarchiv*, **46**, 56–84.

van Essen, U., Kaiser, H. and Spahn, P. B. (1990a) Mikrosimulation statt Tarifanalyse. Eine weitere Klarstellung. *Zeitschrift für Wirtschafts- und Sozialwissenschaften*, **110**, 126–7.

van Essen, U., Kaiser, H. and Spahn, P. B. (1990b) Einkommensteuerreform 1990: Cui bono? Eine Anmerkung. *Zeitschrift für Wirtschafts- und Sozialwissenschaften*, **110**, 115–1.

van Essen, U., Kaiser, H. and Spahn, P. B. (1993) Tax policy on the bifurcation between equity and efficiency: Lessons from the West German Income Tax Reform, 217–35.

Franz, W. (1981) Schätzung regionaler Arbeitsangebotsfunktionen mit Hilfe der Tobit-Methode und des Probit-Verfahrens unter Berücksichtigung des sogenannten 'Sample Selection Bias', *Jahrbuch für Regionalwissenschaft*, **2**, 88–108.

Franz, W. (1985) An Economic Analysis of Female Work Participation, Education, and Fertility: Theory and Empirical Evidence for the Federal Republic of Germany. *Journal of Labor Economics*, **3**, 218–34.

Franz, W. and Kawasaki, S. (1981) Labor Supply of Married Women in the Federal Republic of Germany: Theory and Empirical Results from a New Estimation Procedure. *Empirical Economics*, **6**, 129–43.

Hall, R. E. (1973) Wages, Income and Hours of Work in the U.S. Labor Force, in *Income Maintenance and Labor Supply*, (eds G. G. Cain, and H. W. Watts), New York, pp. 102–62.

Hanefeld, U. (1987) Das Sozio-ökonomische Panel – Grundlagen und Konzeption. Campus, Frankfurt/Main.

Hausman, J. A. (1981) Labor Supply, in *How Taxes Affect Economic Behavior* (eds H. J. Aaron, and J. Pechman), Brookings, Washington DC, pp. 27–72.

[21] See van Essen *et al.* (1988, 1993).

[22] See Kaiser and Spahn (1989), Kaiser *et al.* (1990) and Kaiser (1990).

Hausman, J. A. (1983) Stochastic Problems in the Simulation of Labor Supply, in *Behavioral Simulation Methods in Tax Policy Analysis* (ed. M. Feldstein), University of Chicago Press, Chicago, pp. 47–82.

Hausman, J. A. (1985) The Econometrics of Nonlinear Budget Sets. *Econometrica*, **53**, 1255–82.

Johnson, T. R. and Pencavel, J. H. (1982) Forecasting the Effects of a Negative Income Tax Program. *Industrial and Labor Relations Review*, **35**, 221–34.

Judge, G. G., Griffiths, W. E., Hill, R. C., Lütkepohl, H. and Lee, T. C. (1985) *The Theory and Practice of Econometrics*. Wiley, New York.

Kaiser, H. (1990) *Konsumnachfrage, Arbeitsangebot und optimale Haushaltsbesteuerung – Theoretische Ergebnisse und mikroökonometrische Simulation für die Bundesrepublik Deutschland*. Peter Lang, Frankfurt/Main.

Kaiser, H., van Essen, U. and Spahn, P. B. (1991) Income taxation and the supply of labour in West Germany, in *Jahrbücher für Nationalökonomie und Statistik*, **209**, 87–105.

Kaiser, H. and Spahn, P. B. (1989) On the Efficiency and Distributive Justice of Consumption Taxes – A Study of VAT in West Germany. *Journal of Economics*, **49**, 199–218.

Kaiser, H. and Spahn, P. B. (1991) Verteilungspolitische Beurteilung der Steuerreformen in der Ära Stoltenberg – Einige Klarstellungen, in *Kredit und Kapital*, **24**, 526–31.

Kaiser, H., Wiegard, W. and Zimmermann, H. (1990) Testing the Reliability of Optimal Tax Calculations, *Finanzarchiv*, **48**, 77–96.

Keeley, M. C. (1981) *Labor Supply and Public Policy. A Critical Review*. Academic Press, New York.

Killingsworth, M. R. (1983) *Labor Supply*. Cambridge University Press, Cambridge.

Killingsworth, M. R. and Heckman, J. (1986) Female labor supply, in *Handbook of Labor Economics*, vol.1 (eds O. Ashenfelter, and R. Layard), North-Holland, Amsterdam, pp. 103–204.

King, M. A. (1983), Welfare Analysis of Tax Reforms Using Household Data. *Journal of Public Economics*, **21**, 183–214.

Layard, R., Barton, M. and Zabalza, A. (1980) Married Women's Participation and Hours. *Economica*, **47**, 51–72.

Leu, R. E. and Kugler, P. (1986) Einkommensteuern und Arbeitsangebot in der Schweiz, in *Mikroökonomik des Arbeitsmarktes*, (eds H. Schelbert-Syfrig, N. Blattner, P. Halbherr, and N. Harabi), P. Haupt, Bern, pp. 205–56.

Maddala, G. S. (1983) *Limited Dependent and Qualitative Variables in Econometrics*. Cambridge University Press, Cambridge.

McKenzie, G. W. (1983) *Measuring Economic Welfare*. New York.

Merz, J. (1987a) Das Arbeitsangebot verheirateter Frauen in der Bundesrepublik Deutschland – Eine mikroökonometrische Analyse unter besonderer Berücksichtigung des 'selectivity bias', in *Lebenslagen im Wandel: Analysen 1987* (eds H.-J. Krupp, and U. Hanefeld), Campus, Frankfurt/Main, pp. 126–57.

Merz, J. (1987b) Labor force participation, market wage rate and working hours of married and unmarried women in the Federal Republic of Germany, Sfb 3-Working Paper No. 249, Frankfurt/Main.

Merz, J. (1989) The 1990 German Tax Reform – Microsimulation of Time Allocation Effects in the Formal and Informal economy, Sfb 3-Working Paper No. 288, Frankfurt/Main.

Pencavel, J. (1986) 'Labor Supply of Men', in *Handbook of Labor Economics* (eds O. Ashenfelter, and R. Layard), *vol. 1*, North-Holland, Amsterdam, pp. 3–102.

Samuelson, P. A. (1974) Complementarity – An Essay on the 40th Anniversary of the Hicks – Allen Revolution in Demand Theory. *Journal of Economic Literature*, **12**, 1255–89.

Spahn, P. B., Kaiser, H. and Kassella, T. (1990) Alternative Tax Treatment of Married Couples in West Germany – Distributive and Allocative effects, *Frankfurter Volkswirtschaftliche Diskussionsbeiträge Arbeitspapier* Nr. 7, Frankfurt/Main.

Part Three

Fiscal Reform in Four EEC Countries

Tax rates, progressivity and *de facto* fiscal indexation in ten European countries

Fiorella Padoa Schioppa Kostoris

9.1 INTRODUCTION

It is a common opinion that the possible and perhaps desirable harmonization of European fiscal systems will meet with serious problems, particularly as far as direct taxes are concerned. Difficulties in fiscal harmonization will mainly depend on present intercountry differences concerning effective rather than scheduled tax rates or tax structures. Hence, this chapter tries to evaluate the historical and current heterogeneities and similarities which characterize not only *de lege* but also *de facto* the total burden of taxation on the workers[1] of 10 European countries (eight belonging to the EEC plus Austria and Sweden): for cross-country comparisons in the effective tax rates and structures, an OECD data set for the period 1960–88 is utilized.[2] In section 9.2 it appears that, by the end of the 1980s, European fiscal systems differ in the relative weight assigned to direct relative to indirect taxes and to social security contributions charged on employers, more than in the effective global fiscal pressure, as summarized by the tax wedge.

But the tax wedge (as usually calculated) is proved to be (Padoa Schioppa, 1992b) a specially relevant fiscal parameter only if all tax rates are flat. While this may be an acceptable hypothesis for indirect and social security tax rates, it is certainly not a correct approximation for direct tax rates, the latter being the

---

[1] The limitation is important: direct taxes on capital income are ignored, while personal income taxes on households are supposed to proxy personal income taxes on employees; on the contrary, not only social security contributions paid by employees but also those paid by employers are taken into consideration because the latter are usually backward-shifted on employees' wages (Padoa Schioppa, 1992b); moreover, indirect tax rates are incorporated into the analysis as they are forward-shifted on consumer prices and, thus, have an effect on employees' purchasing power.

[2] A data appendix describing the methodology utilized in the reconstruction of the time series derived from the OECD empirical evidence is available upon request from the author and is presented in the author's *CEPR Discussion Paper* (1991).

sum of an approximately flat tax rate (the employees' social security tax rate) and of a progressive tax rate (the personal income tax rate). Thus, in order to provide a more accurate evaluation of the burden of taxation, it is important to estimate the effective degree of progressivity of direct taxation in the 10 European countries, recalling that this is not a directly available information for most of the years and for most of the countries under examination. Moreover, the various European direct tax systems may also be very heterogeneous in terms of their *de facto*[3] fiscal indexation, again a not immediately observable variable.

A theoretical model, able to identify the effective marginal tax rate of the average taxpayer, the degree of progressivity and *de facto* indexation of direct tax systems is, therefore, described in section 9.3. The model being testable, in section 9.4 some estimations of the effective marginal tax rate, the degree of progressivity and *de facto* fiscal indexation of the 10 European direct tax systems under consideration are illustrated for the time interval 1960–88. These estimates lead us to conclude that everywhere in Europe, except in Denmark, Spain, Sweden (and to a limited extent in France) the degree of progressivity has essentially declined in the 1980s, reaching values close to zero in some small open economies; in the last decade, *de facto* fiscal indexation has been largely adopted (fully or partially, except in Spain), even though it remained in some countries legally prohibited. Consequently, in section 9.5, by looking at the coefficients of variation (between the European countries and across time) of the effective social security contributions, the indirect tax rates, the tax wedge, the direct average and estimated marginal tax rates and the progressivity of direct taxation, it is shown that the harmonization of the burden of taxation on European workers is certainly a more difficult task for direct than for other forms of taxation or for all taxes at the same time, due to 'compensating' differences in tax structures. In the 1990s, however, this fiscal harmonization does not seem to be a utopian goal, as the European effective tax rates and structures appear much closer in the late 1980s than ever in the past.

9.2 FISCAL SYSTEMS IN EUROPE: THE SCHEDULED AND THE EFFECTIVE TAX STRUCTURES AND TAX RATES

From an institutional viewpoint, as indicated by Table 9.1, the cross-country comparison of the burden of taxation on European workers shows many homogeneities, but also several differences. I will concentrate my attention on indirect taxes, social security contributions and personal income taxes, because these are the three major items everywhere.

---

[3] In some periods and some countries the Parliament has introduced a law to index income brackets, tax deductions and tax credits; in other situations, labelled as those where *de facto* indexation has been realized, the Parliament and/or the citizens' behaviour have obtained the same result through different instruments.

9.2.1 Indirect taxes

Starting with indirect taxes, it is well-known that the most important in Europe is the VAT which is a prerequisite for any country intending to join the European Economic Community (EEC). The VAT was first introduced in Luxembourg (which is not of concern[4] in this Chapter), then in Denmark, France and Germany; it was adopted almost everywhere in Europe by 1973, except more recently in some countries like Spain who have been latecomer members of the EEC (row q, Table 9.1). The basic rate does not differ much between countries, as shown by rows p and q, but the tax structure varies a great deal, as indicated by rows n and o: not only does the number of the VAT rates range between a minimum of 1 (in Denmark and the United Kingdom) and a maximum of 6 (in Belgium), but also the dispersion around the basic rate and, hence, the 'implicit' degree of progressivity of the VAT is accordingly different. In any case, the VAT is generally considered very mildly progressive and by some authors (Pechman, 1990) even regressive.

In general, it is assumed that the effective (not the scheduled)[5] indirect tax rate, denoted as T, which includes excise and other indirect taxes besides the VAT, net of government subsidies – for example on exports – is a flat rate in every country.

However, in spite of all the apparent similarities there are two major inter-country differences concerning the indirect tax rate, T. First, the dynamics of the indirect tax rate, T, in the last 30 years has been uneven in the various European countries. In fact, while in some countries T has almost steadily declined (e.g. in Germany, except for a peak in 1968 corresponding to the introduction of the VAT), in others it has consistently grown (e.g. in The Netherlands, Denmark and Sweden). During the 1960–88 interval, T has more often presented either down-turns (e.g. in Belgium between 1965–75, in the United Kingdom between 1969–76, in Austria since 1973 when the VAT was introduced), or upturns (in France since 1977, in Italy since 1975 soon after the introduction of the VAT, and in Spain since 1978). Surprisingly, the introduction of the VAT is not associated to a definite temporal trend in the indirect tax rate, T, less so to a positive trend: in Belgium, France, and Austria T approximately started to decrease precisely when the VAT was enforced and never returned to previous peaks; in Spain it has remained cyclically constant after the introduction of the VAT. The notable exceptions to this unexpected negative correlation between the temporal change of T and the adoption of the VAT are represented by Italy and the United Kingdom, where T has started rising two–three years after the VAT enforcement. Unlike in Italy, in the United Kingdom during the 1980s the observed indirect tax rate has remained approximately constant, as much as most of the other tax rates.

---

[4] The other EEC countries excluded from this study are Ireland, Greece and Portugal, due to data absence or insufficiency.

[5] The scheduled tax rates are legally determined and are described in Table 9.1; the effective tax rates are the ones derived from the OECD data and are illustrated by Tables 9.2–9.4. Many more graphs of these effective tax rates are available upon request from the author and are presented in the author's *CEPR Discussion Paper* (1991c).

Table 9.1. Tax systems in Europe: an institutional perspective in 1988

Tax systems	Belgium	Denmark	France	Germany	Italy	The Netherlands	Spain	United Kingdom	Austria	Sweden
1. Personal income tax schedule	Progressive	Progressive	Progressive	Progressive[g]	Progressive	Progressive	Progressive	Progressive	Progressive	Progressive
a. Number of brackets	25 in 1976 (second-bracket lump-sum tax) 29 in 1979 (second-bracket lump-sum tax) 24 in 1978–82	3	13 before 1982; 14 afterwards	4 ranges of marginal tax rates: first two, flat; third, progressive; fourth, flat	37 in 1982 9 in 1983 6 later	9 in 1974 10 in 1975, 1978–79 13 in 1980 10 in 1981–83 9 in 1984–85	16 in 1976 28 from 1977 to 1980 30 in 1981 34 from 1983 to 1987 with a reduction since 1988	10 in 1977 11 in 1978 7 in 1979 6 from 1981 to 1987, with a reduction since 1988	11 in 1975–81 10 in 1982–83	8 in 1974 11 in 1975 12 in 1976 16 in 1977 15 in 1978 18 in 1980–81 15 in 1982 16 in 1983–84 11 in 1985–88
b. Minimum and maximum marginal rate	0–60% in 1975–83 0–72% in 1978–82 0–86.7% in 1986	14.40–39.60% in 1975+20.2% average local income tax rate, with small changes in the local tax up to 1982; 73.00% maximum global (central + local) rate in 1985 68.00% maximum global rate in 1986	0–60% in 1975–81 0–65% in 1982 0–70.2% in 1983–85 0–58% in 1986 0–56.8% since 1987	0–19–53% in 1977 0–22–56% in 1986–90	10–72% in 1975–82 18–65% in 1983 Maximum rate 76% in 1985 Maximum rate 62% in 1986	25–71% in 1974 20–71% in 1975 20–72% in 1976–79 17–72% in 1980–83 16–72% in 1984–85	15–62% in 1976 15–65% in 1977–81 16.14–66% in 1983 16–65% in 1984–85 8–66% in 1986–87 25–56% since 1988	33–83% in 1977 25–83% in 1978 30–60% in 1980–83 29–60% in 1986–87 27–60% in 1987–88	23–62% in 1975–81 21–62% in 1982–83 1986	7–56% in 1974–75 2–58% in 1977–79 1–58% in 1980–82 0–54% in 1983 0–50% in 1985
c. Marginal tax rate for 80.0% of employees[a]	44.0%	28.8%	25.0%	32.0%	19.0%	31.0%	n.a.	34.0%	33.0%	29.0%

Table 9.1. Tax systems in Europe: an institutional perspective in 1988

Tax systems	Belgium	Denmark	France	Germany	Italy	The Netherlands	Spain	United Kingdom	Austria	Sweden
d. Income brackets indexation	No, few changes since 1979 to account for inflation	Yes, non-discretionary in 1970–83; discretionary thereafter	Discretionary since 1969; partial up to 1982, full but still discretionary later	No, some changes to account for inflation since 1977	No, few changes after 1983 to account for inflation	Discretionarily adjusted approximately by 60%–80% since 1971	No, yearly changes since 1981 to increase progressivity	Discretionary since 1981 but usually enforced	No, only two changes to account for inflation	Yes, non-discretionary in 1979–82; discretionary thereafter
e. Tax credits (TC) and/or tax allowances (TA)[b]	TA, TC	TA, TC	TA	TA	TA, TC	TA	TA, TC	TA	TA, TC	TA, TC
f. Tax allowances proportional to income	No	No	Yes, with ceiling	No	No	No	Yes, regressive up to 1978	No	No, but sharp increases in tax credits since 1978–79	Partly fixed and partly proportional
g. Tax credits and tax allowances indexation	No, few changes to account for inflation	Yes, non-discretionary in 1970–83; discretionary thereafter	No, some changes in the ceiling to account for inflation	No, some changes in 1979 and in 1981	No	Discretionarily adjusted approximately by 60–80% since 1971	No, yearly changes since 1979	Yes, non-discretionary since 1978	No	Yes, non-discretionary in 1979–82; discretionary thereafter

Table 9.1. Tax systems in Europe: an institutional perspective in 1988

Tax systems	Belgium	Denmark	France	Germany	Italy	The Netherlands	Spain	United Kingdom	Austria	Sweden
h. Main structural changes in the last 30 years	1962 Tax reform for the introduction of progressivity. 1988-89: Tax reform to enlarge the tax base and reduce top rates	1987: Tax reform to enlarge the tax base and reduce top rates	1983: Start of a tax restructuring that increased the tax base and reduced top rates	1986-90: Reform programme to widen the tax base, reduce marginal rates and introduce a linear progressive tax scale, significantly affecting the third income bracket[f]	1974: Tax reform for the introduction of the actual progressive tax system 1983: Reduction of number of brackets and top rates	1964: Tax reform for the introduction of the actual progressive tax system 1986: Proposed reform with the intent to simplify the tax structure	1975: Tax reform that introduced the actual progressive tax system 1988: Fiscal reform that enhanced progressivity	1979: Tax reform to enlarge the tax base and reduce top rates	1989: Tax reform to enlarge the tax base, lower and flatten the marginal income tax rates and reduce the number of brackets	1982: Tax reform for the reduction of top rates; 1985: Tax reform to reduce the number of brackets and top rates[f]
II. Social security OSD Schedule[c]	Flat without ceiling	Flat for basic insurance: regressive for supplementary insurance	Flat with ceiling	Flat with ceiling	Flat without ceiling	Mildly regressive with ceiling	Flat within a floor and a ceiling	Progressive with ceiling[d]	Flat with ceiling	Flat without ceiling
i. Employee tax rate	7.50% in 1985-88	3.50% of the personal income tax base +33.40 DKR. in 1985; 58.30 DKR. in 1988	5.80% in 1985 6.60% in 1988	9.60% in 1985 9.35% in 1988	7.50% in 1984 6.86% in 1985	13.1% in 1985 12.8% in 1988	4.80% in 1984-88	6.85% in 1985 Minimum and maximum marginal rate: 5%-9% in 1985-88	10.25% in 1985-88	0.00% in 1985-88

Table 9.1. Tax systems in Europe: an institutional perspective in 1988

l. Employer tax rate	8.86% in 1985–88	64.80 DKR in 1985; 2.50% of the VAT base in 1983	8.20% in 1985–88	9.60% in 1985; 9.35% in 1988	17.97% in 1984; 17.65% in 1985	n.a.	24.31% in 1984–88	6.35% in 1985; Minimum and maximum marginal rate: 5%–10.45% in 1985–88	12.45% in 1985; 12.55% in 1988	19.45% in 1985; 19.55% in 1988
m. Percentage of employees under the ceiling in 1985	100.00%	100.00%	100.00%	95.00%	100.00%	n.a.	90.00%	n.a.	90.00%	100.00%
III. Indirect VAT tax schedule[e]	6 rates	1 rate	4 rates	2 rates	4 rates	2 rates	3 rates	1 rate	3 rates	2 rates
n. Maximum rate	33.00%	No	33.30%	No	38.00%	No	33.00%	No	32.00%	No
o. Minimum rate	1.00%	No	5.50%	7.00%	2.00%	6.00%	6.00%	No	10.00%	12.90%
p. Basic rate	19.00%	22.00%	18.60%	14.00%	18.00%	20.00%	12.00%	15.00%	20.00%	23.50%
q. Year of introduction and basic rate then	1971: 18.00%	1967: 10.00%	1968: 20.00%	1968: 10.00%	1973: 12.00%	1969: 12.00%	1986: 12.00%	1973: 10.00%	1973: 16.00%	1969: 11.00%
r. Basic rate in 1979	16.00%	20.25%	17.60%	13.00%	14.00%	18.00%	No	15.00%	18.00%	20.60%

0 Value Zero.

n.a. Not available.

Sources:

Andersson (1988); Bayar (1989); Hagemann *et al.* (1988); Lipschitz *et al.* (1989); Lopez-Claros (1988); OECD (1976); OECD (1977); OECD (1981a); OECD (1981b); OECD (1986a); OECD (1986b); OECD (1986c); OECD (1989a); OECD (1989b); Padoa Schioppa (1992a); Pechman, (1987); Tanzi (1980).

a All the information refers to 1981 and only to the tax rates levied by the Central Government. The distinction is particularly important for some countries: for example, in Sweden Local Government income taxes are levied at a flat rate of about 30%.

b Data include income and non-income related tax allowances and tax credits with the exception of Denmark, whose tax allowances are only income-related.

c Data include social-security contributions for old age, survivor and disability (OSD) insurances in every country with the exception of France and The Netherlands, whose data include only OS contributions, Spain, whose data include OSD and health insurance contributions, and the United Kingdom, whose data include OSD, injury and unemployment contributions.

d The ceiling on employers' was abolished in 1985.

e All the information in the first four rows (up to p) refers to 1987. VAT is the value added tax.

f Significant changes in the income tax systems have taken place in the 1960s and the 1970s particularly in Germany, Austria and Sweden.

g The German personal income tax schedule presents an upward-sloping marginal tax rate function for one of the income brackets not a step function everywhere.

A second, more general, heterogeneity concerning indirect taxes of various European countries, considers the weight these taxes have on the general tax revenues comprehensive of indirect taxes, social security contributions and income taxes. Although different in the level, the dynamic path of the weight of indirect taxes over the tax bill has almost everywhere not increased in the last 30 years.

9.2.2 Social security contributions

Social security scheduled tax rates for old age, survival and disability pensions (OSD) are essentially similar – although in some respects different – in the various European countries under observation, as confirmed by Table 9.1 (see rows under heading II, i, 1 and m): the OSD tax rate is flat everywhere except in The Netherlands, where it is mildly regressive, in Denmark, where the supplementary insurance is regressive, and in the United Kingdom, where it is partially progressive. In most countries, OSD contributions might become regressive because the marginal social-security tax rate drops to zero at a ceiling wage level (as in France, Germany, The Netherlands, Spain, the United Kingdom, and Austria); observe, however (in row m of Table 9.1), that in practice this is not the case because the ceiling is usually set above the wage level of all employees (with the partial exception of Germany, Spain and Austria).

Therefore, the assumption of a flat, effective (not scheduled) social-security tax rate paid for OSD and other items (health, unemployment, work injuries) both by employees (labelled SL) and by employers (labelled S) adequately corresponds to the facts generally observed in European countries. Note that the effective employees' (or employers') social-security tax rates are larger than the corresponding scheduled OSD, with the possible exception of Denmark because the scheduled tax rates are applied on a tax base different from the one on which S and SL are calculated[6], and with the exception of Spain because in this country – unlike elsewhere – social security contributions are paid only on wage rates exceeding a floor level.

However, important differences in social-security contributions emerge between different European countries, particularly as far as the weight of these contributions on the total tax bill and the relative share paid by employers and by employees are concerned. The maximum weight is observed in France, Italy and Spain; the minimum in Denmark and UK. In recent years, the scheduled OSD employees' tax rate (row i, Table 9.1) and the (observed) SL rate both range between a minimum in Scandinavian countries (Sweden approaching zero since 1975, Denmark) and a maximum in The Netherlands (where, as in most other countries, it has been ever increasing from the 1960s to the beginning of the 1980s); in the starting years under examination, the highest SL rates were ob-

---

[6] These and other technical details concerning the utilized OECD empirical evidence are described in the data appendix mentioned in footnote 2.

served in Italy and Germany. Only in Italy, Sweden and Spain is the OSD scheduled employers' social-security tax rate larger than that of the employees (compare rows 1 and i, Table 9.1), while the two rates present comparable values in all other countries. Some scheduled differences in the OSD contributions charged to employers and to employees are attenuated when looking at the effective *S*/*SL* ratios (e.g. in Italy), while others unexpectedly appear (e.g. in Belgium and Austria). The intercountry difference in the observed employers' social security tax rate, *S*, has been enormous in the past and, though shrinking in the recent years, still remains very large, with *S* ranging between minimum values of 2% in Denmark and 7.5% in the United Kingdom, and maximum values approximately equalling 30% in France, Sweden and Spain.

But the temporal path of the observed employers' social security tax rate is very similar in all European countries, with *S* almost uninterruptedly positively trended since the beginning of the 1960s: an exception is Italy which shows huge cycles in its upward *S* trend, due to frequent reductions of employers' social-security contributions – particularly after 1976 – in the hope of favouring the growth of employment; another exception is Denmark which presents an upturn of *S* in the beginning of the 1980s after a continuous decline in the first 15 years under observation, as part of the Danish fiscal adjustment, combined with a downturn in the already small employees' effective social security tax rate, *SL*, due to a basic reform in the social security system.

9.2.3 Personal income taxes

The scheduled personal income tax systems are also in few respects very similar but in others very different in different European countries, as clarified by Table 9.1 (see all the headings after row I). The observed average personal income tax rate, denoted by *IL*, also varies between maximum values in Scandinavian countries (Denmark, Sweden) and minimum values in Latin countries (Spain, France, Italy).

Everywhere, the personal income tax schedule is progressive and this (step-wise) progressivity is ensured by increasing marginal tax rates for successive income brackets. The number of brackets ranges from a minimum of three in Denmark to a maximum of more than 30 in Italy (before 1983) and Spain (see row a). As is well-known and documented by rows b, c[7] of Table 9.1, the top marginal scheduled tax rates are of only limited importance: it may happen that countries such as Italy with relatively high top marginal tax rates (72% at the beginning of the 1980s) turn out to impose on the majority of taxpayers an effective marginal tax rate among the lowest in Europe (19% for 80% of employees); by contrast, in other countries such as Belgium with similar top marginal tax rates, the majority of taxpayers is subject, *de facto*, to an extremely high marginal tax rate (80% of employees to a marginal tax rate of 44%).

---

[7] One should not forget, however, that row c refers, unlike the OECD data on the effective tax rates, to central-government taxes only and not to general-government taxes.

Consequently, income tax progressivity should be measured through the observed average tax rates borne by different taxpayers earning different levels of income rather than through the scheduled top marginal tax rate. Lacking these cross-section data for most countries and most years within the 1960–88 period considered here, one can use, as a proxy, time-series data on the observed average direct tax rates and on the aggregate nominal and the real wage rates, under the reasonable assumption that the personal income tax system has remained constant over time except in the specific years and for the specific reasons, different in different countries, institutionally known.

Throughout Europe income tax progressivity has always been in existence in the period under examination, except in Italy and Spain, where it was essentially raised by a radical fiscal reform in 1975: in that year, a structural break in personal income taxation occurred in these two countries. At the opposite, during the 1980s most European countries underwent major fiscal changes aimed at decreasing the progressivity of their personal income tax schedule through a broadening of the tax base and a reduction of the top marginal tax rates. From this view point, the leading country has been the United Kingdom, where such a tax reform was adopted in 1979; later, the Thatcher vein has been followed, to some extent, by Sweden, France, Italy, Germany and more recently by Denmark, The Netherlands, Belgium, Spain and Austria (see row h in Table 9.1).

These tax policies of the 1980s, while mainly aiming to raise efficiency and create new incentives to workers and producers, have had – as an important by-product – the capacity to counterbalance the combined effects on fiscal drag of progressivity in personal income taxation and of high inflation. Consequently, some form of *de facto* fiscal indexation was introduced, implying either the constancy of the average personal income tax rate or its growth related to the real wage rate (as it will be specified in sections 9.3 and 9.4).

In some countries the tax reform really inaugurated a new wave of *de facto* fiscal indexation. This is the case of the United Kingdom, where a non-discretionary legal indexation of tax allowances and tax credits has been in existence since 1978 but where income brackets were not indexed at all, only becoming discretionarily indexed after the Thatcher's fiscal reform (see rows d–h, Table 9.1). The observed average personal income tax rate, IL, has been growing ever since 1960 and only stopped increasing precisely around 1979, the year of the fiscal reform.

In other countries, these 'Thatcherian' tax reforms were superimposed on an already existing regime of partial or full fiscal indexation and served the purpose of maintaining, in a new way, the previous regime rather than introducing a radically new one. For example in Sweden, as indicated by rows d–h of Table 9.1, a non-discretionary legal indexation of personal income taxes was put forth in 1979 by the only post-war Swedish Conservative Government; while in 1982 the legal fiscal indexation was fading out being in the process of becoming discretionary, the tax reform of 1982 was able to newly reinforce the existing fiscal regime. The same reasoning appears to hold true for The Netherlands, which started its legal partial fiscal indexation around the beginning of the 1970s (rows d–f, Table 9.1), further reinforcing its *de facto* tax indexation already at the beginning of the 1980s (rows a, b. and g, Table 9.1)

By contrast, in other countries, the fiscal changes of the 1980s have probably restored a much older tax structure. This seems to be the case of France where the tax innovations of the 1980s intervened on a fiscal system which was *de lege* partially and discretionarily indexed since 1969 (in the income brackets, not in the tax allowance components, but tax allowances are in France – unlike in most other European countries – proportional to income, as shown by Table 9.1), *de facto* reinforcing fiscal indexation. A similar process appears to hold true in Italy where the 1983 legal reduction in the number of income brackets and top marginal income tax rates probably led to a degree of effective fiscal indexation comparable to the one which was in existence before the 1974 fiscal reform.

Finally, in other countries, the tax policy inspired by the 'Thatcherian' principles consisted of fine tuning, frequent restructuring of the fiscal systems more than radical modifications. A similar case is provided by Germany, which, though constitutionally opposing any kind of indexation, has introduced, according to Table 9.1, first some changes in income brackets (since 1977) and tax allowances (since 1979), second (in 1986) a more definite programme of reductions in the top marginal tax rates and in the degree of progressivity of the personal income tax schedule: the implications in terms of the constancy of the observed average income tax rate, *IL*, are perhaps unexpected but nonetheless evident in the data. Similarly, Belgium and Austria since 1979 have started to introduce minor variations in the number or in the nominal value of their income brackets and tax deductions to account for inflation, with some consequences for the *de facto* indexation of their personal income taxes.

Lastly, there are other countries which have, over a considerable period, legally and non-discretionarily indexed their personal income tax schedule without adopting (if not very recently) a 'Thatcherian' fiscal reform: notably Denmark, as described in Table 9.1, has not only fully indexed both its income brackets and its tax credits and allowances between 1970 and 1983, later abandoning fiscal indexation precisely to allow the fiscal drag to act as an instrument to reduce public deficits, but it is also the only country in Europe to have legally adjusted the nominal personal income tax to the wage rather than to the consumer price dynamics.

9.2.4 Differences and similarities of effective tax rates in 10 European countries from the 1960s to the 1980s

In order to give a preliminary evaluation on differences and similarities of effective tax rates and tax structures borne by European workers in the 1960s, the 1970s and the 1980s, the following simplifications will be adopted in Table 9.2.

1. Five-year averages of OECD cross-country comparable data will be considered, starting with 1965–69.
2. Only three observed fiscal indicators will be analysed, the direct tax rate, the other tax rates mentioned above, and the sum of the previous two rates, i.e. the so-called tax wedge. In the recent economic literature[8] this tax wedge (denoted as tw in Table 9.2) is considered as the most relevant synhetical index of global fiscal pressure, it being the sum of S, T, IL and SL. But Padoa Schioppa (1990, 1992b) has proved that the tax wedge is the most proper index of global fiscal pressure only if all tax rates are flat. When the latter hypothesis is not consistent with the facts, as it is not for personal income taxes, due to progressivity, the papers just quoted suggest to examine separately the direct tax rate and all the other relevant tax rates. Indeed, if one looks at all taxes levied on labour income, rather than distinguishing the personal income tax rate, IL, from the employees' social security tax rate, SL, the so-called average direct tax rate, denoted by Λ in Table 9.2 and defined as $IL + SL$, is certainly progressive, the direct tax rate being the sum of a progressive (IL) and a flat (SL) tax rate; on the contrary, the employers' social security contributions tax rate, S, the indirect tax rate, T, and the sum of the two, $S + T$,[9] are probably flat, as argued above.
3. Besides supplying this empirical evidence for each of the 10 countries under examination, Table 9.2 also describes the tax wedge, the direct tax rate and the other tax rates for the unweighted average of the eight EEC countries and for the unweighted average of the 10 European countries (including Austria and Sweden) involved in this study.

Table 9.2 indicates that both for the average of the eight EEC countries and for the 10 European countries examined, the direct tax rate, Λ, changed more rapidly over time than the other tax rates ($S + T$), leading to a substantial increase of the tax wedge (tw) from the 1960s to the 1980s.

Each of the 10 European fiscal systems evolved in its own way, starting from heterogeneous 'initial conditions'. However, precisely because the dynamic path was not identical in the various European countries, one gets the impression that nowadays differences in tax rates and tax structures are attenuated relative to the past, though remaining quite strong. For example, in 1965–69 the distance between the minimum and the maximum observed direct tax rate was approximately 1–7 (1 for Spain, 7 for Sweden), while becoming in the late 1980s lower than 1 to 3 (the minimum still in Spain, the maximum in Denmark). A more precise statistical index of intercountry direct tax variability will confirm in section 9.5 this first impression.

[8] Theoretical, empirical and econometric analyses all agree on the importance of the tax wedge from this viewpoint, even when the tax wedge is found to be statistically ineffective on economic agents: see, for example, Tanzi (1980) Nickell and Andrews (1983) Bean *et al.* (1986), Coe and Gagliardi (1985), Dreze and Bean (1991), Knoester and van der Windt (1987).
[9] In the works of Padoa Schioppa (1990, 1992b) it is shown that S and T have the same effect on optimal wage setting and employment, so that the sum, $S+T$, becomes a relevant fiscal index.

Table 9.2 Five-year averages of the sum of the employers' social security and the indirect tax rates $(S + T)$, of the tax wedge (tw), and the average direct tax rate $(\Lambda \equiv IL + SL)$, in 10 European countries

Countries		1965–69	1970–74	1975–79	1980–84	1985–88
Belgium	$S+T$	0.299	0.296	0.296	0.291	0.321
	tw	0.447	0.486	0.550	0.569	0.608
	Λ	0.148	0.190	0.254	0.278	0.287
Denmark[a]	$S+T$	0.202	0.212	0.213	0.233	0.255
	tw	0.453	0.560	0.560	0.592	0.667
	Λ	0.251	0.348	0.347	0.359	0.412
France[b]	$S+T$	0.431	0.418	0.437	0.465	0.487
	tw	0.599	0.588	0.643	0.712	0.759
	Λ	0.168	0.170	0.206	0.247	0.272
Germany	$S+T$	0.272	0.279	0.299	0.310	0.311
	tw	0.531	0.563	0.631	0.639	0.647
	Λ	0.259	0.284	0.332	0.329	0.336
Italy[c]	$S+T$	0.317	0.311	0.319	0.316	0.319
	tw	0.420	0.421	0.451	0.515	0.539
	Λ	0.103	0.110	0.132	0.199	0.220
The Netherlands[d]	$S+T$	0.252	0.267	0.306	0.332	0.353
	tw	0.526	0.593	0.672	0.736	0.750
	Λ	0.274	0.326	0.366	0.404	0.397
Spain[b]	$S+T$	0.243	0.256	0.276	0.357	0.402
	tw	0.283	0.323	0.388	0.509	0.577
	Λ	0.040	0.067	0.112	0.152	0.175
United Kingdom	$S+T$	0.218	0.221	0.231	0.266	0.269
	tw	0.391	0.411	0.448	0.480	0.484
	Λ	0.173	0.190	0.217	0.214	0.215
Austria	$S+T$	0.355	0.371	0.385	0.410	0.423
	tw	0.528	0.569	0.600	0.647	0.666
	Λ	0.173	0.198	0.215	0.237	0.243
Sweden[b]	$S+T$	0.220	0.270	0.398	0.471	0.499
	tw	0.503	0.584	0.738	0.809	0.852
	Λ	0.283	0.314	0.340	0.338	0.353
8 EEC Countries	$S+T$	0.279	0.283	0.297	0.321	0.340
	tw	0.456	0.493	0.543	0.594	0.629
	Λ	0.177	0.211	0.246	0.273	0.289
10 European Countries	$S+T$	0.281	0.290	0.316	0.345	0.364
	tw	0.468	0.510	0.568	0.621	0.655
	Λ	0.187	0.220	0.252	0.276	0.291

Source: OECD data mentioned in Footnote 2.
[a] In Denmark, the first year for which data are available is 1966.
[b] In France, Spain, Austria and Sweden, the last year for which data are available is 1987.
[c] In Italy, the last year for which data are available is 1985.
[d] In The Netherlands, the first year for which data are available is 1987.

Over the entire period under consideration, heterogeneities seem to regard the tax structure, i.e. the weight assigned to direct taxation relative to other taxes, more than the global fiscal pressure. Again this statement will be clarified through a proper statistical index in section 9.5 but it is already apparent from Table 9.2 that very few European countries are characterized either by high or by low fiscal pressure both in direct *and* in other tax rates. Using a ranking of the 10 European countries with regard to $S + T$ on the one side and Λ on the other, it can be seen that in the late 1980s only the United Kingdom presents very low direct tax rates *and* very low other tax rates, showing the minimum tax wedge, while Sweden presents very high direct tax rates *and* very high other tax rates, showing the maximum tax wedge. In most cases the two forms of taxation 'compensate' each other: for example, in Denmark the maximum (among the European countries) of the direct tax rate is combined with the minimum of indirect and employers' social security tax rates; a similar imbalance, although not so strong, appears to hold true in Germany; on the contrary in Spain the minimum (among the European countries) of the direct tax rate is combined with very high indirect and employers' social security tax rates; the same kind of imbalance, although not so strong, arises in France, while Belgium, The Netherlands and, to a limited extent, Italy indicate a more even tax structure.

But Table 9.2 reports only effective average tax rates. It is well-known, however, that this is not a sufficient information when tax rates are progressive, as direct tax rates are, everywhere. Next two sections will, therefore, be devoted to evaluate first analytically and then empirically the degree of progressivity and *de facto* indexation of direct tax systems on labour income in Europe.

9.3 A THEORETICAL MODEL ON DIRECT TAX PROGRESSIVITY AND *DE FACTO* INDEXATION FOR 10 EUROPEAN COUNTRIES

In order to accomplish this task, I will start by presenting a theoretical model able to identify the marginal direct tax rate of the average taxpayer, showing a proper index for effective progressivity and fiscal indexation. In the model I will first consider the basic characteristics of a non-indexed direct tax system, distinguishing the case of the representative individual direct taxation and the case of aggregate direct taxation. I will then examine partially indexed and fully indexed fiscal systems, according to two possible rules of indexation. In any case I will ignore, for simplicity[10], tax allowances or credits. The reader who is not interested in the theoretical model may skip sections 9.3.1–9.3.3, and go directly to the summary provided in 9.3.4.

9.3.1 No indexation in the tax system: individual direct taxation

The direct tax, $\bar{T}$, of an individual, earning a wage, W, is

---

[10] A more general model including tax allowances and credits can be found in my *CEPR Discussion Paper* (1991c).

$$\bar{T} = \beta_0 W_0 + \beta_1(W_1 - W_0) + \beta_2(W_2 - W_1) + \ldots + \beta_N(W - W_{N-1}) + SL\, W$$

$$= (\beta_0 - \beta_1)W_0 + (\beta_1 - \beta_2)W_1 + (\beta_2 - \beta_3)W_2 + \ldots + \beta_N W + SL\, W$$

where β_0 is the tax rate for wages up to W_0; β_1 is the tax rate for the income bracket $W_1 - W_0$ etc.; of course, $W_{i+1} > W_i$ and $\beta_{i+1} > \beta_i$ for any i if income taxation is progressive, while $\beta_{i+1} = \beta_i$ for any i if income taxation is proportional; SL is the employees' flat social security tax rate. In what follows, unless otherwise specified, I will mainly discuss the progressive direct taxation.

The corresponding average direct tax rate is $\bar{\Lambda}$. Using a logarithmic approximation consisting in assuming that the percentage variation $(W_i - W)/W$ can be proxied by $\log(W_i/W)$, the following formula for $\bar{\Lambda}$ is obtained:

$$\bar{\Lambda} = \frac{\bar{T}}{W} = \beta_0\left(1 + \log\frac{W_0}{W}\right) + \beta_1\left(\log\frac{W_1}{W} - \log\frac{W_0}{W}\right) + \ldots - \beta_N\left(\log\frac{W_{N-1}}{W}\right) + SL$$

$$= \beta_0(1 + \log W_0) + \beta_1(\log W_1 - \log W_0) + \beta_2(\log W_2 - \log W_1)$$

$$+ \ldots + \beta_{N-1}(\log W_{N-1} - \log W_{N-2}) - \beta_N \log W_{N-1} + (\beta_N - \beta_0)\log W + SL$$

or

$$\bar{\Lambda} = \hat{\alpha} + \hat{\beta} \log W \tag{9.1}$$

with

$$\hat{\alpha} \equiv SL + \beta_0(1 + \log W_0) + \beta_1 \log(W_1/W_0) + \beta_2 \log(W_2/W_1) + \ldots$$

$$+ \beta_{N-1} \log(W_{N-1}/W_{N-2}) - \beta_N \log W_{N-1} \tag{9.1a}$$

$$\hat{\beta} \equiv \beta_N - \beta_0 \tag{9.1b}$$

The essential point illustrated by equations (9.1), (9.1a) and (9.1b) is that the average direct tax rate of a wage earner, paying progressive income taxes according to the rule illustrated above – which is generally enforced in European countries – is linear in logarithms.

In the specific case of two income brackets only, where $W_{N-1} = W_0$, hence, $W_1 = W$ and $W_i = 0$ for every $i > 1$, the average direct tax rate is

$$\bar{\Lambda} = \bar{\alpha} + \bar{\beta} \log W \tag{9.2}$$

with

$$\bar{\alpha} = \beta_0(1 + \log W_0) - \beta_1 \log W_0 + SL \tag{9.2a}$$

$$\bar{\beta} = \beta_1 - \beta_0 \tag{9.2b}$$

From now on, I will confine myself only to this specific case of two income brackets because it simplifies the calculations without losing the general message. An important point to remark is that when the average direct tax rate is log-linear, the marginal tax rate equals the average plus a constant. Indeed, the marginal tax rate is

$$d(\bar{\Lambda}W)/dW = \bar{\alpha} + \bar{\beta}\log W + \bar{\beta} = \bar{\Lambda} + \bar{\beta} \qquad (9.2c)$$

9.3.2 No indexation in the tax system: aggregate direct taxation

What happens if there are wage earners with different wage levels?

Let me call *TT* the aggregate direct taxes paid by wage earners and *WA* the aggregate wage bill. Assume that there are two types of wage earners: **type 1**, having a wage equal to W^1 and being as many as L^1, and **type 2** having a wage equal to W^2 and being as many as L^2. The average direct tax rate in the economic system, ΛA, is

$$\Lambda A = \frac{TT}{WA} = \frac{L^1 T^1 + L^2 T^2}{L^1 W^1 + L^2 W^2} = \frac{T^1}{W^1}\left(\frac{L^1 W^1}{L^1 W^1 + L^2 W^2}\right) + \frac{T^2}{W^2}\left(\frac{L^2 W^2}{L^2 W^2 + L^1 W^1}\right) \qquad (9.3)$$

The fiscal pressure, ΛA is, therefore, a weighted average of the tax rates on wage earners of type 1 and type 2, with weights equal to the income share of the type 1 (type 2) wage earners, relative to total income.

To give an example, suppose that type 1 wage earners have a wage falling in the second income bracket, while type 2 wage earners have a wage falling in the third income bracket. Hence,

$$\Lambda^1 = \frac{T^1}{W^1} = \beta_1 - \frac{W_0}{W^1}(\beta_1 - \beta_0) + SL = \bar{\alpha} + \bar{\beta}\log W^1$$

$$\Lambda^2 = \frac{T^2}{W^2} = \beta_2 + (\beta_0 - \beta_1)\left(1 + \log\frac{W_0}{W^2}\right) + (\beta_1 - \beta_2)\left(1 + \log\frac{W^1}{W^2}\right) + SL$$

$$= \tilde{\alpha} + (\beta_2 - \beta_0)\log W^2$$

with

$$\tilde{\alpha} = \bar{\alpha} - (\beta_2 - \beta_1)\log W^1$$

The average direct tax rate of type 1 and type 2 wage earners is plotted in Figure 9.1. The aggregate average direct tax rate, ΛA, is higher than the average direct tax rate paid on the average wage because of convexity. The difference between ΛA and $\bar{\Lambda}$ is smaller, the smaller is the wage dispersion around the average wage rate, for a given average wage rate, W.

From now onwards, I will deal only with the case of direct taxation as if all individuals were alike, bearing in mind, however, that the better it approximates the behaviour of the aggregate direct taxation, the lower is the wage dispersion around the average wage rate.

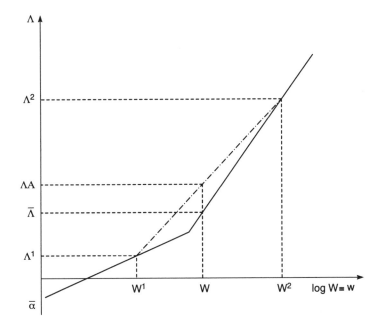

Fig. 9.1 Average direct tax rate of type 1 and type 2 wage earners.

9.3.3 Indexation in the tax system: the representative individual direct taxation

In the European direct tax systems there exist essentially two possible indexes relative to which nominal taxes are adjusted to account for undesirable changes in direct tax rates induced by inflation. One index concerns the wage rate, the other the consumer price. The former is rarely adopted *ex lege*, when indexing direct tax schedules, but it has been legally introduced in Denmark between 1970 and 1983. The latter has been legally adopted more often for example in France since 1969, and, with some adjustments for changes in VAT, in The Netherlands and in Sweden; in the United Kingdom the index used in the fiscal legal indexation is the retail price.

According to the first rule of indexation I will say that there is fiscal indexation if

$$\frac{T(1)}{W(1)} = \frac{T(0)}{W(0)} \quad \text{or} \quad \Lambda(1) = \Lambda(0)$$

where 0 refers to the initial period, while 1 to a subsequent one. This implies that the direct tax rate is constant through time even when the nominal or the real wage is changing.

According to the second rule of indexation, there is fiscal indexation if at time $t = 1$ and $t = 0$ direct taxation in real terms remains constant, provided there have been no institutional changes between date 0 and date 1, and the real wage has not varied. This requires

$$\frac{T(1)}{P(1)} = \frac{T(0)}{P(0)} \quad \text{if} \quad \frac{W(1)}{P(1)} = \frac{W(0)}{P(0)}$$

where P is the consumer price level. Of course, both conditions just mentioned are satisfied when direct taxation is proportional ($\beta_0 = \beta_1 = \ldots = \beta_N$ and $\bar{\Lambda} = \bar{\alpha}$). To see when the same results are obtained in the case of progressive direct taxation, let me first define

$$\frac{W(0)}{P(0)} = WR^0 = \text{real wage at date 0,}$$

$$\frac{W(0)}{P(1)} = WR^1 = \text{real wage at time 0 deflated by time 1 prices,}$$

$$\frac{W(1)}{P(0)} = \hat{W}R^0 = \text{real wage at time 1 deflated by time 0 prices,}$$

$$\frac{W(1)}{P(1)} = WR = \text{real wage at dates 1, 2, \ldots, n,}$$

$$\frac{W_0(0)}{P(0)} = WR_0^0 = \text{first bracket real wage at date 0,}$$

$$\frac{W_0(1)}{P(1)} = WR_0 = \text{first bracket real wage at dates 1, 2, \ldots, n.}$$

Let me show under which conditions the progressive direct tax is indexed, if the adjustment for inflation is done according to the change in the wage rate (first rule). Note that the nominal tax at time 1 is

$$T(1) = \beta_0 W_0(1) + \beta_1 [W(1) - W_0(1)] + SL \cdot W(1)$$

while the nominal tax at time 0 is

$$T(0) = \beta_0 W_0(0) + \beta_1 [W(0) - W_0(0)] + SL \cdot W(0)$$

Thus, according to the first indexation rule, the direct tax system is indexed if

$$\frac{T(0)}{W(0)} = \beta_1 + SL - \frac{(\beta_1 - \beta_0)W_0(0)}{W(0)} = \frac{T(1)}{W(1)} = \beta_1 + SL - \frac{(\beta_1 - \beta_0)W_0(1)}{W(1)};$$

this may hold true if and only if the ratio of the first income bracket to the nominal wage, W_0/W, is constant through time, in which case $W_0(1) = W_0(0) W(1)/W(0)$.

More generally, the ratio of every income bracket relative to the wage rate has to remain constant so that the direct tax incorporating this kind of indexation must have the following form:

$$\bar{T}_i = (\beta_0 - \beta_1) \frac{WR_0^0}{WR^0} WR \cdot P + (\beta_1 + SL)WR \cdot P$$

with

$$\overline{\Lambda}_i = \frac{\overline{T}_i}{W} = \frac{\overline{T}_i}{WR \cdot P} = \text{constant}$$

Let me now show under which conditions the progressive direct tax is indexed, if the adjustment for inflation is done according to the growth rate of prices (second rule). Following this second rule, the tax system is indexed if

$$\frac{T(1)}{P(1)} = (\beta_0 - \beta_1)WR_0 + (\beta_1 + SL)WR = \frac{T(0)}{P(0)} = (\beta_0 - \beta_1)WR_0^0 + (\beta_1 + SL)WR^0$$

These two real taxes are identical, when $WR = WR^0$, if and only if the first bracket nominal wage, i.e. the one with tax rate β_0, is indexed at date 1. Then $W_0(1) = W_0(0)P(1)/P(0)$, so that $WR_0 = WR_0^0$. With N income brackets, each of them must be indexed to consumer prices.

More generally, the real tax is independent from prices if and only if the nominal direct tax, T_i, is conceived as follows:

$$T_i = (\beta_0 - \beta_1)WR_0^0 \cdot P + (\beta_1 + SL)WRP$$

where both T_i, and P refer to any possible time subsequent to the initial one.

The corresponding average direct tax rate is

$$\Lambda_i = \frac{T_i}{W} = \beta_1 + SL + (\beta_0 - \beta_1)\frac{WR_0^0}{WR} = \alpha_i + \overline{\beta}\log WR \qquad (9.4)$$

with

$$\alpha_i = \overline{\alpha} + \overline{\beta}\log P(0) \qquad (9.4a)$$

From now onwards, unless explicitly mentioned, I will analyse fiscal indexation **only with reference to this second kind of adjustment rule**: unlike the former, the latter rule implies that the average direct tax rate is constant when there is a proportional increase in the nominal wage and the consumer price level but it rises if the real wage increases. More precisely, the average direct tax rate with indexed income brackets, Λ_i, is a linear logarithmic function of the real wage, WR.

Note that the indexation of income brackets reduces the average (progressive) direct tax relative to the non-indexed fiscal system, when prices rise, because it avoids the so-called 'bracket creep'. In fact,

$$\Lambda_i = \overline{\alpha} + \overline{\beta}\log P(0) + \overline{\beta}\log W - \overline{\beta}\log P < \overline{\Lambda} = \overline{\alpha} + \overline{\beta}\log W \quad \text{if } P > P(0) \quad (9.4b)$$

Note also that in this indexed fiscal system the marginal tax rate is again equal to the average (Λ_i) plus a constant. Indeed, the marginal direct tax rate is

$$d(\Lambda_i W)/dW = \alpha_i + \overline{\beta}\log WR + \overline{\beta}[1 - (d\log P/d\log W)] = \Lambda_i + \overline{\beta}(1 - q) \quad (9.4c)$$

where q is defined as the consumer price elasticity to wages ($q \equiv dp/dw$) and is supposed to be a non-negative constant ranging between zero and one. It then clearly appears that if $P > P(0)$ and if the price elasticity to wages is non-negative, the marginal direct tax rate is lower when the fiscal system is indexed than it would be if the fiscal system were non-indexed because $\Lambda_i + \bar{\beta}(1-q) < \bar{\Lambda} + \bar{\beta}$.

When fiscal indexation is only partial – perhaps because income brackets are indexed but tax credits or allowances identical for every wage earner are not, or *vice versa* – the average direct tax rate is a log-linear positive function of the nominal wage rate and a negative function of the consumer price, as in the following example, where tax credits and allowances are fixed in dollar terms $[T_0 = kW_0(0)]$. Indeed, in this event the tax is

$$T_{1,i} = (\beta_0 - \beta_1)WR_0^0 \cdot P + (\beta_1 + SL)WR \cdot P - kW_0(0)$$

$$= \{(\beta_0 - \beta_1)[P/P(0)] - k\}W_0(0) + (\beta_1 + SL)WR \cdot P$$

The corresponding average direct tax rate is

$$\Lambda_{1,i} = \beta_1 + SL + \{(\beta_0 - \beta_1)[P/P(0)] - k\}\frac{W_0(0)}{W}$$

$$= \alpha_{1,i} + \bar{\beta} \log WR + k\log W = \alpha_{1,i} + (\bar{\beta}+k) \log W - \bar{\beta} \log P \qquad (9.5)$$

with

$$\alpha_{1,i} = \alpha_i - k[1 + \log W_0(0)] \qquad (9.5a)$$

Four points are worth noting in this, as in other cases of partial indexation: (i) the average direct tax rate is a log-linear function of both the nominal wage and the consumer price level, (ii) the semielasticity of Λ relative to the nominal wage is higher in absolute value than the one relative to the price level, (iii) the direct tax with tax credits is lower than the corresponding without tax credits $(T_i > T_{1,i})$ with $\alpha_i > \alpha_{1,i}$; but (iv) the marginal tax rate may be higher, as $\Lambda_{1,i} + \bar{\beta}(1-q) + k > \Lambda_i + \bar{\beta}(1-q)$, because $W_0 < W$.

9.3.4 A generalized equation for the average direct tax rate

In conclusion, if direct taxation is progressive and progressivity is obtained by charging different marginal tax rates on different wage brackets, the observed average direct tax rate, Λ, in the absence of fiscal indexation, can be approximated by a log-linear function of the nominal wage rate, W (log W is denoted as w). If direct taxation is progressive and fully indexed to the price dynamics (the usual case of fiscal indexation), the corresponding observed average tax rate, Λ, can be approximated by a log-linear function of the real wage rate, WR (log WR, denoted as wr), implying that it increases only if the nominal wage rate grows proportionately more than the consumer price index, P (where $\log P \equiv p$), and remains constant if there is wage indexation ($wr \equiv w - p$ is constant). Moreover, if direct taxation is progressive and only partially indexed, Λ is a log-linear function both of the nominal wage rate, and (with opposite sign) of the consumer price: the semielasticity of Λ relative to W (denoted as β) is in absolute value higher than the semielasticity relative to P (denoted as γ). Finally, if direct taxation is progressive and fully indexed to the wage rather than to the price dynamics (as it used to be the case *ex lege* in Denmark), the observed average tax rate, Λ, is constant. Unless otherwise mentioned, I will always talk about fiscal indexation in the former, not in the latter sense.

Therefore, the general formula derived in this model for the average direct tax rate is

$$\Lambda = \alpha + \beta w - \gamma p \tag{9.6}$$

with $\beta \geqslant \gamma$; $\gamma \geqslant 0$; α can be of any sign but certainly positive if both β and γ equal zero. Equation (9.6) represents a nested form, because four subcases are included. They are:

1. Proportional direct taxation or progressive indexed direct taxation with fiscal indexation obtained by adjusting the nominal tax bill to the wage rate rather than to the consumer price dynamics, with $\beta = \gamma = 0$; $d\Lambda/dw = d\Lambda/dwr = 0$ and Λ is constant.
2. Progressive direct taxation without any indexation in the fiscal system: $\beta > 0$, $\gamma = 0$; $d\Lambda/dw = \beta > 0$ and Λ is positively and uniquely dependent on the nominal wage rate.
3. Progressive direct taxation with full indexation in the fiscal system: $\beta = \gamma > 0$ and Λ is a positive function of the real wage rate; this implies that $d\Lambda/dwr = \beta$ and $d\Lambda/dw = \beta[1 - (dp/dw)]$, with Λ increasing with the nominal wage rate if the latter is not fully indexed, but with constant[11] Λ if there is wage indexation (and $dp/dw \equiv q = 1$).
4. Progressive direct taxation with partial indexation in the fiscal system: $\beta > \gamma > 0$, and Λ is not a function of the real but of the nominal wage rate, besides being a function of the price level; $d\Lambda/dw = \beta - \gamma(dp/dw) > 0$ because $\beta > \gamma$ and $q \leqslant 1$.

Let me now recall two important analytical properties of the Λ equation (9.6). First, when the average direct tax rate is a log-linear function of the nominal wage and the price level, the marginal direct tax rate of the average taxpayer (denoted as N) is simply equal to the average plus a constant. Indeed,

$$N \equiv \frac{d(\Lambda W)}{dW} = \Lambda + W \frac{(\beta - \gamma q)}{W} = \Lambda + (\beta - \gamma q) \tag{9.7}$$

---

[11] Therefore, a flat Λ would include a case of proportional direct taxation (no relation between Λ and w or p); a case of fiscal indexation obtained through readjustments of nominal income brackets and tax deductions to the wage rather than to the consumer price dynamics; finally, a case of perfect indexation (to prices) both of nominal wages and of income brackets and tax deductions ($\beta = \gamma > 0$ and constant wr). Note that in the latter case, unlike in the two previous ones, the constancy of Λ is not combined with $\beta = \gamma = 0$.

Second, when Λ is a log-linear function of W and P, the well-known progressivity index (Jackobsson, 1976)

$$H = 1 - \frac{1 - \text{marginal direct tax rate}}{1 - \text{average direct tax rate}} = \frac{\text{marginal} - \text{average direct tax rate}}{1 - \text{average direct tax rate}} \qquad (9.8)$$

which ranges between 0 (when the marginal tax rate equals the average, at constant Λ) and 1 (when the marginal tax rate approches 100%), takes the simple form of

$$H = \frac{\beta}{1 - \Lambda} \qquad (9.9)$$

9.4 AN ESTIMATE FOR 10 EUROPEAN COUNTRIES OF THE DIRECT TAXATION MARGINAL RATE, PROGRESSIVITY AND *DE FACTO* INDEXATION

Let me now report some estimations on the Λ equation (9.6). While a fully technical discussion on the econometric problems and results related to the regression of equation (9.6) in 10 European countries is found in a parallel paper (Padoa Schioppa, 1991b); here I illustrate in Table 9.3 only the estimated five-year average values of the marginal direct tax rate (N^e) and of the progressivity index (H^e).

It clearly appears from Table 9.3 that in the time interval under examination, the marginal direct tax rate of the average taxpayer, N^e, has increased almost everywhere (the notable exceptions being the United Kingdom, The Netherlands and Austria), but generally less than the average direct tax rate, Λ; on the contrary, the estimated progressivity index, H^e, has remained approximately constant or has mildly risen only up to the mid late 1970s, while declining thereafter in all European countries, except Denmark, Spain, Sweden (and, to a limited extent, France). In some very small and open economies, i.e. in The Netherlands and Austria, effective progressivity of direct taxation has even dropped to zero since the mid-eighties.

Analysing the unweighted average of the eight EEC countries or of the 10 European countries, Table 9.3 seems to indicate that effective progressivity has grown in the late 1980s; this is only due to the presence of an 'outlier', namely to the drastic fiscal adjustment enforced in Denmark in 1984. If the Danish result were not to be considered in evaluating the average of the European countries or if the average were weighted[12] rather than unweighted, the estimated progressivity index, H^e, on an average would decline in Europe over all the 1980s. This would also hold true, *ceteris paribus*, if the time interval for my estimates could be extended up to 1989, given that Denmark has adopted only in the latest years a 'Thatcherian' fiscal reform (Table 9.1).

[12] The reasons why Tables 9.2–9.4 present unweighted rather than the weighted averages and coefficients of variation are twofold: from a theoretical point of view, it is not clear what should be the proper weight for an index like H; from an empirical point of view, even if the weight were arbitrarily chosen to be equal to the percentage of each country's wage bill (or direct tax bill) over the European total, the necessary OECD data in terms of a common currency would be missing for the time interval 1960–88.

Table 9.3: Five-year averages of the estimated marginal direct tax rate of the average taxpayer (N^e) and the estimated progressivity index (H^e) in 10 European countries

Countries		1965–69	1970–74	1975–79	1980–84	1985–88
Belgium	N^e	0.237	0.280	0.329	0.329	0.338
	H^e	0.102	0.107	0.105	0.069	0.070
Denmark[a]	N^e	0.557	0.351	0.351	0.418	0.730
	H^e	0.421	0.0	0.0	0.101	0.544
France[b]	N^e	0.221	0.225	0.254	0.296	0.330
	H^e	0.064	0.061	0.063	0.069	0.075
Germany	N^e	0.331	0.361	0.403	0.399	0.407
	H^e	0.099	0.104	0.107	0.105	0.106
Italy[c]	N^e	0.152	0.164	0.204	0.262	0.271
	H^e	0.058	0.059	0.082	0.079	0.067
The Netherlands[d]	N^e	0.496	0.564	0.606	0.444	0.402
	H^e	0.319	0.352	0.375	0.076	0.0
Spain[b]	N^e	0.207	0.235	0.291	0.333	0.350
	H^e	0.175	0.180	0.201	0.211	0.215
United Kingdom[e]	N^e	0.279	0.272	0.282	0.250	0.243
	H^e	0.061	0.060	0.057	0.036	0.036
Austria[b]	N^e	0.219	0.251	0.273	0.238	0.238
	H^e	0.081	0.085	0.069	0.0	0.0
Sweden[b]	N^e	0.419	0.485	0.525	0.529	0.543
	H^e	0.192	0.247	0.285	0.286	0.293
8 EEC Countries	N^e	0.310	0.310	0.340	0.341	0.385
	H^e	0.162	0.115	0.124	0.093	0.139
10 European Countries	N^e	0.312	0.319	0.352	0.350	0.386
	H^e	0.158	0.126	0.134	0.103	0.141

Source: Padoa Schioppa, F. (1992b).

[a] In Denmark, the first year for which an estimation exists is 1966, because the data are not available before.

[b] In France, Spain, Austria and Sweden, the last year for which an estimation exists is 1987, because the data are not available later.

[c] In Italy, the last year for which an estimation exists is 1985, because the data are not available later.

[d] In The Netherlands, the first year for which an estimation exists is 1967, because the data are not available before.

[e] In the United Kingdom, the first year for which an estimation exists is 1968, due to lags in the estimated equation (9.1), introduced to correct for serial autocorrelation.

In order to understand the econometric results obtained by Padoa Schioppa (1992b) on *de facto* fiscal indexation, a plot of Λ, w and wr for each of the 10 European countries under consideration is presented in Figure 9.2, enabling one to 'observe', along the lines of my theoretical model, the correlation between the change over time of the average direct tax rate, the nominal and the real wage rates.

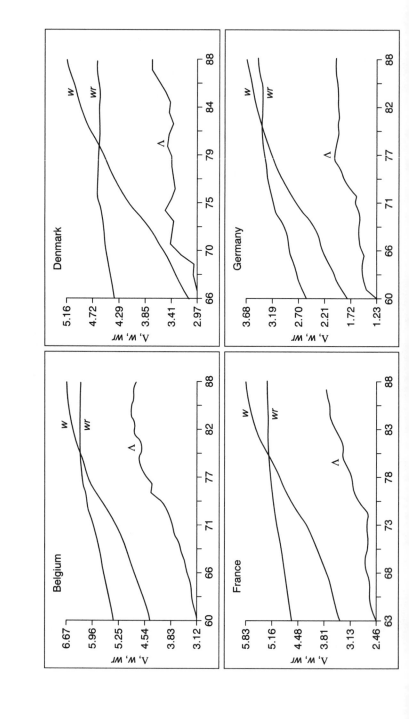

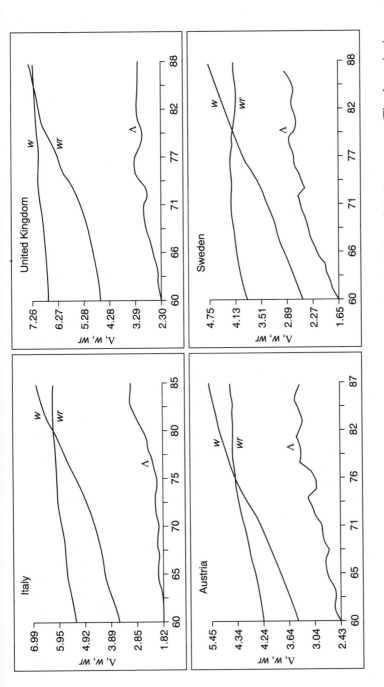

Fig. 9.2 Temporal dynamics of the average direct tax rate (Λ), of the nominal (w) and the real (wr) wage rates. (The dynamics is correct while the levels of Λ, w and wr shown in these graphs are conventional.)

Source: OECD data mentioned in footnote 2.

As expected from the previous discussion based on the scheduled personal income tax system (Table 9.1), in Belgium the direct tax rate, Λ, shows in Figure 9.2 a structural break around 1979. At that time the strong positive correlation apparently existing in the previous years between Λ and the nominal wage rate, w, becomes weaker, while the correlation with the real wage rate, wr, seems to become stronger. Interestingly enough, the econometric tests of Padoa Schioppa (1991b) confirm the opportunity to fix at 1979 a structural break for Λ, while showing that the progressivity index (Table 9.3) has decreased since then, within a fiscal system partially indexed (with $\beta > \gamma \geqslant 0$). Therefore, in the 1980s, the average direct tax rate remains a function of the nominal wage rate and the marginal direct tax rate of the average taxpayer keeps rising, though very slowly.

Given the particular form of the legal income tax indexation in Denmark during the interval 1970–83, it is not suprising to see from Figure 9.2 that Denmark presents a flat direct tax rate in that period, while before 1970 and after 1983 the direct tax rate is increasing with an apparent correlation with w and with wr. The estimation results for Λ, presented in Table 9.3, precisely point out that the Danish direct tax system had a much higher marginal direct tax rate and progressivity index before 1970 and particularly after 1983, being fully indexed to the wage dynamics in the interval 1970–83.

The introduction in France of a partial legal indexation in the personal income tax system, starting in 1969, is certainly observable in Fig. 9.2. This innovation and the 'Thatcherian' fiscal changes adopted since 1983 are also confirmed by the regression results presented in Padoa Schioppa (1992b): but the French direct tax system has probably benefitted *de facto* from some form of partial indexation in the whole period under observation, while the degree of progressivity, according to Table 9.3, has not remarkably changed within and outside the time interval 1969–82.

Germany, as expected from my previous discussion, is a country where legal indexation is prohibited, but following the econometric results of Padoa Schioppa (1992b), *de facto* fiscal indexation has certainly been obtained since 1977 through frequent, small changes in the personal income tax system; moreover, note from Table 9.3 that the marginal tax rate and the degree of progressivity in direct taxation have not been essentially modified during the last 15 years: Figure 9.2 intuitively confirms the validity of these estimates.

In 1975 a fiscal reform largely increasing the progressivity of personal income taxation was enforced in Italy. But in 1983 a kind of 'Thatcherian' structural change was introduced, decreasing the number of income brackets, reducing top marginal tax rates and broadening the tax base. As a consequence, according to my estimates illustrated in Table 9.3, progressivity sharply grew between 1975 and 1982, declining later, while *de facto* fiscal indexation has been obtained since 1983 through the fiscal adjustments for inflation mentioned above: Figure 9.2 hints to the validity of these econometric results.

Like Italy, Spain presents (Figure 9.2) an evident structural break of direct taxation in 1975, highly increasing progressivity in the post-Franco period. Unlike Italy, however, Spain introduced a 'Thatcherian' change in the personal income tax system only in 1988 – too late to affect my estimations ending in the same year; Table 9.3 confirms that in Spain both the marginal direct tax rate and progressivity kept rising in the period under consideration, while fiscal indexation has been probably non-existent.

The Thatcher fiscal reform of 1979 appears – from Figure 9.2, from the estimations of Padoa Schioppa (1992b) and from Table 9.3 – to have implied a structural break of the United Kingdom average direct taxation. According to my econometric results, the direct tax system was highly progressive and *de facto* not indexed at all before 1979 while becoming less progressive and fully indexed in the last decade, when both the marginal direct tax rate of the average taxpayer and progressivity in fact declined.

Table 9.1 tells us that in The Netherlands the personal income tax schedule has been legally but partially and discretionarily indexed since the beginning of the 1970s. Therefore, one is not surprised to observe (from our econometric results and from Figure 9.2) that in this country a correlation between the average direct tax rate and the real wage has *de facto* existed in the whole period under consideration. The same graph indicates that the reduction in the number of income brackets and in some of the marginal income tax rates decided in 1981 have produced around that year a main change in the dynamics of Λ – which, in fact, became approximately constant after 15 years of almost uninterrupted increase. The estimations reported by Table 9.3 further confirm that the marginal direct tax rate and progressivity have dramatically decreased since 1981.

The Austrian direct tax system seems, from Figure 9.2 and from the econometric results partially shown in Table 9.3, to have been affected by a structural break around the end of the 1970s, so that the marginal direct tax rate and progressivity sharply declined in the 1980s as in The Netherlands, while fiscal indexation (non-existent before) was *de facto* adopted in that year, though remaining, as in Germany, *ex lege* prohibited.

Finally, the splitting of the family income as a base for personal income taxation, decided in Sweden in 1971, explains why Figure 9.2 and my econometric results appearing in Padoa Schioppa (1992b) show a structural break of the average direct tax rate at the beginning of the 1970s, when fiscal *de facto* indexation was introduced even if legal indexation was adopted only in 1979 by the conservative government. According to Table 9.3, the marginal direct tax rate has been mildly increasing in the last decade, but, unlike in most other European countries, in Sweden the degree of progressivity of direct taxation kept rising over time, so that it consistently remained among the highest in Europe (today being second only to the Danish degree of progressivity).

9.5 SOME POLICY CONCLUSIONS

Let me now try to go back to the original question set in the introduction: do differences dominate over similarities in the tax systems borne by European workers, so that major problems on fiscal harmonization should be expected? Table 9.4 tries to answer this question by measuring the intercountry tax variability through the unweighted coefficients of variation[13] for the observed employers' social security plus indirect tax rates, for the tax wedge, for the direct average and the estimated marginal tax rates and finally for the effective estimated progressivity of direct taxation; in each of the five-year intervals considered, the coefficients of variation are calculated both within the 10 European countries and within the eight EEC countries.

Table 9.4: Intercountry coefficients of variation[1] on the five-year averages of the sum of the employers' social security and the indirect tax rates ($S + T$), of the tax wedge (tw), of the average (Λ) and the estimated marginal direct tax rates (N^e), and of the estimated progressivity index (H^e)

		1965–69	1970–74	1975–79	1980–84	1985–88
8 EEC Countries	$S + T$	0.26	0.23	0.23	0.22	0.22
	tw	0.21	0.20	0.19	0.16	0.15
	Λ	0.46	0.48	0.39	0.32	0.30
	N^e	0.47	0.40	0.36	0.21	0.40
	H^e	0.84	0.94	0.94	0.56	1.26
10 European Countries	$S + T$	0.25	0.22	0.23	0.23	0.24
	tw	0.19	0.19	0.20	0.19	0.17
	Λ	0.43	0.45	0.36	0.29	0.28
	N^e	0.44	0.39	0.36	0.27	0.40
	H^e	0.79	0.84	0.87	0.82	1.20

Sources: See Tables 9.2 and 9.3.
[1] These coefficients of variation are corrected for the small sample bias.

By definition, the tax wedge, tw, is the logarithmic difference between the real labour cost deflated by the product price at factor costs, $w + S - p + T$, and the net real wage, $w - \Lambda - p$; thus, $tw \equiv \Lambda + S + T$. Therefore, the variance of tw equals the variance of Λ plus the variance of $S + T$ plus two times the corresponding covariance; consequently, the squared coefficient of variation of tw is a weighted average of the squared coefficient of variation of Λ, of the squared coefficient of variation of $S + T$ and of the covariance divided by the mean value of Λ multiplied by the mean value of $S + T$. Hence, the coefficient of variation of the tax wedge between the European countries, indicating the intercountry variability of the global fiscal pressure, can be smaller than both the coefficients of variation of the two components of the tax wedge – the direct tax rate and the other tax rates – only if the various European countries 'compensate' in a different way a form of taxation (for example, the direct one) with another (the non-direct taxation); this is then interpreted to be a sign of heterogeneity in tax structures more than in the global fiscal pressure. By an identical reasoning, effective tax rates and tax

[13] Unlike the variance which is positively related to the mean, the coefficient of variation depurates apparent changes in variability which are, in fact, due to changes in average levels. All the coefficients of variation are unweighted in Table 9.4, for reasons described above.

structures are estimated to become increasingly similar if the intercountry coefficients of variation of $S + T$, Λ and tw decline over time.

With these statistical caveats, the following results are derived from Table 9.4.

1. The cross-country and cross-periods variability of the European tax systems is essentially the same within the eight EEC countries and within the 10 European countries (including Austria and Sweden).

2. In every five-year period analysed here, the maximum inter-country variability regards the direct tax rate, followed by the employers' social security plus the indirect tax rates. The tax wedge differentials are lower, showing that the various European countries differ more in the relative weight assigned to different forms of taxation than in the global fiscal pressure. From a policy viewpoint, this implies that trying to harmonize a subset of taxes even starting from those which are more similar among European countries (i.e. $S + T$) will prove harder than harmonizing the overall fiscal systems; this is because most European countries which will be losers in the direct tax harmonization will be winners in the employers' social security and indirect tax harmonization, and *vice versa*. In other words, a European tax harmonization will be easier if it will concern the tax wedge as a whole, rather than, separately, its components.

3. Over the time period examined by Table 9.4, while the inter-country variability of the employers' social security plus the indirect tax rates $(S + T)$ has not greatly changed, the inter-country differentials in the effective average direct tax rate (Λ) and, consequently, in the effective tax wedge (tw) have enormously decreased, particularly since the mid-seventies. By the end of the 1980s, the intercountry coefficient of variation of Λ is not much larger than the coefficient of variation of $S + T$, whereas the former was almost twice as large as the latter in the 1960s. This leads one to believe that the European fiscal harmonization is possibly easier nowadays than it would have been in the 1960s, although remaining difficult, especially in the direct tax rate component.

4. With regard to direct taxation, differentials in the marginal tax rates of average taxpayers (N^e) and in the effective progressivity (H^e) are as relevant as differentials in the average tax rate (Λ). Table 9.4 indicates that from the mid-sixties to the mid-eighties, the intercountry coefficient of variation of the marginal tax rates has consistently declined, while the intercountry coefficient of variation of progressivity, after reaching a maximum around 1975, has started decreasing as well. Apparently, according to Table 9.4, this shrinking progressivity differentials within Europe has been interrupted in the second half of the 1980s. Such an ackward result is only due to three outliers – Denmark, with an extremely high H^e bound to decrease in the late 1980s (as indicated above), The Netherlands and Austria with a zero H^e. If the coefficient of variation were weighted, rather than being unweighted (as it is in Table 9.4), the variability of progressivity in direct taxation would diminish within Europe in the overall 1980s, given that Denmark, The Netherlands and Austria are very small countries.

These final remarks, then, confirm my previous conclusion: differences in effective tax structures and tax rates regarding European workers exist, particularly in the direct tax component, but they are not very strong and in any case they are weaker nowadays than in the past. Tax harmonization in Europe is an easier task to reach in the 1990s than it would have been in the previous 30 years because *de facto* a large tax convergence has already been obtained in Europe, especially in the last decade.

REFERENCES

Andersson, K. (1988) Tax Reforms in Scandinavia during the 1980s. Paper prepared for the American Association's Annual Meetings, New York, 28–30 December.

Bayar, A. (1989) Une Evaluation de la Reforme Fiscale en Belgique. Paper prepared for the Applied Econometric Association Conference on Fiscal Policy on Modelling, Rome, 30 November – 1 December.

Bean, Ch. R., Layard, P. R. G. and Nickell, S. J. (1986) The Rise in Unemployment: A Multi-Country Study. *Economica* (Supplement) **53**, 1–22.

Coe, D. T. and Gagliardi, F. (1985) Nominal Wage Determination in Ten OECD Economies. OECD Working Paper No. 19.

Dreze, J. H. and Bean, Ch. R. (1991) Europe's Employment Problem: Introduction and Synthesis, in *European Unemployment: Lessons from a Multy-Country Econometric Study* (eds J. H. Dreze and Ch. R. Bean), MIT Press, Cambridge, MA, pp. 1–65.

Hagemann, R. P., Jones, B. R. and Montador, R. B. (1988) *Tax Reform in OECD Countries: Motives, Constraints and Practice*. OECD, Paris.

Jackobsson, U (1976) On the Measurement of the Degree of Progression. *Journal of Public Economics*, **5**, 161–168.

Knoester, A. and van der Windt, N. (1987) Real Wages and Taxation in Ten OECD Countries. *Oxford Bulletin of Economics and Statistics*, Special Issue on Wage Determination and Labour Market Inflexibility, **49**, 151–169.

Lipschitz, L., Kremers, J., Mayer, T. and McDonald, D. (1989) The Federal Republic of Germany. Adjustment in a Surplus Country. *IMF Occasional Paper* No. 64.

Lopez-Claros, A. (1988) The Search for Efficiency in the Adjustment Process: Spain in the 1980s. *IMF Occasional Paper* No. 57.

Nickell, S.J. and Andrews, M. (1983) Trade Unions, Real Wages and Employment in Britain 1951–79, in *The Cause of Unemployment* (eds C. A. Greenhalgh, P. R. G. Layard and A.J. Oswald), Clarendon Press, Oxford, pp. 183–206.

OECD (1976) *The Adjustment of Personal Income Tax Systems for Inflation*. OECD, Paris.

OECD (1977) *The Treatment of Family Units in OECD Member Countries under Tax and Transfer Systems*. OECD, Paris.

OECD (1981a) *The Impact of Consumption Taxes at Different Income Levels*, Studies in Taxation. OECD, Paris.

OECD (1981b) *Income Tax Schedules Distribution of Taxpayers and Revenues*, Studies in Taxation. OECD, Paris.

OECD (1986a) *An Empirical Analysis of Changes in Personal Income Taxes*, Studies in Taxation. OECD, Paris.

OECD (1986b) *The Tax/Benefit Position of Production Workers, 1979–1984*. OECD, Paris.

OECD (1986c) *Personal Income Tax Systems under Changing Economic Conditions*. OECD, Paris.

OECD (1989a) *The Tax/Benefit Position of Production Workers, 1985–1988*. OECD, Paris.

OECD (1989b) *Taxing Consumption*. OECD, Paris.

Padoa Schioppa, F. (1990) Union Wage Setting and Taxation. *Oxford Bulletin of Economics and Statistics*. **52**, 143–167.

Padoa Schioppa, F. (1992a) Eccessi, Insufficienze e Distorsioni del Sistema Pensionistico Italiano in *Il Disavanzo Pubblico in Italia: Natura Strutturale e Politiche di Rientzo*, (eds Ente per gli Studi Monetari, Bancari e Finanziari "Luigi Einaudi"), Il Mulino, Bologna pp. 357–427.

Padoa Schioppa, F. (1992b) A Cross-Country Analysis of the Tax-Push Hypothesis. IMF Working Paper No. 11.

Padoa Schioppa Kostoris, F. (1991) Tax rates, progressivity and de facto fiscal indexation in ten European Countries (CEPR Discussion Paper) No. 587.

Pechman, J. A. (1987) *Comparative Tax Systems: Europe, Canada and Japan*. Tax Analysts, Arlington.

Pechman, J. A (1990) The Future of the Income Tax. *American Economic Review*, **80**, 1–21.

Tanzi, V. (1980) *Inflation and the Personal Income Tax: An International Perspective*. Cambridge University Press, Cambridge.

10

Tax policy at the bifurcation between equity and efficiency: lessons from the German income tax reform

Ulrich van Essen, Helmut Kaiser
and P. Bernd Spahn

10.1 INTRODUCTION

West Germany has experienced a major revision of income taxation in recent times. Its major purpose was to mitigate distortive effects of high marginal tax rates, but it also tried to achieve distributional goals – in particular, a preferenced treatment of families with children and the exemption of tax for taxpayers with very low income. The main features of the reform are briefly sketched in section 10.2.

Although the reform was designed to remove disincentives for the taxpayers, the discussion in the Federal Republic of Germany focused on the distributive consequences of the reform, presumably because they seemed to be more obvious and easier to quantify. Section 10.3 dwells on the trade-off between equity and efficiency. We argue that analyses of pre- and post-reform net income distributions, disregarding changes in labour supply due to the reform, give a first hint on the distributional consequences of the reform. Nevertheless, it is not sufficient to evaluate tax reforms (that aim at lowering the extent of disincentives by reducing marginal tax rates) solely on the basis of this criterion.

In order to capture the allocative effects as well, we use the concept of equivalent variation[1] to evaluate the welfare effects of the reform.

For obvious reasons, 'cash gains/losses' and 'welfare gains/losses' should be assessed on an individual basis. In section 10.4 we argue that tax simulation models based on micro-data are necessary in order to obtain correct results. We comment briefly on the advantages and shortcomings of the existing tax simulation models and introduce our own Frankfurt income tax simulation (FITS) model in section 10.5.

---

[1] This approach was pioneered by Hicks (1941).

In section 10.6 we report on our empirical findings with regard to the distributive and allocative effects of the West German income tax reform. The chapter ends with a summary and conclusion in section 10.7.

10.2 THE WEST GERMAN INCOME TAX REFORM 1986-90

In 1986 an income tax reform was carried out in the United States of America, which Pechman[2] praised as 'the most significant piece of tax legislation enacted since the income tax was converted to a mass tax during World War II'. The basic idea can be summarized by the term 'tax cut cum base broadening'. On the one hand, marginal tax rates were lowered in order to improve economic efficiency; on the other hand, there was an extension of the income tax base by closing loopholes for specific groups of taxpayers. Both aspects combined in rendering the reform approximately revenue-neutral. The US Tax Reform 1986 was held by many economists to be a major step in the direction of comprehensive income taxation as well as removing a significant portion of the distortions generated by the tax system.[3]

The US Tax Reform 1986 clearly served as a model for many other countries. The West German Income Tax Reform 1986-90 pursued the same basic idea but differed in some respects:

1. The reform was not designed to be revenue-neutral. The government aimed not only at lowering marginal tax rates but also at bringing down the absolute tax burden.
2. There was a time lag between the announcement of the cut in marginal tax rates and the announcement of base broadening e.g. by removing a number of special deductions. This proceeding obviously resulted from the political strategy not to reveal the burdens associated with the reform before the general election. As a result, the consciousness about the connection between both parts of the reform was partially lost. Public discussion tended to focus on the distributional consequences with regard to special groups of taxpayers like workers in the automobile and printing industries, nearly totally neglecting the cut in tax rates.
3. Contrary to the US tax reform, where both parties, Democrats and Republicans, stuck together in realizing the reform, the West German income tax reform was enforced by the Christian Democrats and Liberals against the opposition of Social Democrats and Greens. The political debate was mainly on distributional and not on allocative issues.
4. In contrast to the US tax reform, the West German tax reform proceeded in three steps. The first and second steps were realized in 1986 and 1988, respectively, whereas the third step was taken in 1990.

---

[2] Pechman (1987, p. 11).
[3] See e.g. Pechman (1987, p. 17).

Table 10.1 Tax Reforms 1986/88 and 1990 and expected loss in tax revenue

Tax Reforms 1986/88	Vol. (Bil. DM)	Tax Reform 1990	Vol. (Bil. DM)
(a) *Reform of the tax schedule*		(a) *Reform of the tax schedule*	
1. Increase of the basic allowance by DM 540/1080 to DM 4752/9504	3.5	1. Increase of the basic allowance by DM 864/1728 to DM 5616/11232	5.6
2. Reduction of the tax progression	15.1	2. Reduction of the proportional tax rate in the first income bracket from 22% to 19%	6.7
		3. Introduction of the linear-progressive tax schedule	20.7
		4. Reduction of the top marginal tax rate from 56% to 53%	1.0
			1.0
(b) *Other arrangements*		(b) *Other arrangements*	
1. Increase of the child tax allowance by DM 2052–2484	4.8	1. Increase of children allowances by DM 540–3042	2.0
2. Increase of the education allowances to DM 1800/2400/4200	0.6	2. Increase of different allowances for families (especially for those with handicapped household members)	0.3
3. Increase of the household allowance to DM 4752	0.1	3. Increase of the deduction at source of the precautions for self-employed up to DM 4000/8000	0.6
4. Improvements of the allowances for depreciations	0.5	4. Reduction of the corporation tax rate for retained earnings	2.3
Sum	24.6	Sum	39.2

The remainder of this section is devoted to a brief sketch of these three steps of the reform.[4] The main purpose of the first two steps was to provide tax relief for families and for taxpayers with very low income. As can be seen from Table 10.1, the first aim was achieved by a drastic increase in the tax allowances for children and for expenditures on education, the latter by increasing the basic allowance. In comparison, the changes in the tax schedule were rather small (cf. T 86 and T 88 in Figure 10.1). The focal point of the third part of the reform, however, clearly lies in the reduction of marginal tax rates. The top rate was

---

[4] For details of the reform, see van Essen *et al.* (1988, pp. 58–65) or Presse- und Informationsamt der Bundesregierung (1989).

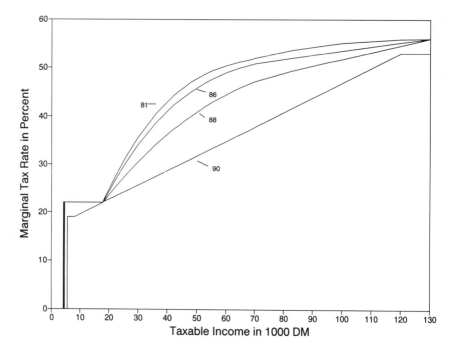

Fig. 10.1   Different income tax schedules for West Germany.

lowered from 56% to 53% and the bottom rate was reduced by 3% as well from 22% to 19%.[5] Figure 10.1 shows that the marginal tax rate function is linear in between.[6]

This reduction in marginal tax rates was, however, combined with broadening the tax base. This was realized by sacking a number of privileges held by special groups of taxpayers. Space limitations do not allow a discussion of all the measures.[7] Nevertheless, we shoul comment briefly on the source taxation of capital income, which was in effect for the first six months of 1989. The introduction of this tax (which was designed to be deductible from the income tax liability) was supposed to raise the tax yield by DM 4.3 billion. Obviously, the government suspected many taxpayers not to declare their interest income cor-

[5] There has been a fierce struggle about lowering the top marginal rate not only between the government and the opposition but also within the coalition. From a theoretical point of view, it looks rather strange that the top marginal tax rate was used as a symbol of distributional justice. One could be suspicious if all participants in the debate clearly understood the difference between marginal and average tax rates. The result of the negotiations was a reduction of both the top and the bottom marginal rate by 3%, which apparently was regarded to be a fair compromise.

[6] For this reason the tax schedule implemented in 1990 is sometimes called 'linear' by mistake. Wiegard, while being in favour of the reduction in marginal tax rates, ironically claims that it would be an interesting topic of research to find out why bulgy forms are less aesthetical than other forms with regard to tax schedules (Wiegard, 1987, p. 246).

[7] See footnote 3.

rectly. The tax was to be transferred by the banks to the fiscal administration without revealing the names of their clients. This feature of the reform led to a massive export of capital.[8] Moreover, source taxation of interest payments was not accepted by large groups of the population so that it had to be abolished just half a year after it had been enacted.[9]

10.3 MEASURING THE EFFECT OF THE REFORM ON EQUITY AND EFFICIENCY

As already mentioned, there was a discrepancy between the aim of the government to stimulate economic growth by removing disincentives generated by the tax system and the public discussion which almost exclusively focused on distributional issues. This is not very surprising if one regards our scarce knowledge about economic behaviour. Economic theory proves to be a useful framework for analysing the effect of taxes on the supply of labour, the accumulation of capital or risk-taking, but only in a few cases are the results unambiguous. Therefore, empirical research proves to be inevitable. In this chapter we concentrate on the assessment of the influence of taxation on labour supply.

Equity and efficiency can be regarded as the main objectives of tax policy. Obviously, there is a trade-off between these two aims. In the extreme, income taxation might leave everybody with the same net income, regardless of how long and how intensive he worked to achieve his income. This levelling of the income distribution would be accompanied by huge disincentives to work. On the other hand, a poll tax turns out to be the first-best solution if the excess burden of income taxation is to be minimized. Clearly, such a tax would not serve in reducing inequality.

Before we discuss the appropriate methods of measuring distributive and allocative effects of tax reforms, two points should be stressed. First, we must emphasize that equity and distributional justice are by no means synonymous.[10] The economist can compare income distributions and conclude that one is more equal than the other. He can (and probably will) have a private opinion about the fairness of different distributions, but it is not his task to recommend one alternative for reason of distributional justice. If, for example, a reform of income taxation ends up in a rise in the concentration of income, this should not be confused with a loss in distributional justice.

[8] The government enacted this feature of the reform although many economists had expected that exactly this would occur (e.g. van Essen *et al.*, 1988).
[9] Obviously, the taxation of interest income was not well understood by the public. Many taxpayers confused the 10% tax on interest income with a 10% tax on savings. But, also, many of those who understood the purpose of the tax correctly opposed it because they believed it to constitute a double taxation of savings. Economists supporting the Schanz–Haig–Simons concept of income taxation clearly have to reject this opinion. The argument is, however, familiar from the literature on the personal consumption tax.
[10] For this argumentation, see also Kaiser and Spahn (1991).

The second point we want to stress is that there is a distinction between a rise in economic welfare and a rise in labour supply. This distinction was rarely made in the public discussion on the West German income tax reform. Economic theory suggests that a reduction in marginal tax rates leads to an improvement in economic welfare, which means that the taxpayer is able to obtain a higher level of utility. Because now there is a smaller substitution effect being generated by the income tax, excess burden is reduced. Lowering the marginal tax rates increases the marginal net wage and, thus, the price of leisure. Labour supply will rise according to the substitution effect. There is, however, an income effect running in the opposite direction. Lowering the marginal tax rates also results in an increase in disposable income, and if leisure is a normal good, this will lead to a reduction in labour supply.

We now turn to the methodological discussion. First, we comment on attempts to evaluate the effects of tax reforms on the distribution of income, disregarding labour supply reactions. In opposition, the allocative impact of tax reforms is usually addressed by measuring the deadweight loss, examining one 'typical' taxpayer. Hence, the distributional aspects are neglected. We demonstrate how both these aspects can be combined by computing the distribution of individual welfare gains.[11]

The evaluation of distributional aspects, without taking labour supply reactions into account, plays a prominent role in tax reform analysis. If done properly, it can be regarded as a good approximation of the distributional effects of a tax reform. Some methods used to evaluate these effects are, however, at least debatable.

One quite common approach is to analyse a typical household, e.g. a couple with two children and an average income. It might be questioned if this type of household is, in fact, typical.[12] Obviously, this is true only for a small fraction of taxpayers. Of course, one can use an infinite number of household types, but without knowing the relative importance of these types a complete analysis of the reform is impossible.

In addition, many income tax reforms include changes in parameters influencing the tax base. If, for example, the deduction for the disabled is increased one has to know if a member of the 'typical' household is disabled if an assessment of the whole reform is intended. For reasons described above, we think that the 'typical household approach' is very unsatisfactory.

Another approach disregards changes in the tax base induced by the reform and only looks at the tax rate schedule. The advantage of this method lies in the possibility to examine the whole range of taxable income. Definite conclusions about income distribution cannot, however, be drawn from this approach for two reasons: firstly, the empirical distribution of taxpayers is not known and, second-

---

[11] This method was proposed by King (1983).

[12] A good example is given by Atkinson and Sutherland (1983, pp. 64–5), who show that only 4% of the families contained in the Family Expenditure Survey are in accordance with the hypothetical families used by the British Government.

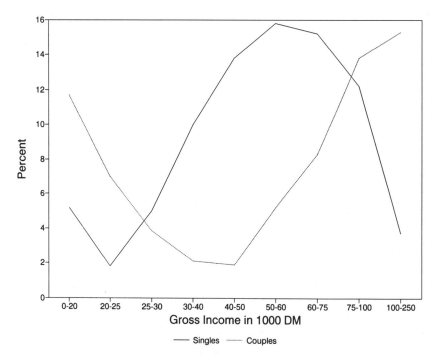

Fig. 10.2 Equivalent variation and cash gain for a change in net wages.

ly, changes in the computation of the tax base are not accounted for. This renders this method inappropriate as well.[13]

We argue that tax simulation models based on micro-data are the appropriate tools for analysing distributional consequences of tax reforms. Before we develop this argument further in section 10.4, something has to be said about the measurement of allocative effects. Figure 10.2 depicts the standard static neoclassical labour supply model. A typical individual maximizes utility (which is supposed to be increasing both in the consumption of leisure f and the consumption of some composite good y) subject to the budget restriction $m_0 y_0$. If the individual does not work at all, he receives non-labour income m_0. The slope of the budget line is equal to the marginal net wage, which depends on the marginal tax rate.[14] The equilibrium before the reform is characterized by point A in Figure 10.2.

A tax reform which reduces the marginal tax rate leads to the new budget constraint $m_1 y_1$, with the new equilibrium at point B.[15] The cash gain (*CG*)

---

[13] Hinterberger and Müller (1988) use this method for an assessment of the income tax reform in West Germany. For a critical analysis of this study, see van Essen *et al.* (1990).

[14] For ease of exposition we assume a constant gross wage and a proportional income tax.

[15] In our example the reduction of the marginal tax rate results in an increase of labour supply. Note, however, that point B might as well lie to the right of point A, implying an increase in leisure consumed.

denotes the result which one obtains if labour supply reactions are ignored. The increase in economic welfare is measured by the equivalent variation (*EV*). This is the amount of money to be given to the taxpayer in the pre-reform situation in order to obtain the utility he achieves as a result of the reform. The equivalent variation, thus, evaluates differences in utility levels in money terms.

This equivalent variation can be computed for every single taxpayer and the distribution of welfare gains and losses can be analysed. But what seems to be straightforward in theory turns out to be rather tricky in practice because utility levels cannot be observed directly. There is, however, a possibility to tackle this problem by 'putting the cart before the horse'. Instead of maximizing a utility function under a budget constraint – the result of which is the Marshallian demand function – we start the analysis with the demand function. The demand of leisure can be estimated empirically as a function of marginal net wage, non-labour income and other socio-economic characteristics.[16] Using Roy's identity, the indirect utility function can be derived from this demand function. The inversion of this indirect utility function $v(y, p)$ yields the expenditure function $e(p, v)$, which indicates the minimum expenditure needed to achieve a given utility level as a function of prices.[17] Equivalent variation induced by a tax reform[18] is defined as the difference between the minimum expenditure needed to achieve the post-reform utility level, given pre-reform marginal net wage $[e(p_0, v_1)]$, and the minimum expenditure needed to achieve the pre-reform utility level, given pre-reform marginal net wage $[e(p_0, v_0)]$.[19]

It should be clear from the exposition that for the computation of equivalent variation on an individual basis, data on marginal tax rates and non-labour incomes are needed for all taxpayers. This calls for a microsimulation model of income taxation.

10.4 TAX SIMULATION MODELS BASED ON MICRO-DATA

Generally, microsimulation models can be characterized by the following three basic ideas:[20]

1. In order to explain human behaviour it is advantageous to dispose of a variety of personal characteristics. Hypotheses on behavioural responses to policy measures can hardly be tested on aggregate data.

---

[16] For details of the estimation procedure and the inclusion of a progressive tax system, see Kaiser *et al.* (1991).

[17] Note that the marginal net wage is the price of leisure in our case.

[18] Of course, equivalent variations can be computed for all changes in prices. A change in income taxation is just a special case.

[19] For computing the equivalent variation, pre-reform prices are used as a reference. One can also use post-reform prices as a reference. The resulting measure is called compensating variation. The compensating variation does, however, not allow a comparison of more than one reform proposal with the pre-reform situation. For details, see Kaiser (1989).

[20] For a detailed analysis of the goals, potentials and limits of microsimulation models see Spahn *et al.* (1992).

2. Politicians are usually interested in the effect of potential changes in the instruments they have at their disposal on the achievement of political goals. Therefore, microsimulation models are well-suited for providing political advice.
3. Even very complicated institutional regulations can be captured by a microsimulation model. In the case of income taxation, in principle, the same computer program can be applied which is used by fiscal authorities in assessing the individual tax liability.

Obviously, microsimulation models exhibit advantages in comparison with models based on grouped or macro-data.[21] As Okner[22] points out, 'it is always possible to aggregate microdata but it is impossible to disaggregate totals.'

One should, however, bear in mind the problems associated with the construction of such models. Hence, Haveman (1978, p. 434) points out: 'While these are significant gains, they come at some cost. The most obvious cost is the sizeable research, manpower, computer, and survey requirements of such modelling efforts. Work with micro-data bases is both time-consuming and inherently frustrating. The potential for calculation and programming errors is very large, and because of the cumulative and linked nature of such models, errors discovered at an earlier stage require the recalculation of estimates developed in later stages. Similarly, minor restructuring of the earlier parts of models (the potential for which is enormous) requires recalculation and often reprogramming of the later stages in the analyses.' Reflecting upon our own research experience, we entirely agree with this statement.

Nevertheless, we hold that microsimulation models are extremely valuable in examining the consequences of changes in complicated institutional regulations, for which the tax system is a typical example.

Therefore, microsimulation models have been very successful in the field of tax reform analysis.[23] Many ministries of finance dispose of microsimulation models.[24] Usually, these models are static and do not account for behavioural responses. While the first qualification should not be too important as long as one is interested in the short-run effects of tax reforms, the second one is serious if tax reforms are carried out in order to increase economic efficiency. One has to bear in mind that assuming no behavioural responses is also a behavioural assumption.[25] Our own model which we are going to describe below is also static but it goes beyond standard models by incorporating labour supply reactions.

Some comments have to be made on the databases of microsimulation models of income taxation. The first claim with regard to the database is that it has to be representative for the population analysed. A sample of income tax returns seems to serve this purpose best. But there are several remarks to be made.

---

[21] For a detailed discussion, see Krupp (1978).

[22] Okner (1978, p. 456).

[23] Merz (1988) provides a survey of the existing tax simulation models in USA and Europe.

[24] Lietmeyer (1986) reports on the experience made within the German Federal Ministry of Finance and describes the models used in other European countries by the fiscal authorities.

[25] See also Nakamura and Nakamura (1990, p. 470).

Analyses of income tax reforms that affect groups of the population that have not yet been covered by the tax are impossible. A solution for this would be e.g. to make social-security benefits taxable income. But for the analysis of all other reforms a database consisting of tax returns would be very promising. For reasons of data protection, researchers are, however, rarely in a position to use such data.[26]

Nearly all tax simulation models are, therefore, based on survey data. Again, we agree with Haveman,[27] who states that 'the weaknesses of such data – misreporting, missing data, inadequate economic or demographic information, and so on – are well-known'. In addition, the execution of population surveys is very expensive which, of course, limits the number of individuals and households included in the sample. As a result, 'there is a conflict between the objectives of making the handling of MTSM as simple and cost-effective as possible and of achieving the accurate and extensive results that are determined principally by the size of the sample'.[28] And last but not the least, 'Survey data are inevitably not up to date.'[29] Nevertheless, researchers have to cope with the existing data and try to replace the missing information by plausible assumptions.

10.5 THE FRANKFURT INCOME TAX SIMULATION (FITS) MODEL

The FITS model was constructed in 1986 by our research group as part of a research project within the Special Collaborative Program 3 (Sonderforschungsbereich 3) at the University of Frankfurt.[30] The structure of the model is shown in Figure 8.3 of Kaiser *et al.* (1993), this volume. It is based on the first wave of the 'Socio-economic Panel' from 1984, which was used as a cross-section database.[31] The model is, however, capable of being adapted to subsequent waves of the panel. Gaps in the database are closed by the use of data from the income tax statistics of the German Federal Office. All deductions, exemptions, etc., contained in the tax code are stored in a special data file.

The first part of the model is very similar to tax simulation models in other countries.[32] Starting from the computation of gross income, the individual income tax liability is computed for each taxpayer. The modular structure of the model and the use of dummy variables for tax constants make it quite convenient to

---

[26] One further qualification has to be made: All relevant information is contained in the tax returns, but not all variables that are interesting for researchers are stored in the data files generated by financial administrations. This renders many simulations impossible.

[27] Haveman (1978, p. 434).

[28] Lietmeyer (1986, p. 143). MTSM stands for microanalytic tax simulation models.

[29] Atkinson *et al.* (1983, p. 66).

[30] For a detailed documentation of the model, see van Essen *et al.* (1986). The model was validated using data from the official income tax statistics (van Essen and Kassella, 1988).

[31] The database comprises about 6000 households with more than 12 000 persons. For details, see Hanefeld (1987).

[32] See e.g. Atkinson and Sutherland (1988). To our knowledge, there is no other microanalytic income tax simulation model in the Federal Republic of Germany based on real micro-data. The model of the Federal Ministry of Finance has been up to now based on synthetic micro-data generated from the income tax statistics.

simulate changes in tax parameters. The output of this part of the model, especially tax liabilities and marginal tax rates, is used for the estimation of labour supply functions in the second part of the model. The procedure outlined in section 10.3 enables us to compute the equivalent variation for each tax-payer in the third part of the model.

The first major application of the FITS model was the simulation of the distributive and allocative effects of the West German Income Tax Reforms 1986–90. In order to insulate the effect of the tax law from the effects generated by inflation and changes in the structure of population, we applied the pre- and post-reform tax law to the same database. In the next section we report on some of our results.

10.6 MEASURING THE IMPACT OF THE WEST GERMAN INCOME TAX REFORM ON INCOME DISTRIBUTION AND ECONOMIC WELFARE

Figure 8.5 of Kaiser *et al.* (1992), this volume, shows the reduction in marginal tax rates resulting from the reform for singles and couples.[33] This figure gives us a hint as to where welfare gains can be expected. The reduction in marginal tax rates is very large for singles earning about DM 50 000 and couples earning about DM 100 000.[34]

Before we turn to the results of welfare analysis we want to report some interesting results obtained by using only the first part of the model. Table 10.2 shows the absolute cash gains resulting from the reform. As one would have expected, cash gains rise with income, from DM 377 for those in the lowest bracket to DM 10 612 for those earning more than DM 100 000 a year. The extent of tax relief also hinges on the occupational status. The self-employed gain considerably more than the employees holding income constant. This is due to some special provisions for the self-employed in the 1990 Tax Law. The table also reflects the strong component of family relief embodied in the reform.

If one uses net income as a basis for comparison, relative cash gains rise with gross income. The use of the tax liability before the reform brings out nearly the opposite result. The choice of the basis for comparison is again a normative question. Someone looking for arguments in favour of the reform will use tax liability. It is not surprising that the Federal Ministry of Finance is among the proponents of this base. Someone trying to show that the reform causes a redistribution 'from the poor to the rich' will prefer income as denominator.

The overall impact on income distribution can be assessed by Lorenz curve analysis. According to our results, the Lorenz curve for net incomes under the

---

[33] Note that the figure depicts effective changes in marginal tax rates, in opposition to the changes in statutory rates resulting from a pure tax schedule analysis.

[34] For couples with very high income the reduction in marginal tax rates must be approximately 3% because of the reduction in the top rate from 56% to 53%. Unfortunately, there are no top-income recipients in the sample.

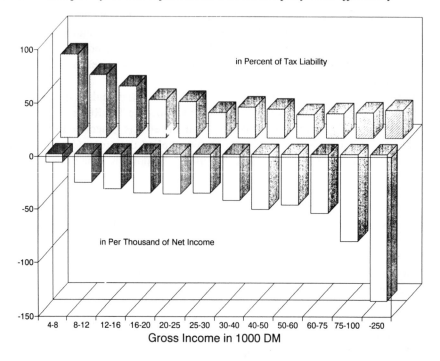

Fig. 10.3 Absolute reduction of marginal tax rates resulting from the Income Tax
Reform 1986–90.

Tax Law 1983 (before the reform) lies above the curve for the Tax Law 1990.
Because both curves do not intersect, one can conclude that the tax law after the
reform is slightly less redistributive. Accordingly, the Gini coefficient increases
from 0.2984 for the pre-reform tax law to 0.3063 for the post-reform tax law.

For the estimation of labour supply the sample was divided into three groups:
singles, married men and married women. This was necessary because in the case
of couples the interdependence of work decisions had to be modelled. In this
chapter we report our results for single persons.[35]

The estimation of labour supply was carried out using a 'second-generation'
labour supply model. These models are characterized by an explicit inclusion of
the tax system and the correction for sample selection and sample truncation
biases. In addition, there is a close connection with utility theory.[36]

In order to include the non-linear budget constraint generated by the progressive tax structure, it was linearized for each individual by constructing the
tangency to the budget line.[37] The slope of the linearized budget constraint is
equal to the marginal net wage; the intersection with the vertical axis is called

---

[35] The results for married men and married women are described in Kaiser and Spahn (1991).
[36] See e.g. Killingsworth (1983, pp. 130–2).
[37] For details of this procedure, see Killingsworth (1983, pp. 332–5).

Table 10.2 Average yearly cash gain caused by the Tax Reforms 1986–90 in DM

					Gross income in DM				
	All tax-payers	0–20000	20001–25000	25001–30000	30001–40000	40001–50000	50001–60000	60001–75000	75001–100000	100000
All taxpayers	2141	377	747	835	1345	1831	3050	3725	4386	10612
Tax payers due to professional position										
Employees	2198	462	633	901	1295	1918	3010	3686	4851	2835
Employers	5288	231	1491	1951	2974	3558	8434	3011	5544	18034
Taxpayers due to number of children										
Without children	1565	365	571	636	1088	1632	3336	2802	5378	10853
One child	2642	539	1288	1215	1698	1774	1632	2471	4547	9800
Two children	3227	552	1216	1922	1969	2138	2024	2757	4641	11308
Three children	8995	754	1456	2166	2434	2416	2569	8091	5078	11784
More than three children	7005	751	1551	2257	2830	2931	3392	3968	5908	24887

Source: Own calculations based on the first wave of the Socio-economic Panel (1984).

virtual non-labour income. Both variables enter the labour supply equation together with several socio-demographic variables.

Accounting for possible biases induced by sample selection, a two-step PROBIT/COLS approach was applied.[38] First, a participation equation had to be estimated by maximum likelihood in order to receive the Heckman correction variable. It can be seen from Table 10.3 that the probability of participating in the labour force rises significantly with non-labour income and declines with age and the degree of physical handicap, as one would have expected from *a priori* reasoning. The probability of doing paid work is greater for foreigners than for Germans, which should be due to the higher percentage of students among the German single persons. The number of children and the level of schooling exhibit no significant influence on the decision to participate in the labour force for that group.

The equation for labour hours supplied[39] was estimated by ordinary least squares (OLS), incorporating the Heckman variable. As can be seen from Table 10.4, both marginal net wage and non-labour income have a negative influence on the number of hours worked. This is also true for the number of children, whereas we observe the opposite for nationality, the degree of physical handicap and age. Schooling, again, seems to have no influence. The Heckman

Table 10.3   Maximum likelihood estimation results for participation rates (using the PROBIT model)

Regressor x_j	Single persons
Intercept	-0.74×10^{-2}
	(-0.12)
Corrected non-labour income in DM	0.33×10^{-4} *
	(7.55)
Number of children under 18 years	0.80×10^{-2}
	(0.16)
Partner working $(1 = yes; 0 = no)$	—
Nationality $(1 = German, 0 = foreigner)$	-0.15 *
	(-2.54)
Schooling $(1 = primary, 4 = university)$	-0.33×10^{-1}
	(-1.54)
Degree of physical handicap $(0-?0\%)$	-0.79×10^{-2} *
	(-5.38)
Age in years	-0.48×10^{-2} *
	(-2.86)
Number of persons	3511

Source: Own calculations on the basis of the first wave of the Socio-economic Panel.
t-values in parentheses; * level of significance 99%.

[38] We, thank Prof. Dr. Joachim Merz (University of Lüneburg) for providing us the appropriate software.
[39] The dependent variable is the number of hours worked per year. Only those who had been employed for the whole year were selected for estimation.

Table 10.4 OLS estimate for hours worked with correction for selection bias

Regressor x_j	Single persons
Intercept	3976.82[*]
	(10.45)
Marginal net wage in DM	21.50[*]
	(−23.29)
Corrected non-labour income in DM	−0.022[*]
	(−2.41)
Number of children under 18 years	−122.75[*]
	(−4.63)
Partner working (1 = yes; 0 = no)	—
Nationality (1 = German, 0 = foreigner)	274.32[*]
	(4.88)
Schooling (1 = primary, 4 = university)	14.68
	(0.91)
Degree of physical handicap (0–100%)	10.26[*]
	(3.65)
Age in years	5.51[*]
	(3.36)
Heckman variable correcting for selection bias μ	−2184.46[*]
	(−4.65)
Adjusted R^a	0.28
Number of persons	1539

Source: Own calculations on the basis of the first wave of the Socio-economic Panel. *t*-values in parentheses; [*] level of significance 99%; [**] level of significance 95%.

variable is significant, indicating that there is indeed a sample selection bias which has to be corrected for.

From the estimated coefficients for marginal net wage and corrected non-labour income, we compute an uncompensated wage elasticity of −0.09 and an income elasticity of −0.20. This results in a compensated wage elasticity of 0.11.[40]

We now turn to the effects induced by the West German income tax reform. The reform raises the total labour supply of singles by 7.62 hours a year, corresponding to 0.1% of labour supply before the reform, according to our results shown in Table 10.5. Although this rise appears to be almost negligible in total, the differences between income classes are remarkable. For recipients of gross income between DM 40 000 and DM 60 000 the increase in the number of hours worked is sizeable. The increase in labour supply observed for this income group coincides with the largest reductions in marginal tax rates. Recipients of very low and very high income tend to work less after the reform.

Finally, we come to the analysis of the welfare effects. As shown in Table 10.5, equivalent variation increases with income and is positive for all taxpayers. The welfare gain resulting from the tax reform can also be expressed by the change

---

[40] All elasticities are evaluated at sample mean.

Table 10.5 Welfare analysis of tax reforms: singles

Total gross income	Yearly cash gains	Equivalent variation	Change in labour supply	Change in labour supply (%)
	in DM	in DM	hours/year	
0–20 000	202	205	− 0.39	− 0.0
20 001–30 000	619	408	− 3.47	− 0.1
30 001–40 000	1123	671	17.51	1.5
40 001–50 000	2191	1075	40.46	1.9
50 001–60 000	3681	2021	41.66	1.8
60 001–75 000	5595	3685	8.80	0.3
75 001–99 999	7971	5600	− 29.90	− 1.6
All households	1274	811	7.62	0.1
Change in excess burden			− 1127	
Change in excess burden (in % of tax yield before reform)			− 18.8	

Source: Own calculations based on the first wave of the Socio-economic Panel (1984).

in excess burden, which is reduced by an equivalent of DM 1127, or 18.8% of the tax collected from the single taxpayers before the reform.

10.7 SUMMARY AND CONCLUSION

A major income tax reform has been enacted in West Germany in recent times. While the basic idea of the reform – reduction in marginal tax rates combined with a closing of loopholes – was the same as in the US Tax Reform 1986 the German reform differed in some respects. The aim of improving economic efficiency by reducing marginal tax rates was combined with the aim of redistributing income in favour of families and recipients of very low income.

The public discussion in Germany on the reform focused on distributional issues and was often based on inappropriate methods like 'typical household' (or 'pure tax schedule') analysis.

Tax simulation models based on micro-data are well-suited to evaluate the effects of tax reform in terms of both cash gain and welfare gain.

The results reported here for singles suggest that there are sizeable cash and welfare gains for this group of taxpayers. Although the change in labour supply is small in total, noticeable increases in the number of working hours were found for those income classes who experience the largest reductions in marginal tax rates.

If the large welfare gains for married women are taken into account (van Essen *et al.*, 1991), one can conclude that the West German income tax reform has brought along considerable welfare gains, presumably at the cost of a slightly less equal distribution of disposable income. In addition, tax relief was given to low-income earners. Many of them are totally exempt from income taxation. There is also a large reduction of the tax burden of families with children.

One remark has to be made, however: the loss in revenue that resulted from the income tax reform was partially compensated for by increases in the excise taxes on gasoline and alcohol, the influence of which has not yet been examined in detail. In our opinion, the integration of indirect taxation – and of the transfer system – into microanalytic simulation models is a promising direction of future research in the area of fiscal-policy modelling.

REFERENCES

Atkinson, A. B., King, M. A. and Sutherland, H. (1983) The Analysis of Personal Taxation and Social Security. *National Institute Economic Review*, **106**, 63–74.

Atkinson, A. B. and Sutherland, H. (1988) (eds) *Tax–Benefit Models*. Occasional Paper 10, London School of Economics, London.

Hanefeld, U. (1987) *Das Sozio-ökonomische Panel. Grundlagen und Konzeption*. Campus Verlag, Frankfurt and New York.

Haveman, R. H. (1978) Economic Effects of Tax-Transfer Policy: The Potentials and Problems of Micro-Data Simulations, in *Problembereiche der Verteilungs- und Sozialpolitik*, (ed. M. Pfaff), Duncker and Humblot Berlin, pp. 417–43.

Hicks, J. R. (1941) The Rehabilitation of Consumer's Surplus. *Review of Economic Studies*, **8**, 108–16.

Hinterberger, F. and Müller, K. (1988) Verteilungswirkungen der Einkommensteuertarifreform 1990. *Zeitschrift für Wirtschafts- und Sozialwissenschaften*, **108**, 355–69.

Kaiser, H. (1989) Zur Messung allokativer und distributiver Effekte wohlfahrtsstaatlicher Maßnahmen. Sonderforschungsbereich 3, Working Paper No. 283, Frankfurt and Mannheim.

Kaiser, H., van Essen, U. and Spahn, P. B. (1993) Income Taxation and the Supply of Labour in West Germany (this volume).

Kaiser, H. and Spahn, P. B. (1991) Verteilungspolitische Beurteilung der Steuerreformen in der Ära Stoltenberg – Einige Klarstellungen. *Kredit und Kapital*, **24**, 526–31.

Killingsworth, M. R. (1983) *Labor Supply*. Cambridge University, Cambridge.

King, M. A. (1983) Welfare Analysis of Tax Reforms Using Household Data. *Journal of Public Economics*, **21**, 183–214.

Krupp, H.-J. (1978) The Pros and Cons of Simulations on the Basis of Individuals or Groups in Micro-Models, in *Problembereiche der Verteilungs- und Sozialpolitik*, (ed. M. Pfaff), Duncker and Humblot, Berlin, pp. 445–52.

Lietmeyer, V. (1986) Microanalytic Tax Simulation Models in Europe: Development and Experience in the German Federal Ministry of Finance, in *Microanalytic Simulation Models to Support Social and Financial Policy*, (eds G. H. Orcutt, J. Merz and H. Quinke), Amsterdam, North-Holland, pp. 139–52.

Merz, J. (1988) Microsimulation – A Survey of Principles, Developments and Applications with Focus on the Static Case and the Static Sfb 3-Microsimulation Model as an Example. Sonderforschungsbereich 3, Working Paper No. 268, Frankfurt and Mannheim.

Nakamura, A. and Nakamura, M. (1990) Modelling Direct and Indirect Impacts of Tax and Transfer Programs on Household Behavior, in *Prospects and Limits of Simulation Models in Tax and Transfer Policy*, (eds J. K. Brunner and H.-G. Petersen), Campus Verlag, Frankfurt and New York, pp. 461–78.

Okner, B. A. (1978) Korreferat zu Hans-Jürgen Krupp: The Pros and Cons of Simulations on the Basis of Individuals or Groups in Micro-Models, in *Problembereiche der Verteilungs- und Sozialpolitik*, (ed. M. Pfaff), Duncker and Humblot, Berlin, pp. 453–6.

Pechman, J. A. (1987) Tax Reform: Theory and Practice. *Economic Perspectives*, **1**, 11–28.

Presse- und Informationsamt der Bundesregierung (1989) Steuerreform 1990. Steuerentlastung–Steuergerechtigkeit–Beschäftigungsimpulse, in *Aktuelle Beiträge zur Wirtschafts- und Finanzpolitik, No. 49*.

Spahn, P. B., Galler, H., Hochmuth, U., Kaiser, H., Kassella, T. and Merz, J. (1992) Mikrostimulation in der Steuerpolitik Wirtschafts- wissenschaftliche Beiträge, Band 66, Heidelberg: Physica.

van Essen, U., Kassella, T. and Landua, M. (1986) Ein Simulationsmodell der Einkommensbesteuerung auf der Basis des Sozio-ökonomischen Panels. Sonderforschungsbereich 3, Working Paper No. 188, Frankfurt and Mannheim.

van Essen, U. and Kassella, T. (1988) Die Einkommensangaben im Sozio-ökonomischen Panel des Sonderforschungsbereiches 3 und ihre Relevanz für steuerpolitische Simulation, in *Aufgaben und Probleme der Einkommensstatistik, Sonderhefte zum Allgemeinen Statistischen Archiv* (ed. U. P. Reich), Heft 26, pp. 133–66.

van Essen, U., Kaiser, H. and Spahn, P. B. (1988) Verteilungswirkungen der Einkommensteurreformen 1986–1990. *Finanzarchiv, N. F.*, **46**, 56–84.

van Essen, U., Kaiser, H. and Spahn, P. B. (1990) Einkommensteuertarifreform 1990: Cui bono? *Zeitschrift für Wirtschafts- und Sozialwissenschaften*, **110**, 115–21.

Wiegard, W. (1987) Reform der Einkommensteuer: Einfacher, gerechter, effizienter? *Wirtschaftsdienst*, **67**, 239–46.

11

Exploring the distribution and incentive effects of tax harmonization

F. Bourguignon, P. A. Chiappori and
R. Hugounenq

11.1 INTRODUCTION: HARMONIZATION AND TAX REFORM

Fiscal harmonization between EEC countries has been an important and some-what controversial issue in France during the last years. The prospect of the unified EEC market in 1992 clearly raises the question of whether the present discrepancies between various national tax–benefit systems may remain un-changed without hampering economic integration. The debate focused, in par-ticular, on whether VAT rates should be harmonized across countries and, in that case, on the consequences of such a harmonization.

The divergences between national indirect tax systems may stem either from their relative weight, their structure, or both. Each system is characterized by a variety of rates, with the consequence that the taxation of any given good or service may vary significantly across countries. In addition, the total amount levied through VAT, as a percentage of GNP, is far from uniform over EEC countries. The distribution of the average weight of VAT and excise taxes ranges from 6% of GDP in the case of Spain to 16.8% in the case of Denmark, with an EEC average of 9.4%, and, as a percentage of total fiscal receipts, from 30.3% (Belgium) to 49.2% (Portugal), with an EEC average of 36.2%. In France, indirect taxes amount to 11.3% of GNP, two points above the EEC average; hence, harmonization, if fully implemented, would probably require a decrease of the same magnitude in the average rate.

The effects of a reform of this kind have been repeatedly investigated; for the case of France, examples are Laisney-Baccouche (1986) and (1989). However, most, if not all, studies consider the issue from a purely welfare viewpoint. Typically, they estimate the induced changes in behaviour and the corresponding efficiency gains (in terms of, for instance, decrease of the deadweight loss for a representative consumer). In contrast, the consequences of a reform of indirect taxation on income distribution have been much less investigated so far. Of course, an immediate argument for this disinterest is that changes in VAT rates do not *per se* significantly alter inequality. Specifically, most studies point out that VAT is slightly progressive (the average rate increases from 8.9% to 10.6% with income), but the overall variations are quite small, so that the impact on inequality is clearly negligible compared to that of direct taxation. One can, hence, consider VAT as an essentially neutral tax – in contrast to income tax or wealth tax,[1] which have major redistributive consequences.

Does this imply that, as far as VAT harmonization is considered, distribution issues are irrelevant? The answer is not immediate. It is clear, indeed, that a 2% decrease of the average VAT rate will considerably affect the receipts of the public sector – remember that VAT in France amounts to almost 45% of the government budget. A decrease in public expenditures of this magnitude is excluded in the short run; hence, a lower average VAT rate will have to be compensated for by an increase in the yield of other taxes. The precise form taken by the compensation is not totally clear. Most likely, however, at least a part of the compensatory amount will be levied through additional taxes on income. A particular feature of the French tax system is the low level of income taxation; income tax represents 8% of GDP and 18.2% of total taxes, whereas the figures are, respectively, 13% and 34.5% for Germany, 13.7% and 37.9% for Italy, and 14.9% and 38.2% for UK. Hence, in the case of France, income tax apparently constitutes a natural source of additional fiscal receipts.[2] Moreover, should the compensation occur merely through an increase in the yield of income tax, this would clearly require a major reform. Indeed, since the average VAT rate is close to 10%, a 2% decrease will cut the corresponding receipts by some 135 billion francs – while the total yield of income tax is approximatively 300 billion.

In this chapter, we investigate the various directions that such a reform could borrow, and its consequences on inequality. The point we are making is neither that VAT harmonization is indispensable, nor that it has to be accompanied by a reform of direct taxation. Both assertions are quite debatable and, probably, excessive. We shall argue, however, that the present French income tax could be considerably improved by such a reform. In this sense, VAT harmonization can rather be seen as an excellent opportunity to carry out changes that, in any case, are clearly needed. Specifically, in what follows, we shall investigate a variety of possible reforms of income tax. The common point is that, in each case, the increase in receipts, in first approximation, will roughly represent 2% of the disposable income and, hence, can be thought of as roughly compensating the VAT rates cut at stake. For each reform, we simulate the consequences on in-

---

[1] Correcting for the differences of saving rates across income classes would lead to a further reduction of progressivity, since differences in marginal propensity to consume roughly compensate for the differences in the effective VAT rates.

[2] It is interesting to remark that the deficits of social security funds have been repeatedly compensated for, during recent years, by a 1% additional tax on all incomes; the recent introduction of the Contribution Sociale Généralisée (CSG) had exactly the same goal.

equality, by estimating the new distribution of income and computing the corresponding inequality indices. In addition, and in order to get a first idea of the outcomes in terms of efficiency, we also estimate the resulting distribution of the marginal rates of taxation. Our conclusion is that a deep reform of the French direct and indirect taxation system has significant room for improving both equality and efficiency, by decreasing simultaneously the inequality indices and the average marginal rates.

This chapter is organized as follows. In the next section, we discuss the basic methodological issues, namely, whether VAT applies to total income or simply to the share of income devoted to (present) consumption. Section 11.3 describes the main features of income tax, and the characteristics of the population sample we use for simulations. The simulations are discussed in section 11.4, where the main results are described. The conclusions are presented in section 11.5.

11.2 SOME METHODOLOGICAL ISSUES

Most empirical studies of redistribution through the tax–benefit system are based on current disposable incomes. If the objective is to evaluate social welfare or to make welfare comparisons across individuals, this choice is quite debatable. In the presence of income variations over time, and assuming some intertemporal arbitrage by income recipients, the relevant concept is either consumption or some measure of 'permanent' income, the former being, in fact, a reasonably good approximation of the latter. The problem in using consumption expenditures, however, is that they relate only indirectly to changes in taxes and benefits based on income, hence, the revealed preference for disposable income in most applied work on distribution.

Things become more intricate when taxes are based on both income and consumption, as is the case here, with the possible distributive effects of a European harmonization of VAT rate compensated by a change in direct income taxation. Faced with the obligation of considering both types of taxes, most of the literature still favours the disposable-income concept. The VAT and other indirect taxes are viewed as a reduction in disposable income, which has a bearing on that part of the income which is not saved. In most countries, indirect taxes are, thus, declared as regressive because, even though they may be mildly progressive with respect to consumption expenditures, the income share of these expenditures decreases with the level of income.

The present section focuses on two points. First, the preceding approach to the distributive effects of indirect taxation, i.e. the correction by saving rates, is theoretically ill-founded. Given the fact that savings are delayed consumption, the VAT should be applied not to current consumption expenditures but to total income. The second point is that a uniform change in the rate of indirect taxation is likely to have distributional effects almost negligible in comparison with those which may arise from the compensating changes in direct taxation rates necessary to maintain overall tax revenues at their original level. Therefore, the real issue is that of direct rather than indirect taxation.

About the first point, the main question to ask is that of the rationale for using disposable income rather than consumption expenditures as a measure of individual welfare. Consider the familiar life-cycle budget constraint:

$$\sum_{t=1}^{T} c_t(1+r)^{-t}(1+v) + W_T(1+r)^{-T} = W_0 + \sum_{t=1}^{T} R_t(1-\tau)(1+r)^{-t} \quad (11.1)$$

where c_t and R_t are, respectively, the real (i.e. net of indirect taxes) consumption and the gross income (i.e. before direct taxes) in period t, v is the indirect tax rate, τ the direct tax rate, r the rate of interest, W_0 the initial amount of wealth and W_T the wealth transmitted by the individual to his/her descendants at the end of his/her lifetime, T. For simplicity, both indirect and direct tax rates are assumed to be constant.

The point to note is that, in the absence of wealth accumulation – i.e. if $W_T(1+r)^{-T} = W_0$ – the budget constraint is homogeneous of degree zero with respect to direct and indirect taxation. In other words, a 1% increase in indirect taxes is rigorously equivalent to a 1% increase in direct taxes. So, the only difference between the two taxes comes essentially from the wealth accumulation process over the whole life cycle. If one were to refer to some steady state of both growth and intergenerational wealth transmission, no net accumulation would take place and the equivalence result would hold rigorously. On the other hand, in the so-called dynamic model (Becker and Barro, 1988), individuals include the welfare of their descendants in their own welfare and the life-cycle model becomes an infinite-horizon model. It may be argued, in this case, that the term in W_T, thus, disappears from the budget constraint and that equivalence does not hold anymore (this conclusion depends, however, on the kind of transversality condition adopted). In any case, it is clear that the difference between the two taxations lies in the fact that the real purchasing power of accumulated wealth is affected by the indirect and not by the direct tax rate.

Instead of considering the entire life cycle, and beyond, in the dynastic case, let us focus on the current period ($t = 1$). Maximizing some utility function under the budget constraint (11.1) yields, in both the dynastic and the life-cycle case,

$$C_1 = F\left[\frac{W_0}{1+v} + \sum_{t=1}^{T} R_t \frac{1-\tau}{1+v}(1+r)^{-t}, r\right] \quad (11.2)$$

for the optimal consumption in period 1. The indirect utility function over the whole life cycle depends on the same arguments as C_1. Total welfare V then may be written as

$$V = g(C_1, r) \quad (11.3)$$

For a given interest rate, current consumption, thus, is some transformation of total welfare. Hence, considering a sample of individuals of **the same age**, cross-sectional differences in current consumption represent, in effect, cross-sectional differences in life-cycle welfare.

By definition of savings, current real consumption is equal to

$$C_1 = R_1(1 - t)(1 - s_1)/(1 + v) \tag{11.4}$$

where s_1 is the saving rate. The right-hand side puts to the forefront the current disposable income so that equation (11.4) provides a justification for using this concept as a basis for welfare comparisons. Note though that, in order to make sense, it must be corrected by the propensity to consume $(1 - s_1)$. If this correction is not explicit, comparing two individuals on the basis of their current disposable incomes is meaningful only insofar as their saving rates may be assumed to be identical. Such an assumption may not be unreasonable if both individuals are of the same age and if their expected future income profiles, starting from the currently observed income, are parallel. It certainly is not justified if individuals are not of the same age or if the current income includes large transitory components.

The important point, in any case, is that equation (11.4) is quite different from the usual practice, which consists of basing interpersonal comparisons on disposable income net of indirect taxes on consumption, i.e.

$$Y_1 = R_1(1 - t)[1 - (1 - s_1)v] \tag{11.5}$$

which has no simple or direct intuitive welfare interpretation. It may be seen that the only case where cross-sectional comparisons based on equation (11.5) give the same relative differences as those based on equation (11.4) is where s_1 and v are linked by a very specific relation across observations, namely,

$$(1 - s_1)/(1 + v)[1 - (1 - s_1)v] = \text{const}$$

Assuming that v is identical across consumers, this requires that all individuals have the same saving rate. In the latter case, however, relative inequality arises only from differences in disposable incomes, indirect taxation being neutral with respect to the distribution of welfare.

In this chapter, we follow the standard practice of using disposable income for assessing the distribution effects of a tax reform, but disposable income is corrected by the indirect tax rate factor $(1 + v)$ as in equation (11.4), rather than equation (11.5). As we ignore cross-sectional differences in saving rates, we also implicitly assume that saving rates are, in fact, identical for all households. Correcting the distribution of disposable incomes by consumption propensities would technically be a simple operation. However, little recent information is available on the relationship between consumption propensity and variables of interest for the present analysis, i.e. income, age and family composition.[3] As

---

[3] Kessler and Masson (1977) give very rough 'guesstimates' of the relationship between savings, income and age, which refer to 1967! More recent, but still incomplete, information may be available in Bloch (1989).

Table 11.1 Apparent VAT rate (percentage of total spending) on consumption expenditures by income and household size

Annual income (thousands 1979 FF)	VAT rate							Number of households (thousands)
	< 24	24–36	36–60	60–96	96–180	> 180	Total	
Household size								
Single	8.9	9.6	10.2	9.8	10.8	10.8	9.7	4034
Single parents	8.8	8.9	9.0	9.8	—	—	9.2	359
Couples with no children	9.1	9.5	9.0	10.5	10.7	10.7	10.1	5291
Couples with one child	9.1	9.9	9.9	10.5	10.9	11.5	10.4	1957
Couples with two children	9.7	8.7	9.9	10.0	10.3	11.0	10.1	1835
Couples with three children	—	9.3	9.7	10.1	10.7	9.1	9.9	670
Couples with more than three children	—	9.7	9.1	10.5	10.1	10.6	10.0	271
Households with three adults or more and no child	8.5	9.3	9.8	10.3	10.3	10.9	10.1	2456
Households with three adults and children	8.5	8.8	9.8	9.9	10.1	9.9	9.9	1991
Total	**8.9**	**9.5**	**9.8**	**10.3**	**10.4**	**10.6**	**10.0**	**18864**
Number of households (thousands)	2601	2125	4620	4610	2464	424	18864	

Source: Bazy-Malausie *et al.* (1982).

shown by the life-cycle model above, another alternative would be to use data on wealth. But, again, cross-tabulations of wealth, earnings, age and family composition are not readily available.

An important consequence of the theoretical arguments above is that the distributional effects of a change in indirect taxation are likely to depend primarily on the way in which this change is compensated for in order to maintain tax receipts at their original level. Following the methodology described above, the distributional impact of taxation is measured by the distribution of the VAT-corrected disposable income, i.e. for an individual i:

$$y_i = R_i(1 - t_i)/(1 + v_i)$$

where t_i and v_i are, respectively, the direct and indirect tax rates faced by individual i.

Assume now that changes in indirect tax rates are to be compensated for by changes in direct tax rates so as to maintain total tax revenues constant – this is the assumption we shall maintain in what follows. The overall redistributive impact of such a measure clearly depends on the possibility to discriminate among agents with different income levels, both with indirect and direct taxation systems. Practically, the income-discriminating power of direct taxes is much higher than that of indirect taxes. An estimate of overall indirect tax rates (v_i) in France is presented in Table 11.1. The average rates vary from 9.6% for low-income households to 10.8% for high-income households. In contrast, direct tax rates (t_i) vary from zero to more than 30% in the top centile of the population. Although this point should really be made at the margin, rather than with average tax rates, it suggests that the distributional impact of a change in the burden of indirect taxes will practically be that of the accompanying reform of the income tax. What really matters then is the scope for such a reform of the direct tax system coupled with a reduction in indirect taxes. This is what we analyse now.

11.3 THE SCOPE FOR PERSONAL INCOME TAX REFORM IN FRANCE

In comparison with personal income tax systems in other countries, the French system is somewhat peculiar. Actually, this facilitates the investigation of the scope for reform since the steps that are necessary to make it comparable to other systems can easily be identified. The main features of the present system are shown in Table 11.2.[4]

The tax unit is the family. Separate taxation of spouses is not allowed; conversely, two individuals living together without being married cannot choose to be taxed jointly. Taxable income is defined as gross income – from employment and other sources – minus two deductions. The first deduction, equal to 10% of

---

[4] In what follows, the CSG is not taken into account.

the gross income (subject to an upper limit applicable to less than 5% of all taxpayers), relates to work expenses and applies only to labour incomes and pensions. The second deduction, equal to 18% of the **gross** income, applies only to wage income and pensions; it is supposed to offset the effects of tax evasion by self-employed individuals or proprietorships. For most wage earners, therefore, taxable income is 72% of the gross income.

Table 11.2   The French Income Tax Schedule (1991)

Taxable annual income (FF)	Marginal tax rate (%)
0–18 140	0
18 140–18 960	5.0
18 960–22 470	9.6
22 470–35 520	14.4
35 520–45 660	19.2
45 660–57 320	24.0
57 320–69 370	28.8
69 370–80 030	33.6
80 030–133 340	38.4
133 340–183 400	43.2
183 400–216 940	49.0
216 940–246 770	53.9
246 770–and above	56.8

The computation of income tax liabilities involves an intermediate step. Taxable income is first divided by the 'quotient familial', which represents the number of persons in the family, with a weight equal to one for the parents, the third child and subsequent children, and equal to 0.5 for the first and the second child.[5] The piecewise linear tax schedule in Table 11.2 is then applied to the corrected 'income per capita' and the total tax is computed by multiplying the result by the quotient familial. If N denotes the quotient, Y the taxable income, and $t(\ )$ the function representing the tax schedule, the total tax liability is given by

$$T = N \cdot t(Y/N)$$

The final tax is then determined by deducting the permissible tax credits (or, in some years, adding extra taxes), which are computed by applying degressive rates to the initial tax, T.

A cursory comparison of the French system with personal income taxes in other developed countries, as described in Pechman (1987) for instance, reveals the following issues:

— joint taxation of labour and other income,
— joint taxation of spouses,
— the size and nature of the deductions,

[5] In single-parent families, all children have a weight equal to one.

— the treatment of family size,
— the shape of the tax schedule,
— the presence and effects of tax credits.

Reforms in the French tax system which could possibly accompany a harmonization of indirect tax rates with the rates observed in partner European countries concern one or more of these six themes. To get some idea about their effects on equity and efficiency, we now examine how a modification of the corresponding features of the French system would alter the distribution of disposable income and the marginal tax rates. This is done on the basis of a representative sample of 2000 French households.[6] Working with a sample of actual households, rather than some arbitrarily defined 'typical' household as is often done, enables one to get a comprehensive view of the effects of a given tax reform. Indeed, the problem with 'typical households' is that one never knows how 'representative' they are.

The simulations that follow assume no behavioural response of households' labour incomes. In that sense, the exercise may be viewed as a purely arithmetical one. However, by emphasizing the effects of a reform on marginal tax rates, we are able to gauge the potential for such behavioural responses and, thus, the efficiency gains or losses. All simulations are made under the restriction that tax receipts are kept constant. Each simulation focuses on a given reform of the income tax system and modifies the VAT rate – assumed to be uniform for simplicity – in order to meet the preceding constraint. Logically, the whole procedure could have been reversed. Starting from a given change in the VAT rate – that required by harmonization – we could have searched for a reform of the income tax that would have kept the total tax receipts constant. The problem in doing so was that of choosing among all combinations of tax reforms achieving that goal or among all the ways to parametrize a given tax reform. Going the other way proved computationally more convenient and provided simple benchmarks for an assessment of possible income tax reforms roughly consistent with the intended change in VAT rates.

The distribution of the sample by income and family size as well as the effects of the present structure of personal income tax and VAT (taken to be 10% of disposable income for all households) is given in Table 11.3. Note that, given the importance of the quotient familial in the French system, it is indeed important to evaluate the effects of a tax reform in terms of both incomes and family sizes. The table shows that, on an average, personal income tax payments are quite low, amounting to 8.8% of the gross income. The tax, however, is strongly progressive: the average tax rate is 28% for the richest families (irrespective of family size) and the richest 10% amount for about half of the total income tax receipts. From the lower half of Table 11.3a, on the other hand, it may be noted

---

[6] All calculations have been performed with the microcomputer software SYSIFF, described in Bourguignon *et al.* (1988). For an example of utilization of the software for a simulation, see Atkinson *et al.* (1988a, b).

that gross income is not a monotonically increasing function of family size. Initially, it rises with size, but large families tend to be poor. Given the treatment of family size under the French tax system, it follows that large families pay relatively less tax due to the progressivity of the tax schedule as well as the quotient familial. However, it should be emphasized that the quotient familial itself is more advantageous for rich than for poor families. The deduction per child is larger for rich families, which may be viewed as a regressive feature of the tax system.

Table 11.3b provides the distribution of the population by range of marginal tax rates (excluding VAT). About 35% of the sample faces a marginal rate of 20%

Table 11.3a   French Income Tax (1991): distributional effects

Population by gross income			
Quantiles	*Average net income*	*Average gross income*	*Average disposable income*
0–10%	14 696	16 140	23 576
10–20%	45 894	53 720	42 545
20–30%	65 308	89 757	61 800
30–40%	80 017	114 497	74 966
40–50%	95 607	137 068	89 745
50–60%	116 152	169 681	105 401
60–70%	138 521	209 286	123 478
70–80%	163 479	249 286	141 183
80–90%	203 237	307 925	169 208
90–95%	265 310	387 242	212 459
95–99%	363 409	528 261	279 077
99–100%	645 718	800 830	442 296
Total	130 487	189 118	112 420

Population by family size				
Quantiles	*Average family size*	*Average gross income*	*Average net income*	*Average disposable income*
0–20%	100	124 409	91 960	73 720
20–30%	113	125 164	89 990	75 278
30–40%	196	178 519	137 840	112 156
40–50%	200	185 382	140 702	114 914
50–60%	209	196 199	142 581	117 830
60–70%	250	244 714	156 092	132 075
70–80%	282	237 524	152 460	134 158
80–90%	300	246 389	156 716	139 244
90–95%	345	246 475	155 526	150 950
95–99%	371	204 044	133 054	142 193
99–100%	480	133 031	86 384	128 666
Total	213	189 118	130 487	112 420

Notes: Net income = gross income − total social security contribution;
disposable income = net income − income tax − VAT + benefits; family size is computed with the following weights: adult = 1 and child = 0.5

Table 11.3b Distribution of households by marginal tax rates (actual French tax–benefit system, 1991)

Marginal tax rate (%)	Gross income	Family size	Population (%)
20 or below	96 787	1.76	35.2
20–40	166 243	2.26	4.8
40–45	95 986	2.78	16.7
46–50	151 542	2.67	12.1
50–55	154 883	2.06	16.2
56–60	191 958	1.90	10.5
60–65	179 642	1.64	2.3
65–80	222 180	2.08	0.8
80–90	108 234	2.16	0.4
Above 90	253 595	2.59	0.9

Marginal rates are computed from gross income, and include social-security contributions, income tax and (means-tested) family benefits but exclude VAT.

or less. Essentially, the tax they pay is confined to VAT, and the effect of the personal income tax in that group can be ignored. Another 50% faces a rate between 20% and 55%. Finally, 4.5% of all households face marginal tax rates of 60% or higher, among which about 1% face rates above 90%. This haphazard distribution of the marginal tax rates reflects the distribution of both gross incomes and family sizes (because of the quotient familial), and the tax–benefit schedule. It suggests that a judgement of the disincentive effects of the personal income tax may be quite misleading if made on the basis of a visual inspection of the tax schedule or some simple summary statistic such as the mean marginal tax rate of the population.

11.4 EQUITY AND EFFICIENCY EFFECTS OF VAT-COMPENSATED REFORMS OF THE INCOME TAX

We now examine a few reforms of the tax system, consisting of compensating a reduction in the VAT rate approximately equal to two to three percentage points by a change in the structure of the income tax. Of course, there are an infinite number of possible tax reforms. In what follows, we consider essentially three of them. The first (RD) is the simplest one. It simply consists of broadening the tax base and increasing tax rates in a way that would maintain the present progressivity of the system. This is essentially done by reducing the deductions which define the taxable income. The second reform (SQF) would take advantage of the necessary increase in income taxation to suppress the quotient familial. A third reform is considered which simultaneously replaces the quotient familial by US-type allowances, reduces the progressivity of the tax schedule (in order to alleviate the effects of suppressing the quotient on marginal rates) and increases family benefits. In this reform (BQ), the tax schedule has two rates, 23% and 43%.

Table 11.4 Gains (+) or losses (−) in disposable income with respect to the actual system (FF)

Quantiles	Population by income deciles		
	SQF	RD	BQ
0–10%	500	715	981
10–20%	890	824	265
20–30%	1104	1101	489
30–40%	1142	900	370
40–50%	294	982	− 432
50–60%	173	809	− 1038
60–70%	34	662	− 1325
70–80%	42	202	− 1431
80–90%	− 372	− 913	− 470
90–95%	− 2098	− 3015	2309
95–99%	− 4626	− 6244	1288
99–100%	− 5562	− 18252	12365

Table 11.5 Gains (+) or losses (−) in disposable income with respect to the actual system (FF)

Quantiles	Population by family size		
	SQF	RD	BQ
0–20%	1556	− 549	953
20–30%	300	− 412	− 105
30–40%	1528	− 586	1000
40–50%	1687	− 648	670
50–60%	1593	− 300	697
60–70%	− 175	− 265	246
70–80%	− 1629	336	− 1350
80–90%	− 2189	399	− 1800
90–95%	− 4553	1045	− 2237
95–99%	− 3455	2029	− 730
99–100%	− 370	2877	3040

Table 11.6 Distribution of households by marginal tax rates

Marginal tax rate (%)	SQF	RD	BQ	Actual
20 or below	35.2	35.2	37.0	35.2
20–40	5.0	4.7	2.8	4.8
40–45	10.7	14.0	14.1	16.7
46–50	14.8	10.0	22.9	12.1
50–55	19.1	15.9	11.9	16.2
56–60	10.8	14.3	7.3	10.5
60–65	2.7	3.1	2.0	2.3
65–80	1.0	1.3	1.0	0.8
80–90	0.2	0.0	0.2	0.4
Above 90	1.2	1.4	1.1	0.9

Marginal rates are computed from gross income, and include social-security contributions, income tax and (means-tested) family benefits.

Although further work is needed for the preceding simulations to lead to the same reduction in the VAT rate, the simulations reported in Tables 11.4–11.6 involve indirect tax rates of a comparable order of magnitude. In any case, as changes in progressivity (inequality measures) and efficiency (mean marginal tax rates) prove to be limited, the reported simulations provide relevant benchmarks.

The results can be summarized as follows. The first reform reduces the deduction from 28% to 16.3%; it allows one to lower the average VAT rate from 10% to 7.2%. This change would clearly increase the redistributive properties of the system, both from high to low incomes and from small to large family sizes. Specifically, the upper-income decile suffers a loss from the reform, while the rest of the population gains. Not surprisingly, the price to pay is a small increase in marginal rates. The second reform – suppressing the quotient – would allow the average VAT rate to be fixed at 8.1%. The rise in progressivity is clear; however, the reform also redistributes from large to small families, and shifts the distribution of marginal rates. The last reform is of special interest. The VAT rate is reduced to 8.2%. The four bottom deciles, together with the top one, gain from the reform. Also, small families (and in particular singles) gain from the reform, but the gain is inversely correlated with income; in particular, very large families in which the average income is low are the principal beneficiaries of the reform. Lastly, the distribution of marginal rates appears more concentrated towards the mean – the latter being itself lower than in the present system.

Table 11.7 provides a few aggregate indicators that summarize the effects of the tax reforms on inequality and marginal tax rates. Inequality is measured by the Gini and the Theil coefficients. As regards marginal tax rates, on the other hand, only the arithmetic and income-weighted mean rates are reported in Table 11.7. As mentioned earlier, what is of interest is the distribution of these rates and alternative summary measures could be used. However, means are sufficient to illustrate the main conclusions of the analysis.

Table 11.7   Effect of simulated tax reforms on income inequality and the mean marginal tax rate

Reform[a]	Inequality of net incomes (%)		Mean marginal tax rate (%)	
	Theil	*Gini*	*(1)*	*(2)*
Actual	17.9	32.7	35.6	40.1
SQF	17.3	32.2	36.2	40.7
RD	17.2	32.1	36.6	41.8
BQ	17.9	32.8	34.9	39.1

(1) Arithmetic mean.
(2) Gross-income-weighted mean.
[a] Keys to reforms:
ACM
RD   Initial deduction reduced from 28% to 16%.
SQF   French tax system without quotient familial
BQ   Main features include (1) two-rates schedule: 0% below 20 000 F, 23% between 20 000 and 100 000 F, 43% above; (2) quotient familial replaced by 10 000 F per child allowances; (3) increased family benefits.

Although more elaborated simulations and calculations are called for, the first results shown in Table 11.7 are rather interesting. They suggest that a reduction in the average, almost uniform, indirect tax rate may indeed provide the opportunity of moving to a new tax system which might **dominate** the present ones from the equity or the efficiency point of view, or from both. A comparison of the actual system with the RD reform, i.e. lower deductions, shows both less inequality and slightly smaller mean marginal tax rates. The drop in inequality is obtained despite the broadening of the tax base because, given the progressivity of the present tax schedule, rich people suffer a larger relative drop in disposable income than middle- or low-income households, due to the proportional increase in taxable incomes. Concerning marginal tax rates, on the other hand, the 12% rise in taxable income increases marginal tax rates by 12% for households who stay in the same tax bracket, and by a little more for those who are raised to a higher bracket; this effect, however, should be traded off with a drop of the VAT rate by almost three percentage points. A simple calculation shows that, on the whole, the RD reform lowers the marginal tax rate of all households who initially were taxed at 20% or below in the margin on their income and raises the marginal tax rate of the others. A rough calculation from Tables 11.5 and 11.7 shows that approximately 70% of households are in the former case. This explains why the increase of mean marginal tax rates (VAT excluded) associated with the RD reform in Table 11.7 is too small to compensate for the drop in VAT rates. Altogether, when VAT is also taken into account, the mean marginal rates are decreased by the reform.

The QF reform, which consists of compensating the drop in the VAT rate by abolishing the quotient familial system, dominates the actual system. The regressivity of the quotient familial system has been analysed in detail in Atkinson *et al.* (1988a). What is interesting in the present results is that, on an average, abolishing the quotient familial does not lead to significantly higher marginal tax rates when this reform is associated with a reduction of the VAT rate. As in the preceding case, the marginal tax rate decreases in poor or middle-income large families and increases in rich families. Although we have not investigated this point, it is possible that the latter effect could be somewhat reduced by introducing some progressivity, with respect to family size, of the lump-sum taxable-income deduction which replaces the quotient familial system. In any case, the fall in inequality that may be obtained, with virtually no increase and, possibly a small drop, in marginal tax rates (due, as before, to the fact that the increase in Table 11.7 is compensated by the lower VAT rate) is worth stressing.

At the other extreme, the BQ reform describes the effects of a policy which would focus on reducing the disincentives introduced by the tax system rather than on enhancing its redistributive power. Abolishing the quotient familial in this reform is accompanied by a modification of the tax schedule which substantially reduces marginal tax rates over a large band of the taxable-income scale. The parameters of this new tax system are calibrated in such a way that the inequality of the distribution of disposable incomes is approximately maintained at its initial level, the gain in progressivity due to eliminating the quotient familial being compensated by the loss due to adopting a flatter tax schedule. The resulting drop in the mean marginal tax rate is substantial, however. It amounts to one percentage point when the mean rate is weighted by gross incomes – to which one should add the two points percentage drop in VAT rates. And, furthermore, the reduction is stronger for high incomes, where the disincentive effects may be more damaging.

11.5 CONCLUSIONS

As mentioned earlier, a more careful analysis of the possible reforms of the income tax system which could be associated with a harmonization of the French indirect tax rates with partner EC countries is certainly needed. The preceding simulations on a sample of households have shown that substantial gains in the overall efficiency of the French tax system could be achieved through such reforms, either by lowering the inequality of the distribution of disposable incomes while maintaining tax disincentives (i.e. the mean marginal tax rate) constant, or by reducing the latter while maintaining the level of inequality constant. A more careful exploration would involve a better characterization of who exactly are the losers and the winners in these reforms, of the precise change in the whole distribution of marginal tax rates instead of mean values, and of the redistribution of income across family sizes. Alternative, more efficient, reforms might also be found by combining the mean parameters of the benchmark simulations performed in this chapter and by adding new parameters. The approximate analysis conducted in this chapter has shown that such a systematic exploration of tax reforms is certainly quite promising.

ACKNOWLEDGEMENTS

This chapter elaborates a previous work by Chiappori (1988) and Bourguignon (1990). We thank G. Weber and I. Walker for useful comments.

REFERENCES

Atkinson, A. B. and Bourguignon, F. (1988) The Design of Taxation and Family Benefits. *Journal of Public Economics* (to appear).

Atkinson, A. B., Bourguignon, F. and Chiappori, P.-A. (1988a) The French Tax–Benefit System and a Comparison with the British System, in *Tax–Benefit Models* (eds A. Atkinson and H. Sutherland), STICERD, London.

Atkinson, A. B., Bourguignon, F. and Chiappori, P.-A. (1988b) What Do We Learn About Tax Reforms from International Comparisons? France and Britain. *European Economic Review*, **32**, 343–52.

Bazy-Malaurie, C., Coutière, A. and Raux, B. (1982) La TVA dans la consommation des ménages. *Economie et Statistiques*, 17–30.

Becker, G. and Barro, R. (1988) A reformulation of the economic theory of fertility, *Quarterly Journal of Economics*, **103**, 1–25.

Bloch, L. (1989) La Croissance française à Choriton 92, *Economic et Statistiques*, **227**, 13–30.

Bourguignon, F., Chiappori, P.-A. and Sastre-Descals, J. (1988) Sysiff: A Simulation Program of the French Tax – Benefit System, in *Tax – Benefit Models* (eds A. Atkinson and H. Sutherland), STICERD, London.

Bourguignon, F. (1990) Taxation of labour income, in *The Personal Income Tax Phoenix from the Ashes*. (eds. S. Crosseu and R. M. Bird), Amsterdam, North–Holland.

Chiappori, P. A. (1988) Distributional Effects of Tax Harmonization: A Preliminary Investigation for France. Document de Travail No 88–10, DELTA, Paris.

Kessler, D. and Masson, A. (1977) Patrimoine et inégalité. CREP (mimeo).

Laisney, F. and Baccouche, R. (1986) Analyse micro-économique de la rèforme de la TVA de Juillet 1982 en France *Annales d'Economie et Statistique*, **2**, 37–74.

Pechman, J. (ed.) (1987) *Comparative Tax Systems: Europe, Canada and Japan*. Tax Analysts, Arlington, Virginia.

12

The European internal market and the welfare of Italian consumers

Vincenzo Patrizi and Nicola Rossi

12.1 INTRODUCTION

In suggesting a programme of action to create a single, integrated internal market within the European Community, the European Commission's 1985 White Paper has paved the way for far-reaching changes in the structure and rates of indirect taxation (value added tax and excise duties on alcohol, tobacco and mineral oils) of EEC member states. These would include, for example, adoption of a two-rate system of VAT, extension of the VAT base to cover the currently zero-rated items as well as large and unprecedented changes in excise duties.[1]

The political debate stimulated by the proposals has, naturally, led to a renewed interest in the distributional and efficiency effects of changes in indirect taxation. Among others, Lee *et al.* (1988) have investigated the impact of the commission's proposals for VAT on the UK Government revenue as well as on the distribution of income. They estimate that the commission's proposals would lead to a rise in indirect tax revenue. Their distributional consequences would, however, depend on the nature of compensatory measures to protect the living standard of poorer households. Symons and Walker (1988) address the same questions in an explicit welfare analysis setting. Their results, based on the estimated demand system discussed in Blundell *et al.* (1988), suggest that the reform would increase the efficiency of the UK indirect tax system. Brugiavini and Weber (1988) replicate the exercise of Blundell *et al.* (1988) on Italian data and apply to the case at hand, the methodology of Ahmad and Stern (1984) for the evaluation of welfare effects of marginal tax changes. They are able to conclude that the commission's proposals appear to move (although not unambiguously) in the direction of an increased social welfare.

---

[1] The package does not, therefore, involve complete uniformity in indirect taxes across all member states. This reflects the commission's emphasis shifting from 'fiscal harmonization' to 'fiscal approximation'. (Lee *et al.*, 1988).

The important point to note about this strand of literature is its reliance on microlevel or individual household level data for the estimation of the structure of consumers' preferences (Blundell, 1988). Apart from avoiding aggregation bias, this approach naturally lends itself to a comprehensive analysis of the distributional effects of tax reforms. However, the quality and quantity of microdata is still far from what is actually needed and, therefore, researchers have to rely (as in Brugiavini and Weber, 1988[2]) on rather limited price variability. As a result, estimates of the parameters of interests and, in particular, of the substitution matrix turn out to be disturbingly imprecise.

Exploring a different avenue of research (pioneered by Jorgenson *et al.*, 1980), in this chapter we set out to provide additional evidence by attempting to exploit the high price variability embodied into aggregate time series while, at the same time, retaining a multi-consumers setting. To this end, we exploit the theory of exact aggregation and base our empirical analysis on the (exactly) aggregate almost-ideal demand system presented in Rossi (1988), whose estimation allows the recovery of individual households' preferences (section 12.2). These are, in turn, used to derive welfare measures (equivalent variations) and, hence, to examine distributional and efficiency effects of the harmonization proposals (sections 12.3 and 12.4).

Lee *et al.* (1988), in reviewing the European Commission proposals, have underlined that (with some exception) their rationale is not to be found in the usual argument about tax differences affecting the pattern of competition. This claim is confined, of course, to the commission's current proposals and does not refer to the entire tax-subsidy system of member countries. In particular, as far as Italy is concerned, it does not take into account the large subsidies to publicly provided services such as public transport, railways, electricity, mail and telephone services which are, of course, also inputs to production. Therefore, in sections 12.3 and 12.4 we extend our analysis beyond the European Commission's proposal and consider also the case for the abolition of subsidies. Section 12.5 concludes the chapter.

The main results of the chapter can be summarized as follows: harmonization of indirect taxes (value added tax and excise duties) could contribute to redistributing the burden of indirect taxation from poor to rich households, thereby reversing the present situation largely due to the regressive role played by excise duties. If, in addition, the abolition of subsidies to publicly provided services is accounted for, the previous result would be substantially strengthened. Apart from the harmonization issue, these results are of interest on their own in as much as they show that the present Italian system of indirect taxation is, as a whole, a regressive one.

---

[2] They exploit the detailed information contained in the 1981, 1983 and 1985 household surveys of the Italian Central Bureau of Statistics. To increase price variability, they use (along with time variation) geographical variation in prices.

12.2 THE STRUCTURE OF HOUSEHOLD PREFERENCES

A preliminary requirement for a meaningful analysis of the distributional effects of relative price changes is given, of course, by a substantial degree of heterogeneity among consumers. This, however, is assumed by representative agent models. At the opposite end of the spectrum, direct estimation of individual households' preferences relies on an impressive amount of information. In between the two extremes stand models based on the concept of exact aggregation due to Lau (1980). In particular, the empirical results referred to in this chapter rely on Rossi's (1988) aggregate version of the almost-ideal (AI) demand system, which can be shown to aggregate exactly over consumers without requiring the notion of a representative consumer. Aggregate expenditure shares turn out to depend on the price vector, on the distribution of expenditures over all consuming units and on the joint distribution of expenditures and household characteristics. Through the latter term, changes in the distribution of expenditures among households with different characteristics produce their impact on aggregate consumer behaviour while, at the same time, allowing the analyst to recover individual preferences.

These are represented by the following expenditure function:

$$\ln e(u^h, p, a^h) = \ln a(p, a^h) + u^h(\beta_0 \Pi_i p_i^{\beta_i}) \tag{12.1}$$

with

$$\ln a(p, a^h) \approx \alpha_0 + \sum_i \alpha_i \ln p_i + 1/2 \sum_i \sum_j \gamma_{ij}^* \ln p_i \ln p_j + \sum_i \sum_n \eta_{in} \ln p_i a_n^h \tag{12.2}$$

where u^h denotes utility for the hth household whose total expenditure is given by y^h and whose socio-demographic characteristics are described by the n-vector a^h. The ith commodity price is denoted by p_i.

The household-specific budget share equations, derived by applying Hotelling's lemma to (12.1), take the following form:

$$w_i^h = \alpha_i + \beta_i \ln[y^h/P^h] + \sum_j \gamma_{ij} \ln p_j + \sum_n \eta_{in} a_n^h + \varepsilon_i^h \tag{12.3}$$

$$\ln P^h = \ln a(p, a^h) \approx \sum_i w_i^h \ln p_i \tag{12.4}$$

where $w_i^h = p_i q_i^h / y^h$ is the ith budget share (q_i^h being the corresponding quantity demanded). In the light of the empirical application, we consider commodity aggregates of individual goods. Therefore, following Lewbel (1986), in equation (12.3) a household-specific error term accounts for aggregation of individual commodities into commodity aggregates.[3] In (equation 12.3) $\gamma_{ij} = 1/2(\gamma_{ij}^* + \gamma_{ji}^*)$

---

[3] In Lewbel (1986), the error term is not household-specific since group price indices are thought to be economy-wide weighted averages of individual prices. If, however, this assumption is extended and an intermediate step (i.e. household-specific-price indices) allowed, then the error term does depend on h.

and in (equation 12.4) following previous applications of the AI demand system, $\log P^h$ is approximated with a Stone price index.

Model (12.3) implies demographic budget share translation (Lewbel, 1985) and significantly (but necessarily) restricts the interaction of household characteristics with expenditure and prices. It belongs to the set of demand functions introduced by Gorman (1981) and allows exact aggregation without requiring the notion of a representative consumer. Letting Y denote aggregate expenditure $(Y = \Sigma_h y^h)$, aggregate budget share equations are given by

$$w_i = \sum_h (y^h/Y)w_i^h$$

$$= \alpha_i + \beta_i[\ln(Y/P)] + \beta_i\left[\left(\sum_h (y^h/Y)\ln(y^h/Y)\right)\right]$$

$$+ \sum_j \gamma_{ij}\ln p_j + \sum_n \eta_{in}\left[\sum_h (y^h/Y)\varepsilon_n^h\right] + \varepsilon_i \qquad (12.5)$$

$$\ln P = \sum_i \sum_h (y^h/Y)w_i^h \ln p_i \qquad (12.6)$$

which define a system of demand equations adding up to total expenditure, homogeneous of degree zero in prices and total expenditure, symmetric in the substitution matrix under a specific set of parametric restrictions.

Note that in (equation 12.5) aggregate expenditure shares depend on the price vector p, on real total expenditure (Y/P), on the distribution of expenditures over all consuming units through the inequality index $[\Sigma_h(y^h/Y)\ln(y^h/Y)]$, and on the joint distribution of expenditures and household characteristics through the term $[\Sigma_h(y^h/Y)a^h]$. Note, furthermore, that estimation of the parameters of equation (12.5) allows one to recover the structure of individual household preferences, thereby providing the basic instrument for applied welfare analysis.

For the purposes of the present chapter the vector a^h has been defined as follows:

a_1^h: region of residence (Northeastern Italy, Northwestern Italy, Central Italy, Southern Italy);

a_2^h: type of residence (urban, non-urban);

a_3^h: professional status of the head of the household (entrepreneur, self-employed in agriculture, self-employed in the industrial sector, self-employed in the service sector, white collar in agriculture, white collar in other sectors, blue collar in agriculture, blue collar in the industrial sector, blue collar in the services sector, pensioner and others);

a_4^h: family size (1, 2, 3, 4, 5, 6, or more).

Characteristics are represented by qualitative variables that allow 528 different types of households in the population at any given level of total expenditure. The reference household is defined as having three components, living in an urban area of Northeastern Italy, whose bread-winner is a blue-collar worker in the industrial sector, with monthly expenditure equal to the national average (2.2 million liras in 1987 prices).

Consumers' expenditure is divided into five broad commodity aggregates:

$i = 1$: food, beverages and spirits;
$i = 2$: clothing and footwear;
$i = 3$: housing, fuel, textiles, china, glassware, miscellaneous household supplies, electric household appliances, radio and TV sets;
$i = 4$: transportation and communications;
$i = 5$: other goods and services.

As far as disaggregate expenditures are concerned, estimation exploited the information contained in the quarterly 1970–84 Italian national accounts as well as those contained in the 1983 survey on family budgets conducted by the Italian National Bureau of Statistics. Furthermore, summary information on the distribution of total expenditure (needed to construct the $\hat{a}_{it}$ variables) was derived from the 1973–84 issues of the same survey.

Details on the estimation procedure and on the econometric results are provided in Patrizi and Rossi (1991). It will suffice here to report income elasticities and compensated own-price elasticities for the reference household (Table 12.1) and to mention the following points. Differences in behaviour with respect to the reference household can be mostly imputed to the following elements: (i) monthly expenditure level; (ii) household size; and (iii) geographical location. It is worth mentioning that, for a given vector of characteristics and for a given level of total expenditure, the professional status of the head of the household plays an absolutely minor role. Therefore, while showing the expected substantial influence of household characteristics on expenditure patterns, empirical results also describe a substantial behavioural homogeneity among social classes, with the exception of pensioners and unemployed.

Table 12.1 Income elasticities (e_i) and compensated own-price elasticities (e_{ij}) for the reference household (reference period: 1984:IV)

	Goods				
	$i = 1$	$i = 2$	$i = 3$	$i = 4$	$i = 5$
e_i	0.5708	2.1405	1.0003	1.0699	1.1031
e_{ii}	− 0.5293	− 0.3705	− 0.3549	− 0.3246	− 0.4266

Note: $i = 1$: food, beverages and spirits; $i = 2$: clothing and footwear; $i = 3$: housing, etc.; $i = 4$: transportations and communications; $i = 5$: other goods and services; the reference household is defined in the text.

12.3 THE INDIRECT TAX-SUBSIDY SYSTEM

A full account of the commission's proposals is far beyond the objective of the present chapter. The interested reader is referred to Lee *et al.* (1988) and, for an

Italian appraisal, to Bollino *et al.* (1988). We shall merely list here the basic assumptions on which welfare calculations of section 12.4 rest.

12.3.1 Excise taxes and duties on alcohol, tobacco and mineral oils

The commission's proposals envisage a harmonized excise duty structure based on the arithmetic average of rates of tax in each member state. In the case of Italy, this would imply vast price changes for selected items; e.g. diesel fuel: -35; petrol: -23; spirits: $+40$; and tobaccos: $+27$.

Table 12.2   Excise duties and value added tax rates (in percentage points)

Commodity aggregates	Excise duties 1987	EEC	Value added 1987	EEC
Food, beverages and spirits	5.2	7.6	8.8	8.3
Clothing and footwear	—	—	10.9	20.0
Housing, fuel, etc.	5.4	1.3	10.9	10.9
Transportation and communications	12.8	8.2	15.4	17.4
Other goods and services	0.5	0.3	10.0	15.3

Table 12.2 reports the proportion of excise duties in price for the five aggregate commodities mentioned in section 12.2, at the end of 1987 and after the harmonization.

12.3.2 Value added tax

The commission proposes that member states should adopt a two-rate system. The standard rate and the reduced rate would lie within 14% and 20% and 4% and 9%, respectively. The latter rate would be applied to certain basic goods and services, including foodstuffs, energy products for heating and lighting, water supplies, pharmaceutical products, books, newspapers and periodicals and passenger transport. Note that, as at the end of 1987 the Italian tax system adopted four VAT tax rates: a standard rate (18%), an increased rate (38%) and two reduced rates of 2 and 9%, respectively.

Table 12.2 reports the VAT rates applicable at the end of 1987 as well as the harmonized rates computed under the working hypothesis that VAT rates will be chosen so as to make up for the revenue loss due to excise and duties harmonization. In particular, we consider as feasible a 6.5–20% choice.[4]

12.3.3 Subsidies to publicly provided services

In their thorough analysis of the European Commission proposals, Lee *et al.* (1988) consider the usual arguments of tax differences being the source of an

---

[4] This choice would imply no change in the **overall** indirect tax revenue. Part of the burden would be, however, shifted from firms to consumers.

unfair cost advantage to producers located in low-tax member states and thereby affecting the pattern of competition. They convincingly argue though that 'this is not an argument which can, in general, be applied to the indirect taxes, VAT and excise duties, which are the subject of the commission's current proposals. VAT is levied according to the destination principle ... Similarly, the majority of excise duties are taxes levied in the country where the goods taxed are finally consumed' (pp. 11–12). Hence, it could be safely concluded that indirect tax differences are not likely to affect significantly the location of production. They mention, as exceptions, the excise duty on mineral oils as well as the case of some exemptions within the structure of VAT.

In the case of Italy, though, we would like to suggest that a further (indirect) significant source of distortion could arise from subsidized prices of publicly provided services such as public transport, railway services, telephone and electricity. Although formally outside the commission's proposals, they form, however, part of the indirect tax subsidy system and apply to non-negligible inputs to production.

Furthermore, they reach, sometimes, unprecedented levels. Comparing selling prices to the average total cost of production, we estimate subsidies to be around 10% for electricity and telephone services, 30% for public transport, 40% for mail services and 80% for railway services (as at the end of 1987).[5] In terms of the commodity aggregates reported in Table 12.2, this would affect only 'housing, fuel, etc.' (with a percentage subsidy of 1.1%) and 'transport and communications' (16.5%). It is not unreasonable to think that a full integration of the Italian economy within the European internal market will require (along with many other things) also dismantling this additional source of distortion.

12.4 WELFARE EFFECTS OF FISCAL HARMONIZATION[6]

We first investigate the impact of the commissions's proposals on household expenditure patterns and government revenue. Table 12.3 presents the estimated budget shares for the reference household and source of government revenue for the same household. We consider two distinct scenarios: (i) VAT and excise duties are modified as mentioned above; and (ii) along with VAT and excise duties changes, subsidies are abolished.

The first thing to note is that the apparently limited variation in budget shares signals non-negligible price responses. Nevertheless, allowing for behavioural responses in estimating the overall change in revenue does not lead to substantial

---

[5] In doing so, we simply recognize that most governments have attempted to make such companies pay for themselves. More importantly, the zero-profit point is the point were natural monopolies may operate if there is effective potential competition (markets are contestable) and sunk costs are not that important.

[6] Empirical results presented in this section have been obtained using INDICE, a user-friendly (personal) computer program designed for the analysis of welfare effects of price changes. Further, information on INDICE may be obtained from the authors.

Table 12.3 Reference household response to harmonization and sources of government revenue

			Goods			
	$i=1$	$i=2$	$i=3$	$i=4$	$i=5$	*Total*
Pre-harmonization						
Budget shares	24.8	8.5	21.8	14.4	30.5	100.0
Government revenue	3.1	0.8	3.1	3.2	2.9	13.1
Post-harmonization (i)						
Budget shares	24.5	8.7	21.2	13.9	31.7	100.0
Government revenue	3.4	1.5	2.3	2.8	4.3	14.3
Δ percentage in Government revenue	2.3	5.3	− 6.1	− 3.1	10.7	9.2
Post-harmonization (ii)						
Budget shares	24.6	8.3	21.0	15.0	31.1	100.0
Government revenue	3.4	1.4	2.5	4.4	4.2	15.9
Δ percentage in Government revenue	2.3	4.6	− 4.6	9.2	9.9	21.4

Note: Budget shares in percentage points. Government revenue in percentage of total expenditure. Government revenue increase in percentage of pre-harmonization level of government revenue.

miscalculations. In case (i) [(ii)] change in government revenue assessed under the assumption of no change in the levels of expenditure on taxed goods and services would be around 8.4% (20.6%) of pre-harmonization Government revenue as opposed to the 'correct' figure of about 9.2% (21.4%). The discrepancy is, however, somewhat larger for selected commodity aggregates.

Government revenue is, however, only part of the story and, as it is well-known, not necessarily the most informative. As a welfare indicator at the individual household level, we consider, therefore, the Hicksian concept of equivalent variation, that is, the minimum payment that would induce the household to forgo the change.[7] Given equation (12.1), it is defined, in relative terms, as

$$ev = [e^h(u^1, p^0, a^h)/e^h(u^1, p^1, a^h) - 1] \approx [(\ln(y^h)^1 - a(p^1, a^h))/(\pi_i p_i^{1 \beta_i})] - \ln(y^h)^1 \tag{12.7}$$

if all prices are set to unity before the change takes place and if the superscripts zero and one denote the pre- and post-reform, respectively.

To allow a comparison of the present situation with respect to the harmonized one, equivalent variations were computed considering as initial situation the one without indirect taxes and letting the change be given by the 1987 tax/subsidy structure, the commission's proposals [case (i)] and the harmonized no-subsidy option [case (ii)], respectively. Table 12.4 reports the equivalent variations for the first of the three mentioned cases and the differences, with respect to the first one, of equivalent variations computed for cases (i) and (ii) above.

A glance at Table 12.4 immediately reveals that the burden of the present (1987) indirect tax structure tends to fall on poorer households living in Northern Italy. If, however, the harmonization proposal took place, the situation would be

---

[7] As opposed to compensating variations, equivalent variations employ a common reference price vector to evaluate all possible tax reforms.

reversed. At the same time, households differing in characteristics other than income would not be appreciably better- or worse-off in relative terms, with the only exception of pensioners and unemployed, who would somewhat be relieved by the reform. The point would be remarkably strengthened by the harmonized no-subsidies option, which would, however, have a much stronger impact on income distribution.

Table 12.4 Relative equivalent variations (percentage points)

	Pre-harmonization	*Harmonization*	
		(i)	*(ii)*
Monthly total expenditure (in million liras)			
1.0	13.4	1.0	1.4
2.2 (Ref. household)	13.2	1.5	2.0
3.0	13.1	1.7	2.3
4.0	13.1	1.8	2.5
5.0	13.0	2.0	2.7
Family size			
1	12.9	1.6	2.1
2	13.2	1.4	1.9
3 (Ref. household)	13.2	1.5	2.0
4	13.2	1.6	2.1
5	13.2	1.5	2.0
≥ 6	12.9	1.7	1.9
Geographical location			
Northeast (Ref. household)	13.2	1.5	2.0
Northwest	13.3	1.4	2.1
Centre	13.2	1.5	2.0
South and islands	13.1	1.6	2.0
Other			
Ref. household	13.2	1.5	2.0
Pensioner	13.0	1.5	1.8
Unemployed	13.1	1.3	1.8

Table 12.4 does not combine changes in welfare for different households into an overall measure of the change in social welfare. This is done in Table 12.5 which, following the lead of King (1983),[8] computes Atkinson's (1970) index of inequality in equivalent total expenditures:

$$W = \begin{cases} \sum_h [y_e^{h^{(1-\varepsilon)}} / (1-\varepsilon)] & (\varepsilon \geqslant 0 = 1) \\ \sum_h \ln y_e^h & (\varepsilon = 1) \end{cases} \qquad (12.8)$$

[8] Atkinson's index is based on additively separable social welfare functions which allow us to avoid the drawbacks of money metric utility although we work with individual equivalent variations. To specify the functional form of a social welfare function, we take a 'single profile' approach (Little, 1952; Samuelson, 1967) which does not require intraprofile restrictions (Arrow, 1963) if only one profile is admitted.

where ε is the relative inequality aversion parameter and y_e^h is the equivalent total expenditure, that is, the expenditure level which, at reference prices, would yield the same index of utility as could be obtained under the given budget constraint. Note that, as shown by King (1983, p. 210), in the present case of almost-ideal preferences, the equivalent income function is straightforwardly related to the equivalent variation function given in equation (12.7).

Table 12.5   Atkinson's (1970) index of inequality for the distribution of equivalent total expenditures

ε	Pre-harmonization	Harmonization	
		(i)	*(ii)*
0.5	5.781	5.731	5.722
1.0	11.716	11.615	11.598
2.0	23.496	23.299	23.271
5.0	49.062	48.751	48.727

Indices of inequality, as given by (equation 12.8), are shown in Table 12.5 for different values of the inequality aversion parameter and for pre- and post-harmonization distributions of equivalent total expenditures. Needless to say, both harmonization proposals represent a move towards a lesser inequality at all levels of the inequality aversion parameter.

12.5 CONCLUDING REMARKS

It is widely recognized that the concern for the overall macroeconomic implications as well as the administrative issues surrounding the fiscal harmonization proposals are likely to play a major role in the future course of the proposals. However, as this chapter has tried to show, fiscal harmonization in Europe is also likely to generate substantial distributional and efficiency effects in member countries.

ACKNOWLEDGEMENT

This chapter is based on the results of a larger research project separately funded by the Italian National Research Council (CNR; Research Project on the Structure and Evolution of the Italian Economy; Grant No. 85.02486.53) and by the Italian National Planning Institute (ISPE). A full report of the results is given in Patrizi and Rossi (1991). We thank L. Bernardi, C. A. Bollino, P. Bosi, V. Ceriani, S. Clement, M. Mare', D. Placentino, D. Rizzi, and the participants of departmental seminars at University College London and Birkbeck College London for their helpful comments on a previous version of this chapter and M. Bella for outstanding research assistance. The usual disclaimer applies.

REFERENCES

Ahmad, E. and Stern, N. (1984) The Theory of Reform and Indian Indirect Taxes. *Journal of Public Economics*, **25**, 259–98.

Arrow, K. J. (1963) *Social Choice and Individual Values*, 2nd edn. Yale University Press, New Haven.

Atkinson, A. B. (1970) On measurement of inequality, *Journal of Economics Theory*, **2**, 244–63.

Blundell, R. (1988) Consumer Behavior: Theory and Empirical Evidence. A Survey. *Economics Journal*, **98**, 16–65.

Blundell, R., Pashardes, P. and Weber, G. (1988) What Do We Learn About Consumer Demand Patterns from Micro Data?, Working Paper 88/10, Institute for Fiscal Studies, London.

Bollino, C. A., Ceriani, V. and Violi, R. (1988) Il Mercato Unico Europe e l'armonizzazione dell'IVA e delle accise. *Politica Economica*, **3**, 315–59.

Brugiavini, A. and Weber, G. (1988), Welfare Effects of Indirect Tax Harmonization: The Case of Italy. University College, London. (mimeo).

Gorman, W. M. (1981), Some Engel Curves, in *Essays in the Theory and Measurement of Consumer Behaviour* (ed. A. S. Deaton) Cambridge University Press, Cambridge.

Jorgenson, D. W., Lau, L. J. and Stoker, T. W. (1980) Welfare Comparisons and Exact Aggregation. *American Economic Review*, **70**, 268–72.

King, M. (1983), Welfare Analysis of Tax Reforms Using Households Data. *Journal of Public Economics*, **21**, 183–214.

Lau, L. (1980) A Note on the Fundamental Theorem of Exact Aggregation. *Economics Letters*, **9**, 119–26.

Lee, C., Pearson, M. and Smith, S. (1988) Fiscal Harmonization: An Analysis of the European Commission's Proposals, Report No. 28, The Institute for Fiscal Studies, London.

Lewbel, A. (1985) A Unified Approach to Incorporating Demographic or Other Effects into Demand Systems. *Review of Economic Studies*, **52**, 1–18.

Lewbel, A. (1986) Grouping Goods Without Separable Utility. Brandeis University, Waltham (mimeo).

Little, I. M. D. (1952) Social Choice and Individual Values. *Journal of Political Economy*, **60**, 422–32.

Patrizi, V. and Rossi, N. (1991) *Preferenze, prezzi relativi e redistribuzione*. Mulino, Bologna, II.

Rossi, N. (1988) Budget Share Demographic Translation and the Aggregate Almost Ideal Demand System. *European Economic Review*, **31**, 1301–18.

Samuelson, P. A. (1967) Arrow's Mathematical Politics, in *Values and Economic Policy: A Symposium* (ed. F. Hook), New York University Press, New York.

Symons, E. and Walker, I. (1988) The Revenue and Welfare Effects of Fiscal Harmonization for the UK, Working Paper No. 88/8, Institute for Fiscal Studies, London.

13

Tax reform within the EEC internal market: empirical analysis with two macroeconomic modelling approaches

Pantelis Capros, Pavlos Karadeloglou
and Gregory Mentzas

13.1 INTRODUCTION

The EEC trade liberalization, which will result in a reduction of import tariffs and export subsidies, as well as in the harmonization of indirect tax system in member states, is among the major issues involved in the process of the completion of the internal market. Macroeconomic empirical evaluations of impacts were first studied and reported in the so-called 'Cecchini report' (Commission of the EEC, 1988). The impact analysis was limited to the large and/or developed countries of the European Community. Independent studies covered two of the small and less developed peripheral economies of EEC, namely Greece and Ireland (Karadeloglou, 1989; Bradley *et al.*, 1989). The macroeconomic analysis of the impacts has been carried out exclusively by means of approaches that follow the neo-Keynesian modelling paradigm, since the model used is the European wide macroeconomic model HERMES.

The Cecchini report recognizes the lack of an approach based on general-equilibrium models and, for this reason, it employs a conceptual analysis as a substitute. The main aim of the present chapter is to contribute empirically towards this direction. The chapter presents a computable general-equilibrium (CGE) model, as well as several model variants, and uses this model for the analysis of impacts of some of the '1992' issues, especially those related to fiscal policy. The CGE model is quite traditional in its design and specification, so that conclusions can be drawn about the kind of results that one should expect if similar CGE models are applied to other European countries. Moreover, these results are compared with those of a neo-Keynesian model which reproduces the behaviour of larger models used in the Cecchini report. The two approaches, namely the CGE and the neo-Keynesian models, share most of the behavioural equations and elasticities, so that their results are directly comparable. The empirical application concerns Greece, but the specification of the models is more general, since it is in accordance with the 'small open economy' hypothesis.

The chapter includes also results of sensitivity analysis, which has been carried out towards two distinct directions: first, since fiscal policy implies changes in the public budget, we introduce in both models public budget balance constraints and study their impacts on the results; secondly, we build variants of the models by formulating alternative clearing mechanisms for the goods and the labour markets.

In our previous related work (Capros *et al.*, 1989, 1990), we have presented evidence that the CGE and the neo-Keynesian modelling approaches provide different results in most issues, especially in fiscal policy ones. However, these results have a certain complementarity: the CGE model has a normative role in the analysis and provides estimates of the long-term impacts, while the neo-Keynesian model has a descriptive role to play and indicates the short- /medium-term disequilibrium pressures. The other model variants, as also stated by Capros *et al.* (1991), are also useful regarding their policy implications: they permit one to study the role of market rigidities and imperfections.

In section 13.2 we present the modelling approaches and the derived model variants that are adopted for the study of tax policy. In section 13.3 we specify and carry out tax policy simulations with the models and present sensitivity analysis results. Basic findings and concluding remarks can be found in section 13.4.

13.2 THE MODELLING APPROACH

13.2.1 Background and model overview

The specification of the behavioural equations of the alternative modelling paradigms used in this chapter is similar to that of the large majority of traditional macroeconomic models. However, each modelling approach retains some special features which are described below. An applied general-equilibrium model is a numerical representation of the basic relationships of the Walrasian general-equilibrium system. In theoretical terms this system has been formalized in the 1950s by K. Arrow and G. Debreu, while a constructive resolution algorithm (referring to the Kakutani theorem) was provided by Scarf in the late 1960s (Scarf, 1969). The literature of empirical general-equilibrium models has taken several directions, ranging from mathematical programming to optimal control and simulation. The computable general-equilibrium model adopted in this paper follows the World Bank school and takes the form of a numerical simulation of the Arrow–Debreu barter model. Conforming to the theoretical framework, **all markets are clearing through prices**. This is termed price adjustment of the markets and in this case prices are determined by equating demand and supply. Similar approaches and applications of CGE modelling can be found in Shoven and Whalley (1972, 1984), Hudson and Jorgenson (1974, 1977), Adelman and Robinson (1978), Taylor and Lysy (1979), Deardorff and Stern (1982), Dervis, *et al.* (1982), Rattso (1982), Lysy (1983), Lewis and Urata (1984), Cordon *et al.* (1985), Blitzer and Eckaus (1986), Devarajan and Sierra (1986), Levy (1987), Kharas and Shashido (1987), Pereira and Shoven (1988), Decaluwe and Martens (1988), de Melo (1988) and Wigle (1988).

On the other hand, the basic elements of neo-Keynesian economic modelling include the rejection of Walrasian competitive equilibrium and reflect the view expressed by Keynes in the book *General Theory* that **equilibrium is obtained via quantity rather than price adjustments**. Market prices are not defined by market equilibrium as in the CGE model. On the contrary, disequilibriums are allowed because of the presence of the capacity utilization and the unemployment rates. Demand determines total production, which, in turn, evaluates the quantity of labour demand. Labour supply is determined by households, while employment is determined as the minimum of supply and demand. Hence, the labour market is not cleared by price adjustments, as it would be in the general-equilibrium framework, but is quantity-adjusted. Markets are imperfectly competitive, the determination of the equilibrium price is rigid and the introduction of a behavioural equation for this price is necessary. The neo-Keynesian model assumes excess supply in all markets and uses supply-oriented equations for determining goods and labour prices. There is a huge economic literature on modelling and applications that follow the neo-Keynesian approach (see Deleau *et al.* (1984) for a standardization of the neo-Keynesian model properties).

The difference between price and quantity adjustment mechanisms is illustrated in the following table:

Price or quantity adjustment of markets

Market M1	Market M2	Market M3
$D = f(p)$	$D = f(p)$	$\underline{D} = f(p)$
$S = g(p)$	$S = D$	$\overline{S} = D$
$D = S$	$p = h(S, D)$	$p = h(S, D)$
		$S = g(p)$
		$U = \overline{S}/S$

If D, S and p denote demand, supply and prices, respectively, it is clear that market type M1 corresponds to a price-adjusted competitive market, while market types M2 and M3 are quantity-adjusted imperfectly competitive ones. In market M2, supply is perfectly elastic and adjusts to demand. In market M3, which is a generalization of market M2, supply is rationed by demand and this affects prices through the rate of disequilibrium U. In the latter case, an excess supply situation is assumed. Market M1 formulation is adopted for the market of goods in typical CGE models. Market M2 is assumed to hold for goods market in models which formulate a cost-dependent price determination. Market M3 is also the typical formulation of most markets represented in neo-Keynesian models. In a multimarket CGE model, all three types of market-clearing formulations may coexist, in the sense that some markets are perfectly competitive, while others are not.

The general-equilibrium model used in this chapter formulates the goods and labour markets following market M1, while the neo-Keynesian model adopts market type M3. Two 'intermediate' variants are also provided which mix formulations M1 with M3. This is summarized below.

Model	Name	Goods market	Labour market
Full-equilibrium model	CGE-00	M1	M1
Goods market equilibrium model	CGE-01	M1	M3
Labour market equilibrium model	CGE-10	M3	M1
Neo-Keynesian model	NKEYNES	M3	M3

The above model variants are traditional in their design, in the sense that they are similar to well-known models proposed in the literature. Examples are as follows: CGE-00 is similar to most CGE models promoted by the World Bank (e.g. de Melo, 1988); CGE-01 is similar to CGE models that formulate short-term behaviour in the labour market (e.g. Bourguignon *et al.*, 1983); CGE-10 is similar to CGE models that assume cost-dependent determination of prices and justify general equilibrium by calling the non-substitution theorem of Paul Samuelson (e.g. Johansen, 1960; Hudson and Jorgenson, 1974, 1977); finally, NKEYNES is a one-sector equivalent of multisectoral macroeconometric models.

The models adopt common assumptions concerning most behavioural equations and elasticities, including production function, consumption, labour supply, factor demand, foreign trade, import and export prices, consumer prices and income distribution and savings identities. The main differences between the CGE-00 and the NKEYNES models are on two points. The first one is concerned with the presence, in the CGE model, of an explicit equation for production, which determines the total supply, which is made equal to demand by adjusting prices. In the neo-Keynesian model the implicit production function serves only for the determination of the demand of production factors while the effective production is determined by demand. The second difference is related to the labour market. The CGE model guarantees full employment by adjusting the wage rate to the varying labour demand and supply. The neo-Keynesian model allows for unemployment and the wage rate is determined by an augmented Phillips curve formula.

The list of equations presented in Table 13.1 is a synthesis of the two modelling approaches described above. By selecting equations from that list, in an adequate manner, one can build the four variants presented above.

Table 13.1 Equations representing a synthesis of the CGE and the neo-Keynesian models

---

(1) $p_m = \alpha_0(p_f e)^{\alpha_1}$

(2) $p_x = \beta_0(p_f e)^{\beta_1} p_v^{\beta_2}$

(3) $p_c = \gamma_0[p_m(1 + t_m)]^{\gamma_1} p_v^{\gamma_2}[(1 + t_v)]^{\gamma_1 + \gamma_2}$

(4) $c = p_v(1 + i - \Delta w/w)$

(5) $V = v_0 e^{gt}[\delta K^{-\rho} + (1 - \delta)L_w^{-\rho}]^{\frac{-1}{\rho}}$

(5a) $V_c = v_0 e^{gt}[\delta K^{-\rho} + (1 - \delta)L_w^{-\rho}]^{\frac{-1}{\rho}}$

(5b) $V = C_p + C_g + I_p + I_g + Z + X - M$

(5c) $U_c = V/V_c$

(5d) $p_v = \pi_0(wL_w/V)^{\pi_1}(cK/V)^{\pi_2}U_c^{\tau}$

(6) $\Delta L_w = \Phi_L[v_0 e^{-gt}(1 - \delta)^{1/\rho}(c/w)^{1/(1+\rho)}V]$

(7) $I_p/K = \Phi_I[v_0 e^{-gt}\delta^{1/\rho}(c/w)^{-1/(1+\rho)}V]$

(8) $L_i = \theta_0 V^{\theta_1}$

(9) $L_s = v_0 N^{v_1}(w/p_c)^{v_2}$

(10) $L_s - L_w - L_i = 0$

(10a) $U_R = (L_s - L_w - L_i)/L_s$

(10b) $\Delta w/w = \lambda_0 + \lambda_1 \Delta p_c/p_c + \lambda_2 U_R + \lambda_3 \Delta(V/L_w)/(V/L_w)$

(11) $M = \varepsilon_0 V^{\varepsilon_1}[p_m(1 + t_m)/p_v]^{\varepsilon_2}$

(12) $X = \delta_0[(p_f e)(1 + t_e)/p_v]^{\delta_1}(p_f e/p_x)^{\delta_2}D_f^{\delta_3}$

(13) $p_x X - p_m M + R_f = \bar{B}$

(14) $\dfrac{C_p}{N} = \mu_0 \left(\dfrac{R_w}{p_c N}\right)^{\mu_1} \left(\dfrac{R_k + R_f}{p_c N}\right)^{\mu_2} \left(\dfrac{W}{p_c N}\right)^{\mu_3}$

(15) $R_w = wL_w(1 - t_w)$

(16) $R_k = (p_v V - wL_w)(1 - t_k)$

(17) $S_p = R_w + R_k + R_f + p_x X t_e - p_c C_p$

(18) $S_g = wL_w t_w + (p_v V - wL_w)t_k + p_c C_p t_v + p_m M t_m - (p_v C_g + p_v I_g + p_x X t_e)$

(19) $p_v Z = S_p + S_g - p_v I_p - (p_x X - p_m M + R_f)$

(20) $V + M = (C_p + C_g + I_p + I_g + X + Z)$

(21) $K = (I_p)_{-1} + (1 - r)K_{-1}$

(22) $W = (S_p)_{-1} + (1 - s)W_{-1}$

(23) $N = N_0 \exp(\lambda t)$

13.2.2 Detailed description of the model

The numerical representation of the above theoretical framework is based on a two-market small open economy (goods and labour), in which two prices are determined: the aggregate price of goods and the wage rate. Since only relative prices affect behaviour in general-equilibrium models, we have considered the nominal interest rate as numéraire. There is a single composite consumption good and three economic agents: households, firms and government. The quantities of inputs used (i.e. capital and labour) are the solutions of a production cost minimization problem, while the production possibility frontier is given by the familiar constant returns to scale CES (constant elasticity of substitution) production function. The behaviour of government, concerning consumption and investment, is assumed exogenous.

The import and export prices depend on the aggregate price of goods, the exogenous international price, p_f, and the exogenous exchange rate e [see equations (1) and (2)]. The consumer price index is an average of domestic and imported deflators, to which an import tariff, t_m, and a value added tax, t_v, are applied, respectively [equation (3)].

The deflated cost of capital is assumed to depend on the difference between an exogenous interest rate, i, and expected inflation of production costs [equation (4)]. Expectations are assumed to be backward-looking.

The determination of domestic supply of goods (V) depends on the theoretical background of the model. In the price adjustment formulation of the goods market, in models CGE-00 and CGE-01, domestic supply (i.e. production) is evaluated by a two-factor CES production function [equation (5)]. In the case of quantity adjustment of the goods market, as in the neo-Keynesian and the CGE-10 models, total production is derived from total demand [equation (5b)]. In this case, equation (5a) evaluates the potential production (V_c) and not the effective one, and a rate of capacities utilization (U_c) is evaluated by equation (5c).

The price of the composite good is determined as the market equilibrium price in the price adjustment formulations and corresponds to equation (20), which guarantees demand–supply equilibrium. In the case of quantity adjustment of the goods market, excess supply is assumed and a supply-oriented determination of prices is adopted. In this case the price of the composite good is evaluated by equation (5d), which applies a mark-up on production cost corrected by disequilibrium pressures in the goods market.

Labour demand of firms (L_w), as well as optimum investment (I_p), are derived from cost minimization behaviour of firms [equations (6) and (7)]. Function Φ denotes the application of an error correction mechanism.

Households determine simultaneously the level of their consumption and the supply of labour force through an implicit utility function that covers both the consumption–saving and the labour–leisure choices. The consumer's decision problem is viewed as that of maximizing an intertemporal utility function subject to an intertemporal budget constraint. The utility level is the total present value of the annual utility derived from the consumption of goods, C_p, and from the consumption of leisure. The latter expresses the supply of labour force by households (L_s), since the total available time is given. The budget constraint is equal to the present value sum of wealth (W) (accumulation of annual savings), salary income and non-salary income. Through wealth, we include explicitly the consumption–saving choice: if the consumer chooses to consume more than usual, savings will be reduced and he will consume less in the next period since the level of wealth will also be reduced. Denoting by R_w and R_k the salary and the non-salary income, respectively, by R_f the net income from abroad and by N the total population, and by assuming a myopic foresight, we derive equations (14) and (9) for consumption and labour supply.

Equation (10) guarantees the equilibrium of demand and supply in the labour market, with L_i representing the number of self-employed persons, which is evaluated proportionally to the level of production in equation (8). Equation (10) is used only in full-employment model variants, namely in models CGE-00 and CGE-10. In the case of variants accepting unemployment, that is the neo-Keynesian and CGE-01 models, equation (10) is replaced by equations (10a) and (10b). The latter is a traditional Phillips curve formulation, which evaluates the wage rate; U_R is the rate of unemployment.

By following the Armington formulation of foreign trade, we derive imports, M, and exports, X, as a function of demand and the relative prices (foreign to domestic) [equations (11) and (12)], where t_m denotes the rate of import tariffs and t_e the rate of export subsidies, while D_f is an exogenous variable representing foreign demand. Identity (13) represents the current account and evaluates its balance, denoted by B.

Identities (15)–(18) correspond to flows of income and evaluate salary income, R_w, non-salary income, R_k, private savings, S_p, and public savings, S_g, the latter being equivalent to the public budget balance. Direct and indirect tax receipts constitute the gross public income. Subsidies together with public investment (exogenous), I_g, and public consumption (exogenous), C_g, form public expenditure. A positive (negative) difference between the gross income and expenditure corresponds to a surplus (deficit) in the public budget. Private savings are given as a difference between private income and consumption.

Equation (19) applies the Walras's law. This equality represents the closure rule of the model. We have adopted the evaluation of stocks variation, Z.

Equation (20) guarantees the equilibrium of demand and supply of goods, as mentioned. The model simulates a dynamic evolution of the economy through the accumulation of capital [equation (21)], the accumulation of wealth [equation (22)], the growth of population [equation (23)] and the time-dependent technical progress that appears in equations (5)–(7). In the current period, both capital and wealth are predetermined from the results of the previous period. This implies that, in the short term, production is constrained by the stock of capital and consumption is constrained by wealth.

In order to build the CGE-00 model, one must select equations (1)–(23) and eliminate equations (5a)–(5d), as well as equations (10a) and (10b). In order to build the neo-Keynesian model (NKEYNES) one must retain equations (5a)–(5d), as well as equations (10a) and (10b), but eliminate equations (5), (20) and (10).

Table 13.2   Values of elasticities

$\alpha_1 = 0.87(6.9)$	$\gamma_1 = 0.23(2.8)$	$g = 0.0027(2.3)$
$\beta_1 = 0.64(2.8)$	$\gamma_2 = 0.63(6.5)$	$\delta = 0.84$
$\beta_2 = 0.37(2.1)$	$\pi_1 = 0.75(6.2)$	$\sigma = 0.10(4.3)$
$\mu_1 = 0.37(8.9)$	$\pi_2 = 0.15(4.1)$	$\delta_1 = 0.17(2.2)$
$\mu_2 = 0.17(2.8)$	$\tau = 0.014(2.3)$	$\delta_2 = 0.75(3.4)$
$\mu_3 = 0.14(3.2)$	$v_1 = 2.71$	$\delta_3 = 0.33(2.3)$
$\varepsilon_1 = 1.12(7.6)$	$v_2 = -0.19$	$\theta_1 = 0.02(1.6)$
$\varepsilon_2 = -0.11(2.8)$	$\lambda_1 = 0.75(4.99)$	$\lambda_2 = -0.01(1.8)$
$\lambda_3 = 0.36(2.2)$	$\zeta_1 = -0.94(3.5)$	$\zeta_2 = -0.0002$

The data used for the empirical estimation of the model are gathered in a database, which mainly consists of the Greek National Accounts for the period 1965–85. The coefficients of the model (Table 13.2) were econometrically estimated using standard techniques, in contrast to the majority of the applied general-equilibrium models, which use 'guesstimates' as elasticities.[1] In addition, we have included anticipation mechanisms and adjustment processes, in order to improve both the dynamic properties of the model and the quality of the econometric equations.

13.3 SCENARIOS AND RESULTS

13.3.1 Scenario definition

The fiscal policy problem investigated concerns the changes in foreign trade tariffs and subsidies implied by the elimination of customs barriers, as well as the harmonization of indirect taxation in the European Community.

The impacts on taxes from the elimination of barriers can be fully assimilated into reductions of both import duties and export subsidies. Moreover, the harmonization of indirect taxes is expected to lead, in Greece, to a decrease of the average rate of VAT as compared to the mean EC level. These effects are represented in the model through exogenous rates, namely the rate of import tariffs, t_m, the rate of export subsidies, t_x, and the rate of indirect taxes, t_v.

The above structural changes are expected to have significant impacts on public sector's borrowing requirements. Import duties and indirect taxes constitute a large share of government's total revenues and their *ex ante* reduction should be smaller than the increased savings which will result from the fall of export subsidies. The importance of the reduction of public revenues and its effects can be evaluated by imposing constraints on the public budget and measuring the macroeconomic impacts of alternative ways of increasing resources. Two ways of financing the reduced resources are examined in this chapter when a public budget constraint is effective: the reduction in public expenditures (public investment or consumption) and the increase in direct taxes on households.

[1] The production and the consumption blocks were estimated using three-stage least squares.

In what follows we analyse the effects of tax policy impacts on the Greek economy by using all model variants and by varying the rates of import tariffs, export subsidies and value added tax rates. We assume a one percentage point reduction in the rates of export subsidies, import tariffs and value added tax.

13.3.2 Results

The results are presented in Tables 13.3–13.8. In each table we present three series of results: the first one corresponds to the case where we do not impose any public budget constraint, while the other two series are obtained after incorporating an explicit public budget constraint[2] in the model. The last two series differ in the choice of the adjustment rule: the first one adopts an adjustment through public expenditures, while the second one corresponds to an adjustment through the salary income tax rate.

Foreign trade liberalization

The direct effects of a foreign trade liberalization, i.e. of a reduction of the rates of both import tariffs and export subsidies are threefold: (a) the economy bears losses in competitiveness, which implies changes towards decreasing exports and increasing imports; (b) the consumer price of goods decreases because of the reduction of import tariffs, the decrease being proportional to the share of imports within total demand; (c) both public revenues (from import duties) and expenditures (in subsidies) are reduced.

Computable general-equilibrium model. Within the mechanism of price clearing of markets, which prevails in the computable general-equilibrium approach, indirect effects are triggered by an upwards shift of the total (i.e. foreign and domestic) supply curve and a downwards shift of the total demand curve. These movements are due to imports and exports, respectively. The result of these shifts is a reduction of the equilibrium price of goods. This implies gains in competitiveness and pushes exports upwards. Thus, at equilibrium, exports may increase.

With consumer prices also decreasing, households perceive increased real wages and augment labour supply. Thus, the equilibrium wage rate is reduced, but its drop is expected to be lower than that of the price of goods.

In the short run, the changes of wages and prices induce an increase in labour demand and a decrease in optimal capital use and, hence, in investment. This is related to the fact that backward-looking anticipations of the wage rate influence the real cost of capital negatively. In the longer term, however, relative factor prices change in favour of capital and, thus, investment is found to have increased (after 2 years). Domestic supply of goods, which depends on capacities and factor mix, is increasing throughout the simulation period. In the short term, the shift

---

[2] The public budget constraint concerns the public sector borrowing requirements as a percentage of nominal GDP.

towards more labour-using technologies sustains domestic supply since this is constrained by capital. In the longer run, investment increases the stock of capital and, hence, domestic supply.

The relaxation of supply constraints feeds a deflationary process, through the market of goods. In the long run, labour-market-determined wages decrease more rapidly than consumer prices, because of lower labour demand, as explained above. This implies losses in real salary income and a decrease in consumption, although significant increases in both real income and consumption occur in the short term. The sign of the change in real non-salary income is uncertain. It depends positively on the growth of output but negatively on the difference between the changes in the wage rate and the price of goods. If the rise in the production cost dominates, real non-salary income is expected to decrease.

The sign of the implications for the balance of the public sector is uncertain. Public revenues are decreasing mainly through import tariffs, but public expenditures are also decreasing through subsidies. In the particular case of Greece, these effects imply an increase in public sector's borrowing requirements (as a percentage of GDP). On the contrary, the current account (as a percentage of GDP) is found to have significantly improved at the end of the period, although it is slightly deficient in the first two years after the shock. Imports are increasing at a rate lower than exports, because imports depend on domestic demand, which is decreasing at the end of the period.

In summary, foreign trade liberalization acts positively on the economy through the relaxation of supply constraints in both the markets of goods and labour. The resulting fall in equilibrium prices improves competitiveness and, thus, the current account. In the short term, net gains in real wages and in real salary income are obtained. However, these vanish in the longer term when capital and investment are reinforced in production because of the evolution of relative factor prices. The public sector bears a part of the costs and its deficit is aggravated. These results are presented in Table 13.3.

Neo-Keynesian model. The main indirect effects are triggered by the decrease in consumer prices. Given the indexation relationship in the Phillips curve, the wage rate is also reduced. This implies diminishing production costs which, in turn, pushes production prices downwards. It is expected, however, that the fall in production prices is less than proportional because there is a delay in adjusting production prices to dropping costs. Such a delay is in accordance with the assumption of imperfectly competitive markets. Moreover, in the case of under-indexation in the Phillips curve, the real wage rate is expected to rise, which acts positively on income and demand. Thus, both a deflationary and a multiplier process are triggered.

Decreasing exports and increasing imports, resulting directly from the shock, imply a reduction of domestic production during the first year of simulation. This is, of course, due to the mechanism of quantity adjustment of domestic production to demand for domestically produced goods. Production capacities being

Table 13.3 Effect on the Greek economy of a one percentage point reduction in the rates of export subsidies and import tariffs, according to CGE-00 and CGE-01 models

	Without public budget constraint		*With public budget constraint*			
			Adjustment by the public investment		*Adjustment by the income tax rate*	
	1st year	*6th year*	*1st year*	*6th year*	*1st year*	*6th year*
	Full-equilibrium model (CGE-00)					
Percentage change[a] in:						
Production price	− 1.473	− 2.414	− 1.418	− 2.304	− 1.379	− 2.168
Wage rate	− 0.740	− 2.071	− 0.713	− 1.979	− 0.695	− 1.881
Consumer price	− 1.156	− 1.874	− 1.121	− 1.799	− 1.096	− 1.708
GDP	0.053	0.018	0.052	0.021	0.051	0.022
Employment	0.017	0.009	0.017	0.012	0.016	0.015
Investment	− 0.229	0.174	− 0.225	0.164	− 0.219	0.162
Consumption	0.069	− 0.087	0.071	− 0.070	− 0.107	− 0.354
Exports	0.506	1.942	0.481	1.833	0.463	1.724
Imports	0.022	0.140	− 0.095	− 0.088	− 0.098	− 0.066
Real salary income	0.480	− 0.185	0.449	− 0.164	− 0.050	− 0.910
Real non-salary income	− 0.560	− 0.521	− 0.529	− 0.481	− 0.507	− 0.421
Difference[a] in:						
PSBR (%GDP)	− 0.130	− 0.251	0.000	0.000	0.000	0.000
Current account (%GDP)	− 0.052	0.116	− 0.018	0.172	− 0.017	0.157
Unemployment rate	0.000	0.000	0.000	0.000	0.000	0.000
	Goods market equilibrium model (CGE-01)					
Percentage change[a] in:						
Production price	− 1.452	− 2.329	− 1.400	− 2.194	− 1.363	− 2.021
Wage rate	− 0.850	− 1.590	− 0.825	− 1.505	− 0.807	− 1.411
Consumer price	− 1.143	− 1.820	− 1.110	− 1.728	− 1.086	− 1.612
GDP	0.112	− 0.322	0.110	− 0.297	0.109	− 0.283
Employment	0.036	− 0.181	0.035	− 0.167	0.035	− 0.159
Investment	− 0.481	0.056	− 0.475	0.055	− 0.471	0.035
Consumption	0.069	− 0.219	0.065	− 0.191	− 0.104	− 0.555
Exports	0.497	1.963	0.473	1.830	0.456	1.695
Imports	− 0.190	0.039	− 0.129	− 0.253	− 0.132	− 0.222
Real salary income	0.374	− 0.130	0.365	− 0.111	− 0.107	− 1.095
Real non-salary income	− 0.419	− 1.061	− 0.390	− 0.974	− 0.370	− 0.865
Difference[a] in:						
PSBR (%GDP)	− 0.123	− 0.334	0.000	0.000	0.000	0.000
Current account (%GDP)	− 0.039	0.152	− 0.006	0.225	− 0.005	0.206
Unemployment rate	− 0.023	0.271	− 0.023	0.254	− 0.023	0.242

[a]Percentage changes and differences refer to the baseline scenario.

practically unchanged, the rate of capacities utilization decreases and, hence, prices are further pushed downwards.

On the production side, given the delay in anticipating wage rate reductions, capital becomes less competitive in the short term. Substitutions occur, then, in favour of employment. These last only one–two years but this is sufficient for contributing positively to the rise of real income and, hence, private consumption. These effects on consumption are reinforced through real wages, which rise because of the fall in consumer price, as mentioned, above, and because of the reduction in the unemployment rate.

The deflationary process, combined with increasing private consumption, triggers the multiplier–accelerator mechanism of the model and provides positive growth prospects for the following years. The process is moderated mainly by pressures on the market of goods which act through an increasing rate of capacity utilization.

The deflationary process is not sufficient for counterbalancing the tax effects on competitiveness in foreign trade. Thus, exports decrease and imports increase, the latter being also pushed upwards by the rise of private consumption. Thus, the deficit of the current account is aggravated. The effects on the public sector's balance are negative. However, these effects are moderated in the longer term because of the increase in public revenues from direct taxation.

In summary, demand pulls production, employment and income. Demand is supported by the wage–price spiral, which leads to deflation and raises real wages. However, delays and inertia in the adjustment that prevail on the production side lead to the reduction of gains for the economy: production prices decrease slowly and foreign trade balance deteriorates. These results are presented in Table 13.4

VAT harmonization

The first type of direct effects from a change in the VAT rate are in the consumer price index. In the case of a 1% reduction of VAT rate, the consumer price index directly decreases (by 0.85%). The consumer price index influences mainly private consumption and, hence, private savings: real income is increased, *ceteris paribus*, and both consumption and savings are upwards readjusted.

Changes in VAT rates influence also public finances. In case of a reduction of the VAT rate, public revenues from indirect taxes are directly decreased.

Computable general-equilibrium model. The decrease in consumer prices, induced by a reduction of the VAT rate, implies higher real income and, thus, an upwards shift of the demand curve. The equilibrium price of goods is, thus, adjusting upwards. In the labour market, the supply of labour is increasing because of higher real wage rates (relatively to consumer prices). The cost of capital, however, increases more than wages, because of the price of goods. Thus, a slight substitution in favour of labour is obtained in production, which allows for an increase in domestic supply of goods. This moderates the initial trends in the market of goods but also in the market of labour through the increase in labour demand. Gross profits are increasing due to higher market prices, and this produces additional income for households. Thus, both salary and non-salary incomes are increasing. The increase in the market prices of goods induces also losses in competitiveness, which further implies decreasing exports and increasing imports. The latter are also pushed upwards by the rise of domestic demand.

The above movements correspond to market readjustments that occur before taking into account the effects of the 'closure rule', which is derived from the Walras identity. In fact, the losses in public revenues and the deterioration of the

Table 13.4 Effect, on the Greek economy, of a one percentage point reduction in the rates of export subsidies and import tariffs, according to CGE-10 and NKEYNES models

	Without public budget constraint		With public budget constraint			
			Adjustment by the public investment		Adjustment by the income tax rate	
	1st year	6th year	1st year	6th year	1st year	6th year
	Labour market equilibrium model (CGE-10)					
Percentage change[a] *in:*						
Production price	− 0.042	− 0.049	− 0.011	− 0.249	− 0.180	− 0.167
Wage rate	− 0.060	− 0.146	− 0.136	− 0.409	− 0.117	− 0.296
Consumer price	− 0.243	− 0.265	− 0.223	− 0.403	− 0.228	− 0.347
GDP	0.035	0.045	− 0.214	− 0.157	− 0.154	− 0.059
Employment	0.007	0.043	0.004	0.010	0.045	0.022
Investment	− 0.068	− 0.070	− 0.684	− 0.371	− 0.535	− 0.205
Consumption	0.117	0.215	0.030	0.070	− 0.155	− 0.012
Exports	− 0.135	− 0.285	− 0.149	− 0.164	− 0.145	− 0.210
Imports	0.156	0.201	− 0.146	− 0.101	− 0.108	0.011
Real salary income	0.199	0.205	0.102	0.035	− 0.439	− 0.261
Real non-salary income	0.256	0.304	− 0.043	0.014	0.029	0.156
Difference[a] *in:*						
PSBR (%GDP)	− 0.108	− 0.074	0.000	0.000	0.000	0.000
Current account (%GDP)	− 0.072	− 0.119	0.007	− 0.031	− 0.002	− 0.063
Unemployment rate	0.000	0.000	0.000	0.000	0.000	0.000
	Disequilibrium model (NKEYNES)					
Percentage change[a] *in:*						
Production price	− 0.127	− 0.040	− 0.110	− 0.159	− 0.114	− 0.116
Wage rate	− 0.284	− 0.128	− 0.459	− 0.267	− 0.415	− 0.212
Consumer price	− 0.297	− 0.260	− 0.286	− 0.342	− 0.289	− 0.313
GDP	− 0.088	0.058	− 0.474	− 0.119	− 0.376	− 0.040
Employment	0.024	0.046	0.023	0.002	0.023	0.017
Investment	− 0.779	− 0.001	− 1.860	− 2.023	− 1.587	− 0.129
Consumption	0.043	0.222	− 0.102	0.102	− 0.349	0.016
Exports	− 0.097	− 0.285	− 0.105	− 0.215	− 0.103	− 0.238
Imports	− 0.007	0.220	− 0.481	− 0.038	− 0.408	0.045
Real salary income	0.070	0.224	− 0.107	0.097	− 0.840	− 0.195
Real non-salary income	0.103	0.317	− 0.362	0.072	− 0.244	0.183
Difference[a] *in:*						
PSBR (%GDP)	− 0.141	− 0.070	0.000	0.000	0.000	0.000
Current account (%GDP)	− 0.030	− 0.123	0.094	− 0.050	0.076	− 0.073
Unemployment rate	− 0.023	− 0.018	− 0.029	0.005	− 0.028	− 0.002

[a]Percentage changes and differences refer to the baseline scenario.

public budget balance are such that a severe reduction of total savings results, these referring to the economy as a whole. Following the model's closure rule, which is based on the adjustment of stocks variation, the reduction of total savings is reflected as a negative variation of stocks, which acts negatively on the demand side.

Figures are such that the implied reduction of demand counterbalances its initial increase, which has been attributed to income. Contractionary effects are produced on the economy, since total aggregated demand is decreasing. This implies a reduction of the equilibrium price of goods. The movements in the labour market being maintained, factor substitutions in production, which are favourable to labour, allow for an increase in domestic production and GDP.

Both demand contraction and production expansion lead to the decrease of market prices of goods. This implies gains in competitiveness and increasing exports. Finally, current-account deficit clearly improves. Because of the Walras identity, a surplus in current account implies a reduction in some of the adjustable domestic expenditures, in our case in stocks variations, and, thus, further contractionary effects are produced.

The fall in market prices of goods is maintained throughout the simulation period. Real wages, however, begin to fall by the middle of the period at a degree that is much lower than that of gross profits. This is due mainly to a slowdown of the labour demand increase, the latter being attributed to the decrease in the cost of capital. The decrease in real wages implies a decrease in income and private consumption.

In summary, the decrease in the VAT rate creates a net surplus in the current account, which, however, is perceived in the general-equilibrium approach as a transfer of wealth towards the rest of the world. Such a transfer leads to losses of income by the domestic economic agents. However, contraction of demand leads also to lower prices at such a degree that net gains in domestic supply and employment are achieved. These results are presented in Table 13.5.

Neo-Keynesian model.   The fall in consumer prices, resulting from the decrease in VAT rates, induces higher income and, thus, private consumption. Following the multiplier–accelerator mechanism of the neo-Keynesian model, the direct increase of about 0.5% in consumption is amplified and finally doubled after the first year. The fall in consumer prices induces, also, a fall in the wage rate via the indexation mechanism within the Phillips curve. Labour costs having been reduced, the production price of goods is also reduced. This leads to gains in competitiveness and, thus, increasing exports as well as a diminishing share of imports. Wages being under-indexed to consumer prices, the relative price of labour is increased and this leads to factor substitutions in favour of capital and, thus, to the rise of investment.

Domestic production, being quantity-adjusted to demand, also increases. However, capacities of production increase less rapidly and, thus, disequilibrium pressures are produced: the rate of capacity utilization rises. This triggers a

Table 13.5 Effect, on the Greek economy, of a one percentage point reduction in the VAT rate, according to CGE-00 and CGE-01 models

	Without public budget constraint		With public budget constraint			
			Adjustment by the public investment		Adjustment by the income tax rate	
	1st year	6th year	1st year	6th year	1st year	6th year
	Full-equilibrium model (CGE-00)					
Percentage change[a] in:						
Production price	− 4.750	− 7.406	− 4.338	− 6.706	− 4.131	− 6.176
Wage rate	− 2.433	− 6.380	− 2.231	− 5.785	− 2.129	− 5.395
Consumer price	− 3.774	− 5.805	− 3.508	− 5.323	− 3.375	− 4.963
GDP	0.175	0.059	0.166	0.083	0.162	0.087
Employment	0.056	0.031	0.053	0.044	0.051	0.046
Investment	− 0.754	0.537	− 0.712	0.474	− 0.697	0.455
Consumption	0.234	− 0.322	0.249	− 0.205	− 0.919	− 1.695
Exports	2.182	7.354	1.987	6.578	1.889	6.102
Imports	− 0.196	0.270	− 0.967	− 0.909	− 0.980	− 0.810
Real salary income	1.516	− 0.559	1.441	− 0.411	− 1.829	− 4.250
Real non-salary income	− 1.787	− 1.586	− 1.551	− 1.328	− 1.432	− 1.093
Difference[a] in:						
PSBR (%GDP)	− 0.867	− 1.320	0.000	0.000	0.000	0.000
Current account (%GDP)	0.000	0.683	0.234	0.960	0.210	0.884
Unemployment rate	0.000	0.000	0.000	0.000	0.000	0.000
	Goods market Equilibrium Model (CGE-01)					
Percentage change[a] in:						
Production price	− 4.677	− 7.138	− 4.277	− 6.373	− 4.073	− 5.757
Wage rate	− 2.783	− 4.838	− 2.585	− 4.356	− 2.484	− 4.017
Consumer price	− 3.726	− 5.634	− 3.469	− 5.107	− 3.337	− 4.690
GDP	0.362	− 1.061	0.353	− 0.888	0.348	− 0.822
Employment	0.115	− 0.593	0.112	− 0.496	0.111	− 0.461
Investment	− 1.557	0.250	− 1.517	0.249	− 1.496	0.172
Consumption	0.214	− 0.746	0.228	− 0.560	− 0.914	− 2.280
Exports	2.147	7.440	1.958	6.566	1.862	6.028
Imports	− 0.325	− 0.035	− 1.076	− 1.376	− 1.091	− 1.242
Real salary income	1.234	− 0.361	1.163	− 0.218	− 2.028	− 4.760
Real non-salary income	− 1.328	− 3.360	− 1.101	− 2.835	− 0.985	− 2.426
Difference[a] in:						
PSBR (%GDP)	− 0.844	− 1.610	0.000	0.000	0.000	0.000
Current account (%GDP)	0.045	0.809	0.273	1.130	0.279	1.030
Unemployment rate	− 0.075	0.885	− 0.750	0.765	− 0.074	0.718

[a]Percentage changes and differences refer to the baseline scenario.

dynamic mechanism that reverses the deflation effects obtained in the short run. After two years, production prices increase although consumer prices are still decreasing. In the same time, the fall in the rate of unemployment, which also shows a disequilibrium pressure, leads to increasing wages and, thus, increasing production costs. This contributes to the rise of production prices. Thus, in the longer run, competitiveness is degraded with reverse consequences on foreign trade. However, real wages sustain the progress of incomes and domestic demand.

The loss of public revenues, produced as a direct effect of the decrease in VAT rates, is partly compensated by increased revenues from direct taxation and

Table 13.6 Effect, on the Greek economy, of a one percentage point reduction in the VAT rate, according to CGE-10 and NKEYNES models

	Without public budget constraint		With public budget constraint			
			Adjustment by the public investment		Adjustment by the income tax rate	
	1st year	6th year	1st year	6th year	1st year	6th year
			Labour market equilibrium model (CGE-10)			
Percentage change[a] in:						
Production price	− 0.359	1.519	− 0.242	0.978	− 0.268	1.176
Wage rate	0.323	1.762	0.037	1.130	0.102	1.373
Consumer price	− 0.965	0.268	− 0.891	− 0.105	− 0.908	0.031
GDP	1.868	1.937	0.914	1.626	1.129	1.774
Employment	0.052	0.396	0.038	0.304	0.407	0.333
Investment	4.055	2.621	1.725	2.363	2.253	2.558
Consumption	1.012	1.885	0.680	1.578	− 0.043	1.450
Exports	0.160	− 0.813	0.108	− 0.459	0.119	− 0.578
Imports	1.311	1.881	0.153	1.373	0.290	1.551
Real salary income	1.366	2.102	0.995	1.716	− 1.103	1.248
Real non-salary income	2.992	3.636	1.839	3.176	2.099	3.399
Difference[a] in:						
PSBR (%GDP)	− 0.409	− 0.107	0.000	0.000	0.000	0.000
Current account (%GDP)	− 0.316	− 0.504	− 0.018	− 0.352	− 0.051	− 0.403
Unemployment rate	0.000	0.000	0.000	0.000	0.000	0.000
			Disequilibrium model (NKEYNES)			
Percentage change[a] in:						
Production price	− 0.519	1.001	− 0.462	0.565	− 0.475	0.715
Wage rate	− 0.099	0.858	− 0.682	0.436	− 0.545	0.588
Consumer price	− 1.067	− 0.086	− 1.031	− 0.384	− 1.039	− 0.283
GDP	1.638	1.888	0.334	1.451	0.640	1.630
Employment	0.083	0.504	0.081	0.353	0.082	0.401
Investment	2.721	2.339	− 0.886	1.875	− 0.036	2.090
Consumption	0.873	1.750	0.386	1.401	− 0.470	1.176
Exports	0.231	− 0.438	0.206	− 0.185	0.212	− 0.265
Imports	1.005	1.737	− 0.592	1.076	− 0.368	1.269
Real salary income	1.121	1.803	0.528	1.433	− 1.982	0.689
Real non-salary income	2.702	3.548	1.122	2.912	1.493	3.179
Difference[a] in:						
PSBR (%GDP)	− 0.471	− 0.164	0.000	0.000	0.000	0.000
Current account (%GDP)	− 0.240	− 0.442	0.173	− 0.258	0.118	− 0.310
Unemployment rate	− 0.044	− 0.242	− 0.066	− 0.160	− 0.061	− 0.186

[a]Percentage changes and differences refer to the baseline scenario.

import tariffs. However, the public budget deficit is aggravated. The current-account deficit is also aggravated despite the short-run gains in competitiveness.

In summary, the neo-Keynesian model simulates a demand-pulled growth. In the short run, this is sustained by a deflation process but this is reversed after two years because of the augmenting disequilibrium pressures in markets of both the goods and labour. Both the current account and public finances deteriorate severely as a result of this process. These results are presented in Table 13.6.

Sensitivity analysis

The introduction of a public budget constraint into the general-equilibrium model does not provide any significant changes in the results. The only noticeable point concerns the case of obtaining public budget balance by adjusting the income tax rate. The resulting higher income tax rate has small negative effects on income and private consumption. For both variants that consider public budget constraint, we must acknowledge the net gains that are obtained in current account.

Concerning the neo-Keynesian model, the incorporation of a public budget constraint produces significant changes in results. However, these changes are mostly quantitative and not qualitative (i.e. signs of simulated changes are not modified). In general, the public budget constraint acts as a moderator of economic impacts by reducing the total demand. This is done by reducing either public expenditure or disposable private income. Comparing with the unconstrained results, the deflation process in production is less important, but at the same time, the disequilibrium pressures and the induced negative effects are less pronounced. Such a situation leads to reduced gains in GDP and employment, but allows for a net improvement of current account. The public policy options that accommodate the public budget objective differ with respect to income distribution.

Consider now the model variants in which only one of the two markets is in price-adjusted equilibrium. Table 13.7 shows that the results obtained with the variant CGE-01 (which formulates price-adjusted equilibrium in the goods markets and unemployment in the labour market) are very close to the results of the full-equilibrium model (CGE-00). On the other hand, Table 13.8 shows that the results obtained with the variant CGE-10 (which formulates wage-adjusted equilibrium in the labour market and quantity adjustment in the goods market) are close to the results of the neo-Keynesian model (NKEYNES). Thus, regarding the model's behaviour, the pattern of adjustment in the goods market is dominating.

By comparing the variants with price adjustment of the goods market, one can conclude that the economy with a perfectly competitive labour market is more efficient. Variant CGE-00 provides higher deflation, GDP, employment and income effects than the CGE-01 variant. In the full-equilibrium variant, the

Table 13.7 Effect, on the Greek economy, of a one percentage point reduction in the rates of export subsidies, import tariffs and VAT, according to CGE-00 and CGE-01 models

	Without public budget constraint		With public budget constraint			
			Adjustment by the public investment		Adjustment by the income tax rate	
	1st year	6th year	1st year	6th year	1st year	6th year
	Full-equilibrium model (CGE-00)					
Percentage change[a] in:						
Production price	− 6.185	− 9.574	− 5.682	− 8.666	− 5.471	− 8.122
Wage rate	− 3.190	− 8.277	− 2.969	− 7.510	− 2.834	− 7.112
Consumer price	− 4.908	− 7.518	− 4.583	− 6.891	− 4.446	− 6.520
GDP	0.226	0.067	0.216	0.097	0.212	0.101
Employment	0.072	0.034	0.069	0.051	0.067	0.053
Investment	− 0.974	0.704	− 0.929	0.627	− 0.911	0.610
Consumption	0.295	− 0.407	0.314	− 0.258	− 1.034	− 2.051
Exports	2.714	9.400	2.471	8.365	2.369	7.863
Imports	− 0.179	0.437	− 1.069	− 0.972	− 1.082	− 0.859
Real salary income	1.967	− 0.765	1.876	− 0.575	− 1.900	− 5.171
Real non-salary income	− 2.355	− 2.060	− 2.064	− 1.715	− 6.302	− 7.893
Difference[a] in:						
PSBR (%GDP)	− 1.010	− 1.590	0.000	0.000	0.000	0.000
Current account (%GDP)	− 0.052	0.829	0.223	1.160	0.229	1.070
Unemployment rate	0.000	0.000	0.000	0.000	0.000	0.000
	Goods market equilibrium model (CGE-01)					
Percentage change[a] in:						
Production price	− 6.088	− 9.215	− 5.602	− 8.205	− 5.392	− 7.548
Wage rate	− 3.628	− 6.233	− 3.385	− 5.611	− 3.280	− 5.253
Consumer price	− 4.845	− 7.288	− 4.531	− 6.591	− 4.396	− 6.145
GDP	0.462	− 1.441	0.451	− 1.208	0.447	− 1.141
Employment	0.147	− 0.804	0.143	− 0.675	0.142	− 0.640
Investment	− 1.985	0.355	− 1.941	0.328	− 1.921	0.235
Consumption	0.269	− 0.975	0.287	− 0.735	− 1.028	− 2.847
Exports	2.667	9.524	2.433	8.336	2.332	7.757
Imports	− 0.342	0.039	− 1.208	− 1.594	− 1.223	− 1.443
Real salary income	1.604	− 0.498	1.518	− 0.325	− 2.157	− 5.863
Real non-salary income	− 1.772	− 4.433	− 1.491	− 3.718	− 1.370	− 3.273
Difference[a] in:						
PSBR (%GDP)	− 0.979	− 1.980	0.000	0.000	0.000	0.000
Current account (%GDP)	0.006	1.000	0.273	1.380	0.279	1.280
Unemployment rate	− 0.095	1.190	− 0.094	1.030	− 0.094	0.981

[a]Percentage changes and differences refer to the baseline scenario.

flexibility of the labour market is such that it allows for higher gains of real wages in the short term, but also leads to higher losses of real wages in the longer term.

Concerning the variants with quantity adjustment of the goods market, results show that the wage-adjusted equilibrium of the labour market allows for higher

Table 13.8 Effect, on the Greek economy, of a one percentage point reduction in the rates of export subsidies, import tariffs and VAT, according to CGE-10 and NKEYNES models

	Without public budget constraint		With public budget constraint			
			Adjustment by the public investment		Adjustment by the income tax rate	
	1st year	6th year	1st year	6th year	1st year	6th year
	Labour market equilibrium model (CGE-10)					
Percentage change[a] *in:*						
Production price	− 0.400	1.471	− 0.253	0.726	− 0.286	0.997
Wage rate	0.265	1.620	− 0.098	0.715	− 0.017	1.061
Consumer price	− 1.205	0.003	− 1.112	− 0.507	− 1.133	− 0.323
GDP	1.902	1.987	0.701	1.463	0.966	1.707
Employment	0.059	0.438	0.041	0.314	0.045	0.354
Investment	3.987	2.562	1.050	1.977	1.702	2.339
Consumption	1.130	2.106	0.711	1.647	− 0.204	1.426
Exports	0.024	− 1.096	− 0.410	− 0.623	− 0.027	− 0.781
Imports	1.470	2.091	0.097	1.265	0.175	1.552
Real salary income	1.569	2.314	1.100	1.751	− 1.552	0.961
Real non-salary income	3.254	3.956	1.800	3.184	2.121	3.549
Difference[a] *in:*						
PSBR (%GDP)	− 0.518	− 0.182	0.000	0.000	0.000	0.000
Current account (%GDP)	− 0.387	− 0.622	− 0.012	− 0.382	− 0.051	− 0.462
Unemployment rate	0.000	0.000	0.000	0.000	0.000	0.000
	Disequilibrium Model (NKEYNES)					
Percentage change[a] *in:*						
Production price	− 0.645	0.965	− 0.571	0.404	− 0.588	0.594
Wage rate	− 0.381	0.737	− 1.132	0.167	− 0.960	0.371
Consumer price	− 1.360	− 0.343	− 1.313	− 0.725	− 1.324	− 0.597
GDP	1.551	1.951	− 0.130	1.328	0.253	1.585
Employment	0.107	0.550	0.104	0.354	0.105	0.415
Investment	1.951	2.349	− 2.700	1.619	− 1.635	1.955
Consumption	0.918	1.978	0.289	1.502	− 0.827	1.183
Exports	0.134	− 0.723	0.101	− 0.400	0.108	− 0.501
Imports	1.001	1.965	− 1.058	1.034	− 0.784	1.307
Real salary income	1.193	2.035	0.426	1.529	− 2.829	0.476
Real non-salary income	2.810	3.880	0.772	2.982	1.236	3.360
Difference[a] *in:*						
PSBR (%GDP)	− 0.613	− 0.235	0.000	0.000	0.000	0.000
Current account (%GDP)	− 0.271	− 0.564	0.265	− 0.307	0.197	− 0.380
Unemployment rate	− 0.066	− 0.259	− 0.095	− 0.155	− 0.089	− 0.187

[a]Percentage changes and differences refer to the baseline scenario.

gains in GDP and income but leads to higher inflation and current-account deficit. Since the neo-Keynesian variant indicates decreasing unemployment as a result of both foreign trade liberalization and VAT rate reduction, it is clear that to reequilibrate the labour market one must raise real wages.

Combined scenario

The combined scenario corresponds to the simultaneous decrease, by one percentage point, of import tariff, export subsidy and VAT rates. All variants of the model provide results that correspond approximately to the sum of the results of the individual scenarios. Thus, in terms of rates of variation, all model variants behave linearly around the solution point.

Table 13.9   Welfare index (difference from baseline)

Model	Without public budget constraint	With public budget constraint	
		Adjustment by the public investment	Adjustment by the income tax rate
Decrease of export subsidies and import tariffs rate by one percentage point			
CGE-00	835	1577	1474
CGE-01	– 459	504	424
CGE-10	– 1310	– 1405	– 1217
NKEYNES	– 1278	– 1395	– 1205
Decrease of VAT rate by one percentage point			
CGE-00	6718	10885	10337
CGE-01	2520	7667	7242
CGE-10	5581	5328	5791
NKEYNES	5844	5430	6030

Welfare comparisons

In order to compare the above results on a common basis, we define a welfare measure as a weighting sum of scenario performances on GDP and on current account. Performances are conceived in terms of differences from a baseline scenario. It is clear that any welfare measure of a macroeconomic impact analysis is sensitive to the way it is defined. Thus, the reader should be aware of the limited scope of the analysis that follows. Table 13.9 presents the welfare measurement results for the two policy scenarios.

For both scenarios, the full-equilibrium model variant provides clearly superior performances compared to other model variants. The price-adjusting competitive markets (of goods and labour) endow the economy with such a flexibility that it is able to take maximum advantage of the fiscal reform. Efficiency is even improved if the fiscal reform is carried out at equal yield, i.e. when accommodating public policy achieves a balance of public sector borrowing requirements as a percentage of GDP. Public investment adjustment, as accommodating policy, performs slightly better than the income tax adjustment option. Concerning the role of the public budget constraint, similar conclusions are drawn with the CGE-01 model variant, in which the market of goods is perfectly competitive.

By comparing performances of model CGE-00 with those of model CGE-01, one can conclude about the important negative role of rigidities or market imperfections in the labour market. Performances clearly degrade in model variant CGE-01, in which the wage rate is determined via a Phillips curve and unemployment is allowed. By incorporating a public budget constraint into the CGE-01 model, performances clearly improve and become superior to those of the models that simulate an imperfectly competitive goods market.

Welfare performances of models CGE-10 and NKEYNES, which have in common an imperfectly competitive situation in the goods market, are similar. The reduction of VAT rates leads to a positive change in the welfare measure, while foreign trade liberalization implies negative changes. This result is due to the demand-driven functioning of the economy, as simulated by these models. The role of labour market imperfections, which constitute the difference between the two models, is much less important, and even opposite in sign, compared to the case of a perfectly competitive goods market. Both scenarios lead to decreasing unemployment in the case of imperfect goods market; thus, to reequilibrate labour supply and demand implies higher real wage rates, which, in turn, induce some losses in economy's performance.

13.4 CONCLUSIONS

In this chapter four variants of a macroeconomic one-sector model of a small open economy have been developed and their parameters econometrically estimated. Model variants differ according to the market-clearing mechanisms concerning the goods and the labour markets. One of the model variants is the full-equilibrium model of the pure CGE tradition and, at the other extreme, one variant is a typical neo-Keynesian model that allows disequilibriums in both the goods and the labour markets. The two other variants mix market-clearing situations.

We ran these models for policy scenarios that assume VAT rate, import tariffs and export subsidies reductions. These are conceived as part of the consequences of the internal market unification of EEC by the end of 1992. Sensitivity analysis is also carried out by assuming alternative accommodating policies of the public sector that aim at reequilibrating the public budget balance.

By comparing the results across the model variants, one can evaluate the role of market imperfections. Moreover, results of the CGE variant have a normative character, in the sense that they indicate whether the policy measures are good or not for the economy. Results of the neo-Keynesian model have a rather descriptive character, in the sense that they indicate eventual disequilibrium problems resulting from the policy measures. The whole exercise we have conducted, demonstrates the ability of the modelling approach to provide conclusions in the sense stated above, i.e. both for the role of market imperfections and for the characterization of the policy measures. Given that the modelling effort was not very important since all variants share most of the equations and one can pass very easily from one variant to another, we conclude that the combined modelling approach we propose in this chapter may be useful also in other policy issues.

The results obtained from the model's variants are significantly different. The dominating source of discrepancy is the way the goods market is clearing. This leads to conclude that both the CGE and the neo-Keynesian modelling approaches must be adopted and that, if a CGE model was available in the Cecchini study, results might be different. In the policy-oriented conclusions stated below, we show a way for combining constructively the results of the two apparently opposite approaches.

By combining results from the models, the sensitivity analyses and the welfare measurements, the following policy-oriented conclusions are drawn:

1. It is clear that measures towards goods market liberalization should be taken for improving economy's efficiency within the 1992 process.
2. It is also clear that these must be accompanied with similar measures in the labour market and especially for eliminating automatic price indexation rules of the wage rate determination.
3. Goods market liberalization is, however, much more important than labour market liberalization regarding the aim to obtain maximum benefits.
4. In any case, the loss of public revenues resulting from the tax cuts involved in the scenarios should be compensated by adequate public policy measures in order to reequilibrate public budget. This improves the efficiency of the economy.
5. If the goods market remains imperfectly competitive, foreign trade liberalization has negative overall impacts on the economy. This is due to demand which is contracted; thus, a compensating policy that aims at sustaining the demand must be envisaged.
6. The necessary funds for implementing such a demand-sustaining policy should come from the rest of the world since, otherwise, the current account would be even more deteriorated. This justifies the doubling of structural funds policy[3] that has been conceived for compensating (in the case of Greece and other countries) the adverse effects of the 1992 process. It is clear that the structural funds policy would have amplifying positive economic results if measures were taken towards market liberalization.
7. VAT rate reductions lead to positive overall results, independently of the market clearing regimes. Efficiency is, however, maximized in the case of perfect markets.
8. From a normative point of view, both measures involved in the 1992 process have positive impacts on the economy. Both measures, however, induce, in the short run, a degradation of current account which is alleviated if public budget reequilibrating measures are taken. In the case of VAT reduction, one should expect also short-term pressures on capacities utilization, which have inflationary implications.

A number of issues remain for further activities in the research area initiated here. These can be classified along the following three directions: The first one

---

[3] Their positive role on productivity and technical progress also justifies these funds.

is related to the analysis of the empirical consequences from the choice of closure rule in the general-equilibrium model. It is known that the closure rule plays a significant role in the determination of policy responses. Its exact impacts, however, remain to be exploited. The second direction concerns the introduction of dynamics in the determination of consumer choices which will contribute to the intertemporal analysis of the welfare implications of policy options. A third, and final, direction concerns the extension of this research towards further elaboration of the financial sector and, in parallel, the introduction of commodity disaggregation and input–output relationships. It is also clear that there is room for much improvement, especially in the area of parameter estimation.

REFERENCES

Adelman, I. and Robinson, S. (1978) *Income Distribution in Developing Countries: A Case Study of Korea*. Oxford University Press, London.

Blitzer, C. R. and Eckaus, R. S. (1986) Energy Economy Interactions in Mexico: A Multiperiod General Equilibrium Model. *Journal of Development Economics*, **21**, 259–81.

Bradley, J., Fitzgerald, J. and O'Sullivan, L. (1989) Medium-Term Review: 1987–92, The Economic and Social Research Institute.

Capros, P., Karadeloglou, P. and Mentzas, G. (1989) Economic Modelling Paradigms: General Equilibrium vs. Keynesian, in *System Modelling and Simulation* (eds. S. Tzafestas, A. Eisinberg and L. Carotenuto), North-Holland, Amsterdam.

Capros, P., Karadeloglou, P. and Mentzas, G. (1990) An Empirical Assessment of Macroeconometric and CGE Approaches in Policy Modelling. *Journal of Policy Modeling*, **7**, 379– 405.

Capros, P., Karadeloglou, P. Mentzas, G. (1991) Market Imperfections in a General Equilibrium Framework: An Empirical Analysis. *Economic Modelling*, **8**, 116–28.

Commission of the EC (1988) The Economics of 1992, *European Economy*, **35** (March).

Cordon, T., Corbo, V. and de Melo, J. (1985) Productivity Growth, External Shocks, and Capital Inflows in Chile: A General Equilibrium Analysis. *Journal of Policy Modeling*, **7**, 379–405.

Deardorff, A. V. and Stern, R. (1982) A Disaggregated Model of World Production and Trade: An Estimated Impact of the Tokyo Round. *Journal of Policy Modeling*, **3**, 127–52.

Deleau, M., Malgrange, P. and Muet, P. A. (1984) A Study of the Short-Run and Long-Run Properties of Macroeconometric Models, in *Contemporary Macroeconomic Modelling* (eds. P. Malgrange and P.A. Muet), Basic Blackwell, Oxford.

de Melo, J. (1988), Computable General Equilibrium Models for Trade Policy analysis in Developing Countries: A Survey. *Journal of Policy Modeling*, **10**, 469–503.

Dervis, K., de Melo, J. and Robinson, S. (1982) *General Equilibrium for Development Policy*. Cambridge University Press, London.

Devarajan, S. and Sierra, H. (1986) *Growth without adjustment: Thailand (1973–82)*. World Bank (mimeo).

Hudson, E. and Jorgenson, D. W. (1974) US Energy Policy and Economic Growth, 1975–2000. *Bell Journal of Economics and Management Science*, **5** 461–514.

Hudson, E. A. and Jorgenson, D. W. (1977) *The Long-term Interindustry Transactions Model: A Simulation Model for Energy and Economic Analysis*. Data Resources, Inc., 27 September, Cambridge, MA.

Johansen, L. (1960) *A Multisectional Study of Economic Growth*, North-Holland, Amsterdam.

Jorgenson, D. W. (1984) Econometric Methods for General Equilibrium Analysis, in *Applied General Equilibrium Analysis* (eds. H. Scarf and J. Shoven), Cambridge University Press, London, pp. 139–202.

Karadeloglou, P. (1989) The Environment and Internal Market: Elaboration of an Integrated Community Strategy for the Protection of the Environment, Economic Development and Employment: Macroeconomic Aspects for Greece. Study carried out for the Commission of the European Communities DGXI, October 1989.

Kharas, H. J. and Shashido, H. (1987) Foreign Borrowing and Macroeconomic Adjustment to External Shocks. *Journal of Development Economics*, **25**, 125–48.

Levy, S. (1987), A Short-Run General Equilibrium Model for a Small Open Economy. *Journal of Development Economics*, **25**, 63–88.

Lewis, J. D. and Shujiro Urata (1984) Anatomy of a Balance-of-Payments Crisis. Application of a Computable General Equilibrium Model to Turkey, 1978–1980 *Economic Modelling*, **1**, 281–303.

Lysy, F. J. (1983) The character of General Equilibrium Models under Alternative Closures, The Johns Hopkins University (mimeo).

Pereira, A. M. and Shoven, J. B. (1988) Survey of Dynamic Computational General Equilibrium Models for Tax Policy Evaluation, *Journal of Policy Modeling*, **10**, 401–36.

Rattso, J. (1982) Different Macroclosures of the Original Johansen Model and Their Impact on Policy Evaluation, *Journal of Policy Modeling*, **4**, 85–97.

Scarf, H. (1969) An Example of an Algorithm for Calculating Equilibrium Prices, *American Economic Review*, **59**.

Shoven, J. B. and Whalley, J. (1972) A General Equilibrium Model of the Effects of Differential Taxation of Income from Capital in the U.S., *Journal of Public Economics*, **1**, 281–322.

Shoven, J. B. and Whalley, J. (1984) Applied General Equilibrium Models of Taxation and International Trade: An Introduction and Survey, *Journal of Economic Literature*, **XXII**, 1007–51.

Taylor, L. and Lysy, F. J. (1979) Vanishing Income Distributions: Keynesian Clues About Model Surprises in the Short Run, *Journal of Development Economics*, **6**, 11–29.

Wigle, R. (1988) General Equilibrium Evaluation of Canada–US Trade Liberalization in a Global Context, *Canadian Journal of Economics*, **XXI**, 539–564.

Index